Contents

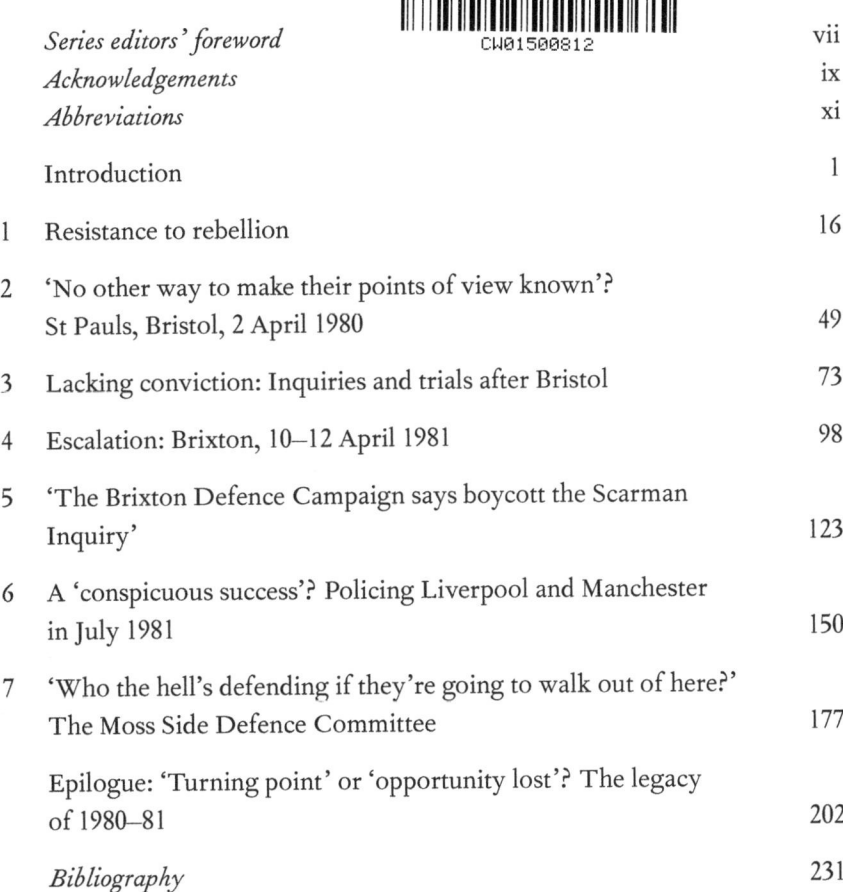

Series editors' foreword

John Solomos, Satnam Virdee,
Aaron Winter

THE STUDY of race, racism and ethnicity has expanded greatly from the end of the twentieth century onwards. This expansion has coincided with a growing awareness of the continuing role that these issues play in contemporary societies all over the globe. *Racism, Resistance and Social Change* is a new series of books that seeks to make a substantial contribution to this growing field of scholarship and research. We are committed to providing a forum for the publication of the highest quality scholarship on race, racism, anti-racism and ethnic relations. As Editors of this series we would like to publish both theoretically driven books and texts with an empirical frame that seek to further develop our understanding of the origins, development and contemporary forms of racisms, racial inequalities and racial and ethnic relations. We welcome work from a range of theoretical and political perspectives and as the series develops we would ideally want to encourage a conversation that goes beyond specific national or geopolitical environments. While we are aware that there are important differences between national and regional research traditions we hope that scholars from a variety of disciplines and multidisciplinary frames will take to opportunity to include their research work in the series.

As the title of the series highlights we would also welcome texts that can address issues about resistance and anti-racism as well as the role of political and policy interventions in this rapidly changing field. The changing forms of racist mobilisation and expression that have come to the fore in recent years have highlighted the need for more reflection and research on the role of political and civil society mobilisations in this field.

We are committed to building on theoretical advances by providing a forum for new and challenging theoretical and empirical studies on the changing morphology of race and racism in contemporary societies.

Acknowledgements

As with any work of this length, it would simply not have been possible to complete such an undertaking without the support of many colleagues, friends and family. Although any remaining faults are mine alone, I would like to thank all those people who have contributed to shaping this project over the last few years.

First, I would like to thank the Arts and Humanities Research Council, the Scouloudi Foundation and the Institute of Historical Research for supporting various stages of this project.

I am indebted to brilliant colleagues at the University of Exeter and elsewhere, particularly Matthias Reiss, Andrew Thorpe, Richard Toye, Gavin Schaffer, David Thackeray and Matthew Rendle, who have constantly provided extremely helpful and constructive feedback and advice, and I am extremely grateful for their support on a wide range of matters over a number of years.

I'd like to thank everyone involved at Manchester University Press and the series editors for their interest and enthusiasm for this project. I'd also like to thank the anonymous readers for their constructive and helpful comments on drafts. Similarly, my thanks go to all those who have offered feedback on aspects of this research presented at various conferences over many years and to those who have made suggestions or comments in general discussions.

Academics, particularly historians, are nothing without their sources; as such, I'd like to thank a range of people for allowing me access to a wealth of material. First, of course, I owe a debt of gratitude to all of those people who were willing to give up some of their time to meet and be interviewed for this book, providing valuable and unique perspectives on the events discussed. John Stevenson generously provided welcome comments and suggestions, further to a great deal of unique materials from his personal collections that formed the basis of discussions of Moss Side in Manchester. Staff and individuals at the Bristol

Records Office (particularly archivist Graham Tratt), the National Archives, the British Library, the Black Cultural Archives (Victoria Northridge), the George Padmore Institute (Sarah Garrod) and the Ahmed Iqbal Ullah Race Relations Resource Centre (Ruth Tait) were always helpful and receptive to my questions and requests, and – despite budgetary and staffing constraints – do terrific work allowing access to otherwise unattainable sources. Similarly, thank you to Information Access Manager Jeff Hines at the Avon and Somerset Constabulary for allowing access to their records, and to the offices of Ben Bradshaw MP who were of great help in my year-long attempts to access government documents.

On a personal note, thanks to my friends for their support over the years. While this includes too many valued and ongoing friendships to name individually here, special thanks must go to Hannah and Will Davies and Luke and Naomi Oates, for providing friendly faces, warm food and a place to sleep after many hours spent in various archives.

Most of all, thank you to my family, to whom I dedicate this book: my parents, Alison and Keith, for their endless support, constantly being my biggest cheerleaders and instilling their children with a love of history; my sister Emma, for her advice, encouragement and insights; and my fiancée Lorna, who has filled my life with love and laughter since we met, while being extremely supportive and understanding of the long working hours that this book has demanded. Their collective love, advice, extremely helpful (and foolhardy!) proofreading and unwavering support have been invaluable – it is no overstatement to say that this book would not exist without them.

Abbreviations

ANL	Anti-Nazi League
BCRE	Bristol Council for Racial Equality
BLM	Black Lives Matter
BPA	Black People's Alliance
CARD	Campaign Against Racial Discrimination
CCRL	Council for Community Relations in Lambeth
CRE	Commission for Racial Equality
DPP	Director of Public Prosecutions
GLC	Greater London Council
GMC	Greater Manchester County Council
IPCC	Independent Police Complaints Commission
IRR	Institute of Race Relations
MCCR	Manchester Council for Community Relations
NCCI	National Committee for Commonwealth Immigrants
NCCL	National Council for Civil Liberties
NF	National Front
PCC	Police and Crime Commissioner
RAR	Rock Against Racism
RRA	Race Relations Act
SPG	Special Patrol Group
TUC	Trades Union Congress
WISC	West Indian Standing Conference

Introduction

13 dead and nothing said, oh what we gonna do?
13 dead and nothing said, oh what this world is coming to.
13 dead and nothing said, don't you know it could happen to you?
Johnny Osbourne – 13 Dead (Nothing Said)

WHEN A house fire on 18 January 1981 in New Cross, South East London, claimed the lives of thirteen black youths, the perceived indifferent response from the police and authorities was considered an apt illustration of the treatment and neglect of black and minority ethnic people in modern Britain. By this time, violent anti-police disorder had already appeared in Bristol, and would reoccur in greater intensity in Brixton three months later, before spreading to numerous locations across England in the summer of 1981. While by no means the first racial disturbances in Britain during the twentieth century – most notably, racist riots occurring in 1919 and 1958 – the nature of anti-police disturbances in 1980–81 differed significantly from previous racially motivated violence; indeed, 1980–81 'marked the beginning of a new era of race relations in Britain'.[1] As Paul Gilroy highlighted, it is important not to overemphasise the uniformity of the 1980–81 disturbances and risk diminishing local circumstances influencing them; accordingly, this book contains detailed studies of three locations, within which similarities allow for some general analysis.[2] It is commonly agreed that the 1980–81 disorders began after 'trigger events' involving police and black Britons, and that areas experiencing such disturbances shared five common characteristics: racial disadvantage and discrimination; high unemployment; widespread deprivation; visible political exclusion and powerlessness; and common mistrust of, and hostility towards, the police.[3] The 2011 disturbances in major English cities provided a stark reminder, if needed, of the impact of such

1

public disorder, and many commentators made direct comparisons to 1980–81 – although these should not be overstated.[4]

Following increased Commonwealth migration after the Second World War, widespread racial discrimination and disadvantage led black and minority ethnic groups to grow frustrated by systems ostensibly protecting them. Whereas older generations had migrated to Britain, often initially demonstrating admiration for the colonial metropole but not always intending to remain permanently, those raised in Britain were influenced by their parents' struggles, rising numbers of racist attacks and a subsequent growth of activism.[5] This mounting sense of discontentment at the state's failings was exacerbated by a police force appearing unaccountable for its actions and treatment of groups on the political fringes, namely working classes and minority ethnic groups. While previous racial disturbances in Britain often saw targeted violence towards these 'outsider' groups, 1980–81 demonstrated a growth in black self-protection and militancy.

This work considers the 1980–81 disturbances and subsequent responses as actions by politically marginalised black Britons, unresolved on how effectively to counter racial discrimination and disadvantage. A dichotomy existed between those favouring state mechanisms – namely public inquiries – and those, more likely involved in anti-police disorders, believing they would be a waste of time or even provide authorities with evidence to use against them. To the latter group, such inquiries 'were perceived as means to legitimate state interests [as opposed to] the apotheosis of democratic pluralism'.[6] Thus, both responses suggest a desire for increased political inclusion, albeit through differing means. Throughout, I suggest the disturbances can be viewed broadly within the 'collective bargaining by riot' framework, while acknowledging the dangers of post-hoc characterisations that overemphasise disorders as coherent, planned actions. However, when considering rationales exhibited during the disturbances and links with longer struggles, such action can be seen as attempts to address and improve their situation. As John Solomos stated: 'not all groups enjoy the same opportunity to participate politically through channels defined as legitimate'.[7] This is encapsulated by a quotation from Mike and Trevor Phillips' *Windrush*: 'People were crying out, like, Come down here and look at us down here, for Christ's sake … We were crying out to the politicians to come'.[8] Therefore, I argue the disorders can be viewed as 'a rational response to genuine grievances'.[9]

While some portray the disturbances as merely expressions of frustration and anger – 'an expressive rather than instrumental form of activity' – this work contends that, although such motivations were present, underlying desires to have their situation addressed were repeatedly demonstrated.[10] However, as Paul

Bagguley and Yasmin Hussain note, 'We cannot simply assume the ideological unity of the crowd before, during or after the riot' – recognised here through discussion of varying motivations/responses.[11] Similarly, it is important to distinguish the anti-police disturbances addressed by this work from the looting and arson, usually undertaken by others, that followed.[12] Some might argue that, prior to the 1980 Bristol disturbance, there were no precursors and therefore no threat upon which to balance 'collective bargaining by riot' actions. However, my contention is that US 'race riots' and Northern Irish 'battlegrounds' provided ample examples.[13]

There has been a long history of settlers relocating to Britain and, as Colin Holmes noted, it is difficult to locate a period within British history where immigration did not take place. Consequently, much has been written on the topic.[14] Increased postwar Commonwealth migration and influences from US social scientists led British counterparts to turn their attention to 'race relations' in the 1950s and 1960s, earning a reputation as a 'race relations industry' – although their approaches came under growing criticism into the 1980s, particularly due to beliefs that studying 'race relations' implied 'naturally occurring populations between whom there are relations'.[15]

During the 1960s and 1970s, numerous writers portrayed the postwar years as a period of laissez-faire immigration, where successive governments did nothing about Commonwealth migration until popular anxiety or migrant labour systems forced the creation of the 1962 Commonwealth Immigrants Act.[16] With the release of government documents, this was subsequently challenged: for example, Bob Carter et al. revealed the state was instrumental in constructing black immigration as a 'problem', and 'racist policies and practices were an integral part of this construction'.[17] Stuart Hall et al.'s seminal work regarding popular moral panic around mugging in the 1970s, a socially constructed 'black crime', highlighted how political and social discourses portrayed black people – supposedly more predisposed to criminality – as a 'social problem' in Britain, incorporating pre-existing views of racial hierarchies.[18] Thus, black immigration was characterised as a problem and, by extension, so were black people themselves – leading to disproportional targeting by the police.[19]

Facing discrimination and racial attacks, minority ethnic groups in Britain organised themselves in self-defence and self-advancement, often influenced by transnational Black Power and Pan-Africanism ideologies; Gilroy has forwarded the 'Black Atlantic' as an arena of transnational cultural construction.[20] David J. Smith noted evidence of a growing coherent political ideology: not to the level of explicitly organising the 1980–81 disturbances, but as a collective response to police and societal oppression.[21] Very little research has thus far been conducted into the British Black Power movement, noted by Rosalind Eleanor Wild in describing her PhD thesis as the only book-length study.[22] Robin Bunce and Paul Field have since published their political biography of prominent activist Darcus Howe, using his life as a framework through which to discuss British Black Power; but this remains an understudied area at risk of being 'written out of history'.[23]

Theories of collective violence

The extensive literature regarding collective violence has gone through numerous developments.[24] Early theories of Gustave Le Bon and Floyd Allport, sharing the viewpoint that human behaviour is reduced to the most primitive characteristics in a crowd, have been criticised by those who question assessments of 'blind and meaningless' mass violence as 'not a deliberately chosen response'.[25] S.D. Reicher furthered such arguments when contending these approaches exclude a social basis for the coherence of crowd behaviour, and do not answer key questions of participation and content. His social identity model, later expressed as Self-Categorization Theory, suggested that crowd behaviour is influenced through people defining themselves as sharing a common social identity and thus learning and exhibiting appropriate shared behaviour.[26]

Later works characterised collective violence as a form of protest within broader political strategies, such as Joe Feagin and Harlan Hahn's study of 1960s US 'ghetto revolts':

> Historically, collective violence has been part of the regular and normal political life of all nations, part of the process by which competing interest groups maintain power, gain power, or lose power in the process of jockeying for influence and control over governmental and other social institutions.[27]

Thus, collective violence is seen as a form of contentious politics, utilised to 'accompany, complement and extend organized peaceful attempts by the same people to accomplish their objectives'.[28] Such arguments were pre-empted by social historians like Eric Hobsbawm, who coined the phrase 'collective bargaining by riot' during discussion of machine-breaking by eighteenth- and early nineteenth-century British workers. Hobsbawm reasoned that such actions were more than simple protests; they wanted and expected to achieve positive results.[29]

However, Michael Keith criticised later works for 'replacing the de-individuated, primitive mob of behaviourism with a coldly calculating, politically conscious unit to be regarded as a lucid social actor on the stage of historical struggle'.[30] Considering it academically questionable to legitimise 1980–81 as part of a broader racial mobilisation through attempts to bestow disorders with post-hoc meaning, he attempted to find an alternative to classifying them either as 'criminal subversion' or 'glorious revolution'. The solution Keith forwarded was to avoid issues relating to common-sense models of causality as blame allocation: 'essentially a call for the need to incorporate a notion of *contingency* into all explanations'.[31] While acknowledging such, my study takes its lead from Gilroy: 'spontaneous struggles may sometimes become violent, but this does not render them irreconcilable with a strategic long-term war of position'.[32]

This book's argument is that 1980–81 can be viewed as a spontaneous response from black Britons to racial violence/discrimination and their lack of political representation, and thus an attempt to further their societal and political position. In his seminal work, E.P. Thompson documented how the British people 'were noted throughout Europe for their turbulence', and the eighteenth and nineteenth centuries were 'punctuated by riot'.[33] In some ways, 1980–81 continued a British tradition of marginalised groups utilising collective violence to address their situation.[34]

Spread of disorder

Sidney Tarrow, through a pioneering empirical study of almost 5,000 Italian protest events, demonstrated how 'protest cycles' emerged and spread before subsequently declining, described as 'a phase of heightened conflict and contention across the social system'.[35] Ruud Koopmans later replaced 'cycle' with 'wave', arguing 'cycle' implied periodically recurring trends, whereas 'wave' merely denoted a 'strong increase and subsequent decrease' in levels of contention.[36] Such theories suggest instances of collective action are not independent; rather, occurring within broader protest. The emergence of protest waves has been attributed to changes in the structure of political opportunities, reducing the 'power disparity between authorities and challengers'.[37]

Relatedly, social diffusion theories posit that, through established social networks, actors in social systems are influenced by certain behaviours of 'contagious' others.[38] Potential actors observe and assess the results of others' actions before making their own decision whether or not to adopt the same behaviour.[39] Daniel J. Myers highlighted how this 'contagion' model has been used in multiple studies of collective behaviours, such as disorders and protest.[40] He categorised such work on contagious influence during collective disorder into two themes: long-term contributions and short-term contagion effects.[41] Long-term contributions include positive results of previous disorders – either real or imagined – and an increased sense of pride towards their social group; short-term contagions provoke others to discuss and consider such action themselves, dubbed by Pamela E. Oliver an 'occasion for deciding'.[42]

In his public inquiry into the 1981 disturbances, Lord Scarman concluded it likely that a 'copycat' element, exacerbated by extensive media coverage, spread disorder nationwide.[43] Such arguments characterise collective disorder as irrational and imitative. Roger Ball examined the 1980 Bristol disturbance, conducting a micro-history of the events leading to a city-based 'mini-wave' of disorder, raising interesting questions relating to the spread of protest more generally.[44] He argued that subsequent disorders in the Bristol area were not the 'copycat' result of an unconscious reaction to media coverage, but rather a rational and evaluative decision-making process, influenced by contagions spread via a social network of peer relationships, education, family links and other factors. This work reaches similar conclusions for disturbances elsewhere in 1981.

1980–81

Less than a year into Margaret Thatcher's divisive Conservative Government, the first confrontation between the public and state appeared on the streets of England; however, this has often been overlooked in favour of an emphasis on later battles with miners and trade unions. For example, Richard Vinen's work portrays the weaknesses of Thatcher's Government in the early 1980s, but the nationwide disturbances that threatened to condemn their policies are awarded just one page's attention.[45] Additionally, as Stephen Brooke highlighted, historians have struggled to consider the 1980s outside of the 'cast of Margaret Thatcher's long shadow'. This work, by no means ignoring the significant impact of Thatcherism, attempts to note developments that are, to some extent, 'independent of', as well as interdependent with immediate political change'.[46]

While some works have examined previous racial disturbances in Britain in the twentieth century, fewer have examined 1980–81 in detail.[47] Studies published soon after events have often been 'heavily influenced by wider political pressures and realities'.[48] Indeed, one collection of responses based on a conference convened by John Benyon in 1982, provides a range of opinions from black activists, social scientists, journalists and senior police and governmental officials, largely conforming to expectations of their respective positions.[49] Similarly, Martin Kettle and Lucy Hodges systematically explored the main disturbances, characterising them as disorganised activity and focusing on the contemporary importance of improving police/community relations; although the broader social and economic situation is not disregarded, attention is focused on policing aspects.[50] Furthermore, Anandi Ramamurthy highlighted how work on 1980–81 has largely focused on sociological analysis of causes of unrest, rather than 'attempts by communities to organise in their defence'.[51] In part, this work aims to address this through examination of organisation before and following disorder, formation of local Defence Committees, and contrasting attitudes towards state-sanctioned public inquiries. It achieves this through study of a range of conventional and recently released archival records, as well as interviews, records of grassroots political organisations, individual and organisational submissions to inquiries, and community periodicals, allowing for examination of perspectives not otherwise represented in official records.

Focus of discussion is predominantly upon local black populations, but some have argued considering underlying aspects of class is more appropriate, portraying disorders as class-based uprisings. Yet, areas of high unemployment such as Yorkshire, Scotland and Newcastle did not experience similar disturbances.[52] Evan Smith demonstrated how 1980–81 was categorised either as acts of class by leftist writers or ethnicity by radical black activists. This work supports Smith's conclusions that a hybrid interpretation is most beneficial to fully understanding the complex nature and causes of these events.[53] However, not claiming to be an all-inclusive exploration of the many different aspects of the disorders, its focus remains firmly upon the involvement and response of black Britons.

John Rex and Sally Tomlinson addressed the relationship between race and class, arguing that, occupying an inferior position throughout aspects such as housing, education and employment, British minority ethnic groups found themselves in an 'underclass': as such, they formed an 'underclass-for-itself', with distinct forms of organisation, culture, political goals and ideology.[54] Such characterisations have since been questioned, notably by Edward Pilkington, whose analysis of the labour market position of minority ethnic groups in Britain queried the notion of an ethnically distinguishable underclass.[55] Class divisions within the black population fostered great hostility, as middle-class black Britons, such as those occupying positions within state 'race relations' institutions, were branded 'sell-outs' or 'careerists' who had abandoned the working-class 'black masses' to further their own agendas.[56] This relationship can be observed throughout responses to 1980–81, as political blackness was often split along class divides. More recently, Satnam Virdee detailed the position of racism and anti-racism in English working-class movements, and how various minority ethnic groups have been designated the 'racialized outsider'.[57]

Britons – black, minority ethnic, and white – participated in the 1980–81 disorders to varying degrees, with Reicher quoting one observer believing 'politically they were all black'.[58] However, analysing arrest and other statistics for Brixton, such as involvement in looting or arson, Keith contended that the notion that 'Black and White regularly fought a united battle on the streets ... becomes virtually untenable'.[59] Different groups took to the streets, but their motivations and actions differed greatly. Similarly, Keith rejected descriptions of 'the average rioter' as either 'black youth' or 'the young'; highlighting that disorders included a broad cross-section of black communities and violent anti-police conflict tended to involve older people, he argued that portrayals of 1980–81 as 'youth rebellion' are attempts to relegate their significance.[60]

Public inquiries

Despite the importance of public inquiries within the British legal system, there is a dearth of academic research on their history. Indeed, the foreword to Jason Beer's 2009 work (erroneously) declared: 'Astonishingly, this is the first book on public inquiries ever to be published.'[61] Public inquiries investigate issues of serious public concern, examining in a public manner events and issues under its remit; consequently playing an important role in the 'theatre of government'.[62] Stephen Sedley provided an alternative definition: 'the organizing of controversy into a form more catholic than litigation but less anarchic than street fighting'.[63] Usually chaired by a prominent judge or lord, a public inquiry accepts evidence from the public and organisations, conducting hearings in a more public forum than typical government mechanisms – thus viewed as a form of discourse with authorities that engages with local communities rather than simply encroaching upon them. There are more requests for inquiries than can be expected to be conducted, due to their cost – time and financially – and their potential to undermine establishment authority. However, as no other apparatus provides the same potential for participation and dialogue between the authorities and public they have been 'Britain's favoured mechanism for ascertaining the facts after any major breakdown or controversy'.[64]

The term 'public inquiry' has a broad meaning within the British legal system and multiple forms are available, such as departmental inquiries established by ministers, or more formal public inquiries through resolution of Parliament. Arguably dating to eleventh-century Domesday surveys, public inquiries began to resemble modern-day incarnations in the mid-nineteenth century.[65] Prior to the introduction of the Inquiries Act 2005, larger public inquiries fell under the remit of the Tribunals and Inquiries (Evidence) Act 1921 – initially enacted to investigate accusations that Ministry of Munitions officials destroyed papers relating to contracts they awarded.[66] The Act specified that if Parliament deemed a tribunal be established into a matter of 'urgent public importance', it should have all the powers, rights and privileges vested in the High Court – such as compelling the production of documents and enforcing witness attendance and examination under oath.[67] A 1966 Royal Commission established that the legal costs of anyone involved in a public inquiry should be met out of public funds, demonstrating both their perceived importance and how their often-spiralling costs somewhat explains reluctance to establish them.[68]

There are many reasons why public inquiries might be established, other than simple attempts to uncover the truth. As well as being an important tool of public accountability, they can depoliticise and remove issues from the political arena and provide the appearance that ministers share public concern, and, while independent from the government, inquiries are still largely under its control in terms of members, reference, and publishing of their reports.[69] Despite their perceived independence, inquiries exist within a political environment, influenced by the intentions, language and scope of those commissioning them, and Angela Hegarty contended that public inquiries are employed 'not as a tool to find truth and establish accountability … but as a way of deflecting criticism and avoiding blame'.[70] Thus, Michael Lipsky and David J. Olson concluded public inquiries create expectations that cannot be fulfilled – certainly true of some reactions towards Lord Scarman's inquiry into the 1981 disturbances.[71]

Despite growing discontent with British authorities, public inquiries – part of that political establishment – were seemingly regarded by some almost as a panacea, whether through genuine belief inquiries would address their issues, or simply as a method to obtain resources and provide a platform for local residents 'to be heard'.[72] Government rejections of most calls for public inquiries, partly due to cost and potentially undermining their authority, have been linked to Thatcherite 'New Right' ideology of a rejection of compromise and movement from apparent postwar consensus politics.[73] Persistent denials of public inquiries into all but the most controversial events demonstrates a calculated governmental response that 'a full public investigation of facts that are likely to help its political opponents is not a price worth paying for the stilling of public clamour'.[74]

Additionally, research has highlighted additional barriers to obtaining public inquiries faced by political 'outsider groups', further noting the 'considerable protection from public scrutiny afforded to the police' and 'the difficulties in securing any form of official condemnation of police action'.[75]

Previous US inquiries into racial disturbances suggested frameworks for British equivalents, but also exemplified their problems. For example, the emphasis placed on security issues by the McCone Commission into the 1965 Watts 'riots' frustrated its social science advisors, and such inquiries were viewed with cynicism as previous investigations had produced 'the same analysis, the same recommendations, and the same inaction'.[76] Indeed, concerns about the potential content of the 1967 Kerner Commission, examining US racial disorders, prompted limitations in its budget, scope and personnel; President Johnson, facing a white backlash, accepted the report but refused to implement its recommendations. Thus, Keith concluded that the Kerner Commission was, to some extent, no more than another pressure group, 'compelled to trade idealism for pragmatism in the art of what is possible'.[77]

Following the Brixton disturbances in April 1981, Home Secretary William Whitelaw announced the establishment of a public inquiry chaired by Lord Leslie Scarman; although a widely respected judge, he did not enjoy support from all.[78] During its eighty-four-year duration, just twenty-four inquiries were held under the Tribunals and Inquiries (Evidence) Act 1921.[79] Scarman's was not one of these, instead established under Section 32 of the Police Act 1964, which gave the Home Secretary powers to establish a 'local inquiry' into 'any matter connected with the policing of any area'. As will be demonstrated, this provoked criticism as it focused investigations onto immediate policing aspects rather than broader social/political conditions or governmental policies.[80] While campaigners had spent years calling for a public inquiry addressing endemic racism, racial disadvantage and police brutality, the one eventually established continued earlier trends of seeking to depoliticise racial aspects.

A note on terminology

'Black' is a term that continues to be contested. As Uvanney Maylor argued, employing collective terminology to describe groups of people with differing backgrounds, cultures and self-identification is extremely problematic.[81] Black had historically been used to describe essentially anyone 'non-white', but, as Yasmin Alibhai-Brown highlighted, there has often been an 'absurd assumption that all whites are part of the same homogenous group'.[82] Similarly, Lucy Bland described, in discussion of miscegenation fears in post-First World War Britain, that 'imprecision as to the labelling of different peoples was indicative of the slippage between ideas of race, ethnicity and culture'.[83] However, despite communities with disparate histories 'from the Caribbean, South Asia, and Africa [being] lumped together', black was used in the 1960s–1980s as a positively empowering term of self-description to incorporate and unite wider groups with 'experiences of colonialism'; as Ramamurthy concluded: 'Black was not simply a skin colour, but a political position'.[84] In recent years, such usage has diminished due to its inability to stress the diversity of cultural identities and the range of ways racism may be experienced.[85] Although not ignoring groups such as British Asians – for instance, disorders in Southall primarily occurred between white skinheads and Asian youth – this work focuses analysis upon anti-police disorders where the prominent ethnic group was the Afro-Caribbean community, and the term black is therefore used to refer to this group.[86] Where discussing common shared experience of people elsewhere defined as 'non-white'/'people of colour', I refer to 'minority ethnic groups' – itself an imperfect term.

Similarly, despite placing 1980–81 within a 'collective bargaining by riot' framework, they are deliberately not referred to as 'riots'. As Charles Tilly noted, the term 'embodies a political judgement rather than an analytical distinction', inherently suggesting criminal and illegitimate actions and removing agency.[87] Kettle and Hodges rightly pointed out that any terminology, including their own titular 'Uprising', contains linguistic baggage, before concluding: ' "riot" will have to do'.[88] With this taken into consideration, this book instead refers to 'disturbances' or 'disorder' conducted by 'participants', although these terms are not without their own issues. It is important to reiterate the undoubted involvement of many individuals who used the opportunity to engage purely in criminal actions under the guise of protest. Thus, where appropriate, such as discussing public reactions or authorities' portrayals of events, 'riots' or 'rioters' are used.

Structure

This book is generally chronologically structured, to examine how events played a role in influencing subsequent actions; while one risk of such an approach is discussion simply becoming narrative, this has attempted to be negated throughout. Three case studies of Bristol, Brixton and Manchester are examined through double-chapter studies, before an epilogue reflects upon the legacy of 1980–81 and relevant subsequent developments.

Chapter 1 provides historical context by considering the situation for black and minority ethnic people in Britain, noting the development of activism and militancy between the growth of postwar Commonwealth migration and outbreak of disorder in Bristol; in effect, acting as a 'roadmap to 1980–81'.

Chapters 2–3 explore the disturbance occurring in the St Pauls area of Bristol on 2 April 1980. A city that authorities deemed a model for 'good race relations', it is shown that the reality was somewhat different. Chapter 2 examines the background to the disorder, subsequently noting how a police withdrawal at the height of disorder led to an increased propensity for 'hard' policing responses. Similarly, chapter 3 observes contrasting local opinion towards the prospect of a state-sanctioned public inquiry and argues that the authorities' focus on law and order, rather than broader social/political aspects, set the template for responses to subsequent disturbances.

Chapters 4–5 study the Brixton disturbances, the most well-known outbreak of disorder in 1981. Chapter 4 examines the formal local Liaison Committee, established in an attempt to improve troubled police/community relations, which broke down prior to disorders due to tensions regarding policing attitudes and tactics. Chapter 5 focuses on the establishment and report of the Scarman public inquiry, which prompted a dichotomous reaction and boycott from some local people and organisations.

Chapter 6 considers the nationwide disturbances in July 1981, specifically Southall, Bradford, Toxteth and Moss Side. It argues that police tactics and equipment were strengthened following previous disturbances, as authorities attempted to prevent public disorder rather than address issues of racism or criticism of their economic and social policies. Chapter 7 provides a detailed examination of the Moss Side Defence Committee, which boycotted the local County Council inquiry into the disturbances.

Finally, the epilogue examines the differing reactions to 1980–81, before providing an overview of its legacy through subsequent developments related to race, policing, protest and public inquiries. While there have been a number of advancements, recent statistics regarding the policing of minority ethnic groups and deaths in police custody demonstrate many of the issues remain unresolved.

Notes

1   Keith, *Race, Riots and Policing*, p. 52. For 1919 racist riots, see: Jenkinson, *Black 1919*; Evans, 'Race Riots'; Murphy, *Racism and Reaction*, pp. 13–42. For 1958, see: Pilkington, *Beyond the Mother Country*; Phillips and Phillips, *Windrush*, pp. 158–80; Miles, 'Riots of 1958'.

2   Gilroy, *Ain't No Black*, p. 237.

3   Solomos, *Black Youth*, p. 237; Benyon, 'Civil Disorder', pp. 33–5.

4   See: Epilogue; Frost and Phillips, '2011 Summer Riots'; Smith, 'Summer of '81'.

5   See: Lea and Young, 'The Riots'.

6   Scraton, 'Official Inquiries', p. 50.

7   Solomos, *Race and Racism*, p. 199.

8   Michael Nesbeth, in Phillips and Phillips, *Windrush*, p. 365.

9   Rowe, *Racialisation of Disorder*, p. 153.

10 For such an argument, see: Waddington, *Liberty and Order*, p. 6.

11 Bagguley and Hussain, *Riotous Citizens*, p. 33.

12 See, for example: Keith, *Race, Riots and Policing*, pp. 101–4; Kettle and Hodges, *Uprising!*, pp. 28–9; Brain, *History of Policing*, p. 68.

13 See, for example: Fogelson, *Los Angeles Riots*; Feagin and Hahn (eds), *Ghetto Revolts*; Sanders and Wood, *Times of Troubles*; Dawson *et al.* (eds), *Northern Ireland Troubles*.

14 Holmes, *John Bull's Island*, p. 3. See, for example: Winder, *Bloody Foreigners*; Hiro, *Black British*; Ramdin, *Reimaging Britain*; Olusoga, *Black and British*.

15 Pilkington, *Racial Disadvantage*, pp. 48–9; Rich, *Race and Empire*, pp. 169–204. Examples of early studies include: Glass, *Newcomers*; Foot, *Immigration and Race*; Deakin, *Citizenship and British Society*.

16 For example, Foot, 'Immigration and the British Labour Movement'; Rose, *Colour and Citizenship*; Freeman and Spencer, 'Black Workers'.

17 Carter *et al.*, 'Racialisation of Black Immigration', 335; Gilroy, *Ain't No Black*.

18 Hall *et al.*, *Policing the Crisis*. See: Gabriel, *Whitewash*, pp. 139–41; Schwarz, *Memories of Empire*; Gilroy and Lawrence, 'Two-Tone Britain', p. 126.

19 Cashmore and McLaughlin (eds), *Policing Black People*, pp. 1–9; Fryer, *Staying Power*, pp. 381–6.

20 Gilroy, *The Black Atlantic*; Tuck, *Malcolm X*; Joseph (ed.), *Black Power Movement*; James, *Pan-African Revolt*; James, *Decolonization from Below*.

21 Smith, 'Policing and Urban Unrest', p. 72.

22 Wild, 'Black Power in Britain'.

23 Bunce and Field, *Darcus Howe*, p. ii.

24 For a recent overview, see: Bagguley and Hussain, *Riotous Citizens*, pp. 11–37. Jacqueline Jenkinson noted rioting has received much attention from historians and sociologists, but often focused on earlier periods than 'modern-day rioting': Jenkinson, *Black 1919*, p. 20.

25 Le Bon, *The Crowd*; Allport, *Social Psychology*. For discussion, see: Joshua *et al.*, *To Ride the Storm*, pp. 11–12; Jenkinson, *Black 1919*, pp. 20–5.

26 Reicher, 'St. Pauls Riot', 18–19.

27 Feagin and Hahn (eds), *Ghetto Revolts*, p. 146.

28 Tilly, 'Collective Violence', p. 343.

29 Hobsbawm, 'The Machine Breakers'. See: Thompson, *English Working Class*, p. 554; Rudé, *The Crowd*.

30 Keith, *Race, Riots and Policing*, p. 88.

31 *Ibid.*, pp. 90–5, emphasis in original.

32 Gilroy, 'Race and Class Formation', cited in *ibid.*, pp. 90–1.

33 Thompson, *English Working Class*, p. 62.

34 See: Stevenson, *Popular Disturbances*; Hampton, *A Radical Reader*. For the dangers of viewing these 'struggles as merely part of a continuous narrative of lower class rebellion in Britain', see: Smith, 'Conflicting Narratives', 25.

35 Tarrow, *Democracy and Disorder*, p. 153.

36 Koopmans, 'Protest in Time and Space', p. 21.

37 See, for example: Tarrow, *Power in Movement*; McAdam, 'Diffusion Processes'; Koopmans, 'Protest Waves'.

38 See: Rogers, *Diffusion of Innovations*; Strang, 'Adding Social Structure'; McPhail and Wohlstein, 'Individual and Collective Behavior'.

39 Oberschall, 'Protest Diffusion'.

40 For example: Hobsbawm and Rudé, *Captain Swing*; Bohstedt, 'Dynamics of Riots', Olzak and Shanahan, 'Deprivation Race Riots'.

41 Myers, 'Collective Violence', 175–8.

42 Oliver, 'Bringing the Crowd Back In', 11.

43 Scarman, *Report*, p. 14.

44 Ball, 'Violent Urban Disturbances'.

45 Vinen, *Thatcher's Britain*, p. 131. They similarly play a minor role in Jackson and Saunders' edited collection *Making Thatcher's Britain*.

46 Brooke, 'Historicizing 1980s Britain', 20, 24.

47 For previous racial disturbances, further to cited works on 1919/1958, see for example: Panayi (ed.), *Racial Violence*; Rowe, *Racialisation of Disorder*.

48 Bloch and Solomos (eds), *Race and Ethnicity*, p. 3.

49 Benyon (ed.), *Scarman and After*.

50 Kettle and Hodges, *Uprising!*

51 Ramamurthy, *Black Star*, p. 121.

52 Vinen, *Thatcher's Britain*, p. 131. For further discussion, and how 'shared experiences of being youth, working-class and living under crisis conditions' led disorder to appear in areas without an appreciable black presence, see: Gilroy and Lawrence, 'Two-Tone Britain'.

53 Smith, 'Conflicting Narratives'. See: Bagguley and Hussain, *Riotous Citizens*, pp. 27–36.

54 Rex and Tomlinson, *Colonial Immigrants*. See: Sivanandan, 'Race, Class and the State'; Hall *et al.*, *Policing the Crisis*.

55 Pilkington, *Racial Disadvantage*, pp. 51–92. See: Daye, *Middle-Class Blacks*; Centre for Contemporary Cultural Studies, *The Empire Strikes Back*.

56 Daye, *Middle-Class Blacks*, p. 3; Rex and Tomlinson, *Colonial Immigrants*; Sivanandan, *Different Hunger*.

57 Virdee, *Racialized Outsider*, pp. 3, 112.

58 Reicher, 'St. Pauls Riot', 15.

59 Keith, *Race, Riots and Policing*, pp. 97, 116. See: Bagguley and Hussain, *Riotous Citizens*, pp. 4–5; Joshua *et al.*, *To Ride the Storm*; Cooper, 'Merseyside Riots'.

60 Keith, *Race, Riots and Policing*, pp. 5, 116–17; Joshua *et al.*, *To Ride the Storm*. For the 'crisis of black youth', see: Solomos, *Black Youth*.

61 Beer, *Public Inquiries*, p. vii. Wraith and Lamb's *Public Inquiries* pre-dates it by some thirty-eight years. See: Elliot and McGuiness, 'Public Inquiry'.

62 For discussion, including of dramaturgy theory, see for example: Grube, 'Drama of Public Accountability'; Hajer, 'Dramaturgy of Policy Deliberation'; Rough, 'Public Inquiries'.

63 Sedley, 'Public Inquiries', 469.

64 Jasanoff, 'Restoring Reason', p. 218.

65 Wraith and Lamb, *Public Inquiries*, pp. 17–21.

66 Beer, *Public Inquiries*, pp. 6–7.

67 Tribunals of Inquiry (Evidence) Act 1921, s 1(1).

68 Royal Commission on Tribunals of Inquiry, *Report*.

69 Woodhouse, 'Judicial Inquiries', 25–6.

70 Keith, *Race, Riots and Policing*, p. 74; Hegarty, 'Public Inquiries', 1149.

71 Lipsky and Olson, *Commission Politics*. See: chapter 5.

72 See: Elliot and McGuiness, 'Public Inquiry', 15.

73 Smith, 'From Consensus to Conflict'.

74 Sedley, 'Public Inquiries', 470.

75 Holdaway, 'Police Accountability', 85; Newburn and Hayman, *Policing, Surveillance and Social Control*, p. 5.

76 Black psychologist Kenneth Clark testifying to the Kerner Commission, referencing reports from investigatory committees into racial disorders in 1919, 1943 and 1965.

77 Keith, *Race, Riots and Policing*, p. 75. See: Hrach, *Riot Report*; Lipsky, 'Riot Commission'; Campbell, 'Commission Studies'.

78 See: chapter 5.

79 See: Beer, *Public Inquiries*, pp. 8–14.

80 Brain, *History of Policing*, p. 68.

81 Maylor, 'Meaning of "Black"?'.

82 Alibhai-Brown, *Who Do We Think We Are?*, p. vii. See: Dyer, 'The Matter of Whiteness'.

83 Bland, 'White Women and Men of Colour', 30; Tabili, *Workers and Racial Difference*, p. 9.

84 Wild, 'Black Power in Britain', p. 8; Tuck, 'Malcolm X's Visit', 88; Ramamurthy, *Black Star*, p. 65.

85 See, for example: Modood and Berthoud (eds), *Ethnic Minorities*; Mason, *Race and Ethnicity*, pp. 16–17.

86 Huq, 'Youth Culture and Antiracism', 45. For Southall, see: Ramamurthy, *Black Star*; Brah, 'The "Asian" in Britain', pp. 55–8.

87 Tilly, *Collective Violence*, pp. 18–19. For discussion, see: Bagguley and Hussain, *Riotous Citizens*, pp. 5–6; Rudé, *The Crowd*, pp. 7–8.

88 Kettle and Hodges, *Uprising!*, p. 10. 'Uprising' was utilised by many community activists, to remove the criminal context and introduce a political perspective.

1

Resistance to rebellion

Well believe me I am speaking broadmindedly,
I am glad to know my Mother Country,
I've been traveling to countries years ago,
But this is the place I wanted to know,
Darling, London, that's the place for me.

Lord Kitchener – London is the Place for Me

Dreams are just an illusion,
Pavements are not gold.
Hatred, hatred and oppression,
Down in the Ghetto.

Misty in Roots – Ghetto of the City

TO UNDERSTAND why disturbances erupted around England in 1980–81, it is necessary to examine the broader historical context. As Michael Keith stressed, 'Such periodization cannot on its own provide an explanation for such conflict, but without it any explanation will inevitably lack plausibility'.[1] This first chapter addresses the history of black and minority ethnic people in Britain following increased Commonwealth migration after the Second World War, and subsequent relationship with an often-hostile society, experiencing widespread discrimination, racial violence and a political consensus to depoliticise and marginalise racial issues. It examines the development of activism and militancy, considering the build-up of antipathy towards the police due to their policies, actions and general rejection of criticism. While discussion within this relatively short chapter unavoidably threatens to afford this history only cursory attention, it illustrates the gradual building of discontent towards a British state offering minority ethnic groups little support, particularly regarding treatment at the hands of the police, as well as highlighting growing black mobilisation.

As an opening chapter, this is, unavoidably, a broad overview of the struggles faced by black and minority ethnic communities in Britain; but engagement with a range of sources and existing literature highlights increasing frustration towards the authorities and growth of self-defence and activism, as it was believed both were becoming increasingly required. The chapter's title, 'Resistance to rebellion', inspired by Ambalavaner Sivanandan, itself provides a basic overview of the change demonstrated through these years.[2] Discussion in this chapter, and indeed entire book, aligns with what Edward Pilkington termed the 'imperialism–racism framework'. Opposed to the 'immigrant–host framework', which suggests minority ethnic groups will be assimilated into the host society after a period of adaption and acceptance, the 'imperialism–racism framework' evokes imperial beliefs of superiority and domination, suggesting that the passing of time will not necessarily see the elimination of racial discrimination.[3]

Many local organisations were established during this period in an attempt to participate in the political process and affect change, although these often went ignored or were marginalised by authorities. As argued throughout, this led some black Britons to conclude that conventional means had failed and the only recourse was militancy and clashes with the police – visual symbols of the state that had repeatedly failed them. Some explanations of 1980–81, especially from authorities downplaying connections with their policies, attempted to portray disorders as 'sheer criminality' from 'rioters' simply wanting 'rewards' of looting or excitement. While disorders themselves were triggered by seemingly spontaneous outbursts, they occurred within broader political activities attempting to combat ongoing racial disadvantage and discrimination. As Ron Ramdin concluded, in previous years, 'the harassed black community offered strong resistance. Rebellion, after a long gestation period, eventually came in the early 1980s'.[4]

Beyond the 'Windrush Generation'

To begin, it is essential to acknowledge the long history of immigration into Britain. Zig Layton-Henry summarised how, 'Throughout its history Britain, especially England, has been a destination for immigrants and refugees', and Peter Fryer highlighted evidence suggesting African soldiers were stationed on Hadrian's Wall and black people were therefore in Britain some 200 years before Anglo-Saxons became the first to be called 'English'.[5] This opposes views suggesting the postwar period saw the 'beginnings of non-white immigration', still espoused by some writers, and others use the appearance at London's

Tilbury Dock of 492 passengers on board the *Empire Windrush* on 22 June 1948 as a 'culturally imagined moment of arrival'.[6] Scholars such as Kennetta Hammond Perry have correctly demonstrated the potential pitfalls of this 'Windrush-as-origins' discourse, which threatens to downplay the role of colonial history upon racism and suggest that postwar Caribbean migration was the main factor leading to the so-called 'colour problem'.[7] Previous incidents of collective racial violence, for instance 1919 racist riots between white and minority ethnic workers in major British seaports such as London, Cardiff and Liverpool, demonstrate how minority ethnic groups were already viewed as a 'problem' within mainland Britain.[8]

Although by no means a postwar creation, immigration was certainly significant during this period. For example, the British population rose by over a million by 1961 due to an influx of European refugees, Irish citizens and British subjects from the West Indies, India and Pakistan.[9] Many were recruited by the government to relieve substantial postwar labour shortages, but official treatment of Commonwealth migrants was noticeably disparate – not to claim European/Irish immigrants easily assimilated into British society, or downplay the often-hostile reaction they received.[10] Arrivals from Ireland were frequently treated by the state essentially as British citizens, as it was deemed too difficult to include them within immigration controls, demonstrated by a 1954 Working Party suggestion that the government should 'argue boldly that the population of the British Isles was essentially one'.[11] Similarly, European immigrants benefited from government initiatives such as favourable publicity campaigns, English language classes and support to join appropriate trade unions – a celebrated symbol of 'Britishness'. Indeed, Kathleen Paul demonstrated that 'interested official departments were committed to ensuring [their] "ultimate absorption into the British community" '.[12]

Conversely, those entering postwar Britain from its colonies acquired limited support. In fact, following the *Windrush*'s arrival, eleven Labour MPs immediately wrote to Prime Minister Clement Attlee fearing the negative consequence such migrants would have upon the 'harmony, strength and cohesion of our public and social life'.[13] As subjects of the British Empire, or 'citizens of the United Kingdom and Colonies' as created by the 1948 British Nationality Act, they should have faced fewer difficulties.[14] As Bill Schwarz noted, such arrivals 'were juridically British, regarded themselves as British, and regularly expressed enthusiasm for diverse aspects of the civilization of the British'.[15] However, the British Colonial Office and colonial governments conspired to limit migration by making the process more difficult, including limiting distribution of passports, increasing application fees and stressing a lack of employment for potential migrants.[16] The perceived need for this was heightened by the 1952 McCarran-Walter Act, which strictly limited immigration from the British West Indies into the United States, redirecting many migrants towards Britain.[17] The dichotomous view of Commonwealth migrants as both 'British citizens' and 'undesirables' reveals attitudes that black people were unable to assimilate into British culture and would thus cause social tension.[18] Through an ongoing process, 'colonial subjects' became 'immigrants' and, as Jodi Burkett concluded, 'The long history of people in former colonies being part of the British Empire was simply erased'.[19] Lacking official support, and being 'visibly distinguishable by the colour of their skins', Commonwealth migrants faced great animosity: 'The coloured migrant, and particularly the Negro, appears to be the supreme and ultimate stranger.'[20]

The legacy of the British Empire upon such discriminatory responses must not be understated; during this period, 'Colonial racism was transformed into indigenous racism' as migrants were seen to belong '*to* the Mother Country but not *in* the Mother Country'.[21] For example, Evan Smith and Marinella Marmo detailed the shocking history of 'virginity tests' conducted upon South Asian women migrating to Britain during 1968–79, which they describe as 'the epitome of an attitude of racial superiority and dominance over the black "other" rooted in Britain's colonial past'.[22] Introducing a class perspective, Satnam Virdee demonstrated that the British working-class helped intensify negative reactions through the racialisation of British nationalism. Minority ethnic migrants were viewed as outsiders and 'a source of cheap "foreign" labour deployed by unscrupulous employers with the intention of undermining the hard-won economic security of the white/British worker'.[23]

The British government escalated negative reactions towards Commonwealth migrants, who bore the brunt of popular discontent regarding rising immigration. As Layton-Henry concluded, 'a more positive early lead by government and political leaders might have done much to assuage public anxieties'.[24] This refutes traditional views of the British state being 'negligible' in the development of postwar racism before 1958 racist riots supposedly forced it into action.[25] Such perspectives were contradicted with the release of contemporary government records; for example, Cabinet Secretary Norman Brook observed in 1955 that an official inquiry into Commonwealth migration 'would not be to find a solution (for it is evident what form control must take) but to enlist a sufficient body of public support for the legislation'.[26] Successive postwar British governments linked minority ethnic people with immigration, therefore escalating popular discontent towards them – such as Winston Churchill's attempts in 1955 to persuade the Conservative Party to adopt the slogan 'Keep England White'.[27] Many have argued this construction was deliberate: 'what was perceived as a race problem had to be disguised as an "immigration" problem – a much more politically and socially acceptable issue'.[28]

The 'immigration problem' took centre-stage in 1958 when racial unrest erupted in Nottingham and Notting Hill, where tensions between white working-class and black residents were inflamed by high rents and overcrowding enforced by slumlords such as Peter Rachman.[29] Over 1,000 people took to the streets of Nottingham on 23 August, with the *Nottingham Evening Post* labelling it 'like a slaughterhouse'.[30] Violence spread to London and, on 30 August, seventeen people were arrested after attacks and petrol bombing of black households in Notting Hill. Reporter Colin Eales described the scene:

> I saw a mob of over 700 men, women and children stretching 200 yards along the road. Young children of ten were treating the whole affair as a great joke and shouting: 'Come on, let's get the blacks' ... a fierce cry rent the air and the mob rushed off ... shouting, 'Kill the niggers!'[31]

Disorders continued for several days and, as it appeared that the police either could not or would not protect them from attacks, black residents began to organise their own self-protection. At one gathering, after three speakers urged the formation of organisations and letter-writing to MPs, Michael de Freitas – who from 1964 would become known as black revolutionary Michael X – instead argued: 'You don't want committees and representatives. What you need is to get a few pieces of iron and a bit of organisation so that tonight when they come in here we can defend ourselves.' Such suggestions received approval from the assembled crowd, and they fought back against their attackers.[32]

During a Cabinet meeting the following week, Conservative Home Secretary Rab Butler indicated that competition for housing and employment had led to violence. However, rather than seeking economic or social policies to ease such competition, he advocated immigration controls and powers to deport 'undesirable immigrants'. Likewise, Minister of Labour Iain Macleod proposed denying passports to potential West Indian migrants who could not prove guaranteed employment.[33] Perry demonstrated how perceived 'un-British' racial violence was popularly blamed on increased immigration and the deviant working class – to avoid blemishing notions of 'the tolerant British' – and a poll conducted shortly afterwards by the *Daily Mail* suggested 85 per cent of respondents supported the introduction of hard-line immigration policies.[34] Thus, such events provided the opportunity to foster and exploit growing anti-immigration sentiment, with far-right groups such as the White Defence League, National Labour Party and Oswald Mosley's Union Movement increasing political activity in the area.[35] Clive Bloom even suggested that the 1958 riots were 'entirely manufactured by white racist groups', but such conclusions underplay existing levels of popular discontent.[36]

On 17 May 1959, Antiguan migrant Kelso Cochrane was murdered in Notting Hill: 'stabbed to death in the sight of help'.[37] His death was the culmination of growing tensions and minor violence, which commentators blamed on those who had 'too easily assumed' conflict would be negated by exemplary sentences the previous summer; Judge Justice Salmon had sentenced nine white youths, who had gone 'nigger hunting', to four years in prison. The authorities' and media response to the 1958 riots – blaming far-right groups, 'hooligan' white working-class 'Teddy Boys' and the migrants themselves – produced scapegoats that avoided addressing growing antipathy.[38] Thus, it was believed not enough had been done to prevent Cochrane's murder and, despite violent warnings, 'little official action has followed … the government has a far greater responsibility than it has yet admitted'.[39] A recurring accusation throughout the period, attitudes grew that the government was not doing enough to protect or improve the situation for minority ethnic Britons. For example, in 1959, Labour MP George Rogers proposed appointing a Select Committee or creating an independent body to examine areas with large immigrant populations and suggest remedies to related issues, but this was rejected by ministers because it might offer recommendations the government deemed unacceptable.[40]

Instead, despite evidence suggesting minimal blame on migrants for sporadic violence, demands increased for immigration controls and even deportations. Accordingly, the Home Secretary publicly announced the Government was examining its options.[41] Events such as these allowed officials to move from private contemplations to openly promoting stricter immigration controls, and blame for racial tension was placed upon those who had migrated into Britain, used as scapegoats for societal issues.[42]

Towards political consensus? Immigration controls and 'race relations'

Ira Katznelson argued that, prior to the 1958 racist riots, 'issues of race were raised only sporadically' by Parliament – a period he refers to as 'pre-political consensus'.[43] Following growing public disquiet, Harold Macmillan's Conservative Government began shutting the 'open-door' approach to immigration by enacting controls in the form of the Commonwealth Immigrants Act 1962, with only bearers of government-issued employment vouchers permitted entrance. Outwardly characterised as an economic necessity, it has correctly been viewed as exclusionary based on race and '*de facto* a measure aimed at immigrants from the newer, non-white Commonwealth'.[44] Labour leader Hugh Gaitskell – who maintained 'principled opposition' against immigration controls – deemed it 'a plain anti-Commonwealth Measure in theory and … a plain anti-colour Measure in practice'.[45] Indeed, Conservative Minister William Deedes later admitted: 'The Bill's real purpose was to restrict the influx of coloured immigrants. We were reluctant to say as much openly.'[46]

Those who were granted entry faced many inequalities in their daily lives, with sociological studies attempting to examine the state of British 'race relations'. For example, a survey was established in 1963 by the think-tank the Institute of Race Relations (IRR), modelled upon an influential US survey conducted twenty years previously.[47] IRR director Philip Mason believed study of US experiences could avoid worsening racial tensions in Britain, contending that increased immigration meant 'a menace once comfortably remote has appeared on the doorstep'.[48] While the 1962 Act restricted immigration, it had not eradicated racial tensions: 'The problem is clearly one that will stay with Britain permanently.'[49] As attempts to decrease racial tensions by simply limiting immigration had failed, the IRR warned that other actions were required – but this was greeted with governmental scepticism, deemed an attempt to 'make trouble' for the authorities.[50] This, despite the government's own Commonwealth Immigration Committee similarly recommending immediate 'legislation and administrative action' to address racial pressures.[51]

Unlike the United States, it has often been argued that no effective civil rights movement existed in Britain.[52] For instance, Erik Bleich claimed there was no 'substantial pressure from ethnic minorities', who 'played surprisingly minor roles' in instigating anti-discrimination legislation.[53] Mike and Trevor Phillips believed constant US comparisons have prompted such conclusions:

> For generations reared on the notion that 'black' leadership was defined by a King or a Malcolm X, or that 'black' organisation could only take the form of a Black Panther movement, the forms of black leadership and organisation which emerged in Britain were ramshackle and unimpressive.[54]

Sivanandan argued that a disjointed migrant population, arriving from different locations with different backgrounds, as well as a 'racial division of labour …

[initially] kept the Asian and Afro-Caribbean workers apart and provided little ground for common struggle'.[55] However, minority ethnic 'self-organisation ... was quick to appear'.[56]

One noteworthy action addressing racial inequality was the 1963 Bristol bus boycott, a successful non-violent boycott of a local bus company refusing to employ minority ethnic workers on front-line services, inspired by its 1955 forerunner in Montgomery, Alabama.[57] Led by local youth officer Paul Stephenson after a potential employee, Guy Bailey, was denied an interview because he was black, the boycott of the Bristol Omnibus Company lasted four months and effectively ended the company's colour bar. Largely overlooked until recent anniversaries, Madge Dresser's work is the only detailed study.[58] Boasting support from influential figures such as renowned anti-racist Sir Learie Constantine and prominent left-wing Bristol MP Tony Benn, the boycott repeatedly permeated Parliament and Labour leader Harold Wilson personally met Stephenson, promising a Labour Government would pass anti-discrimination legislation.

Thus, when Labour returned to government in 1964, so too did its campaign promise of introducing anti-discrimination legislation – Labour's National Executive Committee had committed itself to this just one month after the 1958 racist riots.[59] This attempted to counter failures of previous governments who, in Katznelson's words, 'were convinced that immigration controls and the appointment of an advisory council [would] provide for harmonious race relations'.[60] In contrast, observers such as renowned journalist Bernard Levin contended that limiting immigration increased racism: 'If you talk and behave as if the black man were some kind of virus that must be kept out of the body politic, then it is the shabbiest hypocrisy to preach racial harmony at the same time.'[61]

Labour introduced the 1965 Race Relations Act (RRA), the first British legislation to address racial discrimination and punish incitement to racial hatred.[62] However, the Act was a weak, ineffectual law not addressing the main areas of discrimination in employment and housing. It has since been almost universally criticised as feeble or too narrow; Shamit Saggar recorded widespread condemnation for its 'softly, softly' approach, and Bleich labelled it 'truly a whimper of a law'.[63] Despite obvious failings, the RRA did mark the beginning of anti-discrimination legislation, setting a framework for future laws. Michael Banton thus concluded that the shift in public and governmental debate about racial discrimination was of greater significance than the RRA itself, and Steven Fielding added that, despite clear limitations, 'it did constitute the first legal challenge to white prejudice'.[64]

Despite this, following Gaitskell's death in 1963, Labour opposition to immigration control was not sustained under his successor Harold Wilson. Labour's position was partly influenced by the surprise 1964 Smethwick general election victory of Conservative Peter Griffiths, who defended his supporters' reported use of the slogan 'If you want a nigger neighbour, Vote Labour' as merely 'a manifestation of popular feeling'.[65] Layton-Henry summarised that this 'shattering result ... appeared to show that racial prejudices could be effectively exploited for electoral advantage'.[66] Labour Minister Richard Crossman demonstrated the perceived electoral necessity of movement on race and immigration, affirming that Labour 'felt [it] had to out-trump the Tories by doing what they would have done'.[67] Despite bemoaning being forced into such 'illiberal' actions, Labour later extended restrictions, rushing the 1968 Commonwealth Immigrants Act through Parliament within a week, following a sustained right-wing campaign and media-induced moral panic regarding the potential influx of British Asians from Kenya due to its 'Africanisation policy'.[68] Sivanandan linked this shift with a growth in black militancy, due to mounting disillusion with Labour's immigration policies: 'Blacks were enraged. They had lobbied, petitioned, reasoned, demonstrated – even campaigned alongside whites ... and had made no impact.'[69]

Andrew Geddes argued these developments demonstrated bipartisan agreement that immigration had to be controlled, initiated by Labour to diminish its electoral significance and 'depoliticise race issues', with Douglas Ashford agreeing the RRA represented a cross-party agreement 'to do little or nothing'.[70] The RRA was part of a 'package deal', allowing further immigration restrictions while appearing to reward the disadvantaged immigrant population: 'sops to black interests following racist immigration legislation', as Robert Miles and Annie Phizacklea described.[71] By declaring racial discrimination unacceptable in modern Britain, it was hoped that increased restrictions would be more broadly accepted. However, coupling immigration controls with anti-discrimination legislation further demonstrated that authorities assumed numerical limits on immigration would ease racial tensions. Such a connection characterised immigration as a problem and, by extension, migrants themselves. Those who had hoped the RRA would combat racism and discrimination were left frustrated with a weak law, often useless for addressing their problems. Indeed, heralded as the state's effort to tackle issues faced by minority ethnic Britons, its general ineffectiveness undermined the British legal system.[72]

Discontentment was furthered by the Race Relations Board; tasked with enforcing the RRA and the 'linch-pin on which the success of the whole system will depend'.[73] Despite its importance, the Board's formation was a protracted process with numerous failures and increasing panic to appoint suitable members. Mark Bonham Carter was eventually appointed Chair, the thirty-fifth potential candidate proposed.[74] Despite governmental acknowledgement that the RRA was likely to be immediately tested, initial complaints to the yet un-appointed Board merely received replies that the government disapproved of racial prejudice but currently had 'no power to intervene'.[75] Such responses could have served as only cold comfort to those suffering racial discrimination, despite it having been legally prohibited.

Delays establishing the Board restricted the RRA's immediate short-term effectiveness, but long-term success was constrained by its legislative limitations. The Board could only investigate matters falling within the RRA's narrow remit, and it became immediately clear this was insufficient: 73 per cent of complaints received in the Board's first year were outside the scope of the RRA.[76] Exemplifying its limitations, the first conviction under the RRA was subsequently quashed by the Court of Appeal, which determined that posting pamphlets declaring 'Blacks not wanted here' on a local MP's door could not be deemed distribution to the public: 'It might amount to publication if passers-by could see them, but at the time it had been dark.'[77]

For some, Enoch Powell's infamous 'Rivers of Blood' speech in Birmingham on 20 April 1968 is the embodiment of incitement to racial hatred. Recounting a purported conversation with a constituent fearing a future where 'the black man will have the whip hand over the white man', Powell concluded: 'We must be mad, literally mad, as a nation to be permitting the annual inflow of some 50,000 dependents ... It is like watching a nation busily engaged in heaping up its own funeral pyre.'[78] Despite calls to prosecute Powell under the RRA, Attorney-General Sir Elwyn Jones decided against doing so, believing Powell could easily escape prosecution by simply stating he did not intend to incite racial hatred, and, despite his speech's extensive press coverage, it had not occurred at a public meeting.[79] Tariq Ali, demonstration leader against racial discrimination, concluded the decision made 'a mockery of the whole law and establishes a very bad precedent'.[80]

As Powell escaped punishment, other than removal from the Shadow Cabinet, it appeared to embolden others sharing such beliefs to express them.[81] Estimates suggest that 6,000–7,000 men participated in strikes supporting Powell, a Gallup poll indicated that 74 per cent of the population agreed with his speech, and the swing to the Conservatives in the 1970 election was attributed to it.[82] Camilla Schofield argued that, through various interjections, Powell had helped reframe the myth of the Second World War from the 'People's War' into one of Britain 'permanently under siege', subsequently extended to an assertion of public self-reliance against the liberal state.[83] Powell's 'Rivers of Blood' opened floodgates to similar views, pushed both the Conservatives and Labour towards stricter immigration controls, and altered the political debate; in Burkett's words, 'Powell's speech was about much more than immigration. It was about what it meant to be British, who was included and, most importantly, who was excluded'.[84]

Furthermore, apparent willingness to pursue incitement to racial hatred prosecutions against black activists more readily than white counterparts furthered discontent. Gavin Schaffer reasoned that this was due to the considered language employed by white politicians rather than flagrant racism, but 'it appeared [to observers] that new race relations laws were actually designed to prosecute black Britons'.[85] On the same day that white workers marched in support of Powell, representatives from over fifty organisations formed the Black People's Alliance (BPA), notably holding a conference 'with declarations of unity and of gratitude to Mr. Enoch Powell'.[86] A 'militant front for Black Consciousness and against racialism', it led marches on Downing Street protesting immigration controls, and its obvious dissatisfaction with the state was demonstrated by its exclusion of any organisation that had cooperated with government policy. Both Powell's speech and the BPA prompted a number of militant black organisations appearing across England, clearly deeming the state incapable of delivering progress.[87]

The 1965 RRA was strengthened by Labour in 1968 and 1976, extending anti-discrimination legislation into housing, employment and education; yet, this was still lacking and much damage had been done. Manchester MP Paul Rose complained it had taken ten years for his suggested amendments to be legislated, 'by which time it was too late'.[88] In addition, after the 1968 RRA, government services such as the police were not covered. Even proposals to amend the police discipline code – 'no more than a presentational device' – were dropped after 'intense and deep-seated' opposition from the Police Federation and Police Advisory Board.[89] This was later lamented by former Home Secretary James Callaghan: 'we gave way on it. I regret that we did'.[90] This omission would continue until 2000, when – following the Macpherson public inquiry deeming the police 'institutionally racist' – the 1976 RRA was amended to include them.[91]

Anti-discrimination legislation did not solve many of the issues faced by minority ethnic groups in Britain. Research by the Policy Studies Institute in the 1980s showed that levels of racial discrimination were largely unaffected by legislation, and Tom Rees argued that widespread institutional, cultural and societal discrimination could not be effectively challenged through systems relying upon victim complaints.[92] Community activist Gus John recalled a reluctance to use the law due to its ineffectiveness and lack of 'the political culture that supported its use'.[93] Weak, ineffectual laws prevented advancement due to contentions that issues had been legislatively addressed, leading black and minority ethnic groups to become increasingly disillusioned with the state. As Claus Offe detailed: 'increasingly visible conflict between the promise and experience, form and content of state policies can lead … to a growing difficulty for state policies to win acceptance for the legitimating rules on which political power is based'.[94] In the context of fumbling, half-hearted attempts at anti-discrimination legislation, it is perhaps unsurprising that feeling spread that the British government would not help black and minority ethnic Britons, compelling the development of self-reliant and militant organisations.[95]

Growing activism and militancy

Running concurrent to increasing immigration controls and 'race relations' legislation discussed above was a growth in black political consciousness and activism – influenced by US civil rights struggles and the development of worldwide black consciousness, linked with African liberation.[96] The 'black movement [in Britain] was suffering something of a hiatus' during the 1950s, as radical Pan-African leaders left Britain to lead nationalist movements in Africa and the West Indies, which 'left a vacuum of black militant leadership'.[97] As migrants became more established in Britain and, in turn, racial discrimination was institutionalised, 'the mosaic of unities and organisations would resolve itself into a more holistic, albeit shifting, pattern of black unity and black struggle'.[98]

The 1958 racist riots had given many black Britons their first watershed experience of 'being black in a country that did not welcome black people', prompting self-organisation. Rosalind Eleanor Wild cited a 1959 Special Branch report recording 'no [black] political organisation or activity in the Notting Hill area until September, 1958 [after which] many mushroom organisations sprang up'.[99] This included the West Indian Standing Conference (WISC), established to develop leadership and communication between the existing organisations and community in London. All white members of the WISC's Executive Committee left following the 1962 Commonwealth Immigrants Act, reflecting its leaders' wish to transform into an independent organisation 'free of white participation'. Ramdin concluded that the problem faced by WISC, true of many such organisations, was whether to co-operate with British organisations or seek independence from them: an issue that 'remained unresolved'.[100]

Another organisation formed in the aftermath of the 1958 riots was the Committee of Afro-Asian Caribbean Associations, co-founded by Amy Ashwood Garvey and Claudia Jones. Perry deemed it 'impossible to write about how Afro-Caribbean migrants shaped race politics in the early postwar era without paying attention to [Jones]'. A Trinidadian deported from New York during anti-Communist witch-hunts of the 1950s, Jones established one of the earliest black newspapers in London shortly before the riots, the *West Indian Gazette*.[101] This publication, alongside Jones and tireless Jamaican Pan-Africanist activist Ashwood Garvey, played a key role in shaping an 'imagined diasporic political community' for Commonwealth migrants in Britain.[102] As the 1958 riots demonstrated integration into British society would not be as straightforward as initially hoped, the *West Indian Gazette* played a significant role in publicly voicing the hopes and fears of this community.[103]

Similarly, Jones and Frances Ezzrecco (founder of the Coloured Peoples' Progressive Association) led 'the first ever ... delegation' of Caribbean organisations to the Home Secretary after Cochrane's murder.[104] Moreover, the Coordinating Committee Against Racial Discrimination marched through Birmingham in September 1961 to oppose proposed immigration controls, and the Afro-Asian Caribbean Conference was established from various organisations in January 1962 to challenge what they described as 'legalized apartheid'.[105] Brian David Jacobs concluded such organisations 'marked an important stage in the development of an identifiable black leadership', and Dilip Hiro deemed this a 'highly significant development [as] black and brown immigrants, faced with a threat to their rights, decided to enter the arena of British politics and apply direct pressure to safeguard their interests'.[106] Nonetheless, Paul B. Rich noted that 'no overall black organisation existed politically ... to mount a strong opposition to the 1962 Commonwealth Immigrants Bill'.[107]

Indeed, these developments 'were not, however, matched by the emergence of a black political culture with any purchase on the mainstream political process'.[108] Instead, so-called 'quasi-colonial buffer institutions', such as community relations councils, were created by the government to manage racial issues outside traditional political arenas and disperse political pressure for change by removing 'a layer of potential Black leaders ... into salaried positions'.[109] This has been portrayed as a continuation of Britain's colonial policy; methods of indirect rule in maintaining social control appeared within the metropole, as 'national and local liaison committees were not meant to be spokesmen for the newcomers or organised pressure groups. Rather, their orientation was consensual'.[110] As demonstrated above, authorities could claim issues faced by minority ethnic groups were being addressed, while these institutions were controlled and limited. The Race Relations Board exemplifies this; tasked with enforcing weak legislation, it proved ineffectual and was discredited. Its replacement, the Commission for Racial Equality (CRE), was similarly criticised. Sivanandan accused the Board of being a state attempt to create 'a class of collaborators', and declared 'the CRE took up the Black cause and killed it'.[111] While the CRE appeared more capable than predecessors to enforce anti-discrimination legislation, its members were largely drawn from bodies it replaced, leading to fierce competition and accusations that senior posts were only obtained by white people; in short, guilty of the racial discrimination it was established to combat. Furthermore, by the end of 1981, it had begun only forty-seven investigations into racial discrimination and published reports on twelve.[112] Such statistics do not suggest an effective organisation; through 'institutional buffering', it had 'become the focus of unrealistic expectations and the scapegoat for failing to deliver racial justice'.[113]

Thus, as Layton-Henry concluded, it might be expected that minority ethnic Britons would grow frustrated with weak, ineffective institutions and seek political influence through independent organisations.[114] Such attempts had limited success. For example, the Campaign Against Racial Discrimination (CARD), founded by activists in 1964 following a visit from Martin Luther King, aimed 'to speak for a social and political movement that did not exist'.[115] Aspiring to represent all minority ethnic Britons by uniting activists and organisations, the size of this task was demonstrated through CARD's internal struggles and divisions.[116] One early dispute was the decision of CARD's Chair and Vice-Chair, David Pitt and Hamza Alavi, to accept appointments to the government's National Committee for Commonwealth Immigrants (NCCI). The NCCI had been established in April 1964 to 'promote and co-ordinate' attempts to integrate Commonwealth migrants through voluntary liaison committees around England, of which thirty-nine were listed in 1966.[117] The NCCI was denounced as Labour's attempt to balance harsher immigration controls and, similar to local liaison committees, create a separated space from the political mainstream where issues relating to black and minority ethnic communities 'could thus be ignored with impunity'.[118] Dipak Nandy, member of CARD's executive committee, later characterised the NCCI as generating 'an atmosphere of superficial liberalism and of generalised good-will … Its characteristic style is paralysis and non-statement'.[119] Although themselves later joining the NCCI in an advisory capacity, the WISC decried Pitt and Alavi's involvement with a committee established to 'implement the so-called Integration proposals' of the 1965 White Paper on Commonwealth Immigration, which CARD opposed.[120]

Thus, the NCCI fractured black and minority ethnic organisations, as militant groups abandoned CARD following co-operation with it: 'The government had effectively shut out one area of representative black opinion.'[121] Ramdin contended this was the aim of such bodies, to weaken rising militancy by incorporating leading black figures within the state's own institutions.[122] However, discontent towards CARD's co-operation with the state resulted in increased popularity for militant groups such as the Racial Action Adjustment Society, established by Jan Carew and Michael X following Malcolm X's 1965 visit to London.[123]

The rise of Black Power

In 1979, John Rex stated that 'Nearly all the black leaders I have met make references to war and violence and it is not sufficient merely to dismiss them as extremists'.[124] Ramdin charted the influence of Black Power on organisations appearing in Britain during the 1970s and 1980s, as appearances of prominent Black Power leaders such as Stokely Carmichael and Malcolm X – who symbolically visited Smethwick following its infamous 1964 election and encouraged local minority ethnic people to organise themselves to fight racism – spread the global struggle of the 'exploited against the exploiter'.[125] Subsequently, the British Black Panther Movement warned that, unless the state ensured their protection, black self-defence would instigate US-style racial violence and 'the Thames [will] foam with blood sooner than Enoch Powell envisaged'.[126] Similarly, Sivanandan argued that the Universal Coloured People's Association, whose members talked about killing white people and speakers 'urged coloured nurses to give wrong injections to patients, coloured bus crews not to take the fares of black people … [and] Indian restaurant owners to "put something in the curry"', helped 'stiffen black backs [towards] greater militancy'.[127]

The 'high-water mark' of British Black Power was the trial of the 'Mangrove Nine' in 1971. When police forcibly responded to a protest march – organised by local activists and the Black Panther Movement – against the proposed closure of the Mangrove restaurant in Notting Hill, dubbed 'a resting place in Babylon', the ensuing disorders resulted in nine individuals being charged with incitement to riot.[128] The Mangrove had been targeted by repeated police drugs raids, which always failed to find evidence, and its organised defence was greeted with a heavy-handed police response; Robin Bunce and Paul Field demonstrated this was a 'deliberate [police] strategy to target and decapitate the emerging black power movement'. This was unsuccessful, as the trial ended in acquittal of all nine incitement charges, which 'turned Black Power into a cause célèbre'.[129]

Wild contended that the British Black Power movement, while not preventing discrimination and disadvantage, 'did equip future generations with the ability to recognise such a fate and rebel against it, constructively or otherwise'.[130] Indeed, during the late 1970s, black struggle was waged most fiercely by youth, bringing with them 'not only the traditions of their elders but an experience of their own, which was implacable of racism and impervious to the blandishments of the state'.[131]

Racial violence, the National Front and Anti-Nazi League

The need for self-defence amongst black and minority ethnic communities was heightened in the 1970s with the growth of the far-right National Front (NF). Formed in February 1967 from the British National Party, League of Empire Loyalists and Racial Preservation Society, the NF 'enthusiastically adopted the Powellite idea of repatriating black and Asian immigrants'.[132] Fielding candidates in local elections from 1969, the NF saw a growth of popularity in local election campaigns in 1973 and 1976, obtaining around 20 per cent of the vote in some locations. Despite never winning a contested seat, Ben Bowling asserted that the NF's electoral growth during the mid-1970s demonstrated that ' "race" and the fears of the white electorate could be exploited for political purposes'.[133] Indeed, the visible popularity of the NF promoting racist views encouraged other political parties to harden their own policies, and the Conservative 1979 election victory was cited as due to its tough stance on immigration.[134]

Moreover, combined with Powellite-fuelled immigration panic and the advent of racist 'skinhead' youth culture, the rise of the NF stimulated a growth in racial violence; for example, the term 'Paki-bashing' emerged during 1969–70.[135] Ironically, the NF's association with such violence likely prevented electoral success.[136] In response, self-defence and anti-racist movements developed in combination with left-wing anti-fascism in the mid-to-late 1970s, including the formation of anti-fascist magazine *Searchlight*, anti-racist musicians' campaign Rock Against Racism (RAR), and the Anti-Nazi League (ANL).[137] Despite intensifying racial violence, Labour Home Secretary Merlyn Rees refused requests to investigate, instead expressing 'total confidence in the police'.[138] As Anandi Ramamurthy detailed, in charting Asian Youth Movements, local people thus did not appear to have any choice other than self-organisation: 'The lack of police response to racist attacks and the frequent criminalisation of victims led many young people to see self-defence as the only solution.'[139] The widespread organisation of ANL spreading anti-racism – aimed particularly at youth, believed particularly vulnerable to NF propaganda – and various music carnivals organised with RAR demonstrated, through 'an open celebration of multi-ethnic Britain', that racism was not to be tolerated and the movement's success helped hasten the NF's decline.[140]

Increased conflict

Increased self-organisation and militancy resulted in intensified conflict during the 1970s, combatting racial violence and attempting success where the legal system and state had failed. This saw a number of disorders and deaths, such as Kevin Gately, a student who died during London's Red Lion Square disorders on 15 June 1974. Around 1,000 demonstrators assembled to protest a NF rally, leading to violent conflict and Gately's death from injuries believed inflicted by an officer striking him. Gately's father demanded that 'Only the strongest, fullest inquiry into Kevin's death will satisfy me' and, after the coroner's inquest jury returned a verdict of death by misadventure deemed 'totally unsatisfactory' by campaigners, a public inquiry was established by Labour Home Secretary Roy Jenkins.[141] Chaired by Lord Leslie Scarman, who had previously led an inquiry into Northern Ireland disorders in 1969 and would later investigate the 1981 disturbances, the inquiry solely investigated actions leading to disorder – excluding Gately's death, upon suggestion from police counsel that this had already been settled by the inquest.[142] This mirrored official investigations into 1980–81, which, being deemed an inappropriate platform, refused to examine specific allegations of police misconduct. It appeared to campaigners that, even when state action was forthcoming, the most significant aspects were purposefully omitted. Further to concluding police actions were generally justified by the aggression displayed against them, Scarman did not blame police for Gately's death or criticise the controversial Special Patrol Group, instead advising protestors to 'co-operate with the police'.[143]

Another prominent death was that of Blair Peach, who died following injuries obtained at a demonstration in Southall on 23 April 1979.[144] Peach, a New Zealand-born teacher who had immigrated to London in 1969, was an active member of the ANL and fourteen witnesses claimed to observe an officer hitting him. The Blair Peach Memorial Fund partly funded counsel for the inquest, imploring donations from supporters: 'Whereas all police expenses involved in this case come from public funds, ours we have to raise ourselves.'[145] Coroner Dr John Burton was accused of prejudicing the inquest jury, complaining of 'a widespread campaign to damage the institutions concerned with the law'. Senior civil servants therefore suppressed the release of Burton's account of Peach's death, which overlooked discrepancies in police testimony but claimed some civilian witness statements were not trustworthy, believing this would fuel appeals for a public inquiry.[146] It was considered such inquiries should be reserved for national scandals, partly due to cost and fear of undermining the authority and reputation of the police and government.[147]

A lack of public inquiry into Peach's death prompted other investigations. A National Council for Civil Liberties (NCCL) inquiry, chaired by Oxford professor Michael Dummett, was described by Martin Kettle and Lucy Hodges as 'far and away the most thorough, scrupulous and principled piece of research on any police operation in postwar Britain'.[148] This was despite the police and Home Office refusing to co-operate, even though the inquiry highlighted the importance of police and legal systems acting as 'some rock to cling to' for minority ethnic groups:

> Deprive people of the sense that they enjoy the protection of the law and of the agencies that enforce and administer it, and you destroy their whole feeling of security and any sense that they might otherwise have preserved that they are part of the society within which they live.[149]

Dummett advised Home Secretary William Whitelaw that many people felt alienated from society, but may be reassured by a public inquiry hearing their concerns.[150] The Home Office was not moved to action, privately deeming the NCCL's report a 'tedious correspondence'.[151]

Metropolitan Police Commissioner Sir David McNee appointed Commander John Cass to investigate Peach's death internally, but officer obstruction played a large role in the inability to determine exact events. Cass deemed some officers' testimony 'dubious', 'easily recognisable lies', and believed some 'must have conspired to pervert the course of justice'. Officers reportedly grew or shaved beards before long-delayed identification parades – considered by the *West Indian World* indicative of a 'massive cover-up'.[152] A cold case review in 1999 concluded that, while impossible to identify whom, it was likely that an officer had struck Peach.[153] It is interesting to note that it required the involvement of one of the first black British MPs, Paul Boateng, before this review was obtained.

In the 1970s, conflict intensified between black youth and the police. Fryer suggested this was the 'logical and … inevitable response' to racist attacks where black and minority ethnic people 'had been forced to defend themselves, since nobody else could or would'.[154] One such example, the 1976 Notting Hill

Carnival disorders which injured 500, was blamed on a massive police presence causing local anger that the police had attempted to take over 'their carnival'. The Carnival's roots can be traced to a 1959 event in St Pancras Town Hall, as an assertion of postwar migrants' right to belong in Britain following racist attacks: 'In the same streets through which we'd been hunted by baying crowds we assembled to dance and sing and to say that we were celebrating being alive and being here.'[155] Cecil Gutzmore thus argued police action in 1976 was representative of attacks on black culture, such as music, dress and speech, and that the police considered black youth inherently delinquent.[156] Appeals for a public inquiry into the disorders were characteristically rejected, and, by authorities maintaining this was simply a law and order issue, public discussion of the broader issues was significantly limited.[157] Nonetheless, prominent black British journal *Race Today* presented the disturbances as a seminal moment: 'The open defiance to our rulers and their representatives ... shows that a whole period in the history of our presence here in Britain has come to an end. A new stage is about to emerge.'[158] This new stage would be seen on the streets of England throughout 1980–81.

A changing police force

Concurrently, the police went through many changes in the years preceding 1980–81 in terms of their organisation, public perception and self-image; away from the 'traditional' view of policing that had proliferated in various forms since the 1829 Metropolitan Police Act by Home Secretary Sir Robert Peel.[159] For example, use of new technologies such as panda cars from the mid-1960s led to a decrease of the local 'bobby on the beat', towards officers in fast cars, unfamiliar with changing local communities, who would only appear when trouble was occurring – or, in more extreme views, to cause some.[160] The governmental Edmund-Davies inquiry increased police pay and escalated the number of young officers: in 1980, 36 per cent were eighteen to twenty-five years old.[161] This was coupled with an evolving popular culture image of the police, such as *Starsky & Hutch* and London-based *The Sweeney*, 'perhaps the ultimate celebration of the police breaking the rules in order to obtain a conviction' nevertheless 'always shown to be ultimately in the right'.[162] Thus, young recruits were often attracted by the promise of action, and David J. Smith and Jeremy Gray suggested many found anything else boring in comparison.[163] Areas such as St Pauls and Brixton were accused of being used as training grounds for young inexperienced officers, criticised for being less sympathetic to residents' views and 'quicker to react to things and people they did not understand'.[164] However, Keith stressed the danger of 'cultural generalizations of junior police officers which either provides a rhetorical let-off for their senior colleagues or a convenient scapegoat for analysis of police/Black antagonism'.[165]

Many theories have been proposed regarding police racism.[166] That the existence of 'rotten apples' within the force can be purged through awareness education and training, or that, as racism exists within society, police racism simply reflects that. Yet, multiple studies on police culture during the 1970s and 1980s suggested racism was more prevalent within the police than wider society, and the IRR claimed police did not reflect or reinforce popular morality, instead 'they re-create it – through stereo-typing the black section of society as muggers and criminals and illegal immigrants'.[167] Counterarguments suggested that officers fulfilled their duties without prejudice, regardless of private views, but Bowling and Coretta Phillips displayed that behaviour is affected by holding racially prejudiced attitudes.[168] Stuart Hall deemed 'rotten apples' and 'reflection of society' explanations 'not only cynical but constitutionally unacceptable', arguing they have since been proven incorrect.[169] Theories of 'institutional racism', most prominently espoused by Macpherson's 1999 public inquiry, have become widely accepted.[170]

Major organisational reforms were introduced by the Police Act 1964, endowing more power to chief constables and the Home Secretary, while creating forty-three local police authorities. These consisted of two-thirds elected members of county or borough councils and one-third local magistrates, responsible for maintaining an 'adequate and efficient' police force.[171] Police authorities could raise additional funding through local council tax, set police budgets and – subject to the Home Secretary's approval – remove chief constables, although this was rarely seen. In practice, most authorities did little and usually deferred to the local chief constable's 'professional' expertise: ' "passive and quiescent" committees ... were both unwilling ... and incapable of calling the chief constables to account'.[172] In November 1979, Labour backbencher Jack Straw unsuccessfully attempted to strengthen police authorities' powers and influence over local policing strategies.[173] The police and Conservative Party constantly opposed what they deemed the politicisation of the police, arguing that their political independence was vital to maintain their impartiality.

However, accountability can only exist if functioning mechanisms allow it. Lord Scarman, in his 1981 inquiry, decried the decline of 'policing by consent', concluding that 'a police force which does not consult locally will fail to be efficient'.[174] Timothy Brain summarised that Conservative policy relied upon increased police numbers and harsher sentences, while Labour attempted to increase political control over the police. Criticising both respectively for being in denial or for pursuing political rather than practical solutions, Brain concluded that all parties, including the police, must take responsibility for the failures.[175] Failures there certainly were; polls recorded that public respect for the police almost halved from 83 per cent in 1959 to just 43 per cent in 1989.[176]

Deteriorating police/community relations

Reflecting declining public respect for the police, their actions in this period were routinely criticised for raising tensions with black and minority ethnic communities. For example, saturation policing operations in 'high crime areas', consisting of extra officers descending upon an area to deter criminal activity, was a tactic used frequently in black residential areas, most infamously Brixton's 'Swamp 81' days before the 1981 disorder. Study of such operations concluded that the number of stops conducted was disproportionate to the reasonable suspicion of criminal offences, amounting to a form of harassment.[177]

Increased and disproportionate use of stop and search laws certainly caused widespread resentment amongst young black men. The most infamous was 'sus', the shorthand for suspicious behaviour under the 1824 Vagrancy Act: an arrestable offence without any other crime having to be committed, any witnesses other than two police officers, or even a victim.[178] The police argued such measures were required to combat rising criminality, but black people believed they were unfairly targeted as 'acting suspiciously' – that being young and black on English streets had been made a crime. A disproportionate number of black people were stopped and/or arrested throughout the 1960s and 1970s, during 1977–79 around three-quarters of those arrested under 'sus' were black, and an April 1980 Select Committee inquiry concluded that the total number of black 'sus' arrests did not accurately reflect actual involvement in street crimes.[179]

Several explanations have been forwarded to explain this ethnic disproportionality, including that the black population is generally younger, that higher levels of school exclusions and unemployment resulted in their spending more time on the streets, a residential concentration in high crime areas, and even an elevated rate of 'street crime' offending.[180] Robert Reiner detailed how police activity has always been focused on 'economically marginal elements in society', and young black men often fitted that description in 1970s and 1980s Britain.[181] While, prior to the mid-1970s, evidence indicated black Britons were less likely to be arrested, research after this date showed otherwise. In 1976, police described black crime rates as a problem, despite having noted just four years earlier that 'the West Indian crime rate is much the same as that of the indigenous population' – demonstrating the impact of popular moral panics, such as around the socially constructed crime of 'mugging', building on pre-existing notions of black masculinity and criminality.[182] Furthering an argument pioneered by John Lea and Jock Young, Reiner concluded: 'A vicious cycle of interaction developed between police stereotyping and black vulnerability to the situations that attract police attention.'[183] The police persisted with stops and searches, despite evidence suggesting minimal success in combatting street crime; but its negative effect on police/community relations was, in Scarman's words, 'beyond doubt'.[184]

Development of self-conscious youth cultures and militancy increased discontent towards the police: a 1972 select parliamentary committee on 'Police/ Immigrant relations' was surprised by a WISC submission characterising the situation as 'almost akin to civil war'.[185] A 'Scrap Sus' campaign emerged out of the Black Parents Movement to challenge police harassment of black youth and 'sus' was subsequently repealed after widespread disorders in 1981, demonstrating positive change through a sustained campaign. As Boateng summarised: 'it wasn't black people asking white people to do something for them, it was black people organising to make sure something happened'.[186] Nevertheless, the end of 'sus' did not stop police targeting black people and its replacement, the 'even worse Criminal Attempts Act', was decried as 'one can be charged with intending or conspiring to commit an impossible crime'.[187]

Furthermore, responding to increasing conflicts, the police moved from 'extraordinarily low-key' tactics towards 'hard' policing; considered either advancing police ability to combat public disorder, or an increased paramilitary approach that threatened civil liberties.[188] Senior officers, such as Robert Mark (Metropolitan Police Commissioner 1972–77), had reasoned that maintaining public confidence was more important than dispersing public disorder: 'winning by appearing to lose'. Overlooking Britain's riotous history and consistent with ideas of imperial superiority, it was believed riots, and specialised equipment to combat them, belonged in other, less-civilised countries, and were not a 'British problem'.[189] However, policing transformed into more heavy-handed responses; flooding streets with officers, despite this tactic of 'overpolicing' – deploying deliberately large numbers in an attempt to dissuade disorder – often provoking more problems. By the 1980s, maintaining law and order was deemed more important, prompting widespread demands for specialised equipment influenced by Northern Ireland experiences where street battles led to the dissemination of robust policing responses to public disorder.[190] As Reiner eloquently summarised, 'Darth Vader displaced Dixon in riot control tactics'.[191]

Much criticism was subsequently directed towards the Metropolitan Police's Special Patrol Group (SPG). Formed in 1961 to combat serious public disorder and crime, they were not specialist 'riot police', but critics portrayed them as 'a force within a force'.[192] The negative impact of the SPG on police/community relations is undeniable.[193] Trades Union Congress General Secretary Len Murray criticised the SPG as 'alien to the tradition of this country of leaving policing to a local constabulary with knowledge of and sympathy with the local community'.[194] In stark contrast with 'community policing', which encouraged close relationships with local people, the SPG had a 'burgeoning reputation as an élite, aggressive, unaccountable squad'.[195] Authorities defended their necessity, insisting that an organised mobile taskforce, able to be deployed at short notice, was 'absolutely essential for present day policing'.[196] Metropolitan Commissioner Sir David McNee backed the SPG 'to the hilt' and, the day after Blair Peach's funeral, told a black journalist: 'I understand the concern of your people … But if you keep off the streets of London and behave yourselves you won't have the SPG to worry about.'[197] Statements such as these question whether McNee actually understood concerns. While some, such as radical Labour MP Alex Lyon, campaigned for the SPG to be disbanded, their strength was increased in the late 1970s and the controversial name retained because 'a change would be detrimental to the morale of the Group'.[198]

Boateng concluded that saturation operations, 'sus' laws and the SPG prevented community policing from being effective, as residents could not instantly absorb changes from forceful specialised units to community officers.[199] Nottinghamshire Assistant Chief Constable Geoffrey Dear noted that the 'permanent beat officer' subsequently found their job 'almost impossible', and the IRR dubbed these tactics 'policing against the community'.[200]

Ineffective police complaints

Another area of growing concern was the effectiveness of the police complaints system. The Police Act 1964 introduced a complaints system, albeit investigated by the police themselves; it would take until 1976 before the independent Police Complaints Board was introduced. However, in 1981, its new chair Sir Cyril Phillips described it as having 'kept so low a profile that it has climbed into a ditch'.[201] Indeed, between 1973 and 1978, not a single complaint of racial discrimination by the Metropolitan Police was upheld, and it is perhaps unsurprising that the Board was branded 'a rubber stamp for police cover-ups'.[202]

Under this system, an 'amazingly small number of complaints [were] substantiated', and numerous studies indicated minority ethnic groups were much more likely to complain of police misconduct, but less likely to have complaints substantiated; consequently, and unsurprisingly, they tended to be more pessimistic about the complaints system than white counterparts.[203] Fear of retribution also prevented victims pursuing complaints; for example, a Liverpool Trade Council inquiry suggested police threatened anyone recording officers' numbers.[204] The police investigating their own ranks certainly sparked fervent discontent, especially after growing evidence such investigations were woefully inadequate.

Despite mounting discontentment, the police generally responded to criticism with disdain. Some senior officials appeared personally offended at their officers' conduct being questioned, leading to blanket refusals to investigate accusations, only furthering distrust. For instance, the Police Superintendents' Association of England and Wales declared themselves 'somewhat annoyed' at criticisms they believed 'did not represent the true voice of most of the people'.[205] Demonstrating the increasingly close relationship between the police and 'Party of law and order', several Conservative MPs spoke out against police criticism. Roger Geary asserted that, as the police are inexorably linked with authority, to question the police's integrity was seen to be questioning the legitimacy of the state itself, resulting in the 'tendency to repudiate any allegation of improper police behaviour'.[206]

Consequently, a common criticism was the need for police to be less dismissive of legitimate public concern. Phil Scraton and Kathryn Chadwick considered the authorities' response to serious allegations 'almost neurotic', and even Home Secretary William Whitelaw advised the Police Federation in 1980 that some criticism was rooted in genuine anxiety from 'moderate and thoughtful people'.[207] In his discussion of deaths in police custody, Kettle described the police's questioning the motives of anyone who challenged their actions 'one of the most worrying aspects'.[208] This alarm was undoubtedly shared by those who believed the police simply would not admit their failings, as there appeared no effective judicial method of holding them accountable.

Conclusion

Amongst growing activism and distrust of the police, Margaret Thatcher's Conservative Party returned to government in 1979. Thatcher's rejection of a previous bipartisan consensus was replaced with aggressive tactics and exclusionary policies, which increasingly characterised migrants as the problem.[209] In 1976, then Shadow Home Secretary Whitelaw had told the party conference they would end 'immigration as we have seen it', and Thatcher appeared on television in 1978 sympathising with voters 'afraid that this country might be rather swamped by people with a different culture'.[210] Although her comments were criticised as 'pandering to popular prejudices' – Conservative MP Peter Walker presciently warned 'if you exploit people's worries in a way which shows hostility to minorities, you will do immense damage to racial harmony' – Thatcher's Conservatives immediately gained a 9 per cent poll lead, largely through attracting erstwhile defectors to the NF to return.[211] Yasmin Alibhai-Brown summarised that Thatcher shared Powell's views 'that this island belonged to white people, but unlike him she was able to make this view respectable and admired'.[212] Accordingly, her Government passed the British Nationality Act 1981, which was progressing through Parliament during the 1981 disturbances. This further restricted immigration by depriving black and minority ethnic British nationals the right of abode, and denied automatic citizenship to those born in Britain.[213]

Thatcher's Conservatives also concentrated heavily upon law and order, rejecting arguments that rising crime levels were linked to rising unemployment – which questioned their philosophy and policies – instead focusing upon strengthening the police, and 'New Right' ideology redefined national identity around respect for authority and law and order.[214] The Conservatives' 1979 manifesto promised increased police numbers and 'short, sharp shock' treatment of youth offenders, appealing to many officers who had grown critical of Labour's policies. Indeed, prior to the 1979 election, the Police Federation publicly criticised Labour's record on crime and policing. Brain concluded that, while the content was 'pretty mild stuff', the Federation publicly taking this politicised stance was extremely significant.[215] Alistair Henry similarly contended that the police were 'more explicitly politically active than at any other time'; some Federation members were even concerned they had 'nailed [their] flag for all to see to the Conservative Party mast'.[216]

Accordingly, on the first working day after Conservative election victory, the substantial police pay increase recommended by the 1978 governmental Edmund-Davies inquiry was implemented. Although this simply hastened a step previously agreed by Labour, it further provoked anti-police sentiment at a time of high unemployment and economic difficulty.[217] For many observers, it appeared that the Conservatives and police were converging, and Whitelaw's 'position of putting the police first in any issue of doubt' added to growing concerns over police accountability.[218]

Certainly, this period saw growing questioning of the forces of British law and order. In 1980, the *Daily Star* highlighted how the traditional worldwide image of the 'British bobby', with its reputation for honesty and fair play, was being challenged, raising questions about whether systems of accountability were functioning effectively.[219] Despite continual rejections to hold public inquiries into police actions, demands persisted. This was despite the distrust of the government overseeing such inquiries, and a lack of evidence that past examples had achieved anything; they were nonetheless viewed as key to making advances.

Running parallel to increasing discontent towards the police was a growing militancy and departure from peaceful compliance of earlier generations of migrants.[220] Influenced by transnational radical movements, attitudes had become more cynical to the idea that British authorities would – or even should – be the ones to solve the issues. Earlier generations arrived in postwar Britain, often showing deference to the 'mother country' and not intending to remain indefinitely, but black youth raised in Britain were increasingly disposed to combat racial discrimination and attacks, police mistreatment and a lack of opportunities.[221] Whereas many older or moderate black Britons and organisations retained beliefs that governmental mechanisms such as public inquiries could provide a political voice, younger and more radical groups believed no positive advances would be gained by these. This dichotomy would be demonstrated through differing perceptions of and responses to disorders spreading across England in 1980–81 – believed, by some, to be the only way for their voices to be heard.

Notes

1   Keith, *Race, Riots and Policing*, p. 18.

2   See: Sivanandan, *Different Hunger*, pp. 3–54.

3   Pilkington, *Racial Disadvantage*, pp. 40–2.

4   Ramdin, *Black Working Class*, p. 448.

5   Layton-Henry, *Politics of Immigration*, p. 3; Fryer, *Staying Power*, p. 1. See: Winder, *Bloody Foreigners*; Holmes, *John Bull's Island*; Olusoga, *Black and British*; Cohen, 'Perversions of Inheritance'.

6   See, for example: Goodhart, *British Dream*. For cultural memory of the *Windrush*, see: Mead, '*Empire Windrush*'; Lunn, 'Empire Windrush'; Kushner, *Battle of Britishness*, pp. 163–85.

7   Perry, *London is the Place for Me*, pp. 12–17. See: Hesse, 'Black Britain's Post-Colonial Formations', pp. 96–120; Burkett, *Constructing Post-Imperial Britain*.

8   Walvin, *Passage to Britain*, p. 80. See: Jenkinson, *Black 1919*; Evans, 'Race Riots'; Murphy, *Racism and Reaction*, pp. 13–42; Fryer, *Staying Power*, pp. 298–316.

9   Paul, 'Subjects to Immigrants', pp. 224–5; Holmes, *John Bull's Island*, pp. 210–26.

10 Philip Cohen noted Irish immigrants were singled out by authorities in the 1850s, but in the 1950s 'their arrival was officially hardly noticed', demonstrating how migrant groups deemed 'dangerous' changes over time: Cohen, 'Perversions of Inheritance', p. 14. See: Miles, 'Nationality, Citizenship, and Migration'; Delaney, *Irish in Post-War Britain*; Corbally, 'The Othered Irish'; Holmes, *John Bull's Island*, pp. 246–53.

11 The National Archives (TNA): HO 344/12, W.H. Cornish, 'Working party to consider restriction of right of British subject from overseas to enter and remain in UK'; TNA: HO 344/92, Draft article 'Commonwealth immigration'.

12 Paul, 'Subjects to Immigrants', pp. 225–6, 241. See: Carter *et al.*, 'Racialisation of Black Immigration'; Kay and Miles, 'European Volunteer Workers'; Nocon, 'A Reluctant Welcome?'.

13 Quoted in Carter *et al.*, 'Racialisation of Black Immigration', 335.

14 See: Hansen, 'British Nationality Act'; Deakin, 'British Nationality Act'.

15 Schwarz, 'Post-Colonial Britain', 267; James, 'Black Experience', pp. 377–8.

16 TNA: CO 1032/195, Indian High Commissioner to Commonwealth Relations Office (CRO), 10 May 1958; Pakistan High Commissioner to CRO, 16 May 1958; James, 'Black Experience', p. 369.

17 Holmes, *John Bull's Island*, p. 221; Hiro, *Black British*, pp. 15–16.

18 Malik, *Meaning of Race*, p. 19.

19 Burkett, *Constructing Post-Imperial Britain*, p. 7. See: Katznelson, *Black Men*, pp. 123–51; Carter and Joshi, 'Creation of a Racist Britain'; Carter *et al.*, 'Racialisation of Black Immigration', 335–47; James, 'Black Experience', pp. 349, 377–8.

20 Commonwealth Immigrants Advisory Council, *Second Report*; Patterson, *Dark Strangers*, p. 17. See: Waters, 'Dark Strangers'.

21 Bowling, 'Emergence of Violent Racism', p. 187; James, 'Black Experience', p. 378, emphasis in original. Attitudes of imperial superiority were clearly demonstrated in views of inter-racial sexual relationships displayed during the 1919 racist riots: Bland, 'Miscegenation Fears'; Rowe, 'Sex, "Race" and Riot'.

22 Smith and Marmo, *Subject to Examination*, p. 2. See: Buettner, 'Race and Sex in 1950s Britain'; Gilroy and Lawrence, 'Two-Tone Britain', p. 126.

23 Virdee, *Racialized Outsider*, pp. 102–4; Cohen, 'Perversions of Inheritance', pp. 23–100; Phizacklea and Miles, 'The British Trade Union Movement and Racism'.

24 Layton-Henry, *Politics of Race*, pp. 29–32.

25 For example: Foot, 'Immigration and the British Labour Movement'; Rose, *Colour and Citizenship*; Freeman and Spencer, 'Black Workers'.

26 Paul, 'Subjects to Immigrants', p. 238. See: Miles and Phizacklea, *White Man's Country*; Carter *et al.*, 'Racialisation of Black Immigration'; Carter and Joshi, 'Creation of a Racist Britain'.

27 Macmillan, *Diaries*, p. 382; James, 'Black Experience', pp. 370–1.

28 Paul, *Whitewashing Britain*, p. 134; Carter *et al.*, 'Immigration Policy', 136.

29 James, 'Black Experience', p. 374; Pilkington, *Beyond the Mother Country*; Rowe, *Racialisation of Disorder*, pp. 105–34; Katznelson, 'Nottingham, 1954–68'; Davis, 'New Light on Rachmanism'.

30 Linda Pressly, 'The "Forgotten" Race Riot', *BBC News*, 21 May 2007, http://news.bbc. co.uk/1/hi/uk/6675793.stm (last accessed: 29 August 2013).

31 *Kensington News*, 5 September 1958.

32 Malik, *Michael X.*, p. 76. See: Pilkington, *Beyond the Mother Country*; Phillips and Phillips, *Windrush*, pp. 158–80; Hiro, *Black British*, pp. 38–41.

33 TNA: CAB/128/32, Cabinet Conclusions, 8 September, 11 September 1958.

34 Perry, *London is the Place for Me*, pp. 89–125; *Daily Mail*, 10 September 1958.

35 Layton-Henry, *Politics of Race*, p. 89; Thurlow, *Fascism in Britain*, pp. 212–17.

36 Bloom, *Violent London*, p. 352.

37 *New Statesman*, 23 May 1959; *Searchlight*, May 2006.

38 Jackson, *Policing Youth*, p. 88; Holmes, *John Bull's Island*, p. 259; Pearson, *Hooligan*; Macilwee, *Teddy Boy Wars*.

39 *New Statesman*, 23 May 1959.

40 HC Deb 04 June 1959 vol. 606 c. 369; TNA: CO 1031/2539, Note of Meeting, 2 June 1959.

41 Jacobs, *Black Politics*, p. 33; Rich, *Race and Empire*, pp. 189–90; Gilroy and Lawrence, 'Two-Tone Britain', pp. 126–9.

42 Cashmore, *United Kingdom?*, p. 90; Miles, 'Riots of 1958'.

43 Katznelson, *Black Men*, pp. 123–38.

44 Saggar, *Race and Politics*, p. 105. See: Hansen, *Citizenship and Immigration*, pp. 100–24; Spencer, *British Immigration Policy*, pp. 129–33; Layton-Henry, *Politics of Race*, pp. 30–43; Deakin, 'Commonwealth Immigrants Bill'.

45 HC Deb 16 November 1961 vol. 649 c. 799; Smith and Marmo, *Subject to Examination*, p. 32; Foot, *Immigration and Race*, pp. 174–5.

46 Deedes, *Race without Rancour*, p. 10. See: Solomos, *Black Youth*, pp. 34–7.

47 The IRR's report was published as Rose, *Colour and Citizenship*, and the U.S. survey as Myrdal, *An American Dilemma*.

48 See: Kelley and Tuck (eds), *The Other Special Relationship*.

49 *The Times*, 27 September 1963; TNA: HO 344/92, Philip Mason, 'Survey of Minorities in Britain', 18 June 1963.

50 TNA: HO 344/92, J.M. Roffey to R.F. Wood, 7 September 1962.

51 TNA: HO 376/128, Commonwealth Immigration Committee, 'Coloured Immigration', 30 September 1963.

52 For overviews of the US Civil Rights Movement, see: Newman, *Civil Rights Movement*; Verney, *Black Civil Rights*; Dierenfield, *Civil Rights Movement*.

53 Bleich, *Race Politics*, pp. 59–60.

54 Phillips and Phillips, *Windrush*, p. 353.

55 Sivanandan, *Different Hunger*, p. 5.

56 Goulbourne, *Race Relations*, p. 64. See: Solomos, *Race and Racism*, pp. 202–3; Ramdin, *Black Working Class*; Gilroy, *Ain't No Black*.

57 See: Phibbs, *Montgomery Bus Boycott*; Collier-Thomas and Franklin (eds), *Sisters in the Struggle*.

58 Dresser, *Black and White*.

59 Cited in Layton-Henry, *Politics of Race*, p. 124.

60 Katznelson, *Black Men*, p. 146.

61 *The Times*, 14 February 1978.

62 Hindell, 'Race Relations Bill'; Dean, 'Race Relations Policy'.

63 Saggar, *Race and Politics*, p. 81; Bleich, *Race Politics*, p. 61.

64 Banton, *Promoting Racial Harmony*; Fielding, *Labour Governments*, p. 152.

65 *The Times*, 9 March 1964.

66 Layton-Henry, *Politics of Race*, p. 55; Katznelson, *Black Men*, pp. 146–7.

67 Crossman, *Diaries*, p. 299.

68 Hansen, *Citizenship and Immigration*, pp. 153–78; Steel, *No Entry*; Schofield, *Enoch Powell*, pp. 140–207.

69 Sivanandan, *Different Hunger*, p. 24; Nelson, *Black Atlantic Politics*, p. 240; James, 'Black Experience', p. 377.

70 Geddes, *Politics of Immigration*, pp. 49–51; Ashford, *Policy and Politics*, p. 239; Katznelson, *Black Men*, pp. 139–49; Miles and Phizacklea, *White Man's Country*, pp. 38–78.

71 Miles and Phizacklea (eds), *Racism and Political Action*, p. 24.

72 Mullard, *Black Britain*, pp. 75–88; Layton-Henry, *Politics of Race*, pp. 131–2.

73 TNA: HO 376/161, Frank Soskice to the Earl of Selkirk, 6 December 1965.

74 Peplow, '"Linchpin for Success"?'; Perry, *London is the Place for Me*, pp. 229–37.

75 TNA: CK 2/11, G.M.B. Owen to the Reverend Ronald Crewes, 28 January 1966.

76 Race Relations Board, *Report*, p. 8.

77 *The Times*, 20 December 1966. For attempted prosecutions under the act, see: Schaffer, 'Legislating against Hatred', 258–74.

78 Schofield, *Enoch Powell*; Brooke, '"Rivers of Blood"'; Brown, 'Anecdotal Racism'; Shepherd, *Enoch Powell*.

79 TNA: DPP 2/4504, J.F. Claxton to S. Edwards, 3 May 1968.

80 *The Times*, 3 May 1968.

81 Layton-Henry, *Politics of Race*, pp. 75–6.

82 Virdee, *Racialized Outsider*, p. 115; Lindop, 'Support of Enoch Powell'.

83 Schofield, *Enoch Powell*, p. 210; Rutherford, *Forever England*, pp. 104–38.

84 Burkett, *Constructing Post-Imperial Britain*, p. 5; Katznelson, *Black Men*, p. 181.

85 Schaffer, 'Legislating against Hatred', 274–5; Peplow, '"Linchpin for Success"?'.

86 *The Times*, 29 April 1968, cited in Rhodes, *Black Panthers*, p. 269.

87 Ramdin, *Black Working Class*, pp. 498–9; Hiro, *Black British*, p. 146; Sivanandan, *Different Hunger*, p. 25; Holmes, *John Bull's Island*, pp. 241–2.

88 Rose, *Backbencher's Dilemma*, p. 54.

89 TNA: C(68) 122, James Callaghan, 'Race Relations – The Police', 6 November 1968; TNA: CAB/128/43, Cabinet Conclusions, 12 November 1968.

90 *BBC News*, 8 January 1999.

91 See Epilogue.

92 Smith, 'Policing and Urban Unrest', p. 69; Rees, 'Immigration Policies', p. 90; Pilkington, *Racial Disadvantage*, pp. 237–8; Malik, *Meaning of Race*, pp. 16–25.

93 Interview with Gus John, 19 May 2017.

94 Offe, *Contradictions of the Welfare State*, p. 144.

95 Ramdin, *Black Working Class*, p. 500.

96 Hiro, *Black British*, pp. 76–95; Holmes, *John Bull's Island*, pp. 240–1; Katznelson, 'Nottingham 1954–68'; Smith, 'Conflicting Narratives', 18–20; James, *Decolonization from Below*.

97 Ramdin, *Black Working Class*, pp. 370–1; Pilkington, *Beyond the Mother Country*, p. 141.

98 Sivanandan, *Different Hunger*, p. 8.

99 Wild, 'British Black Power', pp. 33–5; Hiro, *Black British*, pp. 38–41.

100 Ramdin, *Black Working Class*, pp. 410–14; Rich, *Race and Empire*, p. 199.

101 Perry, *London is the Place for Me*, pp. 9–10; James, 'Black Experience', p. 381. For Claudia Jones and the *West Indian Gazette*, see: Sherwood, *Claudia Jones*; Davies, *Left of Karl Marx*.

102 Perry, *London is the Place for Me*, p. 9; Wild, 'British Black Power', pp. 32–3.

103 Schwarz, 'Post-Colonial Britain', 269–70.

104 Pilkington, *Beyond the Mother Country*, p. 143; Perry, *London is the Place for Me*, p. 143.

105 Sivanandan, *Different Hunger*, p. 11; Perry, 'Black Britons and the 1963 March', p. 13.

106 Jacobs, *Black Politics*, p. 33; Hiro, *Black British*, pp. 42–3.

107 Rich, *Race and Empire*, p. 199.

108 Kettle and Hodges, *Uprising!*, p. 60.

109 Daye, *Middle-Class Blacks*, p. 4; Rex and Tomlinson, *Colonial Immigrants*; Katznelson, *Black Men*, pp. 175–88; Sewell, *Black Tribunes*, pp. 50–1; Shukra, 'Black Political Movement'.

110 Katznelson, *Black Men*, p. 177; Rich, *Race and Empire*, p. 11; Malik, *Meaning of Race*, pp. 149–77.

111 Sivanandan, *Different Hunger*, pp. 118–20.

112 Layton-Henry, *Politics of Race*, pp. 137–43.

113 Keith, *Race, Riots and Policing*, p. 172.

114 Layton-Henry, *Politics of Race*, p. 168; Gilroy, *Ain't No Black*, pp. 146–341.

115 Heineman, *Politics of the Powerless*, p. 1.

116 Ramdin, *Black Working Class*, pp. 415–38; Perry, *London is the Place for Me*, pp. 187–243.

117 TNA: CK 2/26, 'Voluntary Liaison Committees', National Committee for Commonwealth Immigrants.

118 Layton-Henry, *Politics of Race*, pp. 128–9.

119 Cited in Katznelson, *Black Men*, pp. 178–9. Alternatively, Bleich commented that NCCI members were 'far from puppets in the government's hand', citing NCCI's Information Officer Martin Ennals' self-description of a Committee opposing governmental policies 'and has said so to the Prime Minister': Bleich, *Race Politics*, p. 67.

120 Cited in Perry, *London is the Place for Me*, p. 221.

121 Sivanandan, *Different Hunger*, p. 17.

122 Ramdin, *Black Working Class*, pp. 496–7. See: Katznelson, *Black Men*, pp. 175–88; Holmes, *John Bull's Island*, p. 239.

123 Holmes, *John Bull's Island*, p. 241; Patterson, *Immigration and Race Relations*, pp. 322–4; Sivanandan, *Different Hunger*, p. 16.

124 Rex, 'Black Militancy', pp. 89–90.

125 Ramdin, *Black Working Class*, pp. 370–456; Virdee, *Racialized Outsider*, p. 120. See: Tuck, *Malcolm X*; Joseph (ed.), *Black Power*.

126 Black Panther Movement circular, 3 October 1968, cited in Sivanandan, *Different Hunger*, p. 26.

127 Sivanandan, *Different Hunger*, p. 21.

128 *Ibid.*, pp. 32–3.

129 Bunce and Field, *Darcus Howe*, pp. 93–135.

130 Wild, 'Black Power in Britain', p. 19.

131 Sivanandan, *Different Hunger*, p. 37; Smith, 'Conflicting Narratives', 20–1.

132 Hiro, *Black British*, p. 254. See: Fielding, *National Front*; Taylor, *National Front*; Layton-Henry, *Politics of Race*, pp. 87–107; Thurlow, *Fascism in Britain*, pp. 245–67.

133 Bowling, 'Emergence of Violent Racism', p. 198.

134 Pilkington, *Racial Disadvantage*, p. 218; Layton-Henry, *Politics of Race*, p. 106.

135 Bowling, 'Emergence of Violent Racism', p. 196.

136 Virdee, *Racialized Outsider*, p. 138; Cohen, 'Perversions of Inheritance', p. 38.

137 Copsey, *Anti-Fascism in Britain*, pp. 115–52; Gilroy, *Ain't No Black*, pp. 120–30.

138 Cited in Bowling, 'Emergence of Violent Racism', p. 201.

139 Ramamurthy, *Black Star*, p. 120.

140 Virdee, *Racialized Outsider*, pp. 136–44; Gilroy and Lawrence, 'Two-Tone Britain', pp. 146–51; Solomos, *Race and Racism*, pp. 211–12. See: Goodyer, *Crisis Music*; Rachel, *Walls Come Tumbling Down*; Renton, *Anti-Nazi League*; Higgs, 'Making Anti-Fascism Anti-Racist'.

141 *The Times*, 17 June 1974, 13 July 1974.

142 See: chapter 5; Ellison and Smyth, *Policing Northern Ireland*, pp. 61–4.

143 Scarman, *Red Lion Square*, p. 43; Brain, *History of Policing*, pp. 12–15; Gilbert, *Only One Died*.

144 Scraton and McCulloch, *Deaths in Custody*, pp. 75–8; Layton-Henry, *Politics of Race*, p. 105.

145 *Morning Star*, 29 October 1979.

146 TNA: HO 299/114, John Burton, 'Blair Peach Inquest: The Unpublished Story'.

147 Keith, *Race, Riots and Policing*, pp. 74–9.

148 Kettle and Hodges, *Uprising!*, p. 77.

149 National Council for Civil Liberties, *Southall*, pp. 11–12.

150 TNA: HO 299/114, Michael Dummett to William Whitelaw, 28 July 1980.

151 TNA: HO 299/114, G.H. Phillips to A.P. Jackson, 27 August 1980.

152 Metropolitan Police Service Publication Scheme (MPS): Investigation into the death of Blair Peach (BP), Cass, 'Second Report', 14 September 1979; Cass, 'Report', 12 July 1979; 'Notes of conference with Director of Public Prosecutions', 25 September 1979; *West Indian World*, 5–11 October 1979.

153 MPS: BP, 'Report', 14 June 1999.

154 Fryer, *Staying Power*, p. 395. See: Layton-Henry, *Politics of Race*, pp. 108–21; McLaughlin, 'Police Accountability'; Ramdin, *Black Working Class*, pp. 453–4; Solomos, *Black Youth*.

155 Phillips and Phillips, *Windrush*, p. 383.

156 Gutzmore, 'Black Masses', p. 208.

157 Joshua *et al.*, *To Ride the Storm*, pp. 60–1; Nelson, *Black Atlantic Politics*, p. 201.

158 *Race Today*, October 1976. For *Race Today*, see: Smith, 'Conflicting Narratives'.

159 See: Critchley, *History of Police*; Taylor, *The New Police*.

160 Emsley, *English Police*, p. 165; Kettle and Hodges, *Uprising!*, pp. 66–7.

161 Benyon, 'Policing Issues', p. 105.

162 Leishman and Mason, *Policing and the Media*, p. 69; Emsley, *English Police*, p. 176.

163 Smith and Gray, *Police in Action*, p. 55.

164 *Jamaican Weekly Gleaner*, 9 April 1980.

165 Keith, *Race, Riots and Policing*, p. 14.

166 For an overview, see: Bowling and Phillips, *Racism, Crime and Justice*, pp. 115–62.

167 Cain, *Policeman's Role*; Reiner, 'Black and Blue'; Holdaway, *Inside the British Police*; Institute of Race Relations, *Police against Black People*, p. 1.

168 Bowling and Phillips, *Racism, Crime and Justice*, pp. 161–2.

169 Hall, 'From Scarman to Stephen Lawrence', 189.

170 Macpherson, *Stephen Lawrence Inquiry*. See: Epilogue.

171 Emsley, *English Police*, p. 174.

172 Reiner, *Politics of the Police*, p. 227; McCabe and Wallington, *The Police*, p. 135, cited in McLaughlin, 'Police Accountability', p. 114.

173 *Police Review*, 23 November 1979; Brain, *History of Policing*, pp. 60–1.

174 Scarman, *Report*, p. 149. See: McLaughlin, 'Police Accountability'.

175 Brain, *History of Policing*, p. 76.

176 Cited in Reiner, *Politics of the Police*, p. 78.

177 Rollo, 'Special Patrol Group', p. 193; Mason, *Race and Ethnicity*, pp. 111–14; Kettle and Hodges, *Uprising!*, pp. 93–4.

178 See: Lawrence, 'The Vagrancy Act'.

179 Cited in Kettle and Hodges, *Uprising!*, p. 91; Carter, *Shattering Illusions*, p. 104; Greaves, 'Brixton Disorders', p. 66.

180 Phillips, 'Ethnic Inequalities', p. 193.

181 Reiner, *Politics of the Police*, p. 94.

182 Solomos, *Black Youth*, pp. 108–9; Bowling and Phillips, *Racism, Crime and Justice*, p. 78; Hall *et al.*, *Policing the Crisis*.

183 Lea and Young, *Law and Order*; Reiner, *Politics of the Police*, p. 95.

184 Scarman, *Report*, p. 87.

185 Cited in Fryer, *Staying Power*, p. 392.

186 Phillips and Phillips, *Windrush*, pp. 306–10. For the Black Parents Movement, see: Alleyne, *Radicals Against Race*, pp. 51–7.

187 Black Cultural Archives, Gutzmore 1/6/1, Brixton Defence Campaign Bulletin No. 2; Marren, *We Shall not be Moved*, pp. 124–5.

188 Brain, *History of Policing*, p. 14. See: Waddington, 'Paramilitary Policing Considered'; Jefferson, *Paramilitary Policing*; Hills, 'Militant Tendencies'.

189 Brain, *History of Policing*, p. 15. See: Stevenson, *Popular Disturbances*; Schwarz, *Memories of Empire*.

190 See: Hillyard, 'Normalisation of Special Powers'.

191 Reiner, *Politics of the Police*, p. 87. 'Dixon' refers to BBC's *Dixon of Dock Green* (1955–76), a series revolving around a sympathetic police constable.

192 Brain, *History of Policing*, p. 13.

193 See, for example: Solomos, *Black Youth*, p. 114; Hall *et al.*, *Policing the Crisis*, pp. 49–50.

194 Cited in Benyon, 'Policing Issues', p. 105.

195 Kettle and Hodges, *Uprising!*, p. 93.

196 MPS: BP, Cass, 'First Report', 12 July 1979.

197 *Guardian*, 15 June 1979.

198 *Daily Telegraph*, 11 March 1980; McNee, *McNee's Law*, p. 89.

199 Boateng, 'Community and Accountability', p. 157.

200 Whitaker, *Police in Society*, p. 68; Kettle and Hodges, *Uprising!*, p. 93.

201 *Guardian*, 19 March 1981; Reiner, *Politics of the Police*, p. 224.

202 Bundred, 'Accountability and the Metropolitan Police', p. 64; *Morning Star*, 12 January 1980.

203 Institute of Race Relations, *Police against Black People*, p. 87. See, for example: Stevens and Willis, 'Ethnic Minorities and Complaints'; Whitaker, *Police in Society*; Maguire and Corbett, *Police Complaints System*; Lambert, *Crime, Police and Race Relations*; Lea and Young, *Law and Order*.

204 *Guardian*, 21 January 1980.

205 *The Times*, 4 March 1980.

206 Geary, 'Deaths in Custody', 36.

207 Scraton and Chadwick, 'Speaking Ill of the Dead', 99–100; *The Times*, 22 May 1980.

208 Kettle, 'Deaths in Custody'.

209 Smith, 'From Consensus to Conflict', 76–7. For the postwar consensus, see: Addison, *Road to 1945*; Toye, ' "Consensus" to "Common Ground" '; Kavanagh, *End of Consensus?*.

210 *The Times*, 6 October 1976; Granada Television, *World in Action*, 30 January 1978.

211 *Sunday Times*, 26 February 1978; Russel, *The Tory Party*, p. 117; Layton-Henry, *Politics of Race*, pp. 150–1.

212 Alibhai-Brown, *Who Do We Think We Are?*, p. xiv. See: Sivanandan, 'Challenging Racism'.

213 Labour was generally in agreement with the need for new legislation. See: Hansen, *Citizenship and Immigration*, pp. 207–21; Hampshire, *Politics of Immigration*, p. 128; James, 'Black Experience', pp. 382–3; Blake, 'British Nationality Act'.

214 Rowe, *Racialisation of Disorder*, pp. 156–7; Mitchell and Russell, 'Race, the New Right and State Policy'; Hall, *The Hard Road to Renewal*.

215 Brain, *History of Policing*, pp. 55, 76.

216 Henry, 'Police and People', p. 9.

217 Emsley, *English Police*, p. 169; Kettle, 'Law and Order', p. 220.

218 Reiner, *Politics of the Police*, p. 89; Brain, *History of Policing*, p. 56.

219 *Daily Star*, 12 March 1980.

220 See, for example: Fryer, *Staying Power*; Goulbourne, *Race Relations*; Layton-Henry, *Politics of Race*.

221 See: Lea and Young, 'The Riots'.

2

'No other way to make their points of view known'? St Pauls, Bristol, 2 April 1980

Then Bristol caught fire,
Smell of burning in the air.

The Selector – Bristol & Miami

T HE DISORDER that erupted in the St Pauls area of Bristol on 2 April 1980 shocked many people. Timothy Brain later epitomised this: 'With the passage of time it is difficult to emphasize just how unexpected the St Paul's riot was.'[1] A viewpoint likely influenced by his having been a Bristol police constable at the time, this was, nevertheless, certainly a widespread reaction. Peter Fryer conversely argued that the disturbances only shocked 'those blind to what had been happening all through the 1970s, and deaf to the many protests and warnings'.[2] Indeed, following increased Commonwealth migration after the Second World War, there had been gradual moves towards self-organisation and militant action as racial discrimination and disadvantage had proliferated, but the state focused more upon stricter immigration controls than combatting racism.

There have been many references to St Pauls in the existing literature, although most as passing mentions of this precursor to the following year's intensified disorders. In the only dedicated work on the events, Harris Joshua *et al.* argued that, although economic and social conditions in St Pauls were significant, police tactics ignited violence that was subsequently fanned by media coverage and shaped by the state's response into a law and order issue.[3] Similarly, Martin Kettle and Lucy Hodges focused primarily on the police's role and authorities' emphasis on prosecuting those deemed responsible.[4] These studies consider many aspects of the disturbance, such as local authorities' housing and education policies, but their focus is not on local organisations and calls for public inquiries as a means of improving levels of public discourse regarding racial discrimination and disadvantage. Additionally, their contemporary publications lack access to subsequently available records.

Examining the response to and impact of this disturbance, this chapter considers a number of aspects through study of local and national records, media representations and interviews with participants. First, it observes previously poor police/community relations in the area, including numerous accusations of police misconduct and growing concern regarding their tactics. It subsequently examines the police action that ignited disorder – a raid on a local café popular with black locals – and resulting disturbance, which saw the police withdraw from the area for nearly four hours, prompting widespread fears of the emergence of police 'no-go' areas, infamous during the Northern Ireland 'Troubles'. The chapter ends by examining how news of the disturbance spread, initially within the city and later elsewhere, concluding that its influence on subsequent disturbances is undeniable.

Bristol

During increased postwar migration, Bristol was deemed an area with 'diverse industries and thus good chances of employment'.[5] Faced with discriminatory housing practices, migrants often had little choice but to flock to the suburb of St Pauls; already infamous for its abundance of brothels before the influx of a West Indian community in the 1950s, it became dubbed 'the jungle'. Ken Pryce's 1979 sociological study of black life in Bristol, notably entitled *Endless Pressure*, recorded that St Pauls was 'regarded as a place of "vice and shame", with a high potential for trouble'.[6] Situated just northeast of the city centre, it quickly became known for its relatively high proportion of black residents. Attracting black people from all over Bristol, it became a meeting place for those with 'nowhere else to go'.[7] Stuart Hall *et al.* termed such locations 'the colony': 'a defensive response to racism experienced by Black Britons during the 1970s … in which an alternative black social life could flourish'.[8] Despite its reputation as a black 'ghetto', Madge Dresser and Peter Fleming countered that official statistics consistently overestimated the black population, comprising only 31 per cent of its total population by 1991.[9] Pryce's study revealed that a single 'community' did not exist, due to divisions and suspicions between different ethnic groups, such as people originating from different Caribbean islands.[10] This is supported by the City Council Housing Department asserting that a constant turnover in population meant 'it was difficult to speak of a "stable community"'.[11] This must be remembered during discussions of 'community leaders' and 'the community's' response.

Adding to existing tensions, unemployment was rife. Exact figures are unknown, due to a lack of recorded statistics, but a 1981 Trades Union Congress (TUC) inquiry argued it was higher than the 35 per cent estimated by the City of Bristol in 1976. Furthermore, the TUC contended that unemployment figures for minority ethnic groups were almost double those of the white population; indeed, numbers of black youth registered unemployed had risen in preceding years but declined for white counterparts. Government investment, when forthcoming, was criticised for being allocated without local consultation. In addition, construction of the M32 motorway in the 1970s further reduced housing standards and fragmented the local community who resented the intrusion upon desires to 'lead much of their social life in the open air and on the streets'.[12] In his study of the area, S.D. Reicher concluded that, while black youth experienced the same kinds of deprivation elsewhere, there was more of a sense in St Pauls of their entire community being under siege.[13] In many ways, it appeared to black residents that their very way of life was under attack.

Fryer contended that a capacity for disorder was a reflection of Bristol's history as a chief slave port. Speaking of Bristol alongside London and Liverpool – areas with extensive slave trade activity that would experience similar disturbances in 1981 – he argued: 'There, if anywhere, the persistent bullying of black people was bound, sooner or later, to provoke rebellion.'[14] Indeed, St Pauls had previously been the location for the devising of the 1963 Bristol bus boycott: a successful non-violent boycott of a local bus company refusing to employ minority ethnic people on front-line services, action by black campaigners and white supporters lasted four months and effectively ended the company's colour bar.[15] Highlighting racial discrimination to the wider public, it repeatedly permeated Parliament and contributed to the passage of the first anti-discriminatory Race Relations Act in 1965.[16] The extent that a city's history of slavery would specifically incite disorder in the 1980s is debatable, whereas their position as port cities with various employment opportunities leading to increased migrant settlement likely played more of a role. Nonetheless, the recent decision to change the name of Bristol's Colston Hall – due to its link with slave trader Edward Colston – demonstrates that a slavery legacy is not soon forgotten.[17]

Police/community relations in St Pauls

The disorder took place against the backdrop of poor relations between the police and black population of St Pauls. More problematically, the police mistakenly believed relations were good – or at least claimed so afterwards in attempts to absolve themselves from responsibility. Brain, a police officer at the time, encapsulated this when later contending that 'there was no history of general disorder or poor police–community relations. Nor was there any noticeable background build-up of tension'.[18] Senior police officials claimed to have had a very good relationship with St Pauls; or that they 'always thought we had'.[19] However, Avon and Somerset Police Authority Chair, Ian Crawford, declared the police had believed relations were improving, but 'apparently they had not improved so much as … thought'.[20] Even to suggest relations were advancing indicates it was known they needed improvement; certainly, Avon and Somerset Chief Constable, Brian Weigh, had warned one year earlier of the possibility of such violence. Nonetheless, Weigh argued that media portrayals of 'continual conflict' between police and black people was incorrect and that the police even acted in a mediatory capacity in some quarrels between ethnic groups; indeed, the Bristol Council for Racial Equality (BCRE) enjoyed close liaison with the Community Relations Officer, Chief Inspector Derek Lane.[21] The BCRE, a local community relations council that liaised with the police and city and county councils, was later described thus: '[They] could not be regarded as the representatives of the immigrant community, as the officers were employed to be advisors, but could be accepted to communicate the black community's views.'[22]

Meanwhile, Owen Henry, West Indian Parents and Friends Association Chair, countered there had never been friendly relations between the police and black residents. He argued that the police were not familiar with residents and communicated wrong information from one area to another, both of which fostered distrust.[23] Robert Reiner's 1974 study of Bristol police noted common hostility towards minority ethnic Britons, with one constable claiming '90 per cent of the force are against coloured immigrants'.[24] Reports after the disturbance showed tensions were rife, and BCRE Chair Bill Nicks recorded previous 'great disquiet' regarding police activities.[25] Local activist and campaigner Simbarashe Tongogara later claimed that the police were 'used as an instrument to terrorise', believing community policing operations were thinly veiled attempts to spy on residents.[26] Despite discontent, the Avon and Somerset Constabulary recorded only nine official complaints from black people in 1980. This, as Assistant Community Relations Officer Peter Courtier pointed out, was somewhat of a false figure due to reluctance to use the official complaints procedure. Echoing criticisms made repeatedly throughout this period, Courtier argued the main reason for this disinclination was belief it would not be productive, or even fear of increased future persecution; both linked to the fact that the police had directly investigated complaints against themselves.[27]

Police Federation Chair Jim Jardine responded that, while much was said about the problems faced by young black people, police difficulties were often forgotten. Arguing that 'a simple exercise of a police power' would be regarded as prejudice and 'add yet another statistic to the complaints against the police', he criticised negative portrayals of the police as a 'classic example of … propaganda'.[28] Jardine, and other senior police, continued to respond to accusations of police misconduct with similar blunt refusals to admit they may be somewhat true. Acknowledging the police's difficulties, local MP Tony Benn reasoned it was unfair to ask the police to 'carry a burden' partly emerging from rising unemployment, social deprivation and other inner-city problems; thus defining the police as the identifiable face of government policies and perceived failings.[29] This was somewhat corroborated when Roy de Freitas, of the African-Caribbean Community Association, claimed the disturbance should be seen as a reflection of broader feelings and frustrations from local black people.[30]

The disturbance

Against this backdrop, the St Pauls disturbance began after a police raid on the Black and White Café, believed to be the site of illegal drinking and cannabis smoking. Despite the café's name implying an attempt to spread a social integrationist message within an area known as the 'frontline', this name in fact originated from its being run by a black husband and white wife.[31] A long-running meeting place for black residents, it had taken on greater significance in recent months due to police closure of similar establishments. Many facilities in St Pauls had been eroded and the café was seen as the last place unemployed youths could gather. Three other prominent meeting places – a disco and two bars – had been shut recently and the Black and White was described as 'the last survivor': De Freitas claimed the general feeling amongst local youth was 'if they close this place, where will we be able to go?'[32] After their other meeting places disappeared, local black youth acted in perceived self-defence, consistent with a departure from peaceful compliance characterising earlier years and generations.[33] In the words of participant Carlton Sharpe: 'We had a perspective now, we don't like what's going on, we don't like what's before – we want to do something about it.'[34]

Precise details differ between accounts, but a generally accepted version of events emerged in the aftermath – later criticised as heavily based on a report by Weigh, who had not arrived until sometime later, demonstrating the prominence awarded to authorities when establishing narratives.[35] Around 3 p.m., a number of officers entered the Black and White searching for the illegal sale of alcohol and drugs; some were plainclothed and several reserve officers with dogs were positioned nearby. The inhabitants were questioned and crates of alcohol seized as evidence. At some point – the reasons vary in different accounts – the growing crowd outside the café became engaged in confrontation with the police, throwing stones and missiles. Police reinforcements were summoned, but vehicles entering the area were overturned and one set on fire. A period variously described as 'uneasy calm' or 'rearmament' followed and, during this time, the majority of the police withdrew to less visible positions – credited by Weigh as having reduced violence. Around 6.30 p.m., riot shields and a breakdown vehicle arrived, and the police attempted to remove the burnt-out car and regain control of the streets. However, they came under such fierce attack that the decision was made to withdraw officers from the area around 7.30 p.m. Police returned at 11 p.m. and, by midnight, the disturbance was over.

Tongogara characterised the raid as 'the usual scenario', but 'because it was a sunny day, lots of young black people quickly turned up and that changed the whole focus'.[36] Certainly, the initial raid was later described by police officials as 'routine', and officers had not anticipated trouble. Yet, police numbers involved suggested they were at least aware of the possibility.[37] When questioned on numbers and the positioning of reserves nearby, senior police officers contended: 'That's prudent. That doesn't mean to say you're expecting trouble.' During a press conference the morning after the disorder, the police initially stated twelve officers had entered the café, rising to '12 to 15' when questioned specifically.[38] This was supported by the Commission for Racial Equality's Paul Stephenson, who placed the number of uniformed police who entered at fourteen. A later memorandum by Home Secretary William Whitelaw based on Weigh's report suggested it was actually twenty, and, during subsequent Crown Court trials, Justice Stocker indicated thirty-nine officers in total were involved.[39] Utilising various sources, Joshua et al. detailed that police briefings specified twenty-four officers were to enter the café, with six posted outside and nine more on stand-by nearby. They concluded that this clearly showed more police were present than recorded by Whitelaw's memorandum, which claimed use of minimum numbers would keep the operation low-key.[40] This contention is supported by the Police Operational Order for the raid, which stated that twenty-two officers would enter, with six posted outside and eight more in reserve nearby. The memorandum also fails to identify the involvement of six Task Force 'A' officers, a local equivalent of infamous mobile support unit the SPG, suggesting attempts to minimise potential criticism of heavy-handed police tactics.[41] Senior police officers stated they did not believe police numbers during the raid to be a material factor in causing the disturbance, but agreed that, once the situation had escalated, there were not enough officers present to 'do what we wanted'.[42]

Response

After the disturbance subsided, questions regarding its cause began in earnest. A crude – if fairly accurate – method of dividing reaction would be between professed surprise from authorities, as opposed to the response of local people or organisations. This was the view of partisan newspaper the *Jamaican Weekly Gleaner*, which claimed: 'trouble was expected by everyone in the area except the police'.[43] Indeed, Bristol City Council leader Claude Draper emphasised his shock, even admitting he believed the telephone call notifying him had been a joke.[44] The national Government appeared particularly surprised that disorder had occurred in Bristol; this 'sleepy, easy-going conservative City' had long been regarded a 'model city' in dealing with inner-city problems, and the Home Office had recently heard a 'glowing report' regarding police relations with the black community.[45] In *The Times*, Fred Emery summarised that 'no one at Westminster would have even shortlisted Bristol as the potential powder keg which many, afterwards, said it had long been'.[46] Yet, one local interviewed on BBC's *Points West* countered: 'I listened to the Home Secretary say about we got good race relations in Bristol. What does he know about it? ... He hasn't been to the black community ... it is only on paper that they says there is good race relations.'[47]

Ron Ramdin argued that collective violence 'was integral to the political struggles' faced by black and minority ethnic communities, and state policies and actions had provoked such resistance that could have occurred at any point in the previous decade.[48] Indeed, at the BCRE's annual meeting Russell Profitt, a black Greater London Councillor, characterised the disturbances as 'a demand for change and black power'.[49] Observers had previously warned of the area's potential for violence, but were disregarded – suggesting that the problems and concerns of black people were not treated as a serious problem. Claiming that they had been warning authorities for more than a decade, the BCRE concluded that the disturbance displayed widespread feelings amongst local black people that there was 'no other way to make their points of view known': now, 'the artificial icing has been ruthlessly removed from the Bristol cake'.[50] As typical government mechanisms seemingly did not allow local black people a means of expressing their views, some undertook violent actions to be heard.

Monique Courtier questioned whether authorities would delve deeper into the issues or simply blame black residents for violence, astutely warning 'this could be just the beginning'.[51] Concerns that black people would be blamed stemmed from previous experience – such as the 1958 racist riots discussed in chapter 1 – and oppressive policing strategies. For example, many local people believed that, despite being illegal, illicit drinking and cannabis smoking did not harm others so did not require a heavy-handed police response.[52] An inquiry conducted by the *Sun* soon after the disorder reported that black youths in St Pauls believed it was evidence of police attempts to suppress their culture. Thus, their violent response to the raid on the Black and White was portrayed as an attempt to protect their culture, under constant attack from the British state. Robert Wilks, brother of the café owner, reasoned: 'I know we can't be treated separately, but there is no need for the police to be heavy-handed.'[53] In the words of Fryer: 'To the black communities the police had become, in effect, an army of occupation charged with the task of keeping black people in their place.'[54] There were even calls to reconsider some laws in order to promote racial harmony. For instance, St Pauls vicar, Reverend Keith Kimber, advocated the decriminalisation of cannabis as he argued laws preventing its use 'grate against the cultural traditions of the immigrants'.[55] The *Sun* itself countered this, contending that people should support the police rather than 'sniping at the very laws which the country has asked them to enforce' – hardly an unsurprising stance from a newspaper that had begun strongly supporting the Conservative Party.[56]

BCRE Chair Bill Nicks linked this drug decriminalisation debate with the widespread belief that black people were predisposed to be unlawful and would not accept British law and order, illustrated by Hall *et al*.'s exploration of 'mugging'.[57] Nicks argued that people in Britain had spent centuries being raised to believe that black people were inferior – 'at best a source of entertainment' – and warned that, until it was fully accepted that British society had changed, this imperial legacy would prevent potential lessons from being learnt.[58]

A 'race riot'?

While newspapers pronounced 'BLACK RIOT' or 'RACE RIOT', the authorities attempted to diminish the racial element.[59] Police Authority Chair, Ian Crawford, asserted that the disorder was not a 'race riot' and senior police officials added: 'it was purely a riot against authority'.[60] Bristol MPs William Waldegrave and Tony Benn similarly declared it was not a case of one community attacking another; rather it was a 'difficult policing problem', and relations between the police and all communities must be considered.[61] The BCRE likewise stressed that it was not a 'race riot' – although it 'undoubtedly had racial implications' – but rather a violent reaction against 'heavy handed and ill-timed' police activities, indicative of the level of frustration felt by black youth towards a 'hostile society'.[62] This is certainly supported by participants themselves, noting that the disorder was 'not a race riot: it was against the police and the way they harass us', and one black teenager declared: 'We took on the police and beat them ... They will never again treat us with contempt.'[63]

Nonetheless, the *Sun* suggested it would be 'absurd' to ignore the racial overtones of an act of rebellion by a predominantly black population against a predominantly white police force.[64] Michael Rowe argued that the media generally described it as a 'black riot', contrasting their reporting with football hooliganism or anti-poll tax disorders, which were not explained in terms of the participants' ethnicity. Citing a *Daily Telegraph* editorial that blamed a lack of parental care, 'race-relations witch-finders and left-wing teachers and social workers', Rowe placed this portrayal firmly within a Thatcherite neoliberal ideology that rejected explanations involving racism or discrimination.[65] Similarly, Joshua *et al.* contended that the authorities' response was shaped by opposition to characterisations that Britain was experiencing US-style racial violence. Thus, in the media's formulation of events, the figure of the 'white rioter' appeared and disappeared at their convenience, diminishing arguments that the disorder had been an uprising against racism.[66] Kettle and Hodges highlighted that the attempted lessening of racial characteristics was seen by black people as a typically British response. In essence, a denial that they faced particular challenges: 'Not to recognize the racial nature of them is to bury one's head in the sand, to lump black people's problems in the same bracket as poor housing and unemployment and to treat outbreaks of violence as aberrations.'[67] Discarding explanations acknowledging racism within British society, this furthered some black people's opinion that traditional political frameworks would not improve their situation, leading others across the country to contemplate similar action.

Police action during disorder

Unsurprisingly, post-disorder attention focused upon the police raid of the café – the event that, it was suggested, 'lit the touch paper'. This interaction acted as the 'flashpoint': the determinant level regarding the outbreak of disorder, according to the theoretical model of the same name.[68] A BCRE press release condemned the nature of the police action, proclaiming that it 'led the Black Community to stand up against this type of police intimidation'.[69]

In contrast, the police repeatedly asserted they did not know why the disturbance erupted. Senior police officials identified that objection to police presence in the area had very quickly escalated, but they 'just wouldn't know' why. Describing accusations that the police's action had been provocative as 'a very subjective statement', a police representative retorted: 'I suppose all police action to some extent is provocative … it depends who you are and what you're doing.'[70] The Police Authority deemed it 'sad' that this 'totally unforeseeable situation' had shattered years of work to improve community relations.[71] As previously noted, it had not been entirely unforeseen.

The raid itself was planned ten days in advance, although at no point was it noted or believed important that it fell upon the local officer's weekly day off – a man known and reasonably well-liked by locals.[72] Had local people faced someone familiar to them and sympathetic with their particular issues, events may not have escalated into disorder. Similarly, the Police Community Relations Officer had not been consulted about the raid, although community representatives apparently had, in a 'temperature-taking exercise': Superintendent Vincent Arkell stated that 'community leaders' attending this meeting claimed 'police–black relations could not have been better'.[73] Clearly, this had been vastly misjudged – either through misunderstanding between police and community 'leaders', or the inherent issue in denoting anybody a 'leader' of an entire community of diverse people. Moreover, Weigh reasoned that previous raids had been carried out at the same time of day without trouble, but later admitted that, as the local school had closed at lunch for Easter holidays, a greater number of assembled youths increased the potential for disorder.[74]

Further to such oversights, Joshua et al. argued that the police removing alcohol from the café was unnecessary – as it had already been photographed for later use as evidence – and added to other potentially provocative actions.[75] However, the Police Operational Order clearly stated the object of the raid was to discover and seize any items relating to the illegal sale or supply of alcohol.[76] Thus, the decision to confiscate items was taken at the planning stage and not at the scene, and many officers carried crates of alcohol from the café into a police van for thirty minutes before serious incidents occurred.[77] Whether officers should have sensed the provocative nature of removing alcohol through an already disgruntled crowd is another question; their operational order showed that they were, to borrow an infamous phrase, simply following orders.

This is not to disregard decisions taken on the day adding to feelings of police provocation. Several witnesses accused officers of failing to produce a search warrant, harassing those inside the café, and even buying or smoking drugs.

While the latter seems unlikely, as Reicher concluded, 'Whether true or not, these perceptions indicate a general feeling about the illegitimacy of the police action'.[78] Defence lawyers during later trials emphasised that the police had no legal right to document innocent people, and the judge agreed these actions would certainly generate animosity. In addition, Joshua et al. argued that, as café customers had offered no resistance and were already outnumbered by police, Arkell's decision to summon additional officers was 'difficult to understand'.[79] The official reason given for these reinforcements was that more alcohol had been found than expected and, with a crowd congregating outside the café, increased numbers would hasten the removal of alcohol and allow more crowd control – although it also amplified tensions. As did two arrests. One man, arrested for the illegal consumption of alcohol, was detained for half an hour before being transferred to the police station. In addition, Bertram Wilks, the café proprietor, was handcuffed and restrained despite being known to the police and unlikely to flee or become violent. Joshua et al. highlighted he could simply have been summonsed to appear later at the police station, and knowledge of this caused every senior officer to later deny ordering his arrest. The Commission for Racial Equality's Paul Stephenson documented that, only a brief time after Wilks had been driven off in police custody, black youths began throwing missiles.[80] In such a volatile atmosphere, the police perhaps would have been wise to err on the side of caution to avoid provocative actions – but, as demonstrated, it appears the police considered disorder unlikely.

Some witnesses recounted that an officer ripped a black youth's trousers while carrying a crate past.[81] Although the police stated conflict was quickly resolved and anger dissipated, that portrayal was questioned by Prince Brown, member of the West Indian Development Council, who had been present and 'had seen the explosion coming'. Brown alleged that actually officers had ignored the youth's request for compensation, instead threatening those present with arrest.[82] Although unlikely for the officer to have simply reimbursed the angry youth from his own pocket, ignoring the complaints provided another apparent example of the police not being held accountable for their actions. The youth responded defiantly to arrest threats, causing the officer to push him with a beer crate, and thus initiate the disturbance.[83]

Numerous eyewitnesses blamed the police's response to initial low-level tensions for subsequent disorder. Partisan publication Out West quoted Arkell's statement, referencing 'a group … hell-bent on causing trouble', before asking: 'Which group? The rioters or the police? Taken out of context, the statement is appropriately double-edged.'[84] Similarly, observers believed that officers marching through the streets with riot shields incited a response from local people: 'If the National Front marched through St Paul's it would have been the same.'[85] As some officers had only been trained to use riot shields in the police station yard immediately prior to deployment, they likely did not have comprehensive experience of their appropriate use. Other accusations of police misconduct appeared, with one telephone call to the police expressing displeasure at police 'running people over' – likely a Northern Irish-inspired attempt to disperse crowds, demonstrated in subsequent disorders.[86] Kettle and Hodges reasoned that, despite the police hoping a show of strength would disperse the crowd, there were insufficient numbers to impose control successfully.[87]

Similarly, Prince Brown stated that police using dogs against crowds 'infuriated the black population'. There was a history of such in the area, and Owen Henry claimed he could not remember any occasion when the police entered St Pauls without dogs.[88] The *Jamaican Weekly Gleaner* recorded that the police had been informed several times that repeated use of dogs branded people as criminals, despite their having committed no crime.[89] Although not meant for crowd control, frequent references to police dogs in testimony and evidence suggest they were used this way; in fact, more than one officer admitted being frightened by the dogs themselves. Using this approach to 'control' St Pauls' residents created the impression that they were treated differently from other British citizens: an inhuman 'other', treated as such.[90] After the disturbance, Weigh acknowledged that the use of dogs required 'very careful consideration', and their provocative nature was a lesson from the disturbance.[91] As discussed in subsequent chapters, such lessons were not readily learnt.

Withdrawal

An aspect garnering much attention was the police withdrawal at the height of disorders, later described as 'a fateful decision'.[92] This drew much criticism contending that the police's primary role was to maintain law and order and protect citizens; their withdrawal was thus viewed as having conceded defeat. Officers stated that their subsequent return to the area was greeted with cheers, residents wishing them well, and even older black tenants apologising for the actions of black youth.[93] While the police were praised for regaining control, observers qualified this by stressing that most of the streets were by then deserted; as one participant stated: 'The police ... did not retake St Paul's: we decided to go home and allow them to move in.'[94]

The decision to withdraw was taken by Chief Constable Brian Weigh, who argued that the 'clearly overwhelmed' police had no other choice; they were not sufficient in number to contain the situation and a maintained police presence would exacerbate it: 'They weren't throwing at anyone else, they were throwing at the police.'[95] This was seemingly vindicated by Detective Sergeant Patrick Ward, who alleged that an interviewed suspect told him: 'There would have been a lot more of you in hospital if you hadn't run away.'[96] Furthermore, Reicher's participant interviews recorded that the message being spread during disorders was 'the object was the police, direct your antagonism that way'.[97] Indeed, twenty-one police cars sustained damage, of which six were destroyed. Adding insult to injury for the police, insurance of police vehicles had reportedly been downgraded the day before the disturbance – ironically, to save money.[98]

It certainly appears that violence was specifically directed, with local Asian-owned shops or those known to employ black workers protected and looting prevented.[99] Injuries and some damages were blamed by participants on accidental crossfire or missing police targets, it was claimed that photographers were targeted only to avoid film being used for police identifications, and the attacks on cars were rationalised as either punishment for apparent endorsement of police harassment or prompted by belief they were unmarked police vehicles.[100] However, many examples exist of non-police damage, such as the Black and White itself being looted and the burning of Lloyds Bank, justified as being 'part of the Establishment we are rebelling against'.[101] Whilst these may simply have been convenient post-hoc rationalisations, the *Sunday Times* noted clear geographical limits of the crowd remaining within St Pauls boundaries, even helping direct traffic through the area.[102] Such focused actions and community mindset certainly fit within the 'collective bargaining by riot' framework, forwarded by Eric Hobsbawm and others, as targeted attempts to obtain positive outcomes for local black people.[103]

A reporter's question summarised criticisms of the police's withdrawal – with the crowd 'left to run wild', were fatalities not more likely? Police representatives dismissed this as conjecture, highlighting that several injuries had occurred while officers were present but they were not aware of any after their departure. Police did confirm more damage had occurred after they withdrew, but argued that their main objective was preservation of life and the 'necessary but regrettable' withdrawal had been 'for the greater good'.[104] This was not likely to placate those who had incurred a large expense from the disorder and subsequent looting, with property-owners reportedly considering suing the police for £750,000 compensation.[105] One shopkeeper summarised widespread sentiment believing that the police had instigated disorder through heavy-handed actions and then retreated, 'leaving us to bear the brunt'.[106] It was argued that, prior to the withdrawal, only police property had been damaged; once they had vacated the area, looting and arson began.[107] Despite being portrayed as black criminality, such looting was seemingly undertaken disproportionately by white people; a pattern that arrest statistics suggest was repeated across the country the following year.[108] The *Daily Mail*, perhaps unsurprisingly given its right-wing political slant, demanded that, 'when society leaves the innocent to struggle against crazed destroyers for four solid hours on their own, [they must be] recompensed, to the last bottle of toffees, out of public funds'.[109] As with other media portrayals, characterisations of the 'innocent' struggling against 'crazed destroyers' leaves little room for nuanced discussion of underlying causes or desired outcomes.

Arguments over their withdrawal highlight the disputed issue of who and what exactly the police's main responsibilities are.[110] Contrary to the criticism he received for the withdrawal, Weigh clearly believed his responsibility rested more on the safety of the public and his officers than material possessions. Unsurprisingly, this view was shared by many officers and the Police Authority 'strongly and unanimously supported' Weigh, arguing that, due to his 'cool and firm leadership, no lives were lost, nor was any serious injury suffered'.[111] Roy de Freitas, of the African-Caribbean Community Association, also praised the withdrawal, dubbing it 'an inspired move' that avoided serious injuries. Believing that anger was directed only towards local merchants who had previously demonstrated contempt for black people whilst also exploiting them, he added: 'Had the police tried to suppress the black anger with force, traders and other people's lives could have been in danger.'[112]

In Parliament, Home Secretary William Whitelaw defended police actions as being 'in the highest traditions' of service and hoped it would be recognised that, regardless of criticisms, 'individual police officers perform their duties with dedication to the service of this country'.[113] He contended that the absence of death or serious injury might go some way to justifying their withdrawal, although others countered that this could simply have been luck. Despite his apparent public backing of Weigh, the *Daily Mail* characterised Whitelaw as being sufficiently 'shaken' by the withdrawal to 'urgently' review the procedures for handling large civil disorders; indeed, Whitelaw later stressed: 'The removal of police protection in this way could not be allowed to happen again.'[114]

Whitelaw also proclaimed that so-called 'no-go' areas would not appear in the country. Widespread fears that such spaces would reach England from the 'Troubles' of Northern Ireland – the most prominent being Free Derry, a self-declared autonomous nationalist area of Northern Ireland between 1969 and 1972 – were highlighted by Whitelaw, who explained the importance for him to say it, 'to be heard to say it, and for it to be realised that that will not happen'.[115] It is not a stretch to believe this was a prominent public fear when newspapers printed headings such as 'We never dreamed that they could come here; that in the England of 1980 we could have "no-go" areas like those of Londonderry'.[116] A further connection across the Irish Sea came from Shadow Home Secretary Merlyn Rees. Previously Northern Ireland Secretary during a particularly turbulent period of 1974–76, he maintained a keen interest in the 'Troubles' and it is reasonable to suggest this influenced his views on policing. He subsequently served as Home Secretary from 1976 to 1979 and, despite the recently elected Conservative Government's policies vociferously promoting law and order, Whitelaw's response can be portrayed in part as a continuation of previous policy, as Rees agreed he fundamentally rejected 'no-go' areas.[117]

As too, seemingly, did the public. The police log of events during St Pauls recorded numerous emergency calls questioning why, despite the 'mob which is running wild like rats', there was 'not a Policeman in sight' – demonstrating the role many callers believed the police should be fulfilling: protecting public and property.[118] Centre-right newspaper *The Times* highlighted that this was especially felt by Conservatives, whose 'intense' shock at the withdrawal expressed 'that classic Tory commitment to the sanctity of property above all else'. Similarly, local Conservative-leaning newspaper the *Western Daily Press* cited several Conservative MPs it believed likely to demand Weigh's resignation over the withdrawal, and Home Affairs Select Committee Secretary Alan Clark condemned the fact that those contacting the police were told 'Sorry we're frightened'.[119] Reportedly, several chief constables privately claimed they would have maintained a presence even at the risk of serious injury or death; many of them would soon have the opportunity to test their conviction when disturbances spread across the country the following year.[120] Following intense criticism of Weigh's withdrawal, they were much less likely to follow his lead and a more robust police response was to follow, examined in chapter 6.

The media's language describing the police withdrawal was similarly unfavourable, portraying it as 'leaving an area of the city unprotected', and adding: 'There was no law, no protection of property or even of the safety of the people.'[121] That other police chiefs were unwilling to comment upon Weigh's decision was used to infer that they believed it was incorrect; although, it is difficult to see what the personal benefit for other chiefs would be for backing Weigh's controversial withdrawal, regardless of their genuine beliefs.[122] Rather than exploring why disorder erupted, questions were asked of the police's failure to preserve law and order and why it took four hours for them to be sufficiently reinforced to return.[123] Some newspapers emphasised Whitelaw's responsibility in fulfilling the Conservative election promise to focus upon law and order and support the police through the 'short, sharp shock' treatment of offenders; they argued he needed to ensure no other British city suffered a similar fate because of police inability to combat a 'roaming band of thugs'.[124] This increased focus upon police procedures and equipment, demanding that they should not be caught out again. Therefore, Weigh's subsequent annual report recorded that organisational lessons had been very quickly implemented, so the police were now adequately trained and equipped to respond appropriately to any recurrence of disorder.[125] The media attention and public discourse, focused upon the police's 'failure' to provide public protection, undoubtedly hastened this process. The state framed reaction to the disturbance around issues of law and order, criminalising those involved and diminishing the discontent at the heart of the disorder. Focus upon law and order was certainly a cross-party response, as Merlyn Rees, again seemingly influenced by Northern Ireland experiences, proposed mobile police units that could deal with such emergencies – overlooking the condemnation of such specialised 'task forces' for being unfamiliar with local situations.[126] With these reactions and perspectives considered, as barrister John Spokes argued, it perhaps 'took considerably more courage to give the order to withdraw than an order to stay'.[127]

Spread of ideas

One aspect of the disturbances not commonly considered is how word spread throughout and beyond St Pauls. Disorder erupted during a period of high tension, amplified by a planned trip to London the next day to protest police harassment following a local youth's court appearance after a London 'sus' arrest.[128] Furthermore, occurring at the beginning of the Easter school holiday, many black youths witnessed the raid and several of those initially inside the café spread news of the police action.[129] This was significant in disseminating information quickly around the area and crowds swelled while the police were still present, increasing both numbers and tensions. This spread of information is exampled by Carlton Sharpe becoming aware of the disturbance when 'my friend's mum said: "something's happening over in St Pauls."'[130]

The Avon and Somerset Constabulary log of events contains many references to how the disturbance affected other areas of the country. Its national importance was highlighted when the Home Office telephoned for an update some six hours into events, requesting to be informed 'should any major developments take place'. One group of citizens in London even proposed assisting the police to regain control.[131] While this offer was acknowledged but declined, the disorder had placed great strain upon the Constabulary. Reinforcements were required from other territorial divisions, and personnel from other police forces either arrived in Bristol or remained on standby at Cheltenham, Leigh Delamare and Exeter.[132] The use of officers unfamiliar with, and to, local people undoubtedly exacerbated tensions in a way that sympathetic community officers might not have.

It was not only police travelling the country due to the disturbances. An emergency telephone call claimed that black people had threatened to have guns delivered to Bristol from Birmingham, Coventry and London. Similarly, a police confidential informant recorded they had heard that coachloads of black people were coming from Birmingham, armed 'to kill the Policemen'; therefore, any coaches heading to Bristol on the M5 motorway were stopped and searched. This was discontinued around 2 a.m. but, after information received at 3.30 a.m. that more than twenty-five vehicles had been 'commandeered' with over 100 black people 'heading for Bristol', motorway checks were immediately reinstated.[133] While high levels of rumour characterise most disorders due to confusion and fear, it appeared, or at least was believed, that events were quickly spreading.

Similarly, reporters quickly became aware of the situation and telephone calls requesting information were logged from *The Times*, *BBC News London* and London's *Evening Standard*. City Councillor Bob Wall noted the prominence awarded to the events in US news bulletins, the BCRE recorded at least one day spent giving interviews to Dutch and Swedish television reporters, and Tongogara spoke with Russian media. Defence lawyer Rudy Narayan concluded that: 'Newspapers, television, the radio and politicians all descended, figuratively speaking, on St Paul's.'[134] Such press coverage was criticised for misrepresenting Bristol, and the satirical treatment of St Pauls by television comedy *Not the Nine O'Clock News* certainly did not paint the city's police in a positive light. City Councillor Trench bemoaned the damaging effect it could have upon the city's economy, suggesting where priorities lay.[135]

The media are often at the forefront of disseminating ideas, especially during such action as rebellion and protest. 'Twitter Revolutions' in Moldova, Iran, Tunisia and Egypt show how influential social media has become, but this is not to say that such ideas could not spread before updating social media at our fingertips.[136] Ruud Koopmans argued that instances of collective action are not independent, occurring within broader protest cycles or waves.[137] St Pauls can be placed within such a framework, as US examples – such as the 1965 Watts disorders in Los Angeles – influenced the action, and itself existed within a spreading youth revolt throughout Europe and served as an example across England.[138] Indeed, a St Pauls resident demonstrated this influence:

> Our history shows us that the dominant community will give us no concessions unless we fight. It happened some years ago in cities in the United States and seems to have done them some good. We have no jobs, no equality of opportunity and if burning a few banks pushes us along the road, then so be it.[139]

Mike Phillips supported the influence that US Civil Rights and Black Power struggles had on those in Britain, as 'we could watch black giants walking the earth'.[140] Clearly portraying Bristol's collective violence as 'collective bargaining by riot' to improve the lives of black people, it also demonstrates that US examples acted as precursors and inspiration for such action.

Fryer argued that St Pauls taught black youth nationwide that they could tactically defeat the police.[141] Authorities appeared aware of this; Diane Abbott, later a Labour MP, recorded that, 'in a novel exercise in community relations', the Metropolitan Police summoned 'key black activists' to warn against replicating the Bristol example.[142] As Brain summarised, 'cross-current transmission of ideas between the Bristol and London Afro-Caribbean communities was possible, indeed likely'.[143] Tongogara depicted the nationwide influence of St Pauls as being due to Bristol's unique role during the 1960s and 1970s: 'Bristol just happened to be this place that, wherever you was in England as black people, you came to it.'[144] Indeed, ideas were spread simply by the movement of people. For example, coachloads of St Pauls residents travelled to London to lobby MPs for a public inquiry – discussed in chapter 3.[145]

Regardless of how information was relayed, it is undeniable that the St Pauls disturbances reverberated across the country. In Lewisham, black youths chanted 'Bristol, Bristol, Bristol' at local police, graffiti within South London correctly predicted 'Bristol now, Brixton next?' and later 'Bristol yesterday, Brixton today', and police statements from the Brixton disturbances, recording crowds shouting 'Remember Bristol!' while charging police lines, demonstrate the significance of St Pauls.[146] Outspoken local police critic Franklin Rapier even spoke at a public meeting organised by the Brixton Defence Campaign 'to link Bristol & Brixton'.[147]

Conclusion

Much post-disorder discussion concentrated on where disorder might appear next. BCRE Chair Bill Nicks argued it would be a mistake to believe St Pauls would not be repeated elsewhere, showing how local challenges were part of wider experiences of racial discrimination.[148] Ray Wardle, Liberal candidate for Bath County Council, voiced this feeling: 'We too have a Black and White Café ... [as does] every inner-city area.'[149] Similar conditions in other cities such as Liverpool, Manchester and London – where disorder would spread the following year – were highlighted as potential sites of disturbances, and thus 'urgent action' was needed.[150] As will be seen, this was not forthcoming.

The first similar disturbance occurred within a day and a few miles of St Pauls when disorder began in Southmead, a northern suburb of Bristol. Roger Ball detailed that this disturbance went 'unnoticed and, more significantly, *unheeded* into obscurity'. After a relatively minor incident on 3 April, the following night saw an increased police presence – reacting against their 'defeat' in St Pauls – and, consequently, increased disorders.[151] The subsequent police report detailed that around 200 youths smashed shop windows and threw stones at police, with thirty-one people being arrested. Several plastic bags were found containing 'milk bottles filled with petrol with rag fuses attached', believed prepared to be thrown at officers.[152] Local MP Michael Colvin believed such disorder the day after St Pauls 'was more than coincidence', and the later court trial of youths charged with disorderly conduct believed it had been 'an attempt to imitate the St Paul's riots'. Colvin requested that the government ensured the Southmead disturbance was not overlooked, and lobbied the City and County Councils to examine the disorder.[153]

Nonetheless, Southmead was largely disregarded, despite Ball explaining that it contained the 'classic' disturbance elements of growth, peak and decline that characterised most disorders in 1980–81. Ball suggested that the 'potent brew' of word of mouth, combined with media reports of the 'successful uprising' in St Pauls, imbued Southmead youth with sufficient confidence to undertake their own uprising. Highlighting Avon County Council's controversial late 1970s policy of transporting youths from St Pauls to secondary schools in other areas of Bristol, including two schools in Southmead, he argued this had the 'inadvertent consequence' of forging direct social links between the youth of St Pauls and Southmead. Ball concluded that Southmead was not purely the 'copycat' result of an unconscious reaction to media coverage, but instead a rational and evaluative decision-making process influenced by 'contagions' spread from St Pauls via a social network of peer relationships, education, family links and others.[154] Southmead youth believed that a similarly positive outcome of conducting their own version of St Pauls was possible, demonstrating that the 'collective bargaining by riot' framework is an apt one. This would be the pattern for disorder to appear across the country the following year, as other areas in Britain followed Bristol's lead.

Disorder in St Pauls certainly shocked many, although seemingly not local black people or those familiar with their situation. In response, the police insisted that they had previously enjoyed a good relationship with black residents – but this has been proven to be at best woefully mistaken or at worst a wilfully disingenuous attempt to avoid criticism and refocus attention onto strengthening the police's ability to respond to public disorder. Their temporary withdrawal during the height of the disorder was generally criticised, further focusing the response onto calls for police to be adequately equipped to combat disturbances appropriately. This shaped stronger responses to subsequent disturbances, ensuring such police 'weaknesses' were not again displayed; but a law and order response largely ignored the discontent behind the disorder. Despite numerous discussions occurring about the best way to study events to obtain any possible lessons, as Roy de Freitas summarised, 'The future depended ... on what [action] actually happened'.[155] As demonstrated by the following chapters, the absence of either governmental public inquiries or substantial action ensured that the immediate future would see recurrences of disorder, when similar disturbances spread across England in 1981.

Notes

1 Brain, *History of Policing*, p. 53.
2 Fryer, *Staying Power*, p. 395. See: chapter 1.
3 Joshua *et al.*, *To Ride the Storm*.
4 Kettle and Hodges, *Uprising!*, pp. 23–38.
5 Dresser and Fleming, *Bristol*, p. 158.
6 Pryce, *Endless Pressure*, p. 26.
7 Kettle and Hodges, *Uprising!*, p. 24.
8 Hall *et al.*, *Policing the Crisis*, p. 351.
9 Dresser and Fleming, *Bristol*, p. 159.
10 For the impact of such divisions, see: Sivanandan, *Different Hunger*, pp. 3–8.
11 Bristol Records Office (BRO) 42714/P/1, Notes by G.J. Woolfe, 7 May 1980.
12 TUC, *Slumbering Volcano?*, pp. 6, 8, 14–16; Kettle and Hodges, *Uprising!*, p. 23.
13 Reicher, 'St. Pauls Riot', 14–15.

14 Fryer, *Staying Power*, p. 399.

15 See: Dresser, *Black and White*.

16 See: Peplow, ' "Linchpin for Success"?'

17 *Guardian*, 26 April 2017.

18 Brain, *History of Policing*, p. 53.

19 BRO: Pol/LG/1/9, 'Report of Press Conference, 3 April 1980'.

20 BRO: 42974/1, City Clerk, 'Notes of a Press Conference'.

21 Avon and Somerset Constabulary, *Annual Report 1980*, p. 2; BCRE, *Annual Report*, p. 21.

22 BRO: 43129 (Box 105), Notes of Meeting, 1 May 1980.

23 'Notes of a Press Conference'.

24 Reiner, 'Race and the Police', 468.

25 'Notes of a Press Conference'.

26 Interview with Simbarashe Tongogara, 4 April 2017. See: Alderson, *Principled Policing*, pp. 122–33.

27 BCRE, *Annual Report*, p. 21. See, for example: Stevens and Willis, 'Ethnic Minorities and Complaints'; Whitaker, *The Police in Society*.

28 *Bristol Evening Post*, 22 May 1980.

29 HC Deb 03 April 1980 vol. 982 c. 663.

30 'Notes of a Press Conference'.

31 Kettle and Hodges, *Uprising!*, p. 24. For symbolic 'frontlines', see: Keith, *Race, Riots and Policing*, pp. 19–50.

32 *Daily Mail*, 5 April 1980; 'Notes of a Press Conference'.

33 See, for example: Fryer, *Staying Power*; Goulbourne, *Race Relations*; Layton-Henry, *Politics of Race*.

34 Interview with Carlton Sharpe, 4 April 2017.

35 See: Joshua *et al.*, *To Ride the Storm*, pp. 56–91.

36 Interview with Tongogara.

37 Joshua *et al.*, *To Ride the Storm*, p. 75.

38 'Report of Press Conference, 3 April 1980'.

39 BRO: 43129 (Box 105), Paul Stephenson, 'Report of Bristol disturbances April 2nd, 1980', 29 April 1980; Whitelaw, 'Serious Disturbances', p. 1; Joshua *et al.*, *To Ride the Storm*, p. 73.

40 Joshua *et al.*, *To Ride the Storm*, pp. 73, 75.

41 BRO: Pol/LG/1/9, Avon and Somerset Constabulary, 'Operational Order, Re: Black and White Cafe'. For the Special Patrol Group, see: chapter 1.

42 'Report of Press Conference, 3 April 1980'.

43 *Jamaican Weekly Gleaner*, 9 April 1980.

44 Kettle and Hodges, *Uprising!*, p. 23.

45 BCRE, *Annual Report*, p. 9; *Daily Mail*, 5 April 1980; Gilroy and Lawrence, 'Two-Tone Britain', p. 123.

46 *The Times*, 5 April 1980.

47 *Points West*, 3 April, cited in Litton and Potter, 'Social Representations', 376–7.

48 Ramdin, *Black Working Class*, p. 503.

49 *Western Daily Press*, 9 July 1981.

50 'Notes of a Press Conference'; BCRE, *Annual Report*, pp. 7, 11, 24.

51 Monique Courtier was married to Assistant Community Relations Officer Peter Courtier: 'Notes of a Press Conference'.

52 Kettle and Hodges, *Uprising!*, p. 24.

53 *Sun*, 5 April 1980.

54 Fryer, *Staying Power*, p. 394.

55 *Western Daily Press*, 9 April 1980.

56 *Sun*, 8 April 1980. For example, on 3 May 1979, the *Sun* ran the front-page headline: 'VOTE TORY THIS TIME'.

57 Hall *et al.*, *Policing the Crisis*.

58 *Jamaican Weekly Gleaner*, 9 April 1980; BCRE, *Annual Report*, p. 7. See: Schwarz, *Memories of Empire*.

59 *Daily Telegraph*, 3 April 1980; *Western Daily Press*, 3 April 1980, emphasis in originals.

60 'Notes of a Press Conference'; 'Report of Press Conference, 3 April 1980'.

61 HC Deb 03 April 1980 vol. 982 cc. 662–3.

62 BCRE, *Annual Report*, p. 24.

63 *The Times*, 5 April 1980; *Sun*, 5 April 1980.

64 *Sun*, 5 April 1980.

65 *Daily Telegraph*, 7 April 1980, cited in Rowe, *Racialisation of Disorder*, pp. 7–8. See: Gilroy and Lawrence, 'Two-Tone Britain', pp. 123–6.

66 Joshua *et al.*, *To Ride the Storm*, pp. 109–11.

67 Kettle and Hodges, *Uprising!*, p. 30.

68 Waddington *et al.*, *Flashpoints*, pp. 166–7. For discussion, see: Bagguley and Hussain, *Riotous Citizens*, pp. 29–31.

69 BRO: 43129 (Box 105), BCRE, Press Release.

70 'Report of Press Conference, 3 April 1980'.

71 BRO: Pol/LG/1/9, Statement by the Avon and Somerset Police Authority.

72 Joshua *et al.*, *To Ride the Storm*, p. 75.

73 BRO: 43129 (Box 105), Bristol Resource Centre, 'St Pauls "Riot" Crown Court Trial', 4 February 1981, p. 2.

74 Whitelaw, 'Serious disturbances', p. 1.

75 Joshua *et al.*, *To Ride the Storm*, p. 76.

76 'Operational Order, Re: Black and White Cafe'.

77 Joshua *et al.*, *To Ride the Storm*, p. 77.

78 Reicher, 'St. Pauls Riot', 6.

79 Joshua *et al.*, *To Ride the Storm*, p. 76.

80 'Report of Bristol Disturbances'.

81 Joshua *et al.*, *To Ride the Storm*, p. 77.

82 'Notes of a Press Conference'.

83 *Jamaican Weekly Gleaner*, 9 April 1980; 'Report of Bristol Disturbances'.

84 *Out West*, 4 March 1981.

85 *Western Daily Press*, 24 February 1981.

86 BRO: Pol/LG/1/9, Avon and Somerset Constabulary, 'Riots St Pauls Area Bristol: Log of Events'. See: chapter 6.

87   Kettle and Hodges, *Uprising!*, p. 27.

88   'Notes of a Press Conference'.

89   *Jamaican Weekly Gleaner*, 9 April 1980.

90   See: Said, *Orientalism*.

91   Kettle and Hodges, *Uprising!*, p. 28.

92   Brain, *History of Policing*, p. 54.

93   *Western Daily Press*, 10 February 1981.

94   *The Times*, 5 April 1980; 'Report of Bristol Disturbances'.

95   Whitelaw, 'Serious Disturbances', p. 5.

96   *Bristol Evening Post*, 25 February 1981.

97   Reicher, 'St. Pauls Riot', 10–11.

98   *Western Daily Press*, 3 April 1980.

99   *Jamaican Weekly Gleaner*, 9 April 1980; 'Report of Bristol Disturbances'.

100 Reicher, 'St. Pauls Riot', 10.

101 *Western Daily Press*, 17 February 1981; *Jamaican Weekly Gleaner*, 9 April 1980.

102 *Sunday Times*, 6 April 1980.

103 Hobsbawm, 'The Machine Breakers'; Thompson, *English Working Class*, p. 554; Rudé, *The Crowd*.

104 'Report of Press Conference, 3 April 1980'.

105 *Daily Mirror*, 23 July 1980.

106 *Western Daily Press*, 9 April 1980.

107 'Notes of a Press Conference'.

108 Kettle and Hodges, *Uprising!*, pp. 28–9; Keith, *Race, Riots and Policing*, pp. 103–4; Cooper, 'Merseyside Riots'.

109 *Daily Mail*, 9 April 1980.

110 See: Brain, *History of Policing*, pp. 141–7; Emsley, *English Police*.

111 *Daily Telegraph*, 24 April 1980.

112 *Western Daily Press*, 23 May 1980.

113 HC Deb 28 April 1980 vol. 983 c. 977.

114 *Daily Mail*, 5 April 1980; Whitelaw, *Memoirs*, p. 242.

115 HC Deb 28 April 1980 vol. 983 c. 973. See: Sanders and Wood, *Times of Troubles*, pp. 103–38.

116 *Sun*, 5 April 1980. See: Keith, 'No-Go Areas'.

117 HC Deb 28 April 1980 vol. 983 c. 972.

118 'Log of Events'.

119 *The Times*, 5 April 1980; *Western Daily Press*, 12 April 1980.

120 Northam, *Shooting in the Dark*, p. 36; Brain, *History of Policing*, p. 54.

121 *The Times*, 29 April 1980; *Sun*, 5 April 1980.

122 *Daily Mail*, 5 April 1980.

123 *Ibid.*; *Sunday Telegraph*, 6 April 1980.

124 *Daily Mail*, 5 April 1980. See: Brain, *History of Policing*, pp. 56–7, 76.

125 Avon and Somerset Constabulary, *Annual Report 1980*, p. 1.

126 *Sun*, 5 April 1980. See: Ellison and Smyth, *Policing Northern Ireland*.

127 *Guardian*, 4 February 1981.

128 *Sunday Times*, 6 April 1980.

129 'Report of Bristol disturbances'.

130 Interview with Sharpe.

131 'Log of Events'.

132 Avon and Somerset Constabulary, *Annual Report 1980*, pp. 2, 39.

133 'Log of Events'.

134 BRO 42974/1, 'Notes on Debate', 15 April 1980; BRO: 43129 (Box 105), Paul Stephenson, 'Bristol Disturbances – April 2nd 1980', 6 May 1980; Interview with Tongogara; *Bristol Evening Post*, 13 March 1981.

135 'Notes on Debate'.

136 See, for example: Christensen, 'Twitter Revolutions?'; Aouragh and Alexander, 'Internet Revolution'; Comninos, 'Twitter Revolutions'.

137 Koopmans, 'Protest in Time and Space', p. 40; Tarrow, *Power in Movement*.

138 The Selector's song 'Bristol & Miami' linked Bristol with the 1980 Miami 'riots'. See: Horne, *Watts Uprising*; Andresen and Van der Steen (eds), *European Youth Revolt*.

139 *The Times*, 5 April 1980.

140 Phillips and Phillips, *Windrush*, p. 232.

141 Fryer, *Staying Power*, p. 399.

142 *The Leveller*, 38 (March 1980).

143 Brain, *History of Policing*, p. 55.

144 Interview with Tongogara.

145 *Bristol Evening Post*, 6 June 1980.

146 'The "Riots"', 223; McNee, *McNee's Law*, p. 111; Kettle and Hodges, *Uprising!*, p. 38; TNA: HO 266/101, Police Statements.

147 Black Cultural Archives, Gutzmore 1/3/1, Minutes of the Brixton Defence Campaign Meeting, 27 May 1981.

148 'Notes of a Press Conference'.

149 BRO 43129 (Box 105), Ray Wardle, Speech to Walcot Ward Liberals, 14 April 1980.

150 Commission for Racial Equality Chair David Lane, cited in *Daily Mirror*, 11 April 1980; *Sun*, 5 April 1980.

151 Ball, 'The "Bristol Riot"', 33–6.

152 Avon and Somerset Constabulary, *Annual Report 1980*, p. 40.

153 BRO 43129 (Box 105), Michael Colvin to Peter Courtier, 25 April 1980; *Bristol Evening Post*, 21 May 1980; HC Deb 28 April 1980 vol. 983 c. 975; BRO 42974/1, Colvin to John Brown, 6 May 1980.

154 Ball, 'The "Bristol Riot"', 36–40. See: Myers, 'Collective Violence'; Oliver, 'Bringing the Crowd Back In'.

155 'Notes of a Press Conference'.

3

Lacking conviction: Inquiries and trials after Bristol

Oh what kind of man could I be,
If I can't talk about what I see?

Eddy Grant – Living On the Front Line

IMMEDIATELY AFTER the 1980 St Pauls anti-police disturbance, there were appeals for an independent public inquiry into why it had happened. For example, Labour Councillor John McLaren identified that Bristol City Council would support an inquiry, provided it was truly independent and had the support of all.[1] Although this idealistic aim should be applauded, satisfying *all* sections of society is a practically impossible task – as will be demonstrated. Home Secretary William Whitelaw initially responded that he wished to receive reports from the Bristol Chief Constable and local MPs before establishing any inquiry, as 'it is right to get the initial reactions first, and then to decide what is best'.[2] At this point, outwardly at least, Whitelaw claimed not to have ruled out the possibility of establishing an inquiry.

This chapter focuses on the divided response to St Pauls, through rejected appeals for a public inquiry and the authorities' alternative reaction, which attempted to divert attention away from governmental policies. There was a clear division of local attitudes between moderates, who desired the societal legitimisation of a public inquiry, and radical or younger groups, more likely to have been involved in disturbances, who believed it would be a diversion or 'whitewash'. Thus, public inquiries were simultaneously viewed by local black people as both a solution and a fraud, demonstrating no unified response. Those desiring a public inquiry believed refusals to grant one demonstrated that authorities did not care about black Britons, or that they were attempting to protect and conceal police misconduct. Other government measures that were implemented – such as select committees turning their focus to the city – were thus boycotted by various groups, who thought their attendance would imply satisfaction with this limited response. Similarly, attempted left-wing inquiries were snubbed by local people who rejected attempts to introduce party politics.

This chapter lastly examines failed court trials to convict twelve locals under the serious charge of riotous assembly. Influenced by criticism directed towards Bristol police for their temporary withdrawal during the disorder, authorities continued their focus upon criminality to the detriment of wider social or political issues, attempting to obtain criminal sentences to reassure the public and deter future violence.[3] This approach was not to prove effective, as numerous disorders appeared across England the following year – blamed, by some, on the absence of a public inquiry into events in Bristol.[4]

A divided local response

Representatives of local community organisations led the calls for a public inquiry. BCRE Chair Bill Nicks suggested that an independent tribunal was needed 'to satisfy the black community', and Owen Henry, Chair of the Bristol West Indian Parents and Friends Association, declared: 'Nothing else other than a public inquiry can put this matter right.'[5] It is likely some believed that a public inquiry into the situation would indicate that the authorities cared about black Britons' problems, therefore legitimising the disturbance as a valid form of protest. Alternatively, Tariq Ali quoted a black youth who claimed a public inquiry was required simply to protect local people from police retaliation: 'They're in a position to take revenge.'[6]

Demonstrating a dichotomous opinion of public inquiries, others, such as St Pauls Carnival organiser Francis Salandy, who ran an advice centre, dismissed ideas of a state-run inquiry, believing the police and white authority would be reflected favourably and that black people could not rely upon white counterparts to act in their interests. Articulating what *The Times* deemed 'a separatist philosophy', Rastafarian Salandy considered issues such as black unemployment a diversion from the inherent racism within British society.[7] Influenced by Black Power self-determination ideology, he referenced Malcolm X when stating 'Discrimination accumulates; chickens come home to roost ... We want the respect of white people, and it's thousands and thousands of years off yet', placing the onus upon black people themselves: 'We have to take responsibility for our own problems.'[8] Emphasising the distrust of authorities, CRE officer Paul Stephenson suggested black residents believed 'a judicial Enquiry would be too restrictive', preferring a Tribunal to sit in Bristol.[9] City Councillor John McLaren agreed, emphasising that those who had lost faith in the authorities 'would not necessarily accept the impartiality of a judicial hearing', and a BCRE Community Relations Officer added that the 'local community … would not necessarily attend that type of meeting'.[10] Similarly, Conservative leader of Avon County Council, Sir Gervas Walker, believed a public inquiry would take too much account of evidence provided by 'the wrong people'.[11] Roy de Freitas, of the African-Caribbean Community Association, claimed an inquiry would 'go over the heads of the black community, although it might satisfy the whites'. Stating that he and other 'older members of the West Indian community' did not want to be involved in violence, they were still glad it had happened: 'For the first time people have been forced to take notice of the black community.' However, notably describing himself as an 'establishment Black' – critics may have labelled him a 'careerist' – he did later record being 'bitterly disappointed' when the Home Office ruled out an inquiry.[12]

Moderate groups, either community workers or self-described 'establishment Blacks', appeared more disposed to argue for the benefits of a public inquiry than younger generations. During a BCRE meeting, black youths even shouted down a solicitor explaining that an amnesty for those charged in connection with the disorder was impossible under English law. *Socialist Challenge*, predictably with a class-based analysis, concluded that this demonstrated growing divisions between 'older West Indians', working through 'pressure groups', and Bristol youth who 'won't beg for their rights. They intend to stand up and fight for them'.[13] Nicks similarly noted that local black youth increasingly felt senior generations did not speak for them or take their views seriously, and attitudes towards public inquiries suggest similar divisions.[14] Further to common notions that youth are more radical than older age groups, this suggests a generational change between migrants arriving in the 'mother country', either desiring to be accepted or not planning to remain indefinitely, and those who, having grown up in Britain, demanded better treatment. As one black youth of St Pauls summarised: 'This is my jungle. I don't like it, but I won't leave it.'[15]

Furthermore, divisions appeared between community workers and black residents. A City Council Housing Department memorandum noted 'some dissension between the acknowledged leaders of the black community and the officers of the B.C.R.E.'; indeed, residents criticised the BCRE's lack of success and communication with St Pauls' residents.[16] The *Guardian* also noted how, unlike local white representatives such as MP Tony Benn, City Councillor John

McLaren or BCRE Chair Bill Nicks, 'black spokesmen are regarding [inquiry] demands with scepticism'.[17] This demonstrates a desire for increased political participation by black Britons themselves, rather than ineffective state organisations acting on their behalf.

Scepticism towards state inquiries was reinforced by the belief that, while previous investigations had identified problems, nothing had been done to resolve them. An interim report emerging from a Bristol CRE-backed inquiry into employment and inequality summarised that inquiry demands were 'in part a tactical manoeuvre to apply pressure to politicians at all levels to respond appropriately to the "riot", in the absence of helpful responses in the past'.[18] This paints such demands as part of broader strategies, arguably including the disorder itself, to achieve political goals and improve the situation of black Britons where other measures had previously failed.

A BCRE meeting soon after the disturbance boasted local support, being well-attended and stimulating great discussion. While the committee called for a public inquiry, a description of the meeting recorded that most of those present believed any possible lessons of the disturbance would either be buried or deliberately misinterpreted by any official inquiry and, regardless, nobody would be willing to learn them. This meeting also demanded that the police drop charges and investigations relating to the disturbance, and several speakers demonstrated a loss of faith in the police. For example, it was alleged that the police had previously assured the BCRE that no further arrests in relation to the disturbance would be made, but subsequent arrests further reduced 'what credence the coloured people could put in Police promises'. Community Relations Officer, Chief Inspector Derek Lane, attempted to respond to this accusation, but his 'valiant attempts' were not accepted by the audience.[19] While this allegation was not wholly accurate, widespread willingness to believe it is noteworthy. Police arrests following the disturbance were interpreted as a campaign directed against black residents in order to regain the authority lost during the police withdrawal. During a meeting one week after the disturbance, Weigh assured the BCRE Committee that house-to-house inquiries had ceased and even offered that local people could visit cells to prove nobody remained detained.[20] However, this was conditional upon black social workers 'accompanying' those wanted for questioning to the police station, and a so-called 'wanted list' of names was created. The police contended this was simply so that social workers could be present to aid those who may be intimidated by the legal system, but to local people it appeared that any apparent concessions by the police were for ulterior motives: to locate suspects.[21]

Deputy Chief Constable Donald Smith informed the BCRE on 29 April that the police did not have the power to grant demands for an amnesty.[22] Despite legislative inability to do so, the apparent police refusal to exonerate participants from legal backlash was deemed a further dismissal of local people's perspective, and an unwillingness to admit mutual culpability. Leslie Wollen, former Community Relations Council Chair, warned Whitelaw that punishing participants would further damage police/community relations, suggesting an amnesty would be 'not only generous but wise':

> nothing would do more to re-establish confidence in the police and our judicial system. Any punishment inflicted is bound to be arbitrary, falling on innocent and guilty, and leaving many yet more guilty to get off free. This will only increase the sense of grievance which many already understandably have and further worsen the relations with the police.[23]

A BCRE Press Release immediately after the disturbances labelled the police's response 'yet another attempt to criminalize the Black Community'.[24] The continued focus upon law and order, to the apparent detriment of community relations, was consistent with the state's broader response.[25]

Whitelaw's 'three-pronged response'

In contrast to those who derided the value of public inquiries, a Bristol City Council debate concluded it was very important to direct the 'bitterness and resentment' of black youths through the 'political machine', otherwise more violence would occur.[26] This further illustrates how those in positions of power seemingly did not appreciate that this 'political machine' was itself believed part of the problem, and how disorder was attempted action on participants' own terms. For example, despite palpable levels of discontent, the Avon and Somerset Constabulary recorded only nine official complaints from black Britons in 1980, due to reluctance to use the official complaints procedure; an extremely low percentage were substantiated, and it was believed that complaints against the police could even increase future persecution.[27]

Governmental action following St Pauls was limited and criticised as an inadequate response. Whitelaw privately told the Cabinet that 'an inquiry would be undesirable' as 'the police would be pilloried to no good purpose'.[28] Martin Kettle and Lucy Hodges argued that Whitelaw 'got himself off the hook of having to announce an inquiry' by outlining a 'three-pronged' response.[29] Local organisations immediately viewed this as a 'tacit refusal' of inquiry demands, arguing that a 'plea for recognition' after St Pauls had been 'fobbed off', and Bristol's Assistant Community Relations Officer Peter Courtier told government officials that 'many local people are confused as there was almost unanimous support in the call for a full independent public inquiry'.[30] Despite demonstrating above that support was far from unanimous, this undoubtedly led to anger from those who believed the Government were still not answering the pleas of local people and even ignoring the collective violence attempting to highlight the disadvantage faced.

A focus on law and order

The first aspect of Whitelaw's 'three-pronged' response was a request for senior government officials to examine 'thoroughly and urgently' arrangements for handling spontaneous public disorder.[31] The CRE detailed that this investigation was subsequently ' "published", i.e. placed in the Library of the House of Commons', clearly showing how little relation this bore to public inquiry demands, as marginalised groups could not even access such discussion:

> The report ... is lodged in the House of Commons Library for the perusal of all with access to that institution. This would seem to indicate that certain matters are either too weighty and complex to be entrusted, or too trivial to be of interest, to ordinary people, and in particular to the black people of inner-city Bristol whose situation brought about the review in the first place.[32]

Kettle and Hodges suggested that the government tactic of framing the response around issues of law and order rather than its social, economic or racial policies demonstrated 'a revealing priority', which attempted to diminish the potential threat to its authority.[33] Similarly, Harris Joshua *et al.* argued that, by focusing foremost upon violence, the authorities further disseminated ideas that it had been an unprovoked attack upon the police by black residents, and thus the solution was to improve police responses to public disorder. In the absence of a public inquiry, the primacy placed upon the Chief Constable's report and later court trials formulated a narrative that removed the social, political and economic dimensions, and discussion was 'reduced to its lowest common denominator – a crisis of law and public order'. Indeed, Joshua *et al.* demonstrated how there was little dispute in public regarding the 'facts' of the disorder and the legitimacy of the 'official' version was not generally questioned, despite resting largely on a highly selective and confused account provided by the Chief Constable.[34] Conservative MP William Waldegrave even used this to reject a public inquiry – despite having initially called for one. He suggested that, as the narrative of events had been largely accepted, there would be nothing for an official inquiry to do except investigate the underlying causes; Waldegrave highlighted several reports already or due to be published seemingly addressing this, and concluded that 'the time has come, not to have more inquiries, but to take the necessary action'.[35] Many locals would likely have agreed with this sentiment, if not necessarily the established narrative of events or the substance of such 'necessary action'. St Pauls was a clear indictment of inadequate government policies, but, rather than reconsider their positions, they instead 'suppress[ed] the symptom of that failure – collective racial violence'.[36]

Some contemporaries challenged this concentration upon law and order. For example, local prominent left-wing Labour MP Tony Benn commented that increasing over-reliance upon the police to 'deal with problems … fundamentally political and economic in character' would not 'constitute a proper answer' to the issues raised.[37] The BCRE implored Whitelaw to examine the underlying reasons behind the disorder thoroughly, arguing 'it would be a tragedy if this unhappy incident was seen simply as a "law and order issue"'.[38] The absence of a public inquiry into conditions producing the disturbance, despite similar conditions existing around the country, suggested that the Government's strategy for dealing with such issues was a 'crude reliance on the police to contain trouble'.[39] When Whitelaw outlined his response, he stated it was important that 'we consider carefully the lessons to be learnt'; in framing the governmental response firmly around issues of law and order, it appears to have been very carefully considered.[40]

A select committee visits Bristol

The second facet of Whitelaw's response was to announce that the Race Relations and Immigration Sub-Committee of the Home Affairs Select Committee would undertake an inquiry into racial disadvantage. However, due to its being a subsection of a House of Commons Select Committee, Whitelaw had no control over the Sub-Committee's actions and they had already independently decided to consider racial disadvantage one month previously.[41] Whitelaw's inclusion of this within his response was thus described as 'A fortuitous use (or misuse?) of an existing body'.[42] Bristol City Clerk John Brown illuminated the subtext when stating that the Sub-Committee's visit to Bristol, undertaken during the process of their inquiry, 'seems to be the Government's response to [appeals for] a full independent public inquiry'.[43] A letter from Brown to Bristol City Councillors detailed the Sub-Committee's visit and examination of 'racial disharmony', although it was not to be limited to St Pauls or even Bristol itself; however, the following day Brown corrected that his letter should have read 'racial disadvantage', not 'disharmony'.[44] Whether a typing mistake or a misunderstanding regarding the Sub-Committee's focus, this clearly suggests investigations into 'racial disharmony' were on the minds of those in Bristol. The BCRE did not believe an inquiry into racial disadvantage was required, already being confirmed multiple times by previous investigations: 'An inquiry was needed to establish remedies for racial discrimination not the fact of it.'[45] The Bristol West Indian Parents and Friends Association agreed, believing this investigation was 'a cover up'.[46]

Any hope that this would provide an opportunity for local people to discuss the April disturbances was quashed when the Sub-Committee clarified it would not examine that 'particular case'.[47] Similarly, notes circulated for the guidance of witnesses stated that oral evidence would be collected in a 'strictly question and answer form', and it would be helpful if witnesses could keep answers as brief as possible. It is not difficult to imagine the frustration of those requesting a public inquiry, complete with its perceived open transparency, to learn that the only opportunity to directly voice opinions or vent frustrations to government officials was in an atmosphere explicitly described as 'not in any way a discussion'.[48]

Moreover, the Sub-Committee's single-day visit was deemed inadequate and 'a failure to appreciate the complexity of the problems'. Bristol City Council leader Claude Draper warned that attempts to limit the amount of time for evidence to be heard would have 'serious repercussions'. If this Sub-Committee visit was a poor response to requests for a public inquiry, being so fleeting added insult to injury. Draper also advised Whitelaw that various organisations might undertake 'other local "enquiries" ... with all the implications that could result from such action' – clearly suggesting such studies may not be impartial and may increase resentment against the authorities.[49] Draper argued that to reject a Government-sanctioned public inquiry, on the basis that it may provoke criticism of the police or authorities, would be counterproductive as local inquiries without government oversight would surely criticise in a far more overtly partisan manner. Conservative MP William Waldegrave countered that, as other inquiries had been planned prior to the Government announcing their response, it was 'quite obvious' that 'whatever happened, there would have been other organisations jumping on the bandwagon'.[50] Also likely is that previous experience, alongside initial Government sluggishness to announce a response, provoked action from other interested parties.

The anger demonstrated by residents during subsequent meetings of the BCRE and St Pauls United Defence Committee – established to provide legal aid to defendants – promoted the tactic of boycotting the Sub-Committee's visit and continuing public inquiry demands. Defence Committee member Roy de Freitas detailed: 'There is a lot of feeling against this committee and it should not come to St Paul's.'[51] It was believed providing evidence to the Sub-Committee, 'a wholly unacceptable response to the community's demand for an independent public inquiry', would appear to legitimise – and therefore be a tacit acceptance of – Whitelaw's response.[52] Local Labour MP Arthur Palmer, while agreeing with the BCRE's objections, implored them to submit evidence to the Sub-Committee, as 'it always pays to use every channel when a protest is to be made'.[53] However, his advice letter was unhelpfully sent two days after the Sub-Committee had visited Bristol.

Sub-Committee Chair, Conservative MP John Wheeler, responded to this criticism with a press statement greatly lamenting the boycott. He emphasised that the Sub-Committee was 'not an organ of the government but an independent body' and that, as Whitelaw had no control over its actions, its visit bore no relation to the public inquiry demands.[54] Attempts to counter criticism, such as scheduling an extra hour of open discussion into its visit, did not appear successful and the Sub-Committee was accused of 'rushing in and rushing out again so it can say it has been to Bristol'.[55]

Thus, when the Sub-Committee visited Bristol on 22 May 1980 it was met with a largely negative response, described by one newspaper as 'A wall of resentment'.[56] The level of anger was such that a police presence was required, keeping a low profile in plainclothes, undoubtedly in an attempt to avoid recurrence of disorder.[57] Despite intentions to hear testimony from local people, more press were present than public – blamed on the visit falling on a Thursday, part of the common working week.[58] It was therefore impossible for many local people, repeatedly calling for an opportunity to make their views known to democratically elected officials, even to attend this unsatisfactory session. It is questionable how many wanted to. The *Daily Telegraph* noted how 'few coloured people were among a mere 50 present ... it was left to mainly white community leaders and counsellors to voice their grievances'.[59] Local black magistrate Fred Walcott pointed out that no participants in the disturbance were present, believing they had stayed away for fear of being identified and targeted by the police; accusations had existed for years that police targeted individuals providing evidence of police misconduct. It is also likely that black youth simply did not believe this meeting was worth attending, as it would not help.[60] Therefore, Walcott insisted that authorities 'must find a means of speaking to them' and St Pauls vicar, Reverend Keith Kimber, further stated 'our voices are no substitute for those of people actually suffering'.[61]

Local authorities and statutory bodies attended and provided evidence, but other organisations boycotted the session and repeated public inquiry demands. Such an inquiry was considered essential as previous select committee proceedings had little positive effect; for instance, the Government's previous rejection of recommendations that 'sus' laws be abolished.[62] This tactic, of refusing to submit evidence unless a public inquiry was held, resulted in local people neither achieving an inquiry nor submitting evidence to the only investigation originating from Westminster. Wheeler accused organisations calling for a boycott of having 'betrayed the ordinary people of the community' by not allowing all available evidence to be presented.[63] Labour City Councillor John McLaren countered that the issue stemmed from Whitelaw's public insistence that this visit was part of the Government's response, thus imposing 'something on the Sub-Committee which was not in its original brief' and suggesting the Government had betrayed St Pauls.[64] Perhaps unsurprising from a political opponent, this response highlights the dissatisfaction towards the Government's response.

Despite the Sub-Committee repeatedly stating that it was not involved in any decisions about public inquiries, the majority present wished to address this — epitomised by a solicitor attending the session, on behalf of a client charged in connection with the disturbances, upon the misunderstanding it was the inquiry being demanded.[65] McLaren declared that the community felt 'snubbed' and, until they were allowed the opportunity to voice their opinions, 'the Sub-Committee's presence in Bristol is a complete and utter waste of time'.[66] Indeed, it had previously been circulated that nothing from the public discussion session would be regarded as evidence or used in the Sub-Committee's report, presumably causing people to question the point of making their feelings known.[67] Moreover, an ad-hoc group of young black St Pauls residents had offered to submit oral evidence to the Sub-Committee — suggesting that not all black youth shunned authority investigations — but they were apparently ignored.[68]

The Sub-Committee claimed its visit to Bristol was the opportunity for 'ordinary people to make their points', but the parameters set meant few accepted this. Indeed, Draper appeared to summarise the mood of the session correctly when remarking: 'You are not going to get anywhere this morning, are you?'[69]

This episode demonstrates both the importance awarded to a more collaborative public inquiry, as well as conversely furthering opinions that authorities' actions would not have positive results.

City/County Council partnership

The final of Whitelaw's 'three-pronged' response was another action that required little from him. Informing Parliament that he welcomed Avon County Council and Bristol City Council's decision to jointly examine improving community relations, he declared that experts from all government departments concerned would 'play a full part'. The Bristol City Clerk was informed Whitelaw believed that, alongside the Sub-Committee's investigations, this represented 'the best way forward in tackling the complex and delicate issues'. However, Whitelaw privately told the Cabinet this joint examination 'might not, in fact, achieve much'.[70] Furthermore, with the exception of the local department of the Manpower Services Commission, the 'full part' played by government departments in reality amounted to very little; a Home Office representative even admitted his department 'did not profess to know any answers to the problem or be able to provide solutions'.[71]

Local Trades Union Congress inquiry

Significantly, there was no publicly accessible inquiry, and two-thirds of Whitelaw's response to events in St Pauls were unconnected to the national Government and had already begun before he even publicly addressed the situation. In an effort to frame the response around aspects of law and order instead of governmental policies, the only response spearheaded by Whitelaw himself was of how the police would deal with future outbreaks of disorder. Whitelaw admitted to the Cabinet that 'There would, undoubtedly, be criticism of the actions of the Chief Constable and of the decision not to hold a full public inquiry'.[72] For example, Conservative MP Nicholas Budgen questioned Whitelaw what 'specific action – as opposed to discussion – is anticipated', to which Whitelaw vaguely replied improved community relations and police recruitment, and that the communities involved must 'adopt a sensible attitude'.[73] Nevertheless, a private note to Prime Minister Margaret Thatcher conveyed that Whitelaw's announcement in Parliament 'went off very well' and nobody was 'disposed to argue seriously for a public enquiry' – despite Benn and Waldegrave already having done so. The note concluded, somewhat optimistically: 'I think that the Home Secretary has successfully put this matter to bed for the time being.'[74] That was not to be the case.

Reacting against a perceived lack of governmental action, local groups and organisations launched their own inquiries. Responding to comments by local Labour MP Arthur Palmer that governmental responses took time, the CRE-backed inquiry into employment and inequality retorted: 'This is cold comfort for the black population of inner-city Bristol, denied even minimal access to what is purportedly being said and done (behind closed doors) on their behalf.'[75]

On 24 April, the General Committee of the Bristol West Constituency Labour Party passed a resolution calling for a Trade Union and Labour Movement-organised public inquiry.[76] This sentiment was repeated during a St Pauls Ward Labour Party meeting in May, where many members believed that a full public inquiry should be supplemented with a local inquiry led by Trades and Labour groups.[77] However, Labour member Trevor Morgan, describing this 'meeting of cranks, well-intentioned do-gooders and weaklings' as a 'shambolic rambling catastrophe', stressed it should not be seen as an indication of what the 'alienated poor of St. Paul's' wanted because they were 'not in the room or anywhere near the meeting'.[78] Nonetheless, a TUC inquiry was launched, boasting the involvement of Professor Michael Dummett – who had received plaudits for the diligence and integrity of the inquiry he chaired into the death of campaigner Blair Peach following head trauma, widely believed inflicted by a police officer during a 1979 demonstration against the NF.[79] The TUC inquiry was chaired by London Labour MP Ian Mikardo; although not a Bristol local, likely to have been more accepted, he did have a history concerning minority ethnic groups. The son of Jewish immigrants, Mikardo previously attempted to tackle relations between the police and ethnic communities within the London Borough of Tower Hamlets, spearheading a pilot scheme to improve confidence in the police by establishing a public body to investigate every alleged incident of racism. This scheme was, in his words, 'sabotaged' by the police who disliked 'the concept of the accountability of the police to the public who pay their wages'.[80] Moreover, he had certainly earned his reputation as an ardent socialist; Bristol City Councillor Bob Wall's description of Mikardo, a 'fairly controversial figure of the Left', was not unfair.[81]

If not self-evident, it became quickly apparent that party politics would play a key role in this inquiry. A poster appealing for witnesses accused Industry Secretary Keith Joseph of stealing jobs and Thatcher of stealing children's milk – referencing her withdrawal of free school milk whilst Education Secretary – questioning: 'Who are the real looters'?[82] Such blatant politicking was criticised; local people felt 'political parties should be kept out of it', and local activist and campaigner Simbarashe Tongogara later noted that they viewed 'radical white organisations' with scepticism as 'they had agendas, and they tried to push those agendas'.[83] This view was visibly demonstrated by the lack of support awarded a left-wing protest march: cancelled, due to lack of numbers. The *Western Daily Press* reported that 'half-a-dozen white extremists' were told by local black youth that people objected to attempts to 'cash in on a cause'.[84] It is not hard to imagine why local people, some of whom had violently protested the figurehead of a perceived unsympathetic state, did not want their plight undermined by party politics. A submission to the TUC's inquiry made the same point: 'Amongst many people in St Pauls there was a resentment at these "politicos" jumping on the bandwagon.'[85] This was further exhibited by the poor response to the inquiry. Local newspapers described how St Pauls gave the inquiry 'a massive cold shoulder' as the response had been 'virtually nil': only fifty people, around half of them black, provided oral evidence. The TUC believed black residents had been discouraged by the intimidating formal atmosphere of the inquiry, but attempts to meet people in the relaxed environment of their own homes had only been achieved a few times.[86]

Additionally, lacking judicial powers, the inquiry failed to obtain co-operation from the police or Conservative councillors – somewhat unsurprisingly, given its overtly political slant. Ron Thomas, Bristol TUC Secretary, stated 'It will be a denial of what we expect in a democracy if the [police] refuse to meet us' – likely mirroring black Britons' opinion.[87] While angered by this snub, Mikardo defended the low public turnout because 'they just feel an inquiry, whoever does it, is part of the establishment'.[88] This point is, of course, also true of public inquiries, highlighting reservations towards all government investigations – but constant calls for a public inquiry suggests the eminence awarded to these measures, imbued with sufficient powers to summon witnesses.

Regardless, the TUC Report still managed to reach controversial conclusions, including the blunt accusation that 'whatever denials and assurances are made, it is clear that the police hold deep, racist views, which are expressed when they harass black people'.[89] This charge was strongly denied by Bristol police, and Assistant Chief Constable Walter Girven countered that no evidence was provided to support such a claim.[90] However, Thomas suggested this was due to the police investigating complaints against themselves, deemed: 'like the devil investigating sin'.[91]

The TUC inquiry made sixty-four recommendations, covering housing, education and community relations, including improved co-operation between City and County Councils and closer consultation with local residents through a community liaison committee. The Report was hoped to be a call for action, characterised by its title of *Slumbering Volcano*: '[Bristol] is a slumbering volcano and, if nobody does anything about it, it will erupt again.'[92] While Bristol itself would not similarly 'erupt' in 1981, disorder did spread across England.

'Riot' court trials

Continuing the authorities' focus upon law and order, persons charged in connection with the disturbance began to appear in Bristol Magistrates Court; between April and the end of November, over 130 people were arrested, ninety of whom faced charges in court, although the majority were minor offences, even including looting toilet paper.[93] The St Pauls United Defence Committee had been established to provide legal aid to defendants, and Tongogara, through connection with reggae band Misty in Roots and the 1979 Southall disorder, acquired the representation of lawyer Paul Boateng, who became involved alongside other prominent lawyers Rudy Narayan and Gareth Peirce, and activist Darcus Howe. Events in Bristol were playing out on a national stage; in the words of Tongogara: 'it was happening in St Pauls now, but it might … it did happen everywhere else within a short space of time'.[94]

Sixteen defendants, whom even prosecution lawyers admitted had been selected somewhat arbitrarily, faced the more serious charge of riotous assembly. Magistrates allowed twelve of these charges to stand, with eleven being black. Journalist Crispin Aubrey implied that the reason for the substitution of these defendants' lesser charges with riotous assembly was due to 'considerable political pressure on the police to justify their retreat'.[95] Defence lawyer Rudy Narayan similarly suggested that, due to immediate intense public questioning of why the disturbances occurred, authorities had to be seen to be responding: 'A script had to be written, actors found to perform it and possibly even a crucifixion arranged.'[96] Carlton Sharpe, a defendant in the trial, described how authorities 'had to collect bodies', and Tongogara believed this 'shot in the dark' trial was an attempt to 'criminalise [black] people in a blatant way', occurring because establishment figures 'had to appease the rest of society that no, we weren't going into anarchy'.[97]

The defendants' committal proceedings on 16 June were met with a protest march from St Pauls, demonstrating against their arrest. The police, through 'Operation Discord', aimed to ensure court appearances occurred with the 'minimum of disruption', although the name of the operation alone suggests they anticipated some discontentment.[98] Indeed, 'Noisy disturbances' erupted, during which £900 of damage was inflicted upon the court buildings, and police reinforcements were called to prevent disturbances in the street.[99] The melee inside the courtroom included defendants and some members of the public, leading to David Royal being charged with obstructing a police officer, while others were reprimanded and at least one person ordered from the public gallery.[100] One of the defendants, Clinton Brown, recalled demonstrations outside the court every time they appeared, including a violent clash with police in October 1980 after another defendant, Franklin Rapier, was imprisoned for contempt after branding proceedings a 'kangaroo court'.[101]

Observers believed this was a sign of worse to come and lawyer Peirce, representing six of the twelve defendants, wrote a strongly worded letter to Director of Public Prosecutions (DPP) Sir Thomas Hetherington, warning the charges were 'intensely speculative' and would result in 'extended trials' worsening relations.[102] Peirce would become a noted human rights solicitor addressing high profile injustices, including the successful overturning of life sentences for the men charged with the murder of PC Keith Blakelock during the Broadwater Farm disturbances in North London on 6 October 1985.[103] However, her warnings did not prevent the accused in Bristol standing trial, which commenced on 3 February 1981.

One reason for the lengthy interval before the trials began was jury selection. In the week prior to the St Pauls trial, not a single black juror sat amongst the 108 people on juries in the Bristol Crown Courts.[104] This under-representation was not a new phenomenon, and previous research in Birmingham suggested there should have been twelve to fifteen times more black people on juries than there actually were.[105] The defence counsel thus exercised their right to reject jury candidates in order to obtain an 'accurate reflection of the local population'.[106] Out of a possible thirty-six rejections, three allocated for each defendant, thirty-four potential jurors – mostly older white men – were vetoed on sight, which resulted in four black or Asian jurors.[107] Lord Denning, Master of the Rolls, later reasoned that the eventual collapse of the trial was due to the jury's composition. Kettle and Hodges deemed this a fair assessment, although the system had not been abused as Denning suggested; rather, it was the first time Denning had observed skin colour being a factor in jury selection.[108] Denning later criticised 'packed' juries, believing black jurors would not convict black defendants because ethnically diverse Britons 'no longer share the same standards of conduct' – which led to him apologising and retiring early.[109]

Whilst not abusing the system, St Pauls defence lawyers clearly attempted to limit discrimination from jurors who would not understand or relate to issues faced by black Britons. This tactic had been previously attempted by Darcus Howe and Ian Macdonald in the trial of the 'Mangrove Nine' in 1971. After a demonstration against repeated police raids on the Mangrove restaurant in Notting Hill led to charges including conspiracy to incite a riot, the accused unsuccessfully argued that their right to be tried by a jury of peers meant an all-black jury was required to understand their situation fully.[110] This legacy, and involvement of the same figures, demonstrates that St Pauls existed within a broader movement.

Another aspect delaying proceedings was the time taken for police to write up their case; one local newspaper described the police file as eighteen inches high and containing over 600 pages of witness statements.[111] The majority of evidence used in the trial was of the police, and a great number of inconsistencies arose, such as incorrectly dated or altered statements.[112] Officers did not bring notebooks into court, despite this being common practice and the events being described having occurred ten months previously, and defence lawyers accused the police of ordering officers not to bring notebooks so their testimony could not be checked. The majority of officer statements were written after their being briefed by senior police, during discussion with colleagues, and having seen photographs and videos of the disturbances. Thus, defence lawyers argued that the police had enough time to fabricate a consistent response. This allegation was repudiated by the police; but, within broader contexts of police corruption throughout the period – including revelations regarding police actions during the miners' strike and Hillsborough disaster – it is, at least, a possibility.[113]

During the trials, it was also alleged that there was a police attempt to frame one of the defendants; Franklin Rapier, an outspoken police critic, was considered a spokesperson for the local community, having had numerous violent exchanges with the police.[114] For example, Detective Constable Bernard Mattock inserted a personal sighting of Rapier leading a crowd into his testimony after its initial submission, which was suspected of being fabricated in a concerted attempt to discredit and frame Rapier. During cross-examination, Mattock agreed with defence lawyer Narayan that this was an important part of his evidence, not something to be inserted later merely as an afterthought. Portraying it as an omission that he had quickly rectified, Mattock defended that he had had a 'very busy day' and, 'Quite frankly, I had a lot to put in that statement'.[115] Equally, Police Sergeant Terence Crees was questioned at length about his statement, completed in two separate sessions. Narayan similarly accused Crees of having altered his statement after discussions with fellow officers, alleging that, by the second session, Crees 'had to write a script of the police line'. Crees denied this, arguing that other duties had stopped him finishing his statement in a single session.[116] Attempts to discredit the police's testimony were clearly a defence tactic, as other officers were similarly accused of perjury.[117]

Rapier himself believed, or at least attempted to convince the jury, he was victim of a 'frame up' by the nineteen officers giving evidence against him.[118] Narayan claimed Rapier was accused 'by at least 29,000 police officers of tearing down St Paul's single handedly' – this hyperbolic figure apparently only a 'slight exaggeration'.[119] Wiping tears from his eyes during testimony, Rapier stated 'I knew nothing about a riot. I did not take part in it. I had no reason to riot against anybody'.[120] However, fellow defendant Brown recently recalled that he and Rapier 'stood outside the cafe with bottles and said nobody is getting out'. Laughing while remembering Rapier's emotional testimony, Brown described them as 'crocodile tears'.[121] Whether Rapier actually believed it was a 'frame up' is known only by him; regardless, the widespread belief clearly existed that the police would indeed frame people to defend themselves and persecute their vocal critics.

Despite accusations of police perjury, Judge Stocker refused to submit details to the DPP because 'this has not been an investigation of police practice', before commending the 'perfectly plain' fact of officers acting 'with great courage and gallantry in very difficult and dangerous circumstances'.[122] Police behaviour was not under legal debate in the Bristol courts, despite local people wishing it had been. This mirrors later disorders, where inquiries largely overlooked frequent accusations of police misconduct, as they were deemed inappropriate arenas for investigating such allegations – despite widespread discontent and distrust of the police complaints system.[123]

After six weeks and an estimated £500,000 – incidentally, the same cost as damage caused by the disorders – the trial collapsed when five defendants were acquitted and the jury was deadlocked on most of the remainder.[124] Defence counsel Edward Rees suggested that trial expenses could have been put to better use, Narayan decried how 'Half a million pounds of taxpayers' money has gone down the drain', and partisan publication *Caribbean Times* claimed more money was spent on this 'Trial of Vengeance' than had been invested in St Pauls over twenty-five years.[125] Bristol's Assistant Community Relations Officer Peter Courtier described the trial as 'farcical', alleged several officers believed it had been a mistake, and reasoned that it had exacerbated poor relations between the police and black youth in St Pauls. He concluded that a 'golden opportunity' had been lost, as any positive consequences of the disorder had been hindered by unjustified trials when 'even the police admit they lost control'.[126] Narayan claimed there was sufficient reason for an investigation into how the 'shabby prosecution' had been mounted upon 'shabby evidence', and Joshua *et al.* later agreed the trial was based upon 'what seems to be appallingly flawed evidence'.[127] BCRE's Graham Reid concluded that the wording used to deny the local community a public inquiry, 'A great circus … which would have wasted time and probably not have clarified very much', was an appropriate description of the trial.[128]

Weigh stated he was happy the case had been appropriately brought before the court and all evidence properly given.[129] Yet, prior to the trials, charges of affray had been believed easier to prove due to evidence of direct involvement in fighting. An unnamed detective, who provided evidence in the trial, later suggested it had been 'a huge waste of money' that would have had more chance of succeeding if lesser charges had been pursued: 'they were too heavy … But hindsight is a wonderful thing'.[130] Indeed, Kettle and Hodges concluded this was probably the key factor in the trial's collapse, as did some contemporary commentators: 'is not the idea of "riotous assembly" … a recipe for hung juries?'[131]

Regardless, the authorities' belief that the disorder was a 'direct and deliberate challenge to police authority by a large number of people acting together' resulted in certainty that riot was the correct charge.[132] DPP Hetherington subsequently defended their decision, arguing that 'we thought that the evidence was good enough to get a conviction for riot and we thought it was in the public interest to prosecute as hard as we could those who in our view had been responsible'.[133] Answering calls for a public inquiry were seemingly not deemed sufficiently within public interest. Defence lawyers argued that, by legal definitions of 'riot', it had been the police who 'acted together' and 'shared a common purpose', not the crowd – although Joshua *et al.* reasoned such arguments were inadmissible in a court environment 'in which the dice are heavily loaded' in the police's favour.[134]

Nonetheless, praise was bestowed upon Judge Stocker's handling of the 'potentially volatile' situation. Approaching the trial in a manner unbefitting the usual formality of the legal system, he tolerated defendants regularly arriving late, or reading newspapers and completing crossword puzzles while in the dock – one defendant even apparently fell asleep. The *Guardian* highlighted the determined effort to avoid any further disturbances similar to those seen at the committal proceedings.[135] This, however, did not transfer to other officials' attitudes towards those attending the trials, who regularly faced locked doors, discouraging comments, and a lack of space: 'It required no little determination to enter the *public* gallery'.[136] This was a very apt representation of how black Britons felt they were being systematically denied access to the legal system.

As the final verdicts were announced, Rapier leapt to his feet and thanked the jury. The presiding juror asked to say something, but Stocker warned 'It would be better if you didn't'.[137] What might have been said is unclear; but the care Stocker took to prevent further escalating tensions is obvious. Defendant Sharpe recalled the 'relief' at the verdict, believing those on trial 'would have got the whole wrath for ... everything' if found guilty.[138] A celebrating crowd of several hundred people stopped traffic as they gathered outside the courtroom and some jurors, black and white, were seen shaking hands with freshly acquitted defendants. The *Sun* reported '*Three of the jurors joined in the celebrations*' – a statement seeming to suggest potential collusion in the verdicts.[139] Brown later admitted that at least three of the four minority ethnic jurors were known by some defendants, and two lived in St Pauls. Furthermore, he and Rapier had even followed two female jurors from the court to discuss the case: 'Some of them we knew all right, but we never said ... I was looking at between three and seven years in prison.' One officer, who gave evidence at the trial, was 'not at all surprised' later to learn that the two defendants had conversed with jurors: 'They weren't stupid people.'[140]

Post-trial champagne revelries continued at the Black and White Café itself, the site where disorder began. This symbolic action again demonstrated that the disturbances came to represent the struggle of a local black community against perceived oppression. A plan quickly emerged for a large street party to mark the disorder's anniversary, described by Rapier as a 'freedom day ... Every decent citizen of any colour should be there'.[141] Clearly exhibiting a sense of victory, defence barrister Sibghat Kadri declared: 'What happened here is something people should be proud of.'[142] On the other hand, Police Authority Chair, Ian Crawford, was 'appalled' at the suggestion, warning racial hatred could be incited by celebrating 'an incident most Bristolians are ashamed of'.[143] It was suggested the date should be changed to make clear that it was a celebration of the acquittals, not the disorder – but this was rejected. Such specific actions show the pride of a local rebellion against a police force deemed oppressive. In the end, a 'loud but uneventful party' on 2 April 1981, from which the police kept a low profile, passed without incident.[144]

Considerable local pressure was exhorted on the authorities that outstanding charges should be dropped against the remaining four defendants, and local MPs Palmer and Waldegrave met with the Attorney-General to stress the benefits such action would have on community relations in St Pauls.[145] BCRE

Senior Community Relations Officer Carmen Beckford agreed, informing the Attorney-General that trials had worsened relations, but 'it is now best to forget the past and work for a better future for all'.[146] This view was seemingly accepted by Hetherington as, when announcing that all remaining charges would be dropped, he cited advice provided by Weigh that doing so would promote racial harmony in Bristol as an important factor in this decision.[147]

The decision was nonetheless criticised by those deeming it worrying that racial harmony had been cited as a reason not to proceed with re-trials. Right-leaning newspapers argued there 'cannot be a trade-off' between racial harmony and justice, as 'The law ... is not there to promote other ideals, however desirable. For to do so is to dabble in politics'. They further argued that such a precedent would allow the situation where 'if a white man hits a police man you charge him; if a black man does the same you don't'.[148] Conservative MP John Carlisle added that 'The coloured population may use this as a protection or shield', and, rather than promoting racial harmony, it may even 'antagonise some people against ethnic minorities'.[149] Just five days after Hetherington's declaration that all remaining charges would be dropped, disorders began in Brixton, prompting accusations that a lack of sentences had emboldened others.[150] It is difficult to argue wholly against this, considering the way that disturbances would spread across England in 1981.

Conclusion

In the aftermath of 2 April 1980, the governmental reaction was not sufficient to appease those calling for a public inquiry and Whitelaw's 'three-pronged response' was inadequate. As the CRE-backed inquiry into employment and inequality summarised: 'Five months on from "riots" that supposedly shook the nation, those who most need shaking, those responsible for and empowered with providing social resources for black people, have managed to avoid significant commitment to the expressed wishes of the people themselves.'[151] Therefore, a Select Committee and local organisations took it upon themselves to attempt such inquiries. These had differing levels of support and success, but ultimately could not appease local people or alter the views of the Government who instead focused their response upon criminality and law and order. However, appeals for a public inquiry were far from universal – many locals believed such investigations would be a 'whitewash' or even used to target and punish black Britons. The level of distrust towards the authorities is clearly demonstrated by this dichotomous response.

Despite refusals to grant an inquiry and the perceived lack of a meaningful response from central government, Bristol local authorities and police appeared to respond to the disorder. To improve poor community relations, a planned Community Involvement Department was implemented early, liaison was increased with local groups and organisations such as the BCRE, and community officers on foot policed the area more often.[152] In July 1980, the St Pauls festival, an annual 'joyous' event celebrating and bringing together different communities in the area – but criticised for later becoming commercialised when the city council realised its economic worth – passed without incident.[153] Some attributed this to the deliberate police tactic of not appearing prominently, as opposed to 'swamping' Brixton following initial disturbances there in April 1981, and officers were praised for attempts to 'join in the festive spirit'.[154] This tactic was repeated in July 1981 as, while disorders spread across England, more than 15,000 people attended the Bristol festival climax and witnessed local officers' 'superb' efforts to join in.[155] An altered police approach and community liaison could go some way to explaining why Bristol, in 1981, remained peaceful.

St Pauls provided an example to black Britons that the police could be resisted, and the lack of effective governmental response or inquiry into the disorder furthered discontentment within sections of black communities, increasingly willing to combat police discrimination violently. Outbursts of disorder would spread around the country in 1981, beginning with Brixton almost exactly one year after St Pauls.

Notes

1 Bristol Records Office (BRO): 42974/1, City Clerk, 'Notes of a Press Conference'.

2 HC Deb 03 April 1980 vol. 982 cc. 663–4.

3 See: chapter 2.

4 *Western Daily Press*, 24 July 1981.

5 'Notes of a Press Conference'; *Western Daily Press*, 23 May 1980.

6 *Socialist Challenge*, 10 April 1980.

7 *The Times*, 7 July 1980. For Rastafari, see: Gilroy, *Ain't No Black*, pp. 187–92; Edmonds, *Rastafari*.

8 *Observer*, 6 April 1980; *Daily Mail*, 28 March 1981. See, for example: Marable, *Malcolm X*; Tuck, *Malcolm X*.

9 BRO: 43129 (Box 105), Paul Stephenson, 'Report of Bristol disturbances April 2nd, 1980', 29 April 1980.

10 *Guardian*, 16 April 1980; BRO: 43129 (Box 105), Notes of Meeting, 1 May 1980.

11 'Notes of a Press Conference'.

12 BRO: 42974/1, Notes of a Press Conference, 10 April 1980; *Daily Mail*, 5 April 1980; *Daily Telegraph*, 23 May 1980; *Evening Post*, 20 June 1980. See: Rex and Tomlinson, *Colonial Immigrants*; Sivanandan, *Different Hunger*.

13 *Socialist Challenge*, 24 April 1980.

14 *Daily Mail*, 5 April 1980.

15 *Western Daily Press*, 9 April 1980. See: Fryer, *Staying Power*; Layton-Henry, *Politics of Race*; Lea and Young, 'The Riots'.

16 BRO: 42974/1, Housing Department Memorandum, 17 April 1980; O.H. Page, 'Notes from the Meeting of the BCRE', 17 April 1980.

17 *Guardian*, 5 April 1980.

18 BRO: 32080/TC1/10/8, Bristol Resource Centre, 'Race, Employment and Inequality in the Bristol Area: An Action Research and Education Project sponsored by the Commission for Racial Equality: Interim Report' (1980), p. 25.

19 'Notes from the Meeting of the BCRE'.

20 BCRE, *Annual Report*, p. 25.

21 Joshua *et al.*, *To Ride the Storm*, p. 130; BCRE, *Annual Report*, pp. 25–6.

22 BRO: 43129 (Box 105), Paul Stephenson, 'Bristol Disturbances – April 2nd 1980', 6 May 1980.

23 BRO: 43129 (Box 106), Leslie Wollen to William Whitelaw, 25 April 1980; Wollen to Carmen Beckford, 25 April 1980.

24 BRO: 43129 (Box 105), BCRE, 'Press Release'.

25 See: chapter 5.

26 BRO: 42974/1, 'Notes on Debate', 15 April 1980.

27 BCRE, Annual Report, p. 21. See: Institute of Race Relations, *Police against Black People*, p. 87.

28 The National Archives (TNA): CAB 128/67/17, Cabinet Conclusions, 24 April 1980.

29 Kettle and Hodges, *Uprising!*, p. 32.

30 BCRE, *Annual Report*, p. 27; 'Race, Employment and Inequality', p. 25; BRO: 43129 (Box 105), Peter Courtier to David Natzler, 15 May 1980.

31 HC Deb 28 April 1980 vol. 983 cc. 971–2.

32 'Race, Employment and Inequality', pp. 25–6.

33 Kettle and Hodges, *Uprising!*, p. 32.

34 Joshua *et al.*, *To Ride the Storm*, pp. 56–91. For this in relation to Brixton, see: Keith, *Race, Riots and Policing*, p. 78.

35 HC Deb 03 July 1980 vol. 987 c. 1748.

36 Joshua *et al.*, *To Ride the Storm*, pp. 190–92.

37 HC Deb 28 April 1980 vol. 983 c. 974.

38 BRO: 42974/1, BCRE to Whitelaw, 14 April 1980.

39 Phillips and Phillips, *Windrush*, p. 362.

40 HC Deb 28 April 1980 vol. 983 c. 978.

41 BRO: 43129 (Box 105), John Wheeler, 'Sub-Committee on Race Relations & Immigration Visit to Bristol', 14 May 1980; Graham W. Reid, 'Report of House of Commons Home Affairs Sub-Committee on Race Relations and Immigration Day Trip to Bristol'.

42 'Race, Employment and Inequality', p. 25.

43 BRO: 42974/1, John Brown to Michael Colvin, 12 May 1980.

44 BRO: 42974/1, Brown to Councillors, 6 May 1980; Brown to R.W. Wall, 7 May 1980.

45 BRO: 43129 (Box 105), Bill Nicks, 'Sub-Committee on Race Relations & Immigration visit to Bristol Thursday 22nd May'.

46 Henry to Natzler, 14 May 1980.

47 BRO: 42974/1, 'Race Relations and Immigration Sub-Committee', 30 April 1980.

48 BRO: 42974/1, I.C. Bryan, 'Notes for the Guidance of Witnesses', p. 2.

49 BRO: 42974/1, Claude Draper to Whitelaw, 13 May 1980; 'Race Relations and Immigration Sub-Committee'.

50 Waldegrave to Brown, 16 May 1980.

51 *Western Daily Press*, 15 May 1980.

52 BRO: 43129 (Box 105), St Pauls United Defence Committee, Press Release, 14 May 1980; 'Sub-Committee on Race Relations & Immigration'; BCRE, *Annual Report*, 28.

53 BRO: 43129 (Box 106), Arthur Palmer to Courtier, 24 May 1980.

54 'Sub-Committee on Race Relations & Immigration Visit to Bristol'.

55 BRO: 43129 (Box 106), Home Affairs Committee, 'Race Relations and Immigration Sub-Committee Visit to Bristol on Thursday 22nd May'; Natzler to Courtier, 16 May 1980; *Bristol Evening Post*, 19 May 1980.

56 *Daily Mail*, 23 May 1980.

57 'Race Relations and Immigration Sub-Committee'.

58 'Home Affairs Sub-Committee'.

59 *Daily Telegraph*, 23 May 1980.

60 Kettle and Hodges, *Uprising!*, p. 34.

61 *Guardian*, 23 May 1980; *Western Daily Press*, 5 June 1980.

62 BCRE, *Annual Report*, p. 28; 'Race, Employment and Inequality', p. 25.

63 *Western Daily Press*, 23 May 1980.

64 'Home Affairs Sub-Committee'.

65 *Ibid.*

66 *Daily Telegraph*, 23 May 1980.

67 *Guardian*, 21 May 1980.

68 'Race, Employment and Inequality', p. 18.

69 *Bristol Evening Post*, 22 May 1980.

70 HC Deb 28 April 1980 vol. 983 c. 972; BRO: 42974/1, C.J. Stewart to Brown, 28 April 1980; Cabinet Conclusions, 24 April 1980.

71 Cited in Joshua *et al.*, *To Ride the Storm*, p. 132.

72 Cabinet Conclusions, 24 April 1980.

73 HC Deb 28 April 1980 vol. 983 c. 981.

74 TNA: PREM 19/484, Note for Prime Minister, 28 April 1980.

75 'Race, Employment and Inequality', p. 29.

76 BRO: 42974/1, R.A. Fehler, pp. Mike Hodkinson to Lord Mayor of Bristol, 6 May 1980.

77 'Notes on Debate'.

78 BRO: 43129 (Box 106), Trevor Morgan, 'Report on Ashley and St. Paul's Meeting', 15 May 1980.

79 National Council for Civil Liberties, *Southall 23 April 1979*. See: chapter 1; Kettle and Hodges, *Uprising!*, pp. 76–8.

80 Mikardo, *Back-Bencher*, pp. 6, 213–15.

81 *Bristol Evening Post*, 13 November 1980. See: Seyd, *Rise and Fall*.

82 BRO: 32080/TC1/10/8, TUC and Labour Party poster. See: Vinen, *Thatcher's Britain*, p. 77.

83 *Guardian*, 10 July 1980; Interview with Simbarashe Tongogara, 4 April 2017.

84 *Western Daily Press*, 12 April 1980. For how the left were often viewed as 'the *white* Left', see: Rodrigues, 'The Riots of '81'.

85 BRO: 3208/TC1/10/8, Submission to the TUC Inquiry on behalf of Bristol District Labour Party.

86 *Bristol Evening Post*, 21 November 1980; *Daily Telegraph*, 24 July 1981.

87 *Bristol Evening Post*, 15 January 1981.

88 *Western Daily Press*, 24 July 1981.

89 TUC, *Slumbering Volcano?*, p. 36.

90 *Daily Telegraph*, 24 July 1981.

91 *Bristol Journal*, 31 October 1980.

92 Mikardo cited in *The Times*, 24 July 1981.

93 BCRE, *Annual Report*, p. 27. For trial proceedings, see: Joshua *et al.*, *To Ride the Storm*, pp. 148–84; Kettle and Hodges, *Uprising!*, pp. 34–8.

94 Interview with Tongogara.

95 *New Statesman*, 27 March 1981.

96 *Bristol Evening Post*, 13 March 1981.

97 Interview with Carlton Sharpe, 4 April 2017; Interview with Tongogara.

98 BRO: Pol/IO/7/8, Avon and Somerset Constabulary, 'Operational Discord', 13 June 1980.

99 *Guardian*, 21 March 1981.

100 *Western Daily Press*, 8 April 1981, 17 June 1980.

101 *Bristol Evening Post*, 28 April 2011.

102 *New Statesman*, 27 March 1981.

103 Rose, *Climate of Fear*, pp. 201–3.

104 BRO: 43129 (Box 105), BCRE, 'Bristol Crown Courts, Jury Monitoring, Monday, 26.1.81 – Friday, 30.1.81'.

105 Cited in Joshua *et al.*, *To Ride the Storm*, p. 167.

106 BCRE, *Annual Report*, p. 27.

107 Joshua *et al.*, *To Ride the Storm*, p. 167; Kettle and Hodges, *Uprising!*, pp. 36–7.

108 Kettle and Hodges, *Uprising!*, p. 36.

109 *The Times*, 22 May 1982, cited in Rowe, *Racialisation of Disorder*, pp. 8–9.

110 Bunce and Field, *Darcus Howe*, pp. 124–5; Fryer, *Staying Power*, p. 394.

111 *Western Daily Press*, 18 February 1981.

112 Joshua *et al.*, *To Ride the Storm*, pp. 153–7.

113 See, for example: Harvey *et al.*, *The Miners' Strike*; Scraton, *Hillsborough*.

114 *Bristol Evening Post*, 28 April 2011.

115 *Bristol Evening Post*, 10 February 1981.

116 *Bristol Evening Post*, 12 February 1981.

117 *Bristol Evening Post*, 14 February 1981.

118 *Bristol Evening Post*, 6 March 1981.

119 *Guardian*, 7 March 1981.

120 *Bristol Evening Post*, 6 March 1981.

121 *Bristol Evening Post*, 28 April 2011.

122 *Guardian*, 21 March 1981.

123 See: chapters 5 and 7.

124 *Daily Mail*, 21 March 1981.

125 *Western Daily Press*, 12 March 1981; *Guardian*, 21 March 1981; *Caribbean Times*, 2 April 1981.

126 *Guardian*, 21 March 1981; *Bristol Evening Post*, 21 March 1981.

127 *Guardian*, 21 March 1981; Joshua *et al.*, *To Ride the Storm*, p. 184.

128 BCRE, *Annual Report*, p. 27.

129 *Guardian*, 21 March 1981.

130 *Bristol Evening Post*, 28 April 2011.

131 Kettle and Hodges, *Uprising!*, p. 35; *Daily Telegraph*, 7 April 1981.

132 *Guardian*, 21 March 1981.

133 *The Times*, 11 May 1981.

134 Joshua *et al.*, *To Ride the Storm*, pp. 143–8, 181–4.

135 *Guardian*, 21 March 1981.

136 BCRE, *Annual Report*, p. 28, emphasis in original.

137 *Guardian*, 21 March 1981; *Bristol Evening Post*, 20 March 1981; *Daily Mail*, 21 March 1981.

138 Interview with Sharpe.

139 *Sun*, 21 March 1981, emphasis in original.

140 *Bristol Evening Post*, 27 April 2011, 28 April 2011.

141 *Bristol Evening Post*, 21 March 1981.

142 Kettle and Hodges, *Uprising!*, p. 38.

143 *Western Daily Press*, 23 March 1981.

144 *Western Daily Press*, 3 April 1981.

145 BRO: 43129 (Box 106), Palmer to Beckford, 3 April 1981.

146 BRO: 43129 (Box 106), Beckford to Sir Michael Havers, 31 March 1981.

147 *The Times*, 7 April 1981.

148 *Western Daily Press*, 7 April 1981; *Daily Telegraph*, 7 April 1981.

149 *Bristol Evening Post*, 8 April 1981.

150 Kettle and Hodges, *Uprising!*, p. 38.

151 'Race, Employment and Inequality', p. 29.

152 BCRE, *Annual Report*, p. 34; Whitelaw, 'Serious Disturbances', pp. 8–9.

153 Interview with Tongogara. See: Dresser and Fleming, *Bristol*, p. 169.

154 *The Times*, 7 July 1980.

155 *Bristol Evening Post*, 6 July 1981.

4

Escalation: Brixton, 10–12 April 1981

You can crush us, you can bruise us,
But you'll have to answer to the guns of Brixton.

The Clash – The Guns of Brixton

D ESPITE WARNINGS of growing frustration from black Britons, violently
expressed by Bristol's 1980 anti-police disorder, the police and Government
did little to change their tactics or attitudes. Repeatedly rejecting calls for a public
inquiry, the authorities seemed to believe the worst was over and, as John Benyon
and John Solomos summarised, appeared to view that disturbance as 'a strange
aberration in social behaviour'. In Brixton, South London, in April 1981, one
year after the similar shock of Bristol, such 'complacent interpretations were
rudely shattered'.[1] At odds with previous government portrayals of Bristol
being a 'model city' for tackling inner-city problems, Home Secretary William
Whitelaw would later reflect that:

> The St Paul's district of Bristol was known to be a difficult area from
> a policing point of view. But this very fact meant that we in the Home
> Office, and indeed in the police service as a whole, failed to recognize
> this disturbance for the warning signal of danger which it turned out
> to be.[2]

However, not everyone failed to identify the potential for disorder to spread.
A poll in Brixton shortly after St Pauls showed that 70 per cent of respondents
had little or no confidence in the police, and two-thirds deemed it likely that
disorder would be repeated.[3] As Ron Ramdin later concluded, the events of St
Pauls 'had echoed a wave of deep-seated resentment among black people across
Britain'.[4]

This disorder has undoubtedly received the most attention from academics compared with others in 1980–81, although Michael Keith, in one of the most detailed theoretical and ethnographic accounts, highlighted a common gap between academic explanations of the disturbances and the empirical reality of what happened.[5] Study of recently released records of Lord Scarman's public inquiry into events and grassroots political organisations allows this chapter to chart Brixton's history of troubled police/community relations and the impact that perspectives of this poor relationship itself had upon deployed officers in the area, who often depicted local people purely as criminals. Examining attempted formal police/community liaison prior to the disturbances, which broke down due to tensions regarding policing attitudes and tactics, the chapter notes how provocative police actions and the detrimental effect of saturation-policing operations, further to the influence of events elsewhere, led to the most well-known outbreak of disorder in 1980–81.

In the period between St Pauls and Brixton, another event occurred furthering belief the authorities simply did not care about black Britons: a house fire in New Cross, South East London, on 18 January 1981, killed thirteen black youths. The police were accused of not investigating seriously claims it had been arson. Other black homes in the area had been attacked, a black community centre had been burnt down, and 'the entire community, not just the anguished parents, were convinced that the fire had been started by fascists'.[6] Despite racist letters having been sent to the homeowner and an unexploded incendiary device being found outside the house, subsequent forensic evidence did not support initial reports of a firebomb; nonetheless, this belief permeated the local community and the police were criticised for portraying the fire as self-inflicted.[7] David J. Smith and Jeremy Gray observed the police investigation and, while concluding the police were 'probably right' that the fire had been accidentally started by a houseguest rather than a racist attack, they criticised the poorly handled investigation. This included unfounded police beliefs that black residents would not co-operate with investigations, failure to convince locals they were investigating the possibility it was racially motivated, and failure to alleviate fears black people were under attack.[8]

Perceived police indifference to the tragedy led to the organisation of the Black People's Day of Action on 2 March 1981, a protest march attended by an estimated 6,000–15,000 people saying 'We're here. Look at us ... We're hurting, and you're not doing anything about it, you're pretending it hasn't happened'.[9] The march was organised by the New Cross Massacre Action Committee and figures such as John La Rose, founder of the first Caribbean publishing house in England, New Beacon Books, and activist Darcus Howe.[10] Howe had been a prominent member of the British Black Panthers, coming to national attention in 1970 as one of the 'Mangrove Nine' who successfully defended against incitement to riot charges.[11] Beginning in 1982, Howe became a well-known broadcaster and his transformation from Black Power 'terrorist' in the 1970s to respected commentator by the mid-1980s suggests in part 1980–81 allowed him a platform previously denied. The response to the New Cross Fire demonstrated a growing collective consciousness within the black community:

> a sense of solidarity … and a collective perception of threats to themselves from various forces in society, symbolised most strongly by the threat that they feel is posed to them by the police … it was a collective political response to events which were remote from the personal lives of many of the people taking part.[12]

Alongside the 1980 St Pauls disturbance, this response confirmed that a new level of black resistance had emerged.[13] Indeed, 'It was no wonder that black youths walked south London with a swagger after the New Cross march'.[14] Playwright and actor Kwame Kwei-Armah deemed it a 'formative moment', and even Metropolitan Police Commissioner, Sir David McNee, concluded that the event 'brought about a change of mood and a sense of unity within the black community not previously seen'.[15] The increased willingness and ability to organise and protest towards a common goal would be seen throughout the disturbances in 1981, beginning in Brixton.

Brixton

Similar to St Pauls, Brixton experienced a growth in postwar Commonwealth migration, notably the 1948 arrival of the *Empire Windrush* leading to migrants settling in the area due to affordable housing. By the late 1970s, Brixton was a classic example of urban decline and, by 1981, the unemployment rate for black males under nineteen was 55 per cent. In his subsequent public inquiry into the disorders, Lord Scarman noted that this, combined with prevalent racial discrimination, resulted in widespread discontentment. Brixton exhibited 'many of the features of other decaying inner city areas' such as poor local facilities – particularly in housing, leisure and recreation.[16] However, this raises the question: if Brixton was in many ways typical, why did it become the epicentre of the next disorder?

One reason was provocative police tactics and actions. Scarman contended it was 'regrettably also true' that Brixton's socioeconomic conditions attracted some people to a life of crime – particularly robbery, car theft and pick-pocketing.[17] Yet, not all observers agreed unemployment and other social issues were linked with a rise in crime, especially right-wing figures. Prime Minister Margaret Thatcher particularly rejected this argument because, as well as undermining her economic policies at a time of weakness for her Government, it would 'suggest that individuals do not possess ultimate responsibility for their behaviour' – contrary to the individualism integral to Thatcherite ideology.[18] Still, as Timothy Brain pointed out, it appeared Thatcher accepted the link between crime, disorder and unemployment when she later appointed Michael Heseltine 'Minister for Liverpool', tasked with restoring the city's prosperity following its own disturbances in July 1981. Brain did contend, though, that this appeared more aimed at neutralising internal threats from economically liberal Conservatives than a clear attempt at social improvement through interventionist economics.[19]

Police statistics indicated that violent crime and robberies increased by 138 per cent within Brixton during 1976–80, with police suggesting black people 'were disproportionately involved'.[20] This led to increased use of tactics such as stops and searches, often targeting black Britons; Kettle and Hodges demonstrated that figures supplied to Scarman suggested black residents were stopped disproportionately to their overall numbers and, once stopped, were more likely to be arrested. They deemed it 'strange' that Scarman's inquiry subsequently 'failed to investigate the matter further'.[21] Peter Bleksley, a Metropolitan police officer in 1981, later claimed that 'sus' – the shorthand for suspicious behaviour under the 1824 Vagrancy Act – was used 'to basically "fit up" and brutalise people that we didn't like'.[22] Whether or not such allegations are accurate, the detrimental effect of 'sus' on police/community relations is clear – but it was not the only policy causing discontentment.[23] In 1980, 1,469 people – black and white – were arrested under 'sus' throughout London: equivalent to only one-third of stops of black people in Brixton alone.

Police in Brixton had to tackle rising crime levels, while attempting to retain the confidence of the community.[24] This was an extremely difficult task, made more so by inherent prejudices and racial discrimination. Michael Keith demonstrated how the labelling and criminalisation of areas such as Brixton affects how these areas are viewed by deployed officers and their relationships with residents, as well as the significance of such confrontational 'symbolic locations'.[25] Bleksley further claimed that 'Racism was compulsory in the police'.[26] While there is no evidence to support claims that racism was a career requirement, such attitudes certainly permeated the police to some degree.

Police/community relations

Further to increased and disproportionate stops and searches, specific Brixton circumstances also caused discontentment, as the area had a history of troubled relations between the police and black residents. Joseph Hunte's 1966 study suggested 'that sergeants and constables do leave stations with the express purpose of going nigger hunting'; Commander Alex Marnoch, who worked in Brixton at the time, admitted such accusations were 'basically true'.[27] Similarly, Wayne Haynes, survivor of the New Cross Fire, described his experiences with local police:

> They could do whatever they want, basically, and they did … if they didn't like your face, if your face didn't fit, or you was a bit too lippy, as most black kids are, you'd get a little kicking. Maybe then you'd get taken down the cell and get a good kicking … And that's just how it was.[28]

Conversely, the police blamed attitudes of Brixton residents for their own hardened opinions: 'I have seen the most liberal and left wing people come down here and within months completely change their attitudes. The hatred on the streets is so awful that you have to conform to the views of the rest of the group to survive.'[29] A cycle of hostility between the police and local people had existed for many years, now heightened by the impact of St Pauls and New Cross.

Brixton also had a history of community activism attempting to improve the situation for black Britons, being home to black activists, radical bookstores, cafés and record shops. Council worker and local activist Devon Thomas attributed the formation of these organisations to second-generation migrants, less likely to leave the country and more determined to fight inequality.[30] For instance, the Council for Community Relations in Lambeth (CCRL) recounted how, in 1976, the police knocked a young pregnant woman to the ground while questioning a middle-aged black man. George Greaves, CCRL Principal Community Relations Officer, recounted that 'So intense was the anger generated … that they marched as a body to Brixton Police Station to complain … it was a spontaneous demonstration without any prompting from community leaders or community activists'. Greaves underscored that the significance of this, that black youths were 'no longer prepared to rely on intermediaries to win for them the justice which they felt was being denied', was not lost on those familiar with the area.[31] Indeed, this demonstrates how black Britons – youths in particular – were increasingly willing to protest perceived injustice.

Successive police commanders in Brixton attempted methods of community policing; championed by Devon and Cornwall Chief Constable, John Alderson, this included using home beat officers and forging links with local communities.[32] However, Merseyside Chief Constable Kenneth Oxford contended community policing should not be seen as 'the panacea for all problems', as similar approaches had previously been employed.[33] Similarly, Paul Gilroy reasoned that evidence, showing Devon and Cornwall police also utilised the same 'fire-brigade' coercive tactics as elsewhere, 'makes nonsense of the view of community policing as a miraculous cure-all for urban ailments'.[34] Despite such criticism, a 1983 study by Sandra Jones and Michael Levi of two forces utilising opposing policing techniques – Devon and Cornwall and Manchester – showed that Alderson's community policing approach resulted in a high public approval and more accurate police perception of their public standing, suggesting a closer relationship between the police and public. While critics have countered that policing 'tranquil rural counties' like Devon and Cornwall was arguably easier than large cities such as Manchester or London, Jones and Levi's study indicated that the relatively large city of Plymouth saw better results than the relatively small town of Wigan, suggesting it was not purely a matter of size.[35] Regardless, community policing efforts were hamstrung by a lack of police staff. In an attempt to bolster low numbers, the increasingly unpopular SPG was sporadically drafted into the area – indeed, Metropolitan Police Assistant Commissioner Wilford Gibson argued the SPG existed to solve such shortages.[36] Scarman later noted the SPG's negative impact:

> They provoked the hostility of young black people, who felt they were being hunted irrespective of their innocence or guilt. And their hostility infected older members of the community, who, hearing the stories of many innocent young black people who had been stopped and searched, began themselves to lose confidence in, and respect for, the police.[37]

Community policing was not likely to succeed when coupled with the SPG, as it was impossible for residents to separate the two approaches.[38]

Community Liaison Committee

As part of community policing strategies of forging strong community links, attempts were made to improve relations between the police and black residents. Due to the socioeconomic situation in Brixton, Scarman concluded that black youths' contact with the police was framed around viewing them as 'visible symbols of the authority of a society which has failed to bring them its benefits or do them justice'.[39] For policing by consent to be effective, positive police/community relations are vital, particularly in such a volatile environment.[40] Recognising this, a formal Liaison Committee between the police and local community organisations, fronted by the CCRL, was established in 1978.

Amongst other topics, the Committee's initial meeting discussed the policing of NF demonstrations. More accurately, community organisations attempted to discuss this, but police refused, believing it was solely the responsibility of Brixton Commander Leonard Adams to determine policing levels.[41] Typifying the general police view, Alan Goodson, President of the Association of Chief Police Officers (1979–80), later argued that, whilst chief constables consulted the community, 'he and he alone has [the] responsibility' of deciding upon operational enforcement of the law.[42]

Despite this dispute – deferred for discussion at later meetings – its first meeting suggested the Liaison Committee could be effective. Three days later, a SPG-led saturation operation commenced in Brixton. Adams had not informed community representatives beforehand, because he believed 'any resultant publicity would alert the criminal factions'.[43] This angered local people who did not believe the police saw liaison as a two-way process: 'The police appear to want help (and therefore agreement) from the community but only on their own terms.' The CCRL argued that agreement relied upon trust between the police and community but that trust and, by extension, consent, had deteriorated.[44]

Adding to dissatisfaction, three CCRL members were arrested in relation to an assault on two plainclothed officers in a Clapham pub. Dubbed the 'Sheepskin Saga', the only apparent connection between the suspects and the three arrested was that they were black and wore sheepskin coats.[45] Lambeth Council leader Ted Knight claimed that police entering CCRL offices to make these arrests was a 'calculated decision', demonstrating the 'state of police minds when dealing with sensitive issues'.[46] Knight's own ideology must be noted; widely known as 'Red Ted', he had been previously expelled from the Labour Party due to links with newspaper *Socialist Outlook*, where some contributors were 'known for their previous association with the Trotskyist Revolutionary Communist Party'.[47]

A member of the 'London left', he gained a national reputation for police criticism, and his opposition to Thatcher and the Conservatives would be seen in efforts to prevent the Government limiting council budgets in 1984 by simply refusing to set one, leading to a five-year ban from office.[48] Regardless of their intentions, involvement of such controversial figures in debates about policing often seemed to legitimise claims that there was a concerted effort to undermine the authorities. Indeed, Knight reportedly received an abusive telephone call blaming him for the Brixton disturbances – before he had even become aware of them.[49]

Following the 'Sheepskin Saga', the CCRL was contacted by dismayed local people who had believed such an organisation would be immune to police harassment, but this demonstrated otherwise.[50] Consequently, the CCRL withdrew from the Liaison Committee the following day, citing the police's 'flagrant disregard for people's rights and dignity and their utter contempt for black people'.[51] Condemning the lack of formal mechanisms for voicing criticism of policing policies – opposed to specific complaints of misconduct – it argued that institutional racism affected police tactics but the police were unwilling to accept this.[52] It also urged Knight to establish an inquiry into the state of police/community relations in Lambeth, which he agreed to; given his political views, he did not require much convincing.[53]

The CCRL's withdrawal initiated an escalating correspondence with Adams, each blaming the other for the Committee's breakdown. Adams decried the decision 'not to support' the Committee, to which the CCRL retorted it had been its suggestion to establish it in the first place, and its decision to withdraw was 'not taken lightly or recklessly'.[54] During this dispute, another police operation utilising the SPG was similarly criticised by the CCRL. Adams curtly responded that the majority of the population welcomed the police's presence to uphold law and order, and this was worth the negative effect upon some sections of the community, describing objections as frequently 'subjective rather than objective'.[55] Dismissal of criticism, often from those with genuine complaints of harassment and discrimination, added to growing feelings of discontentment.

The police did receive support from local residents welcoming SPG-led operations, notably most often from businesses and elderly people appreciating added security. As might be expected, some letters, purportedly expressing support for the police, were actually thinly veiled attacks on the black population. One such letter claimed problems were caused by 'youths who do not really belong here', ending with a plea for the SPG 'to help make this once again a pleasant place to live in for God knows what they are doing to this Country of ours'.[56]

Other letters alleged that those protesting the 'very sensible decision' to deploy the SPG were seeking 'special privileges for various racial and ethnic minorities', while another declared that 'nut case left wingers and do gooders' should 'piss off to Russia'.[57] Similar letters were sent to Knight personally, attacking his criticism of the police. For instance, one proclaimed that 'Nobody with respect for law and order would regard police questioning as "harassment" '.[58] The theme was often repeated that those criticising the police wished to overthrow law and order, and the argument went that those campaigning for less intrusive police actions would alter their views if they were to be mugged.[59] An obvious retort seems to be that people espousing such views similarly might have been a little more sympathetic to police criticism, if they were stopped and searched to the same levels black residents were.

Adams defended use of the SPG, arguing that, if police actions were continuously questioned, it would hearten criminal factions and the public would 'lose faith where officers appear to be required to fight crime with one arm tied behind their backs'.[60] The CCRL replied, 'a little surprised at the vehemence' of Adams' argument, countering that objections are to be expected when a group believes it is being discriminated against; 'It does not make these objections invalid'. Rejecting accusations of carelessly criticising the police, the CCRL blamed the police for ignoring suggested improvements, which had been one reason for its withdrawal from the Liaison Committee.[61] Communication between Adams and the CCRL subsequently deteriorated into the theatre of local newspaper *South London Press*, likely further damaging police/community relations. The CCRL also foreshadowed later events, warning:

> The long-term consequences of your policy are that you will increasingly have to rely on coercion rather than consent. This could ultimately degenerate into open and physical conflict between the police and some sections of the community in which people, both from the community and the police will be injured.[62]

A further deployment of the SPG in Brixton did see Adams informing the CCRL prior to its implementation, even offering to meet and discuss the operation – seemingly a step towards collaboration. However, Adams' letter suggested that, regardless of any concerns raised, the deployment would proceed as planned.[63] Therefore, the CCRL responded that, while remaining opposed to the SPG, there seemed 'little point' in meeting as the decision had already been made.[64] Related to this, three of the four local MPs also wrote to Adams opposing the

SPG, concluding that their repeated use demonstrated that the police lacked sufficient numbers of officers. These were Labour politicians; consistent with previous trends, the only local MP refusing to question the police's tactics was a Conservative.[65]

Due in part to rising hostilities after the CCRL's withdrawal from the Liaison Committee, Lambeth Council passed a resolution on 21 March 1979 to establish an inquiry into police/community relations. This was established largely in response to calls from the CCRL and a previous report into 'Police Conduct in Lambeth', which proposed a local inquiry due to repeated governmental refusals to grant a public inquiry.[66] This inquiry's task was made immediately more difficult when Adams withdrew police co-operation, claiming anti-police bias – deemed 'specious reasons' by the Scrap Sus Campaign.[67] Whilst acknowledging he would be duty-bound to participate in a Home Office inquiry, Adams contended this local inquiry would leave him, as the 'accused person to be judged by my accusers, without the rights and protection you are saying the police are denying the public. Clearly that would be a totally unfair system'.[68]

The inquiry's Report was published in January 1981, describing SPG excursions into Brixton as an 'Army of Occupation' and deeming the situation 'extremely grave' with unrest possible. Occupational policing was in some ways a continuation of colonial policing practices; for example, John Rex noted the appointment in the early 1960s of a former colonial officer as 'Liaison Officer for Coloured People' in Birmingham, demonstrating the perceived link between such roles.[69] The Report made a number of recommendations to improve relations between the police and black people, including the immediate repeal of 'sus' laws and ceasing any further SPG deployment. Robin Bunce and Paul Field summarised how these 'devastating conclusions' were nonetheless ignored by police and politicians.[70] They were not ignored by local people, exacerbating discontent towards the political process; William Shelton, Streatham's Conservative MP, later stressed this by citing the Report as having greatly increased hostility towards the police.[71] It is therefore perhaps unsurprising that, just three months after authorities disregarded the inquiry's findings, collective violence materialised in Brixton.

Nonetheless, there did appear to be some police recognition that local relations had become particularly poor. By this time, Commander Brian Fairbairn had replaced Adams, stating his desire to increase liaison between senior officers and elected representatives of Lambeth Council.[72] Knight responded with criticism that police had again recently forced themselves into CCRL offices, and that such actions would mean invariably 'follow[ing] in … Adams' footsteps of leaving such relationships in tatters'.[73] Knight recorded being 'constantly reassured by local community organisations' that use of the SPG was preventing relations from improving, and, as such, suggested reforming the Liaison Committee. After additional correspondence, in which Fairbairn declared willingness to discuss any facet of policing with the CCRL, the potential for gradual improvement of the situation appeared to be growing.[74]

'Swamp 81'

Undermining these cautious advances, on 6 April 1981 the police launched the plainclothed saturation operation 'Swamp 81', which Chief Superintendent Sidney Nicholson later described as 'an experiment' in reducing crime.[75] Keith noted the operation's additional intention to boost morale of officers working in the difficult climate of Brixton; indeed, Detective Chief Superintendent Jeremy Plowman later deemed the operation a success because 'It motivated officers'.[76]

Reflecting the operation's title, and referencing Thatcher's 1978 televised declaration that 'people are really rather afraid that this country might be rather swamped by people with a different culture', Fryer described Brixton as 'well and truly swamped'.[77] Plowman, taking responsibility for Swamp 81's nomen-clature, suggested it was named after another operation occurring three years previously: potentially aligning even closer with Thatcher's comments.[78] Swamp 81 was widely viewed as a direct reply to the Black People's Day of Action, demonstrating the police's desire to regain control of the streets: Gilroy dubbed it a 'revenge swamping'.[79] Brixton residents, even those deemed 'respectable', commented on the increased police presence and believed the operation to be a display of police authority; 'a boast (after the New Cross march) that no one but the Met would rule the streets'.[80] To some local black Britons, it appeared that peaceful attempts to protest perceived police misconduct or indifferent treatment were greeted with nothing other than a show of police force, escalating feelings that responding in kind was required to effect change.

The police defended Swamp 81 as a necessary response to Brixton's high crime rate. However, Fairbairn deliberately did not employ the SPG, due to concerns raised by representatives of community organisations, and actually had not utilised them since becoming Commander; the first time he did was during the disorders, at which point he acknowledged being 'very glad to have them'.[81] Despite Fairbairn's seeming willingness to be receptive of the antipathy towards the SPG, local people were again not given prior information about the operation, apparently a continuation of the belief previously verbalised by

Adams: 'No good general ever declares his forces in a prelude to any kind of attack.'[82] Evoking military language and war-like comparisons suggests the police amalgamated the Brixton population into a singular criminal enemy, rather than as constituents requiring their protection. This failure to consult community organisations beforehand was later condemned by Scarman's inquiry, and Kettle and Hodges agreed that Adams' statement and subsequent police actions 'spoke volumes on senior police attitudes'.[83]

Describing it as 'a serious mistake' that was 'poured [onto an existing] combustible mixture', contemporary and lasting opinion has condemned Swamp 81 as at best mistimed and at worst wilfully irresponsible.[84] Despite the operation's significance for the ensuing disturbances, and revealing police mindsets, the head of the local CID quoted reduced crime figures and thus considered it 'a resounding success'.[85] It is hard to see how Swamp 81 could possibly be viewed as such when, in the words of the Brixton Defence Campaign, deployment of 'prowling plain-clothed jackals ... succeeded only in provoking the black community of Brixton into an Uprising'.[86] Moreover, Michael Rowe later contested that, although police claimed street robberies and burglaries halved during the operation, little apparent consideration was paid to the possibility that such crimes were just displaced to a nearby locality.[87]

This response is symbolic of the police's broader attitude towards relations with black Britons. The success of Swamp 81 was outwardly measured purely on its statistical reduction in local crime; the fact that it had increased black discontentment towards the police and led to violent protests was seemingly disregarded. The apparent police desire to be visibly controlling the streets of Brixton was deemed representative of the semi-covert racism that characterised many of the police's actions, leading to collective violence occurring just days after Swamp 81's commencement.

Once Swamp 81 began, various observers described that tensions in the area dramatically increased. Considering the noticeably enlarged police numbers on the streets, additional instances of police raids on properties, and stops and searches, this is hardly surprising. Police described uneasy feelings in their dealings with local people and an unwillingness to be seen having 'normal' conversations with officers.[88] A few days into the operation, local organisations were 'overwhelmed' by black youths protesting police actions and Darcus Howe believed that 'the place was going to explode', having observed multiple scuffles between black youth and the so-called 'sneaker squad' plainclothed police.[89] In total, 120 officers made 943 stops in Brixton, of which over two-thirds were under 21 and over half were black: disproportionate in a community described as

36 per cent 'non-white'. Of these 943, 118 persons were arrested and just 75 charges followed.[90] If judged by its own aims of arresting burglars and robbers, this operation had not been a success and instead led to 868 law-abiding people suffering the inconvenience and indignity of being searched.[91] One observer encapsulated this, commenting that, 'as a white person safe in a position of some authority', their negative reaction to increased police numbers and actions indicated how much more threatened and resentful black residents must have felt.[92]

Brixton disturbances

Following tensions between black youths and the police on 9 April, Courtney Laws, Director of the Brixton Neighbourhood Community Association, attempted to contact Community Liaison Officer Superintendent MacLennan to discuss the situation, but was unable to do so.[93] MacLennan later stated he attempted to telephone Laws back, but could not reach him and subsequently left on weekend leave.[94] As with St Pauls, the officer most familiar with/to local people, whose presence may have diffused some of the tensions through familiarity with their situation and grievances, was absent when disorder began.[95]

The 'flashpoint' incident in Brixton, described by Brain as 'an innocent action intended well', shows the extent of police distrust.[96] Around 6 p.m. on 10 April, PC Stephen Margiotta stopped Michael Bailey, a black youth, believing him to be acting suspiciously.[97] After a short struggle, Margiotta discovered that Bailey had been stabbed in the back. Witness statements suggest Bailey had been stabbed during a confrontation with two other youths, and a later hospital examination recorded a one-and-a-half-inch wound.[98] Bailey denied knowing who had stabbed him and told police that, even if he did, he would not identify them.[99] A stabbed black youth still refused to co-operate with the police – although, there may have been other reasons why Bailey did not want to provide evidence about this incident.

A crowd gathered and, believing officers were attempting an arrest, became hostile and Bailey fled to a local house, begging for help. After applying a rudimentary dressing to his wound and being informed by Bailey that 'blacks' had stabbed him, the house's family called a minicab bound for the hospital.[100] This travelled only a short distance before police stopped it, examined Bailey's wound, and called for an ambulance. Scarman noted this call was made at 6.24 p.m., although his published Report did not record the officer's exact phrasing: 'We think we might have a dead "n" here.'[101] Before long, a crowd of black youths, estimated by officers at the time as 100 but subsequently as 30–40, surrounded the scene and, believing the police were attacking Bailey or not obtaining medical help because he was black, seized Bailey.[102] A Detective Inspector later posited that, as the officer applying direct pressure to the wound to prevent serious bleeding needed to be above Bailey, those entering the scene might have assumed officers were attacking him.[103] Officers reportedly attempted to inform the crowd an ambulance had been called and they were administering first aid, but the crowd paid no attention, believing Bailey was being left to die.[104] PC Simon Lock recounted warning the crowd that their moving Bailey could be fatal; nonetheless, the crowd responded that 'they could look after their own'.[105] The effort taken to remove an injured youth from officers visibly illustrates the level of distrust. Bailey was subsequently bundled into a passing car, which took him to a nearby hospital.[106]

This event, far from unique on the streets of Brixton, could feasibly have ended at this point with the only wider consequence being increased resentment between local black youth and the police. However, this occasion, in Scarman's words, 'ended with a sinister twist'.[107] A large crowd of black youths had assembled, as well as numerous officers following calls for assistance and high numbers already in the area, becoming involved in hostilities. 'Inevitably', in Brain's view, an arrest was made for threatening behaviour, causing youths to begin throwing stones and the police to attempt dispersing the crowd.[108] Due to increased tensions noted by numerous officers resulting from Swamp 81 and events with Bailey, it would likely have been prudent for officers to withdraw to allow anger towards the police to calm. This was, however, not consistent with a force that saw the answer to the area's problems being high levels of invasive policing, and thus many black residents accused police of an attempted show of force rather than a proportional response to the situation.

Police/community meeting

After this initial disorder died down, a community meeting was organised by Chief Superintendent Nicholson in an attempt to defuse the situation and correct some rumours spreading about the day's events. Accompanied by Head of the Community Relations Branch Commander Malcolm Ferguson, representatives of local community organisations met the police between 9 p.m. and 1 a.m., during which the police declared an intention to increase their presence in the area in response to disorders.[109] While this was accepted, those present at the meeting expressed concern at police tactics and recommended that numbers should be reduced to defuse tensions.[110] Courtney Laws detailed that the police firmly indicated their determination to uphold law and order, including preventing so-called 'no-go' areas – locations, made infamous by the Northern Ireland 'Troubles', where police feared to tread.[111] This robust response was likely motivated by previous criticism of Bristol Chief Constable Brian Weigh, after his decision to withdraw from St Pauls was portrayed as admitting defeat. Therefore, despite warnings, the police declined suggestions to discontinue the invasive Swamp 81. Scarman later deemed its continuation 'unwise' and, according to Howe, the police had 'refused to take the only action that could have averted serious disorder'.[112]

Compared with the Liaison Committee's chequered history, this meeting could be seen as the police attempting to communicate with representatives of community organisations in a manner not previously undertaken; however, such meetings were usual police procedure during disorders, and they remained unwilling to implement the suggestions and requests of community representatives. Moreover, attendance at this meeting demonstrated local desire to remain active in the political process but, as Paul Boateng later concluded, it would be wrong to characterise it as representative of the policing style championed by Alderson: 'If the community is to be consulted and then have its advice rejected ... then community policing is a nonsense.'[113]

Further to growing tensions surrounding the increased police presence, the proliferation of numerous rumours had also exacerbated hostilities. Later police statements claimed 'many members of the population had misunderstood the situation', and numerous witness statements reference widely-believed rumours that officers had not helped the injured Bailey, or even that he had died from his injuries.[114] Michael Rowbottom, *Independent Radio News* reporter, claimed he spoke to police and black youths that night and both independently agreed it had been 'a big confusion'.[115] The persistence of rumours was demonstrated by schoolchildren maintaining such stories after the weekend, seemingly 'not eager to believe' rebuttals of such allegations.[116] If the police truly believed these rumours could be quashed by senior officers simply telling representatives of community organisations they were incorrect, they vastly underestimated the level of distrust that existed.

These were not the only rumours circulating Brixton that weekend. Less plausible rumours included that the police themselves had stabbed Bailey, that the police had pre-warned local hospitals to expect civilian casualties that weekend, and that Brixton's home beat officers were ordered out of Brixton.[117] This rumour implied that officers known to locals had been wilfully removed in order to utilise 'specialist' units such as the SPG, causing a 'feeling of invasion and oppression'.[118] While the accuracy of this rumour is questionable, the negative image of the SPG appears unmistakable. Despite police attempts for such rumours to be dispelled, they clearly endured and proliferated. The manager of a local pub later argued that, had the rumours been dispelled, tensions may have decreased and 'the mood of the people who became involved in the outburst ... would have been very different'.[119] Whether this would have been the case will, of course, never be known – but the largest disorders were yet to come.

Further disorder

On Saturday 11 April, the police's decision to continue Swamp 81 and even bolster police numbers resulted in an atmosphere 'so tense you could cut it with a knife'.[120] The public deemed the 'overbearing' police presence a 'very provocative gesture' from a force 'out for revenge' and endeavouring to 're-establish [their] rule of the streets'.[121] Rather than attempting reconciliation with local people, or realising that continued invasive tactics were escalating pre-existing tensions, the police met the low-level initial disturbance with increased numbers. Instead of intimidating locals, this prompted a swelling of numbers on the streets, 'as if to meet the challenge'. As one observer recognised, 'Brixton is not the sort of area where large numbers of police can be poured into the streets without creating a mood of high tension and expectation'.[122] This was accompanied by the fact that, similar to Community Liaison Officer Superintendent MacLennan's absence, the two local beat officers familiar to the residents were both off duty.[123] This, alongside other police actions, led Courtney Laws to claim that 'a child would have handled the situation better'.[124]

Scarman's public inquiry later rejected arguments that the police should have reduced their heavy presence; despite agreeing that numbers 'must have heightened tension to some degree ... The risk had to be taken'.[125] This demonstrates the authority mindset, which could not consider – or be observed considering – that a strategic withdrawal might calm the crowd by removing the obvious target for their anger, despite this having occurred in St Pauls. The events of that Saturday evening would demonstrate that 'the risk' of maintaining police numbers in Brixton certainly did not pay off.

After a morning of increased tensions, a further seemingly minor incident – officers searching a minicab for drugs – erupted into disorder, initiating scenes 'the like of which had not previously been seen in this century in Britain'.[126] The officers' decision to search the innocent minicab driver, despite a large crowd having gathered, was questioned; under the circumstances, a hostile reaction from the assembled black crowd was certainly predictable.[127] The Brixton Defence Campaign, established to support those arrested in relation to the disorder, accused the police of inciting the crowd and instigating the disorders through provocative actions.[128] Scarman concluded that the officers 'failed to recognise real danger signals or to strike the correct balance between enforcing the law and keeping the peace'; but, the 'important question' was not whether they had acted foolishly or even unlawfully, but why the event initiated disturbances.[129] By focusing on the public disorder aspect, seemingly overlooking the routine heavy-handed police tactics employed against innocent residents, Scarman may have unwittingly answered his own question.

During the minicab search, officers attempted to arrest a young black man who was allegedly simply telling officers to leave the driver alone.[130] Howe recalled that a few days prior, a local black youth had asked what he was going to do regarding the police's behaviour and actions, to which Howe had replied: 'What can I do?' This youth was seemingly the same person arrested after remonstrating with the police about their tactics.[131] This is a clear demonstration of the intent behind the disturbances; a local black youth had appealed to a famed civil liberties campaigner attempting to effect change and, after being told nothing could be done, took action into his own hands. Similarly, George Greaves argued this event was 'the straw that broke the camel's back', with observers reacting the only way they felt they could: 'Their complaints in the past, formal and informal, about police misconduct had gone unheeded, and as no one was helping them … they had to seek their own solution.'[132]

This seemingly routine police search led to major disorder: 'An orgy of burning and looting took place' that night and following day.[133] Despite not being shocked by the disorders themselves, local community workers did confess surprise at their scale and ferocity.[134] 'Bloody Saturday' resulted in 82 arrests, 279 officers and 45 members of the public reported injured, 117 vehicles – including 56 police vehicles – damaged or destroyed, and 145 premises damaged.[135] Police actions and allegations of misconduct during the disorders are addressed in the following chapter, but the general outcome was, as Scarman later summarised, 'that the scars of what had happened would linger in Brixton, and particularly in the relationship between the police and the public, for a long time to come'.[136]

Conclusion

As with Bristol, the events of Brixton quickly spread – initially within the area, and then further afield. This was fostered by high levels of media attention: just as they had undoubtedly played a role in spreading public consciousness of St Pauls, the media was even more involved in Brixton as improvements in technology allowed television cameras to be on the forefront of public disorder in a way previously unobtainable. Brain stated that television coverage 'imprint[ed] it in the collective consciousness of the nation', and Benyon and Solomos concluded that millions of people 'saw for themselves the fury that had been unleashed'.[137] Keen to document events, the police logged queries from media organisations questioning if there had been outbreaks of violence early on the Saturday morning, with reporters being surprised when the answer at that point was no.[138] Certainly, the speed that photographers and journalists arrived on the scene once disorders began on 'Bloody Saturday' suggests they were expecting it. Their presence was even recorded as having played a role: cameras focused upon Brixton created an air of inevitability that trouble would erupt.[139]

The media's power was clear to all involved, and, when utilised to disseminate and further a political message, was a potentially useful instrument. Such tactics in Brixton were possibly influenced by the US Civil Rights Movement, which often provoked arrests to gain publicity. A notable example of this approach, highly controversial within the Movement, was the use of children on front-line demonstrations in Birmingham, Alabama, in 1963. A lack of local volunteers forced the Southern Christian Leadership Conference to enlist local youth, and their involvement attracted much public attention and sympathy after graphic images were broadcast of the authorities' forceful response.[140]

In Brixton, participants appeared eager to exploit the influence of the media through demands for televised interviews and continued coverage. One participant succinctly summarised, 'We must reach the world Press, everybody's got to know the oppression we've been under'.[141] Additionally, the police accused local people of attempting to provoke officers and document police retaliation. The underlying tone of many such accusations implied these tactics to be foreign to British ideals of 'fair play', despite such justice being absent from the police treatment of minority ethnic groups, and suggested the influence of 'New Right' constructions of national identity and a continuation of colonial policing mindsets.[142] However, the mainstream media largely focused upon violence towards the police, depicting startling and sympathetic images of attacks on unprotected officers, while attempts to document aggressive police responses seemingly did not sway public opinion. Greg Lanning highlighted how the majority of media coverage focused on the reaction of white authorities, rather than of black Britons affected by events; for example, police officials and anti-immigration Conservative MPs received far more coverage than local residents did.[143]

One result of the spread of events through media and word-of-mouth was people travelling to Brixton to observe or participate, especially on the Saturday night. Numerous witness reports claimed those involved were not recognisable to locals so must have come in from other areas, viewing it as an opportunity of 'getting their own back' on the police for past events.[144] Whilst doubtless occurring to some extent, these were likely also attempts to reduce blame upon local people – or, alternatively, government policies, leading to widespread accusations that outside agitators had initially planned the disorders. For instance, Metropolitan Police Commissioner, Sir David McNee, was quoted on 12 April suggesting that outside troublemakers might be behind the events. He later conceded that there was no evidence to support such theories, claiming his supposition was due to being 'caught … on the wrong foot' by the media: 'Act in haste, repent at leisure'.[145] As Graham Murdock highlighted, blaming outsiders or political agitators for initial outbreaks has 'been advanced to explain almost all the disorders that have occurred in Britain since the Gordon Riots of 1780'.[146] It has been demonstrated, in US studies of responses to disorders, that such 'outside agitators' arguments are used to deflect attention away from social, economic or policing concerns.[147] It certainly furthered local levels of anger. Such suggestions, deemed 'laughable' by locals, appeared to affirm paternalistic views and removed the agency of events from those local people who had violently protested police harassment: 'As if we couldn't have put on a riot without a white outsider to show us how. It's typical.'[148]

Additionally, the antecedent of Bristol did not appear to be far from people's minds. For both participants and vocal critics, St Pauls represented an important foundation for the Brixton disturbances. For participants, it was an example to follow, and shouts of 'Remember Bristol!' rang out as Brixton crowds charged police lines.[149] Alternatively, those condemning the disorders believed they were the result of no criminal prosecutions having arisen from St Pauls, fostering beliefs that, as Bristol 'got away with it', so too could Brixton.[150] Local MP John Fraser recalled a conversation during initial disorders suggesting the situation could escalate into a 'mini Bristol'.[151] This was somewhat of an understatement, and the Brixton disturbances themselves would fuel spreading disorder across the country a few months later.

Brixton was to erupt once more on 15 July as, 'incredibly, the police staged a raid on eleven houses in the heart of the front line in Brixton's Railton Road where the hottest fighting had taken place'.[152] 176 officers, with 391 in reserve, descended upon properties ostensibly searching for unlawful drinking and petrol bombs that were never found.[153] McNee, who agreed to the action 'in the full knowledge that tension in the area was running high' and that this 'was a potential flashpoint for further disorder', nonetheless believed that not to have acted upon their information would have been 'tantamount to burying my head in the sand'.[154] These raids, resulting in five charged with possession of cannabis and one with obstruction, ignited a further night of disorder, and the Metropolitan Police subsequently paid compensation of £8,500 for damages. Such a poorly planned raid, so soon after April's disturbances and while many other areas were engaged in similar disorder, clearly highlighted a police force slow to change their practices. The Brixton Defence Campaign even claimed it was a police effort to provoke further disturbances, to bolster their demands for increased riot equipment.[155]

When Home Secretary William Whitelaw informed Parliament about the damage caused during these raids, he stated it would not be appropriate for him to comment – to which MPs loudly inquired 'Why not?' Pointing to ongoing internal investigations that he did not wish to pre-empt, it is likely Whitelaw simply did not wish to entertain discussion questioning police actions. However, when local MP John Fraser viewed the scene, he 'could come to no conclusion other than that a large number of policemen had deliberately set out to wreck the houses'.[156] It can certainly be suggested that these raids were revenge for the anti-police violence, and an attempt to reassert authority upon an area where it had been challenged three months previously; even McNee later admitted these actions 'smacked of revenge'.[157]

An internal police inquiry concluded that, while compensation would be paid to homeowners, officers involved were essentially absolved of any blame, and the DPP likewise decided to take no action regarding formal complaints.[158] Conversely, a Police Complaints Board investigation found 'serious lapses from professional standards' and an 'institutional disregard for the niceties of the law', concluding that the improprieties shown in this operation could mirror a general lack of professionalism.[159] Thus, questions were raised about why the internal inquiry and DPP had not reached similar conclusions, and what this suggested about their investigations into previous accusations against the police. Indeed, the Greater London Council Police Committee Vice-Chair warned Whitelaw that 'nothing less than a full public inquiry ... will be adequate' to dissuade 'the belief that while lawlessness by black people is met with C.S. gas and rubber bullets, lawlessness by police officers will be met with silence and evasion'.[160]

Almost exactly one year after St Pauls, and just five days after all related charges had been dropped, a warm April weekend in Brixton saw an escalation from a tense situation into the largest disorder witnessed on British streets since the Second World War. The police had identified that relations with black residents were poor, and entered into a formal Liaison Committee with representatives of the local community. While such efforts were commended, general police attitudes and policies undermined this measure and resulted in the committee disbanding. Mirroring similar situations in St Pauls and later Manchester, this undoubtedly increased discontent as representatives of the community were seen by the wider population to have attempted reconciliation with the police, only to end such efforts frustrated by a lack of collaboration. Such moderate attempts at increased political participation were rebuffed, leading some to conclude that collective violence was the only strategy that could achieve positive results. The resulting disturbances led to the establishment of the Scarman Inquiry, the independent public inquiry that had been called for after St Pauls. However, it overlooked accusations of police misconduct, and a boycott, organised by the Brixton Defence Campaign, was supported by many local people.

Notes

1 Benyon and Solomos (eds), 'British Urban Unrest', p. 3.

2 Whitelaw, *Memoirs*, p. 242.

3 *The Times*, 10 April 1980.

4 Ramdin, *Black Working Class*, p. 505.

5 Keith, *Race, Riots and Policing*.

6 Fryer, *Staying Power*, p. 398; Kettle and Hodges, *Uprising!*, p. 62.

7 McNee, *McNee's Law*, p. 126; Sivanandan, *Different Hunger*, pp. 47–8.

8 Smith and Gray, *Police in Action*, pp. 158–62.

9 Ros Howells, in Phillips and Phillips, *Windrush*, p. 339.

10 Layton-Henry, *Politics of Race*, p. 114; Phillips and Phillips, *Windrush*, p. 361; Fryer, *Staying Power*, p. 398. For New Beacon Books and related movements, see: Alleyne, *Radicals Against Race*.

11 See: Bunce and Field, *Darcus Howe*.

12 Smith, 'Policing and Urban Unrest', p. 72.

13 See: Sivanandan, *Different Hunger*, pp. 3–54.

14 Phillips and Phillips, *Windrush*, p. 356; Kettle and Hodges, *Uprising!*, pp. 62–3; Ramdin, *Black Working Class*, p. 506.

15 *BBC News*, 18 January 2011; McNee, *McNee's Law*, p. 126.

16 Scarman, *Report*, pp. 18–29, 194.

17   *Ibid.*, pp. 35–6.
18   Solomos, *Race and Racism*, p. 174; Brain, *History of Policing*, p. 76. See: Vinen, *Thatcher's Britain*, pp. 101–33.
19   Brain, *History of Policing*, p. 76.
20   Scarman, *Report*, pp. 83–4.
21   Kettle and Hodges, *Uprising!*, p. 89. See: Carter, *Shattering Illusions*, p. 104; Greaves, 'Brixton Disorders', p. 66.
22   *BBC London News*, 11 April 2011. See: Lawrence, 'The Vagrancy Act'.
23   See, for example: Solomos, *Black Youth*, p. 109; Phillips and Phillips, *Windrush*, pp. 302–3.
24   Layton-Henry, *Politics of Race*, p. 162.
25   Keith, *Race, Riots and Policing*, pp. 19–50, 199–200.
26   *BBC London News*, 11 April 2011.
27   Hunte, *Nigger-Hunting in England?*, p. 12; Keith, *Race, Riots and Policing*, p. 24.
28   Wayne Haynes, in Phillips and Phillips, *Windrush*, p. 301.
29   Peter Lawrence, in Keith, *Race, Riots and Policing*, p. 130.
30   Thomas, 'Black Initiatives in Brixton', p. 185. See: Sivanandan, *Different Hunger*, p. 37; Smith, 'Conflicting Narratives', 20.
31   The National Archives (TNA): HO 266/90, Council for Community Relations in Lambeth (CCRL), 'Constitution'; Greaves, 'Brixton Disorders', p. 64.
32   Brain, *History of Policing*, p. 65. See: Alderson, *Principled Policing*, pp. 122–33.
33   Oxford, 'Policing by Consent', pp. 114–17.
34   Gilroy, 'Myth of Black Criminality', p. 111.
35   Jones and Levi, 'Police and the Majority'; Reiner, *Politics of the Police*, p. 136.
36   TNA: HO 266/90, W.H. Gibson to John Timmey, 26 April 1979.
37   Scarman, *Report*, p. 87. See, for example: Solomos, *Black Youth*, p. 114; Hall *et al.*, *Policing the Crisis*, pp. 49–50.
38   Boateng, 'Community and Accountability', p. 157.
39   Scarman, *Report*, p. 29.
40   See: Kettle and Hodges, *Uprising!*, pp. 65–7.
41   TNA: HO 266/90, CCRL/Police Liaison Committee, Minutes of meeting held on Monday 30 October 1978.
42   Goodson, 'Police and the Public', p. 144.
43   TNA: HO 266/96, Police Submissions (P.S.) 19A.
44   TNA: HO 266/90, CCRL, Materials submitted to Scarman Inquiry.
45   Scarman, *Report*, pp. 88–9.
46   TNA: HO 266/90, 'Notes of meeting at Brixton Police Station on 21 March 1979'.
47   Crick, *March of Militant*, p. 15.
48   Sofer, *London Left*, p. 45; Seyd, *Rise and Fall*, p. 140.
49   TNA: HO 266/103, Other Submissions (O.S.) 124.
50   Greaves, 'Brixton Disorders', p. 65.
51   TNA: HO 266/90, Gerlin Bean to Ted Knight, 15 February 1979.
52   CCRL, Materials submitted to Scarman Inquiry.
53   Bean to Knight, 15 February 1979.

54 TNA: HO 266/90, Leonard Adams to George Greaves, 5 March 1979; Greaves to Adams, 8 March 1979.

55 TNA: HO 266/90, Greaves to Adams, 19 November 1979; Adams to Greaves, 22 November 1979.

56 TNA: HO 266/90, Unsigned letter, 24 July 1980.

57 TNA: HO 266/90, P.A. Lindsay to Adams, 30 July 1980; Unsigned letter, 13 August 1980.

58 TNA: HO 266/90, Unsigned to Knight, 6 December 1978.

59 TNA: HO 266/90, Police note, 23 July 1980.

60 Adams to Greaves, 22 November 1979.

61 TNA: HO 266/90, Greaves to Adams, 7 December 1979.

62 TNA: HO 266/90, Greaves to Adams, 7 February 1980.

63 TNA: HO 266/90, Adams to Greaves, 10 July 1980.

64 TNA: HO 266/90, Greaves to Adams, 17 July 1980.

65 TNA: HO 266/90, John Fraser, John Tilley, and Stuart Holland to Adams, 17 July 1980. See: Brain, *History of Policing*, pp. 55, 76; Henry, 'Police and People in London', p. 9.

66 TNA: HO 266/90, Working Party on Police and Community Relations in Lambeth.

67 Black Cultural Archives (BCA): Gutzmore/1/5/1, Scrap Sus Campaign, 'Let the police be accountable: Evidence and Recommendations to the Inquiry into Community/Police Relations in Lambeth', 4 February 1980.

68 'Notes of meeting at Brixton Police Station'.

69 Rex, 'Life in the Ghetto', p. 103. See: Institute of Race Relations, *Policing against Black People*; Fryer, *Staying Power*, pp. 393–4.

70 Bunce and Field, *Darcus Howe*, pp. 209–10.

71 HC Deb 13 April 1981 vol. 3 c. 24.

72 TNA: HO 266/96, Brian Fairbairn to Knight, 20 November 1980.

73 TNA: HO 266/96, Knight to Fairbairn, 26 November 1980.

74 TNA: HO 266/96, Knight to Fairbairn, 7 January 1981; Fairbairn to Greaves, 19 January 1981, 24 April 1981.

75 TNA: HO 266/97, P.S. 8.

76 Keith, *Race, Riots and Policing*, p. 132.

77 Granada Television, *World in Action*, 30 January 1978; Fryer, *Staying Power*, p. 398.

78 TNA: HO 266/97, P.S. 11.

79 Paul Gilroy, in Phillips and Phillips, *Windrush*, p. 358.

80 *New Statesman*, 17 April 1981.

81 TNA: HO 266/96, P.S. 5A.

82 This statement has often been incorrectly referenced as referring to Swamp 81; it was actually Adams' response to a previous SPG operation: Bunce and Field, *Darcus Howe*, p. 209.

83 Scarman, *Report*, pp. 109–10; Kettle and Hodges, *Uprising!*, pp. 94–5.

84 Scarman, *Report*, p. 46; Brain, *History of Policing*, p. 76.

85 *New Standard*, 13 April 1981.

86 BCA: Gutzmore/1/6/1, Brixton Defence Campaign Bulletin No. 1.

87 Rowe, *Policing, Race and Racism*, pp. 82–3.

88 TNA: HO 266/103, O.S. 258; TNA: HO 266/96, P.S. 12.

89 Bunce and Field, *Darcus Howe*, pp. 211–12.

90 Benyon, 'Policing Issues', p. 24; Scarman, *Report*, pp. 95–6; Bowling and Phillips, *Racism, Crime and Justice*, pp. 139–40.

91 Benyon, 'Policing Issues', p. 101.

92 TNA: HO 266/103, O.S. 77.

93 TNA: HO 266/99, P.S. 360; P.S. 358; TNA: HO 266/96, P.S. 43.

94 TNA: HO 266/96, P.S. 1; Scarman, *Report*, p. 96.

95 See: chapter 2.

96 Brain, *History of Policing*, p. 66. See: Waddington *et al.*, *Flashpoints*.

97 TNA: HO 266/97, P.S. 13.

98 TNA: HO 266/103, O.S. 161; O.S. 136; TNA: HO 266/98, O.S. 854.

99 TNA: HO 266/98, O.S. 17.

100 TNA: HO 266/98, O.S. 18; O.S. 31.

101 Scarman, *Report*, p. 40; TNA: HO 266/73, Police Tape Transcripts, 10 April 1981.

102 Police Tape Transcripts, 10 April 1981; P.S. 12.

103 TNA: HO 266/98, P.S. 29.

104 P.S. 12; TNA: HO 266/98, P.S. 85(1). The belief that no ambulance was called can still be observed in recent recollections: Alex Wheatle, 3 October 2009, www.storyvault.com/video/view/brixton_riots_1981 (last accessed: 6 October 2016).

105 TNA: HO 266/98, P.S. 223(2); P.S. 85(1).

106 P.S. 12; TNA: HO 266/98, O.S. 852.

107 Scarman, *Report*, p. 46.

108 Brain, *History of Policing*, p. 66.

109 Scarman, *Report*, pp. 43–4; P.S. 11.

110 P.S. 1; P.S. 8; Scarman, *Report*, p. 44.

111 TNA: HO 266/104, O.S. 167. See: Keith, 'No-Go Areas'.

112 Scarman, *Report*, p. 46; Bunce and Field, *Darcus Howe*, p. 212.

113 Boateng, 'Community and Accountability', p. 158.

114 TNA: HO 266/97, P.S. 15; O.S. 136; TNA: HO 266/103, O.S. 97; TNA: HO 266/104, O.S. 28; TNA: HO 266/100, C 33.

115 TNA: HO 266/103; O.S. 97B.

116 O.S. 136.

117 TNA: HO 266/104, O.S. 96A; TNA: HO 266/103, O.S. 124.

118 O.S. 96A.

119 O.S. 28.

120 TNA: HO 266/99, P.S 432; TNA: HO 266/100, A 306.

121 *Daily Mirror*, 13 April 1981; TNA: HO 266/103, O.S. 46; O.S. 237; O.S. 178.

122 O.S. 178; O.S. 46; TNA: HO 266/103, O.S. 46A; TNA: HO 266/104, O.S. 147.

123 O.S. 147.

124 O.S. 167.

125 Scarman, *Report*, p. 46.

126 *Ibid.*, p. 13.

127 Phillips and Phillips, *Windrush*, p. 360.

128 BCA: Gutzmore/1/6/1, Brixton Defence Campaign Bulletin No. 3.

129 Scarman, *Report*, p. 67.

130 TNA: HO 266/103, O.S. 40.

131 Bunce and Field, *Darcus Howe*, pp. 211–12.

132 Greaves, 'Brixton Disorders', p. 68.

133 Phillips and Phillips, *Windrush*, p. 360.

134 Greaves, 'Brixton Disorders', p. 67.

135 *Time*, 20 April 1981; Scarman, *Report*, p. 65.

136 Scarman, *Report*, p. 65.

137 Brain, *History of Policing*, p. 68; Benyon and Solomos (eds), 'British Urban Unrest', p. 3. See: Murdock, 'Reporting the Riots'.

138 TNA: HO 266/98, P.S. 6; TNA: HO 266/100, O.S. 122.

139 TNA: HO 266/96, P.S. 18.

140 See: McWhorter, *Carry Me Home*; Eskew, *But for Birmingham*, pp. 259–98.

141 Clare, 'Eyewitness in Brixton', p. 49; O.S. 96A.

142 See: Rowe, *Racialisation of Disorder*, pp. 156–7; Mitchell and Russell, 'Race, the New Right and State Policy'.

143 Lanning, 'The Brixton Tapes', 183.

144 TNA: HO 266/100, C 250; TNA: HO 266/99, P.S. 104; TNA: HO 266/103, O.S. 186.

145 McNee, *McNee's Law*, p. 115.

146 Murdock, 'Reporting the Riots', p. 84.

147 Edelman, *Politics as Symbolic Action*, and Lipsky and Olson, *Commission Politics*, cited in Solomos, *Race and Racism*, p. 167.

148 *The Leveller*, 1–14 May, p. 10; *New Statesman*, 17 April 1981. See: Schwarz, *Memories of Empire*.

149 TNA: HO 266/101, A 599; A 526.

150 TNA: HO 266/138, Unsigned to Scarman, 25 April 1981.

151 O.S. 97.

152 Phillips and Phillips, *Windrush*, p. 365.

153 Benyon and Solomos (eds), 'British Urban Unrest', p. 4; Keith, *Race, Riots and Policing*, pp. 131–2.

154 McNee, *McNee's Law*, p. 120.

155 BCA: Gutzmore/1/6/1, Brixton Defence Campaign Bulletin No. 2. See: chapter 6.

156 HC Deb 16 July 1981, vol. 8, cc. 1398, 1425.

157 McNee, *McNee's Law*, p. 120.

158 HL Deb 29 October 1981 vol. 424 cc. 1127–32.

159 Cited in Benyon and Solomos (eds), 'British Urban Unrest', pp. 4–5.

160 BCA: McKenley/3/1, Steven Bundred to William Whitelaw, 21 July 1981.

5

'The Brixton Defence Campaign says
boycott the Scarman Inquiry'

Now in the streets there is violence,
And lots of work to be done.

Eddy Grant – Electric Avenue

ON 12 April 1981, Home Secretary William Whitelaw and Metropolitan Police Commissioner Sir David McNee visited Brixton to assess the situation following the ferocity of 'Bloody Saturday' anti-police disorders the previous night. Described as 'tense and shaken', Whitelaw reportedly remarked 'how completely and utterly senseless this is', later likening scenes to the London Blitz.[1] This reaction was perhaps not surprising upon witnessing what was, at that point, the most significant outbreak of twentieth-century civil disorder in Britain. However, the fact that Whitelaw could not make sense of the disturbances seems itself partly illustrative as to why they occurred: the very highest levels of British government simply could not perceive the levels of discontent leading to such action.

The reception greeting this establishment delegation was predictably unfavourable. Crowds shouted abuse, chanted 'Sieg Heil Fascist Pigs' with clenched fist salutes, and some threw missiles. Whitelaw himself later acknowledged their presence increased tensions, but 'it was essential that we were there personally'.[2] Clearly indicating the crowd's mood, one protestor loudly questioned 'Why haven't you been here before?'[3] For people who had grown frustrated with the British state's inability or unwillingness to address their situation, it appeared that collective violence had made authorities pay attention – quite literally overnight. Thus, participants stated they would continue such actions: 'This will go on until they listen to us.'[4] As Alex Wheatle summarised in a 2011 interview: 'For the first time, we were actually taken notice of by the wider world.'[5] The world certainly took notice; the scale of Brixton, magnified by media coverage, provoked a particularly strong response. For most people, this was largely of shock, with Lord Scarman summarising in his subsequent public inquiry that 'the British people watched with horror and incredulity'.[6] This was not, however, a universal reaction.

This chapter addresses various responses to the Brixton disturbances; like Bristol the previous year, the authorities and media focused upon the criminality and law and order aspects, leading to repeated calls for the police to be further equipped to respond to such disorder. Yet, unlike St Pauls, due to the scale of events and proximity to Westminster, Whitelaw established a public inquiry. Hence, this chapter discusses Scarman's inquiry through in-depth examination of recently released inquiry records, such as police radio messages and witness statements, and papers of grassroots political organisations, to explore numerous accusations of police misconduct not included in his Report, addressing some of the gaps between submitted evidence and what was published as official record. Scarman chose not to examine such accusations, suggesting his inquiry could not provide necessary safeguards and that allegations should be directed through the police complaints system. However, this system had lost the faith of marginalised groups, who believed it was ineffective; indeed, minority ethnic complainants were less likely to have accusations substantiated than white counterparts.[7] Therefore, for those people believing a government-endorsed public inquiry would expose and investigate police racism, it appeared yet a further denial of full participation in the British political process. Conversely, many local groups, such as the Brixton Defence Campaign established to support those arrested in relation to the disorder, vociferously boycotted the inquiry as they believed it would be a 'whitewash' and that any evidence provided would actually be used against black defendants.

Scarman concluded that the Brixton disorders originated spontaneously as 'an outburst of anger and resentment' against police action, quickly becoming a 'riot', the purpose of which was to attack the police.[8] This was the recollection of participant Alex Wheatle, who later argued that local black youth had reached a point of despair, 'and when you have got no hope you're just going to react and you're not going to care about the consequences'.[9] Thus, while senior police officials later commended officers for their bravery against 'sustained and sickening violence', exclamations from the crowds such as 'That's one to us!' following police injury clearly illustrate that participants viewed events as attempted retribution for previous police action.[10]

Similar to testimonies following the 1980 St Pauls disorder, witness statements support suggestions that violence was specifically targeted towards the police.

For example, one youth throwing a missile at an ambulance was chastised and reminded to focus attacks on the police, and a freelance photographer recounted how youths were instructed to 'Leave him alone, he's not a pig'.[11] Such actions exhibit traits of what S.D. Reicher expressed in his study of St Pauls. His social identity model suggests individuals are able to act as one in crowd events due to sharing a common social identity: in this case, Brixton residents attempting to 'defend' their community against perceived police 'attack'.[12] This is encapsulated by local Reverend Robert Nind who, after speaking with participants, summarised: 'There was plainly at work a common mind to stake out a territory and prevent the police from invading it.'[13]

Obviously, this was not the reaction of the entire Brixton population, or the proportion involved would have been much higher – but it was for those believing no other recourse was available to protest the racism and disadvantage faced by black Britons: 'When we pleaded and screamed and cried that police were abusing us in police cells no one listened.'[14] Despite low participation figures, the *Guardian* claimed that the reaction of the local black community was 'four square behind the youths'.[15] However, some black residents, particularly older generations, expressed 'shame and embarrassment' regarding the actions of the youth, fearing the repercussions it would generate – even allegedly suggesting the army should 'clear them away with tear gas'.[16] A generational divide was evident on numerous occasions. For example, older generations were angrily condemned by younger counterparts for talking to police and, while some individuals categorised as 'community leaders' did appear to have certain levels of influence, there were multiple reports of older black males unable to stop the assembled youths. Younger black Britons, who had grown up witnessing and experiencing largely unchallenged discrimination, especially within education, employment and from the police, were more willing to combat unequal treatment. As Ambalavaner Sivanandan noted: 'The time was long gone when black people, with an eye to returning home, would put up with repression: they were settlers now. And state racism had pushed them into higher and more militant forms of resistance.'[17]

The 'law and order' response

The immediate political response was steadfastly to condemn violence and reaffirm total support for the police, who were widely praised for displaying 'great bravery' in the face of 'such criminality'. Prime Minister Margaret Thatcher proclaimed 'nothing, but nothing, justifies what happened', and Whitelaw echoed, 'Whatever grievances individuals or communities feel they suffer, such violence … cannot and will not be condoned'. Conservative MP David Mellor furthered this by declaring it 'grossly wrong and unfair to talk about social protest', when the disturbances should be viewed as 'sheer criminality'.[18] This was consistent with a Government favouring the conservative portrayal of the disorder as a rejection of law and order, rather than a liberal or radical reading of events that viewed the disturbances as attempts to address 'basic flaws' within society.[19]

While Whitelaw conceded that many participants were British-born, he also argued that others 'came here between 1957 and 1962, and all of us who were in the House at that time bear a similar share of the responsibility'.[20] Staunchly retaining long-standing attitudes that racial harmony could best be achieved through stricter controls, this reaction clearly portrayed immigration, and thus migrants themselves, as the cause of disorder.[21] Michael Rowe highlighted how, combined with denials of Britain's history of similar unrest, such arguments demonstrate the broader Conservative perspective: 'disorder is not a result of ineffective social policies and economic distribution, but is instead explicable by the personal characteristics of the participants, the desire for excitement, or greed for loot'.[22]

A focus on law and order and criminality, especially largely unconnected looting, threatened to suppress the discontent at the heart of initial disorder. Many commentators have noted that looting was generally conducted by persons not involved in anti-police disturbances, and often by white people arriving after the Saturday evening television news. Michael Keith analysed arrest statistics for Brixton, concluding there were two disturbances: first, a localised confrontation with the police involving locals, and second, the looting and criminality some distance from the first.[23] A similar basic pattern can be observed in comparable disturbances occurring during the period. Reflecting upon the 'waves of violence' that had swept through Europe the previous year, notably in Zurich and Berlin, Ralf Dahrendorf illuminated many similarities between them and Brixton. These included specific incidents having turned into broader conflict between youths and police, and that 'Demonstrations which turned violent provide a cover for looting, though quite often stealing goods is not the primary purpose of most'.[24] While the primary purpose of the Brixton disturbances has been contested, authorities certainly concentrated the response upon law and order rather than complaints of black Britons, as with other disorders in 1980–81.

This focus was strengthened by comparisons between Brixton and warfare. Further to Whitelaw's Blitz allusions, numerous police and public witnesses described the disorder as reminiscent of a battlefield, comparable with the Northern Ireland 'Troubles', and 'like a war'.[25] Even Scarman's official Report repeatedly likened Brixton to warfare.[26] It is not difficult to see why such kept appearing, not least that many locals had already described being 'under siege' by the police: add street disorder to feelings of occupation, and warfare comparisons appear increasingly apt. Thus, a large focus of the response was on how to improve the police's reaction to future disorders. Police radio transcripts recorded that at points police possessed neither the equipment nor numbers to go on the offensive against large crowds, and many witness statements commented on a need to strengthen police equipment and training.[27]

John Clare, a BBC reporter present in Brixton, concluded such warfare comparisons led to the supremacy of the 'wrong' lessons: that the police needed to be given enhanced weaponry and that black people were 'an alien, potentially revolutionary wedge'. Clare further criticised Scarman for helping proliferate such views:

> Horror and incredulity might well have been the feelings of a policeman cowering behind his riot shield as he watched the bricks and petrol bombs rain down upon him … However, that is not the vantage point from which the Report is supposedly written … far from stepping back from what happened and judging it coolly, [Scarman] has propelled himself into the very thick of it and been overcome by the smoke.[28]

John Benyon also claimed many commentators tended to exaggerate the scale of disorder, for 'sometimes nefarious' reasons. Emphasising that the disturbances included less than 1 per cent of the Brixton population, he stated 'This is not to seek to minimise the significance of the disorders, rather to place them in perspective'.[29] Despite the relatively small numbers involved, the Brixton disorders disseminated beliefs that the police desperately needed advancements in training and equipment; the impact of this is discussed in chapter 6.

Scarman Inquiry

Similar to his response following St Pauls, Whitelaw vociferously supported the police after the Brixton disturbances; unlike St Pauls, he also announced the establishment of a public inquiry headed by Lord Leslie Scarman. The scale, severity and even location of Brixton ensured such an inquiry was necessary – a meeting between Thatcher and senior ministers agreed 'there would have to be an inquiry' – although its very existence was simultaneously criticised as appearing to legitimise violence.[30] A widely respected judge, Scarman himself recorded his 'considerable experience of the administrative and organisational problems of enquiries of this sort', having previously resided over inquiries into Northern Ireland disturbances of August 1969 and the 1974 Red Lion Square disorders.[31] Whitelaw later recorded that Scarman's Northern Irish experience was influential in his appointment, as he had familiarity with 'similar circumstances'.[32] Despite appearing to be an obvious choice, he was not universally supported. A prevalent opinion existed that, in the Red Lion Square inquiry, Scarman had wrongly absolved the police of responsibility for the death of Kevin Gately, also backing the controversial SPG.[33] The same judge examining multiple police-related events encouraged beliefs that this inquiry would produce no different outcome than previous investigations: as the Brixton Defence Campaign stated, 'Scarman has a history which we can't afford to ignore'.[34]

Conversely, Conservatives and right-wing commentators believed Scarman was too left-wing, notably demonstrated by disagreement with his 1977 inquiry into the Grunwick dispute, a two-year strike by a small number of Asian women regarding union recognition at a small North London film processing plant, which garnered widespread support. Scarman had recommended both union recognition and the reinstatement of workers dismissed for supporting strike action, but this was rejected by the Conservative Party and right-wing groups. The eventual resolution, ending in defeat for the strikers, has been viewed as a major political and ideological victory for the Conservatives, paving the way for their 1979 election success and subsequent curbing of union power throughout the 1980s.[35] Scarman was thus criticised from both sides, being simultaneously too left-wing and not radical enough.

Rather than falling under the Tribunals and Inquiries (Evidence) Act 1921, which had established more wide-ranging public inquiries, Scarman was appointed to hold a 'local inquiry' into policing in Brixton under Section 32 of the Police Act 1964. By design, it would have an increased focus on policing rather than broader social, political, and economic issues.[36] As Timothy Brain concluded, it 'certainly suited the Conservative government, already under fire for rising unemployment and cuts in unemployment benefit, to have the main focus on the police'.[37] McNee shared this view, suggesting that, during the first turbulent years of Thatcherite policies, it was an effort to protect the Government at the expense of the police – a view perhaps unsurprising from the head of that organisation:

I was, to say the least, unhappy ... Some faults certainly lay at our door but there were faults elsewhere too ... An inquiry covering [policy] matters could lead to an embarrassing outcome at a time when the Government's fortunes were low. Was it for these reasons that the police were put into the dock?[38]

Establishing the inquiry under the Police Act was similarly criticised by Labour Shadow Home Secretary Roy Hattersley, and a joint statement on behalf of local community groups the Brixton Neighbourhood Community Organisation, Melting Pot Foundation and Brixton Domino Working Men's Social Club claimed a wider-ranging inquiry, including 'one or more ... Privy Councillors from the Black Commonwealth', would have 'allayed the scepticism of many members of the Black Community'.[39] Scarman countered that his inquiry would 'undoubtedly' examine underlying causes of disorder, as Section 32 was very wide in any matter connected with policing of the area.[40] McNee nonetheless labelled such arguments 'moonshine', believing 'the police were to be the political scapegoats', and Scarman himself later acknowledged that his inquiry required further research to have placed it within its broader social setting.[41]

A meeting between Thatcher and senior ministers concluded it would be ideal for the inquiry to be conducted in private – clearly demonstrating the desire to keep it out of the political mainstream and avoid public scrutiny. Whitelaw suggested Scarman might disagree – and, indeed, he did. The following day, Scarman declared that virtually all of the inquiry would be held in public, as he 'deprecate[d] enquiries of this sort in private'.[42] It is unclear whether Scarman conversed with Whitelaw prior to making this announcement; if not, it is possible this created animosity, potentially affecting the Government's view of his Report.

Nevertheless, after years spent demanding governmental action to address the concerns of politically marginalised black Britons, a public inquiry eventually materialised. Arthur Palmer, Labour MP for Bristol North-East, reminded Whitelaw that he and others had appealed for a similar inquiry after St Pauls, but Whitelaw refused to admit that Brixton showed it had been 'a mistake' not to hold one, arguing it 'was far wider and of far more depth than was the case in Bristol'.[43] Rather than admit potential links, Whitelaw appeared to claim Brixton was such a different situation that no good would have come from an earlier inquiry. Richard Davis, representing the Bristol West Indian Parents and Friends Association, countered that a Bristol public inquiry would have meant 'we probably would not have seen the present succession of disturbances throughout the country'.[44] While impossible to say, it has been demonstrated how refusals for inquiry demands in St Pauls undoubtedly added to discontentment.

'The danger of Scarman'

Brian Jacobs concluded that, while some militant black organisations refused to provide evidence to Scarman's inquiry, most 'seem to have believed that Scarman provided them with an opportunity to express their concern'.[45] However, support was far from universal – reflecting the dichotomous attitude towards governmental inquiries.

One prominent critic was the Brixton Defence Campaign, 'an organisation of black (African and Asian) groups and individuals' formed to mobilise 'the black community to be fully involved in the legal and political defence of those arrested/charged/injured as a result of the Uprising'.[46] It was established following three previous failed attempts to form a Defence Committee by, in the Campaign's words, 'so called leaders' who 'had no credibility and nothing to say'.[47] Indeed, the *Leveller* had highlighted how no cohesive response formed in the disorder's immediate aftermath, observing that unabated anger 'remains unchannelled, and suspicions and recriminations are dividing the black community'.[48] The Defence Campaign organised public meetings – from which the distrusted press 'MUST BE KEPT OUT' – and discussions with other organisations, hoping to coordinate a collective and sustained response 'with other black communities – of both Asian and African descent'. Despite this stated aim, the Brixton Black Women's Group recalled hostility towards them from the Defence Campaign, and experiencing a 'fight to be heard'.[49] Nevertheless, this union of minority ethnic groups demonstrated how, in this period, 'Black was not simply a skin colour, but a political position'.[50] Seeking to involve Brixton youth that had taken to the streets, this group's militancy was highlighted by repeated assertions that members must be representatives of black organisations and black individuals only; even black people representing 'white organisations' were banned.[51] Jeff Rodrigues, writing in *Marxism Today*, alleged that this was due to white left-wing activists attending public meetings, calling for the defeat of the Conservative Government 'rather than listen[ing] to the views and ideas of the black people'.[52]

The Defence Campaign accused Scarman of being a means for the Government to strengthen 'riot' legislation – ultimately occurring as the Public Order Act 1986 – through giving 'subtle legitimacy to the totally racist view ...

that the Brixton Uprising was simply a confrontation between, on the one hand, fundamentally blameless forces of law and order, and, on the other, mainly black criminals!'[53] Minutes of a Defence Campaign meeting record that it boycotted Scarman because 'supporting the inquiry is likely to alienate sections of the community we are interested in mobilising', and thus it 'must be totally discredited and the community mobilised against it'.[54] Therefore, on posters distributed through Brixton, the Defence Campaign warned residents that providing evidence to Scarman 'represents a clear and present danger to defendants yet to stand trial', as there was no guarantee of immunity for witnesses or those incriminated by others' evidence. The inquiry was thus deemed 'a grave danger to the black community' and 'a deadly weapon aimed at our hearts'.[55]

The Defence Campaign organised protests against Scarman, advising picketers how to avoid being arrested for obstruction, and preparing posters and suggesting spray-paint to convey their message.[56] Moreover, it wrote to organisations and individuals believed to be intending to provide evidence to Scarman, warning against doing so.[57] Some of the Defence Campaign's fiercest criticism was directed at black people and organisations who attempted co-operation with the authorities: a clear sign of the divisions between those believing collaboration would be of benefit and those considering such mechanisms to be a fraudulent diversionary tactic. It accused 'betrayers of the people who call themselves "leaders" … [of] persistently working against the interests of the Black community' by supporting Scarman: 'a carrot dangled before our eyes upon which far too many have said that they intend to bite'.[58] For example, the Brixton Neighbourhood Community Organisation, Melting Pot Foundation and Brixton Domino Working Men's Social Club released a joint statement declaring their intent to provide evidence to Scarman, and urging others to do similar. It argued that, despite legitimate concerns, 'this Inquiry presents an opportunity to the Black Community to draw to the attention of the world their sufferings'.[59] The Defence Campaign bluntly responded: 'They are HANGING the community by their actions.'[60] Highlighting these 'enemies inside the community', and claiming their previous attempts at liaison with the police showed them to be 'traitors and informers, who represent nobody in the community but themselves', the Defence Campaign concluded 'we must not be afraid to expose and isolate them'.[61] The Defence Campaign was similarly to disown active lawyer Rudy Narayan who, having even initially led the Brixton defence, was denounced one year later for his 'craven opportunism in support of the Metropolitan Police as they carry on their campaign to criminalise the black community' whilst standing for election as the Labour Party candidate in Handsworth, Birmingham.[62] Certainly, divisions within the black population were demonstrated through criticism of 'sell-outs' who had abandoned the 'black masses' to further their own careers.[63]

The Brixton People's Inquiry

Despite boycotting Scarman's inquiry, the Defence Campaign did criticise the rejections of 'repeated requests' for a public inquiry 'into police brutality and malpractice' over the previous five years. Condemning the state for overlooking previous evidence such as the Lambeth Council inquiry into police/community relations, which described police operations in Brixton as an 'Army of Occupation', the Defence Campaign concluded 'the state has no basis for even claiming to be ignorant'.[64] Indeed, it believed this Report was more valuable than anything Scarman could produce because 'Black people in the Borough were actively involved in collecting and giving evidence'.[65]

Nevertheless, as it argued Scarman 'does not have the confidence of local people', the Defence Campaign sought to establish its own inquiry, financed by local organisations, trade unions and the Labour Party, claiming that 1,700 individuals were prepared to give evidence to this 'local peoples' enquiry'.[66] It was hoped it would 'capture support of the black community by including as wide a section of the community as possible', presenting demands for 'ways in which our situation can be improved'. While noted that an independent inquiry taking place after Scarman would likely be ineffective, it 'need not be rushed' as it was not being forwarded in competition to Scarman.[67] Prominent activists such as Darcus Howe, Paul Boateng and Linton Kwesi Johnson were suggested for membership of the inquiry, which would produce a report and recommendations; however, such inquiries were never completed.

Police action during disorders

Recently released police radio messages sent during the disturbances and statements taken subsequently reveal police actions and misconduct absent from Scarman's published inquiry report, highlighting a continued lack of access for black Britons as his account of events was based almost exclusively on police reports.[68] Police messages, statements and interviews suggest officers' attitudes, although it must be noted that many were submitted *after* Scarman's inquiry was announced. Nonetheless, some officers were more careful about potentially incriminating or inflammatory remarks than others: for example, one particularly memorable police statement complained about 'a fat ugly white woman' taking photographs during disorders.[69]

Confusion and retaliation

It is immediately apparent from police radio messages the great deal of confusion amongst officers and often no real knowledge of who, if anyone, was in charge. Even during Whitelaw's visit, an event surely demanding increased security, officers complained of not being briefed or aware of overall policy. Scarman himself described accounts of police activities as appearing 'awfully haphazard'.[70] Police communications also reveal confusion inherent in deploying officers to an unfamiliar area, such as one officer complaining of being 'a stranger here'.[71] This phrasing highlights the deeper issue of how a police lack of familiarity with the area, and with the local population themselves, escalated issues both before and during disorders. The lack of specific instruction or general strategy, combined with fear of serious injury, undoubtedly led some officers to undertake unsanctioned actions. Civilian accounts record officers telling observers that senior police did not know what they were doing, even ignoring their orders.[72] Police injuries likely led to attempts for vengeance, particularly from younger officers. It appears that the numerous accusations of police misconduct emerged partly because officers were confused, fearful and growing frustrated at a lack of coherent instruction from superiors. However, one observer claimed that, as fresh officers arrived on the scene, they were immediately shown injured officers before being ordered to clear the streets – demonstrating a police attitude for vengeance.[73]

One recurring criticism was of officers throwing bricks and bottles back at the crowd, having an antagonistic effect. While police defended these actions as necessary to 'keep [rioters] at a distance', Scarman deemed allegations of police using unlawful weapons 'particularly worrying'.[74] However, no individual officer subsequently received any form of punishment. Contrasting with the authorities' focus on criminality and law and order, it appeared the police were not being held accountable for their own riotous actions. Such incendiary tactics were ultimately unsuccessful as, rather than intimidating crowds, onlookers observed they appeared to provoke a response.

Another criticism regarded use of fire hoses, described by Brain as an improvised copying of tactics officially used only in Northern Ireland and Europe.[75] Chief Superintendent John Robinson believed 'extraordinary measures' were required to prevent firefighters from retreating and leaving fires raging; commandeering a hose, he ordered other officers to do the same and water was directed at the crowd. Upon being told by a senior fire officer that hoses should not be used for crowd control, Robinson countered that it was necessary to prevent police and firefighters being overrun.[76] A *Time Out* article relayed a conversation between their reporter and a firefighter, who maintained 'It doesn't matter what happens we can't turn the hoses on people. That makes us enemies as well'.[77] Despite Scarman characterising Robinson's tactics as a unique reaction to a particularly calamitous situation, police statements reveal that hoses were used more often and for much longer than suggested in his Report. Multiple uses of hoses against the crowd are recorded, and, contradicting the three minutes stated by a senior officer, one officer claimed he used a hose against the crowd for half an hour, only stopping when his arm grew tired.[78] Nonetheless, Scarman did not reach any judgements on such methods or criticise Robinson's actions, and McNee even singled Robinson out for praise as a 'brave and outstanding police officer' who 'prevented disaster' through his actions.[79]

A further controversial police tactic, 'widely known' to be antagonistic, was the use of dogs for crowd control.[80] Teresa Nind, wife of local Reverend Robert Nind, recorded that her warning that using dogs would further damage police/community relations was greeted by an officer with the response: 'I don't care about race relations. Fucking old bitch, piss off.'[81] Scarman's Report suggested that dogs had only been at the scene because dog handlers had simply responded to general calls for urgent assistance. As such, no disciplinary action followed and he simply recommended the introduction of arrangements to prevent such confusion.[82] However, police transcripts of radio messages clearly record that, a short time after disorder began on Saturday, a specific request was made for 'more assistance and in particular dog units'.[83] Moreover, one eyewitness claimed to have seen police dog handlers removing their epaulettes to prevent identification, demonstrating police awareness of the contentious presence of dog units.[84] Clearly, it was believed at the time that dogs could effectively control increasingly hostile crowds, regardless of later attempts to claim otherwise. As with other contentious activities, Scarman's Report supported the police and overlooked potential misconduct.

No police withdrawal

Various suggestions were made that a police withdrawal may have decreased tensions, such as ITN reporter Michael Oliver describing visible police cordons 'as a red rag to a bull to all the young people'.[85] Whether being shouted, amplified by megaphone, or relayed by those claiming to represent the crowd, a constantly communicated message was that participants wanted the police out of the area, and that this would quell disorder. On 'Bloody Saturday', local councillors John Boyle and Stewart Lansley, black community worker Tony Morgan, and journalist John Clare all passed behind the barricades to discuss grievances and objectives with participants. They all subsequently considered that, if the police had made even a limited withdrawal, tensions would have decreased and disorder reduced; for instance, Clare recorded that participants clearly specified the principal desire for police to leave Brixton.[86] The police, however, refused to see their authority undermined as it had been through withdrawal in St Pauls. Thus, one civilian observer succinctly described the scene: 'The trouble seemed to continue merely because there was something to fight against.'[87]

There were some isolated police attempts to withdraw. After initial outbursts, police radio messages record controllers advising officers to abandon attempted arrests and withdraw if numbers surrounding them were too high.[88] In addition, senior officers at the scene did withdraw some police, viewed and praised by some commentators as an attempt to calm the situation.[89] Similarly, plainclothed officers, a small number of uniformed officers, and all conspicuously marked police vehicles were removed, apparently in attempts to calm the situation as their presence was stimulating anger.[90] Alternatively, police radio messages suggest such withdrawals were actually in response to decreasing levels of disorder, rather than attempts to diffuse tensions. For example, the optimistic message of 'I'm thinking of withdrawing units, because it's got relatively calm' was greeted with 'I think we're beating it then'.[91]

Despite consistently being advised that a withdrawal would likely decrease tensions, senior officials adamantly opposed mass police withdrawal, believing the situation would deteriorate as it 'would give [rioters] the impression they've got a victory'.[92] Further to characterising the disturbance as mindless criminality rather than targeted action against the police, the view that police must not facilitate criminal actions was countered by accusations that they ignored the vast majority of looting. While ninety-two burglary and robbery crimes were reported on 11 April, only twelve related arrests were made.[93] As Councillor Lansley concluded, 'the police apparently chose to ignore this in order to concentrate their numbers in an area of relative calm'.[94] Prioritising battling the crowds, seemingly worsened by their mere presence, the police were determined not to allow their authority to be questioned. Again, Scarman backed police actions and rejected criticism they had ignored looting, believing this illustrated limited police resources.[95]

Thus, senior police ordered 'do not consider withdrawing', and deployed officers were only permitted to vacate an area if immediately replaced – despite it being unclear how many police were deployed or where they actually were.[96] When advised to withdraw by community workers, Brixton Police Commander Brian Fairbairn steadfastly refused. He argued that his primary duty was to clear the streets, that he refused to accept 'no-go' areas, and it was his decision alone what to do.[97] Refusal to remove officers was undoubtedly influenced by the withdrawal – and resultant criticism – at St Pauls the previous year. Reverend Nind recorded that Fairbairn openly told him as much: 'We will not do what they did in Bristol. We are not going to withdraw at all.'[98] As Mike Phillips described, Bristol police had been viewed as 'ninnies for their withdrawal, inefficient for their failure to bring in reinforcements, and undermined by their concern about community relations. The Met wouldn't let it happen'.[99] This steadfast refusal to see their authority undermined was demonstrated succinctly by a police spokesperson: 'The only people who control the streets of London are the Met.'[100] Despite arguments that a police withdrawal had actually limited the extent of St Pauls by removing the focus of the crowd's attack – 'winning by appearing to lose', a traditional police tactic for handling public disorder – police in Brixton firmly placed combatting the crowd ahead of tactical withdrawals. As Peter Squires and Peter Kennison later concluded, this altered approach of 'aggressive and confrontational policing may well be losing, even as it appears to win'.[101]

Notwithstanding its negative effect upon community relations, Fairbairn's determination to face the crowds was praised by both sides of the House. Home Secretary William Whitelaw and Shadow Home Secretary Roy Hattersley claimed recommendations for police to withdraw and abandon law-abiding residents were 'wholly misplaced', and Fairbairn was 'entirely and absolutely right' to reject these suggestions.[102] These responses are not surprising from two authority figures with potentially a lot to lose politically through criticising strong police action. Whitelaw, seen as the 'acceptable face' of Thatcherism who disagreed with some of her policies, needed to remain free from Thatcher's wrath as she attempted to remove 'wets' – those who opposed hard-line policies – from her Government. Similarly, Hattersley represented the moderate side of the Labour Party and, contrasting with Michael Meacher's left-wing radicalism, would later beat him to deputy leader in 1983.[103]

Scarman also supported Fairbairn's refusal to withdraw as he disagreed such action would lessen the fury of the crowd, labelling such arguments as misdirected.[104] Therefore, there was wide authority support for the police decision not to withdraw, despite indications it would likely have lessened tensions and ample evidence suggesting that the police presence sparked disturbances in the first place. As well as seeming to misinterpret the nature of disorder, deliberately or otherwise, this apparent snub of their expressed wishes further increased local people's anger.

Accusations of police misconduct

In addition to occasions where Scarman appeared to support the police's version of events, he also sidestepped addressing direct accusations of police wrongdoing. Charles Tilly has discussed the contested boundaries in distinction between actions by authorities viewed as legitimate 'force' and illegitimate 'violence'.[105] Upon reading the witness statements and submissions to the Scarman Inquiry, it is hard not to be struck by the sheer number of complaints of police misconduct, over-reaction or brutality not appearing in the published Report. As one witness, providing evidence to Scarman, concluded: 'I have been so shocked by what I have seen the police do I do not feel now that I would turn to the police if I was in trouble.'[106] Similar to other official investigations, Scarman maintained his inquiry was not the appropriate place to investigate such accusations; instead, he generally rejected criticism suggesting the police over-reacted in their handling of the disturbances. He suggested the courts or police disciplinary proceedings were the correct avenues for allegations, regardless of growing sentiment and supporting evidence these were inadequate systems and discriminated against black complainants. Despite the level of criticism against police handling of the disorder, only nineteen official complaints were made, highlighting belief that the complaints system was a waste of time.[107] For some black Britons, it was hoped that a public inquiry would provide adequate investigations into specific accusations of police misconduct, but even Scarman himself would later acknowledge that his Report was widely criticised for not doing so.[108]

When all accusations of police impropriety are combined, quite a different situation emerges than the version generally suggested by Scarman's Report, demonstrating how narratives rely upon authorities' accounts. It must not be forgotten that some accusations were undoubtedly fuelled by motives other than attempts to chronicle factual events, and, as Benyon highlighted, an observer only sees a portion of what occurs and that view itself is in the midst of riotous confusion.[109] Nonetheless, the high volume of accusations are surely worthy of consideration, reflecting growing discontent.

The most common accusation of police misconduct during the Brixton disturbances was discriminatorily targeting attacks on black Britons. Numerous accounts were submitted of police approaching large groups and choosing to search or attack only the black residents; for example, one instance saw officers pushing five white people aside to get to a black man, whom they set dogs upon, kicked and hit with batons. Another resident observed three officers who 'aggressively searched' a black man, whilst politely asking a nearby white man to return home. When an officer was witnessed holding a dustbin lid and large stick, shouting 'Come on then, you black bastards, let's have you!', one witness expressed: 'This did not seem to me to be the correct way for a policeman to behave.'[110] There are numerous accusations of people being called 'black bastards' or 'black shit', police telling black residents 'your lot' caused the disorders, and one particularly descriptive account of a senior police officer shouting at a black prisoner in a mock accent, 'something like a bad actor from the Black and White Minstrel show'.[111]

Furthermore, numerous accounts of unwarranted police violence appeared, generally but not exclusively directed against black Britons. Accusations of police attacking and kicking seemingly innocent people are frequent, one describing how two youths 'did not resist arrest, mainly because they had been beaten incapable'.[112] Another observer recalled the crowd warning him the police would attack anyone in the vicinity, because 'remember what happened to Blair Peach at Southall'.[113] This linking of Brixton with previous incidents demonstrates how events were part of a longer battle with the police: 'we felt in Brixton that "Hey, they're killing people in the streets now!" – and so, this is when we really began to resist'.[114] Similarly, police actions were linked to their previous behaviour in the area. Whether provoked or not, the police response was perceived to be heavy-handed, seemingly confirming mounting suspicions of previous misconduct.

A large proportion of accusations were directed towards younger officers. A Probation Officer with the Inner London Probation Aftercare Service, who spent 'Bloody Saturday' on police placement, stated how 'very young' officers seemed excited and proud of their actions, claiming to hear a constable boasting: 'it was a bit naughty, we have been dashing into squats and batting anyone in sight'.[115] Additionally, Councillor Ted Knight claimed overhearing messages from a superintendent concerned because 'most of his men' had only two weeks' service experience but that, regardless, they were ordered into the area.[116] The left-wing and anti-police leanings of 'Red Ted' must be acknowledged when assessing such accusations, absent from official police transcripts made available as records of the Scarman Inquiry.[117] Nevertheless, numerous witness statements refer to older, more experienced officers attempting to prevent younger colleagues from attacking people. Indeed, the relationship between younger, generally more aggressive officers and their older, usually more moderate colleagues has interesting parallels with black youth and older generations.

Alongside accounts of police misconduct, the police endeavouring to avoid disciplinary actions caused much discontent. Some officers were apparently aware of cameras and potential witnesses, thus stopping their attacks to prevent being documented. One witness statement described officers exiting an unmarked police van, brandishing truncheons, lead piping and pickaxe handles to ambush a nearby youth, claiming this attack only halted when BBC employees were spotted. Similarly, accounts emerged of an arrested black man being attacked with truncheons, punches and kicks in a police van, only stopping when emerging into public view.[118] Whether such accusations are actually true, that they were widely believed by local people is important for two reasons: first, by indicating the negative opinion of the police as many locals deemed such actions probable; and second, that it further spread perceptions that existing systems were inadequate to address police misconduct. Thus, frustration that Scarman avoided examining such accusations in his public inquiry was further heightened.

In opposition to numerous submissions criticising police action, supportive statements also appeared. Similar to earlier letters supporting police actions in the area, clear racial sentiments were apparent. Strong police action was forwarded as the only protection for locals against violent 'outsiders', and it was even suggested that Martial Law should be implemented to protect the law and order that 'these immigrants are out to try and break'.[119] Other similar statements claimed that 'Perfectly justified' questioning of black people should not be regarded as harassment because there would be less need to question them if they committed fewer crimes.[120] This grouping of the entire black community into a singular criminal whole compounded the discontent caused by such targeting. Those questioning 'Why should anybody else get upset when there are more police about?' clearly had a different relationship with the police than most black residents.[121]

The belief that police deserved 'no criticism from any quarter' was consequently extended to criticism of Scarman's inquiry.[122] One writer, describing herself as an 'ordinary member of the public' and the wife of a police officer – seemingly not believing this relationship might influence her opinions – declared that people were 'sick and tired of hearing all these weak, feeble excuses' for the disorder, concluding that Scarman's inquiry was an insult to the police and public.[123] This was a view shared by other writers, not deeming the problems faced by black people as having warranted a violent response or specialised government inquiry. One letter even alleged that any recommendations seen to be favouring black people would provoke extreme anger from 'native' Britons, warning Scarman: 'When "your" riots start again (this time with whites in the lead) I hope you can live with yourself.'[124] The possibility of this radical response was somewhat legitimised by accounts during the disorder of gangs of white people gathering to exact 'revenge'.[125]

Despite not addressing specific cases, Scarman concluded he had 'little doubt' from the amount of submitted evidence there were instances of police misconduct.[126] However, he maintained that his inquiry was not the place to investigate specific incidents of police wrongdoing. Thus, he disappointed those who wished to see the police held accountable for their actions and who believed a public inquiry, in the seeming absence of effective or impartial mechanisms, could have achieved this.

Scarman Report

Scarman's terms of reference were widened in July to include spreading disorder. Although cursory visits were undertaken to Birmingham, Coventry, Wolverhampton and Liverpool, in reality other locations did not receive the same level of scrutiny, and it was noted Scarman 'clearly was, and feels he was' more comfortable with Brixton investigations than elsewhere.[127] John Rex unfavourably compared Scarman's inquiry to the 1967 Kerner Commission into US racial disorders, which had collected vast quantities of social science evidence, including teams of researchers interviewing participants, allowing their voices to be added to the analysis – although this investigation was not without its critics.[128] Rex pointed out that Scarman was not a social scientist and was 'totally unequipped' to consider all the disturbances in England, so resultant attempts to obtain similar evidence were 'both random and trivial'.[129] Scarman later defended his inquiry, highlighting the comparatively few people involved and short timeframe.[130] While legitimate points, it is unlikely such explanations would appease those disappointed with his inquiry.

Similarly, some claimed Scarman's inquiry was established purely as a political exercise in being seen to be doing something, but that his eventual report would not be taken notice of, published after public interest had waned:

The scenario was familiar. Both the law-and-order lobby and its liberal critics would be reassured that the outbreak was not being ignored, the politically weak black community would be divided, the media would soon lose interest – and in the autumn there would be a judicious report on race relations in the inner city to place along side all the other judicious reports on the same subject in the Home Office library.[131]

However, Benyon argued that, due to the continuing disorders in 1981 and Scarman's ability to inspire the confidence of many Brixton locals during his inquiry, it was impossible for the Government not to respond to its findings.[132] This was, of course, not the opinion of the Defence Campaign and those they maintained that they represented.

Scarman's Report was published on 25 November 1981, with a largely liberal tone as Scarman concluded the disorders emerged out of political, social and economic disadvantage, and widespread racial discrimination. At times, Scarman also hinted at a radical interpretation, stating that some participants believed disorders were an effective way of protesting and making their voices heard.[133] In many ways it was, in the words of Hugo Young, 'a rare artefact of the Thatcher years couched in pre-Thatcherite language'.[134] Paul Rich described Scarman's view as resembling that of the mid-Victorian era; untouched by 'the last phase of imperial expansion, Scarman was especially concerned with the "plight" of the ethnic minority communities in the inner cities'.[135] Yet, many aspects demonstrated a more conservative response, such as suggesting the 'thrill' of participation and 'reward' of looting as possible motives, maintaining there could be no excuse for violence. Moreover, Benyon highlighted how Scarman's Report generally perpetuated interpretations that these disorders were exceptional threats to British law and order, demanding exceptional responses through police training, tactics and equipment.[136] Layton-Henry described it a 'diplomatic report', in which everyone could find things with which they both agreed and disagreed, and Police Federation Vice-Chair Basil Griffiths criticised the impossible aspiration to 'be all things to all people'.[137] Keith concluded that any judicial inquiry is doomed to shortcomings rendering its conclusions disappointing, such as an inherent favourable view of authorities, but Scarman's focus became too general: 'In striving for the universal, Lord Scarman neglects the particular.'[138]

Scarman examined many aspects and policies, but his recommendations largely focused on the police. Although much discontent had been directed towards them, this emphasis was criticised, as it appeared to be concentrating upon the consequences, rather than causes, of disadvantage.[139] Thatcher's handwritten note on a summary of its contents claimed: 'I'm afraid the report seems highly critical of the police.'[140] Despite this, in light of the level of criticism, Scarman was not overcritical.[141] For example, as with his 1974 Red Lion Square

Inquiry, Scarman refused to advise the dissolution of the infamous SPG, and allocated some blame to local 'community leaders'.

Most notably, Scarman stated that the Metropolitan Police's policies were not racist, but that 'racial prejudice' and proclivity for 'harassment' existed in some officers.[142] He suggested introducing a specific disciplinary offence to tackle racist conduct, but the Government did not accept its need. The Police Federation and Police Superintendents' Association opposed this measure because they believed it was already covered under the existing Police Disciplinary Code, and 'were not prepared in the interests of fostering good community relations to allow the offence to be specifically incorporated'.[143] Benyon deemed this response 'difficult to understand', but Griffiths believed it 'particularly unfair that policemen should be placed in jeopardy in this way when the same complaint is so often levelled against members of other public bodies'.[144] The police appeared unwilling to 'set an example' or be held to a higher standard.

Scarman infamously concluded that '"Institutional racism" does not exist in Britain: but racial disadvantage and its nasty associate, racial discrimination, have not yet been eliminated'.[145] Herman Ouseley, Lambeth's Principal Race Relations Officer, retorted that such rejection left the Report 'fundamentally flawed', and Simon Holdaway and Megan O'Neill later questioned how individual racism could be isolated from institutional racism, when individuals make up those institutions.[146] Scarman's lack of a detailed definition of 'institutional racism' has been criticised, as he focused on knowing policies or intentional actions rather than an unwitting consequence of years of predominantly white institutions.[147] Scarman's conclusions were thus deemed characteristic of 'the blinkered approach to matters about race which can affect even well-meaning white people'.[148]

Further to changes in police training and efforts to recruit more black officers, Scarman, stopping short of increasing local police authorities' power, encouraged more consultation and connections between the authorities and residents. Keith argued the reasoning behind this was to produce an arena in which black Britons' grievances could be addressed, to 'institutionalize conflict, taking it off the streets and into the committee room'.[149] Or, in Anandi Ramamurthy's words, 'the establishment of a whole array of community participation projects and systems which were eventually to buy many activists off the streets'.[150] Militant groups, such as the Defence Campaign who repeatedly criticised those who liaised with the police, remained opposed to 'community policing' techniques, portraying them as a means of convincing an oppressed group to trust their oppressor. They claimed that post-disorders events in Brixton, ostensibly police attempts at improving local relations such as a West Indies XI versus Brixton Police cricket match, were 'exercises in psychological warfare and community control' aimed at 'sabotaging and weakening our struggle'.[151] A Home Office Circular was later published requiring chief constables and police authorities to work together to form 'community-based consultation bodies', but details and whose responsibility it was for actually establishing them were left vague.[152]

Nonetheless, the police seemed to respond positively to the Report. McNee conceded 'some of the criticisms must be right', and Police Federation magazine *Police* even deemed it fair: hardly a response to placate radical black organisations or individuals suspecting Scarman would go easy on the police.[153] The Police Federation announced it would back a new independent body to investigate police complaints, but senior police officials later contended that no system would ever fully satisfy critics, even suggesting that officers felt the 'oppressive' complaints procedure was actually unfair against them. As previously, police officials repeatedly exhibited beliefs that discontent came from minor sections of society, whereas the 'average man' was not particularly concerned.[154] This language of exclusion could be read against the marginalised group attempting to voice their protest through the collective violence of 1980–81. Indeed, Scarman believed the only way to restore faith in the complaints system was through an independent investigations service.[155] While some baulked at the potential expense, Paul Boateng cited the costs of the disorders, concluding that 'when one looks at the question of cost, one must bear in mind the costs of the crisis of confidence which the present arrangements have generated'.[156]

Conclusion

When the Scarman Report was published, it received a generally favourable response. Muhammad Anwar cited an Opinion Research Centre poll suggesting 'massive support' for Scarman's proposals – although, the majority of those respondents were white.[157] Mary Venner summarised newspaper reaction as largely positive, but seemingly in agreement that some aspects could have been improved, such as suggestions for preventing further disturbances, solving policing issues or positive action to counteract racial discrimination.[158] On the other hand, boycotters and those who deemed public inquiries a waste of time believed their views had been vindicated. For example, prominent activist Darcus Howe described the Report as a 'failure' that was 'way off beam' due to the lack of radical suggestions regarding police power, and the Defence Campaign dubbed this 'powerful anti-Black statement ... the most successful diversionary mechanism that the state could have constructed'.[159]

Despite a public inquiry examining the Brixton disorders – a seeming victory for campaigners and potential symbol of further inclusion in the political process – it largely ignored accusations of police misconduct and its conclusions were deemed disappointing. Scarman himself later noted criticism his Report received, agreeing his recommendations regarding 'positive discrimination' should have been more explicit regarding the need for affirmative action to combat and surmount racial disadvantage: 'Perhaps I did not see far enough, or maybe for once in my life I was mealy-mouthed, and for that I do indeed apologise.'[160] Many contributions at a later conference discussing Scarman's Report criticised it for failing to ensure appropriate action would be taken after placing a number of issues on the political agenda.[161] John Lea blamed the mechanism of public inquiries for lacking the ability to generate 'any shift in the structure of social power': 'Recommendations are made and then the inquiry packs its bags and moves on ... Once Scarman had packed his bags, what then was to stop policing returning to its grim normality?'[162] Scarman countered that, although he believed it accomplished more than this, 'Even if the Report has achieved no more than an awakening, it would have served a useful purpose'.[163] However, if Scarman's Report was a 'call for action', there was little evidence such had taken place.[164]

Before Scarman published his Report, further disorders appeared around the country, seeming to lend some credence to Enoch Powell's warning following Brixton that the Government and country 'have seen nothing yet'.[165] The authorities' response to Brixton, focused more upon criminality and police equipment/training than addressing issues faced by black Britons, did not appear to give much hope that their situation would be improved. As John Solomos concluded: 'Having spent the whole summer denying any link between its policies and the riots', the Government was not likely to immediately implement the economic and social policy proposals outlined by Scarman.[166] Nonetheless, Harry Goulbourne suggested that 'Brixton led to the recognition that the police needed to be more accountable to the communities they ostensibly serve'.[167] For those areas of the country witnessing disorders in summer 1981, the potential lessons of Brixton were not learnt or implemented quickly enough.

Notes

1   *Sunday Mirror*, 31 October 1982; Whitelaw, *Memoirs*, p. 243.
2   Whitelaw, *Memoirs*, p. 243.

3 The National Archives (TNA): HO 266/138, Elizabeth Balsom to Lord Scarman, 23 April 1981.

4 The view of one Brixton participant, quoted in Roberts and Drury, *Police out of Brixton!*, p. 1.

5 *BBC London News*, 11 April 2011.

6 Scarman, *Report*, p. 13.

7 See, for example: Stevens and Willis, 'Ethnic Minorities and Complaints'; Whitaker, *Police in Society*; Maguire and Corbett, *Police Complaints System*.

8 Scarman, *Report*, pp. 77–8.

9 *BBC London News*, 11 April 2011.

10 TNA: HO 266/101, A 226.

11 TNA: HO 266/103, Other Submissions (O.S.) 124; TNA: HO 266/100, A 180.

12 Reicher, 'St. Pauls Riot', 18.

13 TNA: HO 266/104, O.S. 96.

14 Words of Alex Wheatle, *Huffington Post*, 11 April 2013.

15 *Guardian*, 18 April 1981.

16 TNA: HO 266/96, Police Submissions (P.S.) 44; TNA: HO 266/99, P.S. 218; Black Cultural Archives (BCA), Uprisings/1/6, Statement by Reverend Denis Paterson, 28 April 1981.

17 Sivanandan, *Different Hunger*, pp. 19–20.

18 Thatcher MSS (digital collection), TV Interview for ITN, 13 April 1981; HC Deb 13 April 1981 vol. 3 cc. 21–6.

19 See: Benyon, 'Civil Disorder'.

20 HC Deb 13 April 1981 vol. 3 c. 30.

21 See: chapter 1.

22 Rowe, *Racialisation of Disorder*, p. 180.

23 Keith, *Race, Riots and Policing*, pp. 101–4. See: Kettle and Hodges, *Uprising!*, pp. 28–9; Brain, *History of Policing*, p. 68.

24 TNA: HO 266/138, Ralf Dahrendorf to Scarman, 14 April 1981. See: Andresen and Van der Steen (eds), *European Youth Revolt*. For 'protest waves', see: Koopmans, 'Protest in Time and Space'; McAdam, 'Diffusion Processes'.

25 TNA: HO 266/76, Police Tape Transcripts, 11 April 1981; TNA: HO 266/103, O.S. 186; O.S. 178; O.S. 185. See: Sanders and Wood, *Times of Troubles*; Dawson et al. (eds), *Northern Ireland Troubles*.

26 Scarman, *Report*, pp. 13–14.

27 TNA: HO 266/77, Police Tape Transcripts, 11 April 1981.

28 Clare, 'Eyewitness in Brixton', pp. 50–2.

29 Benyon, 'Going through the Motions', 409.

30 TNA: PREM 19/484, Clive Whitmore to John Halliday, 13 April 1981; HC Deb 13 April 1981 vol. 3 c. 28.

31 TNA: HO 266/72, Transcript of interview with Scarman, *World At One*, 14 April 1981. See, for example: Ellison and Smyth, *Policing Northern Ireland*, pp. 61–4; Gilbert, *Only One Died*.

32 Whitelaw, *Memoirs*, p. 245.

33 Scarman, *Red Lion Square Disorders*; *Guardian*, 28 February 1975.

34 BCA: Gutzmore/1/6/1, Brixton Defence Campaign Bulletin 1.

35 See: McGowan, 'Grunwick'; Sivanandan, *Different Hunger*, pp. 126–31.

36 See: Beer, *Public Inquiries*; Elliot and McGuiness, 'Public Inquiry', 17–18.

37 Brain, *History of Policing*, p. 68. See: Cannadine, *Thatcher*, pp. 28–38.

38 McNee, *McNee's Law*, pp. 117–19.

39 TNA: HO 266/72, Transcript: PM Programme, *BBC Radio Four*, 14 April 1981; BCA: Gutzmore/1/2/11, Statement, 15 June 1981.

40 Transcript of interview with Scarman.

41 McNee, *McNee's Law*, p. 118; *The Times*, 25 November 1982.

42 TNA: PREM 19/484, Whitmore to Halliday, 13 April 1981; Transcript of interview with Scarman.

43 HC Deb 13 April 1981 vol. 3 c. 29. See: chapter 3.

44 *Western Daily Press*, 24 July 1981.

45 Jacobs, *Black Politics*, p. 145.

46 BCA: Gutzmore/1/2/3, Outgoing letter calling for 'Black Community Support'. 'Uprising' was utilised by many community activists, to remove the criminal context of 'riot' and introduce a political perspective.

47 BCA: Gutzmore/1/6/1, Brixton Defence Campaign Bulletins 1 & 4.

48 *The Leveller*, 1–14 May, p. 11.

49 BCA: Gutzmore/1/3/1, Minutes of the Brixton Defence Campaign Meeting, 3 June 1981, emphasis in original; Thomlinson, *Race, Ethnicity and the Women's Movement*, p. 88.

50 Ramamurthy, *Black Star*, p. 65. See: Modood and Berthoud (eds), *Ethnic Minorities*; Maylor, 'Meaning of "Black"?'.

51 BCA: Gutzmore/1/3/1, Minutes of the Brixton Defence Campaign Meeting, 20 May 1981, 27 May 1981.

52 Rodrigues, 'The Riots of '81', 22.

53 BCA: Gutzmore/1/1/2, Brixton Defence Campaign, 'The Brixton Defence Campaign says – Boycott the Scarman Inquiry'. See: Scraton, 'Official Inquiries', p. 50.

54 BCA: Gutzmore/1/3/1, Minutes of the Brixton Defence Campaign Meeting, 6 May 1981.

55 'Boycott the Scarman Inquiry'.

56 BCA: Gutzmore/1/3/1, Minutes of the Brixton Defence Campaign Meeting, 10 June 1981, 3 June 1981.

57 BCA: Gutzmore/1/2/5, Outgoing letters to those intending to give evidence.

58 Brixton Defence Campaign Bulletins 1 & 4; 'Boycott the Scarman Inquiry'.

59 BCA: Gutzmore/1/2/11, Statement, 15 June 1981.

60 BCA: Gutzmore/1/7/4, Brixton Defence Campaign poster, emphasis in original.

61 BCA: Gutzmore/1/6/1, Brixton Defence Campaign Bulletin 3.

62 Brixton Defence Campaign Bulletin 4.

63 See: Rex and Tomlinson, *Colonial Immigrants*; Sivanandan, *Different Hunger*.

64 'Boycott the Scarman Inquiry'; TNA: HO 266/90, Working Party on Police and Community Relations in Lambeth.

65 Brixton Defence Campaign Bulletin 1.

66 BCA: Gutzmore/1/5/5, 'Brixton People's Enquiry'; Brixton Defence Campaign Meeting, 20 May 1981.

67 Brixton Defence Campaign Meeting, 27 May 1981.
68 Keith, *Race, Riots and Policing*, p. 78.
69 TNA: HO 266/100, A 377.
70 TNA: HO 266/14, Scarman, 'Transcripts of Public Hearings, Twelfth Day'.
71 TNA: HO 266/76, Police Tape Transcripts, 11 April 1981.
72 TNA: HO 266/103, O.S. 124; TNA: HO 266/104, O.S. 153.
73 TNA: HO 266/103, Unknown.
74 TNA: HO 266/89, P.S. 31; Scarman, *Report*, p. 112.
75 Brain, *History of Policing*, pp. 66–7.
76 Scarman, *Report*, pp. 63–4; TNA: HO 266/97; P.S. 7.
77 *Time Out*, 17–23 April 1981, p. 10.
78 TNA: HO 266/100, A 117.
79 McNee, *McNee's Law*, pp. 113–14.
80 O.S. 178; TNA: HO 266/103, O.S. 159.
81 TNA: HO 266/104, O.S. 49.
82 Scarman, *Report*, p. 113.
83 TNA: HO 266/74, Police Tape Transcripts, 11 April 1981.
84 TNA: HO 266/105, O.S. 155.
85 TNA: HO 266/104, O.S. 127.
86 Clare, 'Eyewitness in Brixton', p. 49.
87 TNA: HO 266/103, O.S. 237.
88 TNA: HO 266/73, Police Tape Transcripts, 10 April 1981.
89 TNA: HO 266/104, O.S. 167; Brain, *History of Policing*, p. 66.
90 TNA: HO 266/74, Police Tape Transcripts, 11 April 1981; TNA: HO 266/96, P.S. 9; TNA: HO 266/76, Police Tape Transcripts, 11 April 1981.
91 TNA: HO 266/73, Police Tape Transcripts, 10 April 1981.
92 TNA: HO 266/97, P.S. 8; TNA: HO 266/77, Police Tape Transcripts, 11 April 1981.
93 TNA: HO 266/92, Metropolitan Police, *The Brixton Disorders*.
94 TNA: HO 266/76, Police Tape Transcripts, 11 April 1981; TNA: HO 266/104, O.S. 147.
95 Scarman, *Report*, p. 118.
96 TNA: HO 266/77, Police Tape Transcripts, 11 April 1981.
97 TNA: HO 266/104, O.S. 175; O.S. 194; O.S. 147. See: Keith, 'No-Go Areas'.
98 O.S. 96.
99 *New Statesman*, 17 April 1981.
100 *Sunday Telegraph*, 12 April 1981.
101 Squires and Kennison, *Shooting to Kill?*, p. 159; Reiner, *Politics of the Police*, p. 87.
102 HC Deb 13 April 1981 vol. 3 cc. 21–2.
103 See: Garnett and Aitken, *Willie Whitelaw*, pp. 268–74; Baston, 'Roy Hattersley', pp. 227–8.
104 Scarman, *Report*, p. 114.
105 Tilly, *Collective Violence*, pp. 27–8.
106 TNA: HO 266/105, O.S. 135.
107 Metropolitan Police, *The Brixton Disorders*.
108 Scarman, 'An Epilogue', p. 259.

109 Benyon, 'Perceptions and Distortions', p. 37.

110 TNA: HO 266/103, Unknown; TNA: HO 266/104, O.S. 96A; O.S. 186.

111 TNA: HO 266/103, O.S. 161, O.S. 186; O.S. 153; Unknown; O.S. 35.

112 TNA: HO 266/103, O.S. 25.

113 TNA: HO 266/258, O.S. 258. See: Scraton and McCulloch, *Deaths in Custody*, pp. 75–8.

114 Alex Wheatle, 29 March 2009, www.storyvault.com/video/view/brixton_just_before_ the_1981_riots (last accessed: 6 October 2016).

115 TNA: HO 266/103, O.S. 168.

116 TNA: HO 266/89, Police radio messages overheard by Edward Knight on Saturday 11 April.

117 Crick, *March of Militant*, p. 15; Sofer, *London Left Takeover*, p. 45.

118 TNA: HO 266/103, Unknown; O.S. 186.

119 TNA: HO 266/104, O.S. 33.

120 TNA: HO 266/138, G. Archer to Scarman, 13 April 1981.

121 TNA: HO 266/104, O.S. 45.

122 *Ibid.*

123 TNA: HO 266/138, Jean Critchley to Scarman.

124 TNA: HO 266/138, Dorothy Bell to Scarman, 25 November 1981.

125 TNA: HO 266/101, A 172; TNA: HO 266/79, Police Tape Transcripts, 12 April 1981.

126 Scarman, *Report*, p. 112.

127 TNA: PREM 19/484, Record of discussion between Scarman and Sir Brian Crossland Cubbon, 5 October 1981.

128 National Advisory Commission on Civil Disorders, *Report*. See: Feagin and Hahn (eds), *Ghetto Revolts*; Hrach, *Riot Report*; Lipsky, 'Riot Commission'.

129 Rex, 'Disadvantage and Discrimination', p. 191.

130 Scarman, 'An Epilogue', p. 259.

131 *Observer*, 13 September 1981.

132 Benyon, 'Going through the Motions', 415.

133 Scarman, *Report*, p. 36.

134 Young, *One of Us*, p. 234.

135 Rich, *Race and Empire*, pp. 212–3.

136 Benyon, 'Going through the Motions', 415.

137 Layton-Henry, *Politics of Race*, p. 163; Griffiths, 'One-Tier Policing', p. 125.

138 Keith, *Race, Riots and Policing*, p. 78.

139 Profitt, 'Equal Respect', p. 204; Rex, 'Disadvantage and Discrimination', p. 191.

140 TNA: PREM 19/1521, Note to Thatcher, 2 November 1981.

141 Brain, *History of Policing*, p. 72.

142 Scarman, *Report*, p. 98.

143 Layton-Henry, *Politics of Race*, p. 164.

144 Benyon, 'Policing Issues', p. 104; Griffiths, 'One-Tier Policing', pp. 131–2.

145 Scarman, *Report*, p. 209.

146 *The Times*, 26 November 1981; Holdaway and O'Neill, 'Institutional Racism after Macpherson', 358.

147 Layton-Henry, *Politics of Race*, p. 163; Reiner, *Politics of the Police*, p. 162; Scraton, *Power, Conflict and Criminalisation*, p. 30.

148 Greaves, 'Brixton Disorders', p. 71.

149 Keith, *Race, Riots and Policing*, p. 173.

150 Ramamurthy, *Black Star*, p. 147.

151 Brixton Defence Campaign Bulletin 3.

152 Brain, *History of Policing*, p. 73.

153 Benyon, 'The Riots, Lord Scarman and the Political Agenda', pp. 8–9.

154 Goodson, 'Police and the Public', p. 147; Griffiths, 'One-Tier Policing', pp. 130–1.

155 Scarman, *Report*, p. 183.

156 Boateng, 'Community and Accountability', p. 156.

157 Anwar, 'Public Reaction to the Scarman Report', 371–3

158 Venner, 'What the Papers Said About Scarman'. See: Neal, 'Scarman Report'.

159 *The Times*, 26 November 1981; Brixton Defence Campaign poster; Thomas, 'Black Initiatives in Brixton', p. 190.

160 Scarman, 'The Quest for Social Justice', pp. 127–8.

161 Benyon, 'The Riots, Lord Scarman and the Political Agenda', p. 11.

162 Lea, 'Brixton to Bradford', p. 188.

163 Scarman, 'An Epilogue', p. 261.

164 Benyon, 'Scarman and After', pp. 234–5.

165 HC Deb 13 April 1981 vol. 3 c. 24.

166 Solomos, *Race and Racism*, p. 174.

167 Goulbourne, *Race Relations*, p. 69.

6

A 'conspicuous success'? Policing Liverpool and Manchester in July 1981

It was April 1981, Down in the ghetto of Brixton,
That the Babylon cause such a friction,
That it bring about a great insurrection,
And it spread all over the nation,
It was truly an historical occasion.

Linton Kwesi Johnson – Di Great Insohreckshan

O N 27 April 1981, Home Secretary William Whitelaw sent a report to Prime Minister Margaret Thatcher outlining the likelihood of public disorder occurring that year, concluding that, following anti-police disorders in Bristol in 1980 and Brixton in 1981, 'further violence in the ethnic minority communities is likely'.[1] Less than three months later, while Lord Scarman was conducting his public inquiry into Brixton, further disturbances spread across the country, portrayed as 'A country-wide movement of resistance' by community organisation the Brixton Defence Campaign.[2] After disorder reached numerous locations in July, even the most ardent could no longer claim Bristol or Brixton were isolated local incidents that bore no broader significance: Manchester Chief Constable James Anderton admitted: 'all of us have been overtaken somewhat disastrously by events'.[3] Timothy Brain described how this 'amazing series of riots ... swept England', and recent research by Roger Ball suggested that almost 200 daily disorders occurred around England in July alone.[4]

This chapter examines some key policing developments of these disorders, focusing upon Toxteth, Liverpool and Moss Side, Manchester through interviews and original local records.[5] Reaction to previous disturbances strengthened police tactics and riot control equipment, with this transformation demonstrated by the first use of CS gas within mainland Britain and suggestions of arming the police or mobilising the army. Radical black groups even alleged the police instigated the July disorders to justify enhanced equipment and 'stronger' police tactics.[6] In Moss Side, during a contentious meeting between local community organisations and the police, apparent advances in the police/community relationship were alleged to have actually been a ploy to justify a forceful police response to disorder, employing tactics modelled upon Northern Ireland examples – including using police vehicles to disperse crowds, and 'snatch squads' targeting influential participants. Authorities framed the disturbances around law and order, rather than addressing broader issues of racism, discrimination, or their economic and social policies. Anderton's actions were described by Whitelaw as a 'conspicuous success', but did little to improve poor police/black relations at the heart of the spreading disturbances.

Southall and Bradford: 3 and 11 July

The first disturbances of summer 1981 erupted on the evening of 3 July in Southall, West London, where local Asian youths clashed with skinheads. The area had witnessed racial incidents in previous years, such as the 1976 racist murder of teenager Gurdip Singh Chaggar and Blair Peach's death during an anti-NF demonstration in 1979.[7] Following Chaggar's death, while Asian elders maintained traditional attempts to protest racial violence through conventional political channels, local youths organised a march to the local police station and radical organisations emerged, including the influential Southall Youth Movement.[8] Therefore, when, in July 1981, an Oi! punk concert in a local pub, recently sued for barring minority ethnic customers, attracted groups of skinheads – who smashed windows, attacked locals, and shouted NF slogans – local Asian youth fought back. The resulting violence saw five hours of disorders, 120 people injured and the pub burnt down. Although the police were attacked when perceived to be protecting the skinheads, hostilities initially occurred exclusively between white skinheads and Asian youth; unlike the other anti-police disorders in 'inner city areas where the prominent minority were black Afro-Caribbeans' examined throughout.[9]

In Bradford on 11 July, as disorders spread across the country, local Asian youths from the United Black Youth League prepared petrol bombs for community self-defence in case of racial violence. Although never used, twelve young men were arrested and charged with their production, becoming known as the 'Bradford 12'. On trial for 'conspiracy to make explosives … for unlawful purposes' – charges which 'did not require evidence of any particular crime having been committed' – the defendants all claimed self-defence, allowing them to document evidence of racial violence and discrimination against minority ethnic groups in the area. After an eight-week trial, all defendants were cleared and solicitor Gareth Peirce concluded: 'the jury accepted the proposition that a society should afford protection to all its citizens and that if it did not, as the evidence they heard showed clearly that it does not, then those unprotected can arm themselves'.[10]

Scarman similarly commented that, distinct from black Britons protesting police harassment, the British Asian community's main complaint was that the police 'do not do sufficient' to protect them.[11] These examples complement discussion throughout this book, as a self-defence movement had emerged due to the failures of the authorities to prevent racial violence and discrimination, which formed an integral part of a minority ethnic political consciousness and the unifying term 'black politics'.[12]

Toxteth, Liverpool: 3–11 July

Concurrently, disorder appeared in Toxteth, Liverpool, where 468 officers were injured, 500 people arrested and at least seventy buildings demolished. Again, alleged police misconduct was the initiator. In response to officers questioning Leroy Alphonse Cooper, a black youth erroneously suspected of stealing a motorcycle, eight police vehicles had arrived: an inflammatory action, surely influenced by increased tensions following Brixton. This excessive response incensed locals, and representatives of the community accused the police of both instigating and escalating the disturbances through their actions. Police cordoning provided an obvious target, and suggestions that a reduced police presence would remove this visible focal point for the crowd's anger went unheeded. Officers were also accused of shouting racist slogans and otherwise provoking the crowd, with some police reportedly removing their identifying numbers to prevent subsequent identification.[13]

Toxteth shared a number of similarities with other inner-city areas experiencing disorder. For example, during 1971–81, black unemployment increased 100 per cent for men and 95 per cent for women.[14] In addition, discontent towards the police and belief they targeted black youths was prevalent, with accusations they planted drugs on youths and conducted 'coon races' where the first officer to arrest a black person won a pot of money.[15] Numerous observers noted that preceding hostility in 1971 towards a police 'task force' almost led to disturbances and fear of 'civil war in the city'.[16] William E. Nelson, Jr, documented growing conflict between police and black Britons in Liverpool, including an increasing black resistance through organised protests, such as a sit-in at a local Methodist Youth Centre shortly before the 1981 disturbances.[17] An interview with a resident after the disorder reasoned that a growing sense of discontent had led to increased militancy:

> People had got to the point where they felt they had no territory, where they felt their rights, liberties, and personal freedoms were impinged upon so much that they actually confronted it and said excuse me I have a right to stand on this street ... In this case issues like fair economic conditions and employment were there, but on that day it was more you get out, we've had enough of this.[18]

Following initial disorder in early July 1981, a lower-profile police approach – an apparent effort to liaise with residents – helped reduce tensions.[19] However, representatives of the community criticised Chief Constable Kenneth Oxford's general policing policies and the Liverpool 8 Defence Committee – a local name for the area referring to Toxteth's postal district – demanded his dismissal, believing him to be the main impediment to improved police/community relations.[20] Significantly, officers deployed from other forces during disorders reportedly had friendlier relations with the community than local police; at odds with other examples, where the presence of familiar community officers – known and often relatively popular with locals – may have eased tensions, this was likely partly due to a Chief Constable who argued against the very idea of 'community policing'.[21]

Oxford had clashed with the local population and police authority regarding tactics, seemingly in denial at the extent of dissatisfaction towards the police. For example, his 1980 Annual Report stated that local police/community relations were 'in a very healthy position and I do not foresee any difficulties in the future'.[22] This was despite the Merseyside Community Relations Council severing relations with the police in 1980, believing the established liaison scheme had no value and the police refused to admit racist attitudes existed within their ranks.[23] Liverpool County Council representatives claimed that previous police authority attempts to commence constructive discussion with senior officers had failed, and they hoped that, following disorders, the police would become more receptive.[24] Police Committee Chair, Margaret Simey, routinely criticised Oxford's tactics, believing that politicians granting police extended powers removed 'effective democratic scrutiny'. Having gained a reputation for outspoken views on policing, she remarked that local people would have been 'apathetic fools' if they had not protested.[25] Despite her comments drawing extensive criticism, others clearly shared her position, believing collective violence was required for their voices to be heard once alternative avenues of registering protest had seemingly failed or been denied to them.

Governmental visits and a 'Minister for Merseyside'

On 7 July, Whitelaw visited Liverpool and drew comparisons with Northern Ireland experience, having 'the same pessimism, the same anxieties and the same need to maintain outward calm and good humour while internally suffering deep depression and self-doubt'.[26] Thatcher also visited Liverpool, meeting local police, government, church representatives, and representatives of community organisations and local youth. Informing locals she was there to hear their frank thoughts, she appeared shocked by the response – recording being 'amazed' and 'appalled' at the hostility displayed towards the police.[27] In a swipe at the media, she also noted 'The press were rather confused when, contrary to what they had been expecting, the youngsters told them that I had indeed listened'. A personal meeting with the head of Government would certainly have left some believing the disturbances had quickly improved their levels of political participation. However, Thatcher detailed the resources previously 'poured into Liverpool' and maintained that policing issues were about crime, not skin colour.[28] Indeed, she told local authority representatives they must support the police, as society would crumble if law and order could not be maintained.[29] Thatcher informed Oxford and senior officers they had her complete support and whatever equipment was required to handle disorders would be provided.[30] Even if Thatcher had listened to complaints of local people, governmental support remained firmly behind the police. She urged black Britons 'not to resort to violence or to try to live in separate communities from the rest of us', but general attitudes from authorities pushed some of them towards this.[31]

Thatcher's Merseyside meetings ended by concluding that, while problems had been identified fifteen years ago, the belief that 'if people were given good homes and good schooling, this would give them the basis they needed for a satisfactory life' had not been wholly correct: 'We should have to think again'.[32] Yet, this rethinking of attitudes did not include a basic change in economic policy, as such would publicly admit her Government shouldered some blame for the disorders.[33] Consequently, Thatcher's Government 'responded in a pragmatic, if financially limited, way'.[34] She appointed Michael Heseltine 'Minister for

Merseyside', to head a ministerial task force addressing the problems of inner-cities – appearing to suggest Thatcher accepted a link between crime, disorder and unemployment, even if she would not admit it publicly and undermine her economic policies. Heseltine stressed the need to be seen showing real concern 'without raising expensive and largely unfulfillable expectations ... and particularly without giving the impression that local communities can secure for their areas expenditure with riots'.[35] Nevertheless, the title of his resultant private Cabinet Report, 'It Took a Riot', clearly suggests the only reason Merseyside was receiving added attention was the disturbances.[36]

'Tooling-up': police equipment

During Toxteth disorders, officers were confronted with bricks, various missiles and petrol bombs. Dave Potts, then a twenty-year-old constable, recalled being issued 'a very flimsy riot visor ... a cricket box and a set of football shin pads'; Oxford himself later deemed the police's response 'totally and utterly inadequate'.[37] To combat increasing disorder, reinforcements were obtained from police forces across England. Such practices would later become more streamlined, demonstrated during the 1984–85 miners' strike where the National Reporting Centre at New Scotland Yard controlled 20,000 officers drawn from fifty of the UK's fifty-two forces. This allowed the Government to control the police's strike response, undermining the partially democratically elected police authorities.[38]

At 2:15 a.m. on 6 July, Merseyside officers became the first to use CS gas within mainland Britain, firing 25–30 grenades. All forces in Britain since the mid-1960s had access to small stocks of this equipment, another aspect of the disturbances following Northern Irish antecedents.[39] Officers allegedly caused injuries by firing canisters incorrectly, wilfully or accidentally, directly at crowds.[40] This 'attempted murder' – in the words of the Brixton Defence Campaign – was severely criticised by the local police authority and representatives of the community, accusing the officers of employing dangerous equipment without sufficient training and using cartridges intended for penetrating buildings rather than crowd control.[41] Despite this, Oxford was unapologetic about his officers' undisciplined response.[42] Later recognising opinion that use of CS gas, baton rounds and water cannons was 'repressive and an over-reaction', he nonetheless defended their necessity as an emergency response after the 'staggering number of [police] injuries'.[43] Whitelaw later revealed Oxford had telephoned him in the early hours to approve use of CS gas, but Whitelaw believed such decisions must be made by individuals with situational knowledge – leading him to eradicate approval requirements and further empower local chief constables – 'So, amazing as it seems now, I turned over and went to sleep'.[44]

A recurring theme throughout 1980–81 was the focus on law and order, to the detriment of particular problems facing the black population, encouraging the 'paramilitarisation' of policing.[45] Liberal Liverpool City Council leader, Sir Trevor Jones, appealed for troops to be put on standby, 'If the police cannot cope'.[46] Similarly, local Conservative MP Anthony Sheen contended that the Government, 'being the Party of law and order', needed to make it clear they would do what was necessary.[47] Whitelaw, one of the more liberal members of Thatcher's Government, reportedly could not rule out the 'highly undesirable' use of troops to combat 'extreme ferocity'. Although portrayed in the press as a 'radical departure from the passive tactics generally used by British policemen', John Benyon outlined that soldiers had been utilised in Northern Ireland for almost twenty years and had intervened in twenty-four separate disturbances between 1869 and 1908.[48] Regardless, their appearance would certainly have been signifi- cant. Despite a Military Liaison Officer reportedly being drafted into Brixton police station during disturbances in case troops were required, and Scarman later declaring this 'awful requirement' was close to necessary when 'that thin blue line' was almost overwhelmed, neither the army nor armed police would appear on the streets of England in 1981.[49] However, significantly transformed tactics, and riot control equipment and CS gas, became commonplace.

Amongst others, Benyon blamed this response on the media's and politicians' portrayal of the disorders: 'They were interpreted as exceptional threats to law and order which required exceptional responses.'[50] For example, Thatcher warned journalists that 'The veneer of civilization is very thin', and an unnamed senior official was quoted claiming 'we are facing anarchy'.[51] Graham Murdock analysed media responses to use of CS gas in Toxteth, concluding it was presented as 'an entirely necessary and justified step, given the violence of the rioters and the inadequacy of standard police equipment'. He also made the significant point, applicable to all suggestions that increased police powers and equipment were needed to combat disorders, that 'This perspective comprehensively wrong-foots the counter arguments that tough policing may be a cause of rioting rather than a cure for it'.[52]

Thatcher and Whitelaw agreed the 'use of troops could not be contemplated: if necessary, the police should be properly equipped, and even armed, before such a step was taken'.[53] To that end, Whitelaw organised with Defence Secretary John Nott police acquisition of 'more offensive types of equipment'. Nott expressed 'considerable reservations' about arming police forces with weapons, not least that it would limit the army's ability to aid the Royal Ulster Constabulary in replacing weapons.[54] A Home Affairs Select Committee brief stated that Northern Irish experience had shown the dangers of rubber or plastic bullets, concluding that further thought should be given to their use.[55] Additionally, as officers had suffered a large number of head and neck injuries, better-suited helmets and visors were requisitioned. Based on similar design to those used by army 'snatch squads' in Northern Ireland, their use during subsequent Moss Side disturbances were believed to have greatly reduced police injuries.[56] By 9 July, almost 1,800 were available to the police, with 2,000 more requested.[57] In November 1981, a working group published a report on 'Protective Clothing and Equipment', supporting these developments and further recommended baton rounds, stronger body armour, and increased protection for police vehicles. By 1983, despite links to at least eleven deaths in Northern Ireland, police forces in Britain had stockpiled around 10,000 rubber bullets.[58]

Whitelaw had met with police representatives after the Brixton disturbances, who all agreed that water cannons or plastic bullets were undesirable; however, spreading disorder in July transformed their position.[59] For example, senior Merseyside officers advised Thatcher that water cannons were 'now a necessary part of the equipment', and 'a lot of urgent thought' must be given to how police responded to disorder.[60] Furthermore, the Police Federation, who in 1980 were adamant that the image of the traditional British police 'should be maintained at all costs', were by 1981 demanding 'proper riot equipment'.[61] Incidents involving a proportionally small number of people led authorities to swing towards such changes, regardless of negative effects on community relations. Indeed, David Waddington later described the increasing militarisation of the police, which 'occurred without public debate or accountability', as tending towards provoking rather than quelling public unrest.[62]

The 1981 disturbances caused the authorities to alter their approach to public disorder.[63] This focused upon criminality, combat equipment and tactics to deal with disorder rather than addressing underlying causes or undermining govern-mental social and economic policies. Across the aisle, Shadow Home Secretary Roy Hattersley summarised Labour's view that, in such serious situations, use of imperfect means such as CS gas was 'infinitely better than the risk of death and injury'. Nevertheless, he warned that championing stronger police powers 'wins cheap cheers, but it can have wide and potentially disastrous consequences'.[64] Proponent of 'community policing', Devon and Cornwall Chief Constable John Alderson similarly argued against increased police militarisation: 'We must not advance the police response too far ahead of the situation. It is even worth a few million pounds of destruction rather than get pushed too far down that road.'[65] Alderson's was not a widely held opinion amongst authorities, with the majority aligning behind Thatcher's public pronouncement: 'We have to give the Police all the equipment and protection they want.'[66] The effects of this stance can be seen in the response to subsequent disorder in neighbouring Manchester.

Moss Side, Manchester: 7–11 July

Moss Side is an inner-city area of Manchester, home in the 1980s to a large Afro-Caribbean community and a level of black unemployment deemed 'pretty grim'.[67] Rather than simply stating the need for increased investment, a general criticism was the lack of consultation with residents on what the area required. However, any local community centre or group was required to fall within the confines of the government, which critics suggested limited their usefulness and impact. A former youth worker detailed that many youths in the area had seemingly given up on life, with questions regarding their future greeted with responses such as 'I can't think about the future' or 'I suppose I'll die eventually'.[68] Moss Side contained many black residents plainly disillusioned with the role and worth of the British Government, best illustrated by poor housing standards prompting residents to present bottled cockroaches to the Housing Department in protest.[69] Although discussing a different location, Stephen Brooke's observations are of relevance: 'everyday experience, emotion and space formed an affective ecology … which helped shape and was shaped by a particular culture of democracy'.[70]

Linbert Spencer, Director of Operations at the Greater Manchester Youth Association, described the relationship between the police and local youth as 'two gangs who thought they owned the patch'.[71] Similar to St Pauls, Brixton and Toxteth, Moss Side had a reputation for a high crime rate and subsequently high levels of invasive policing. The Moss Side Defence Committee – established to support those arrested in relation to the disturbances – argued that this 'myth of Moss Side' rested upon implicit racist assumptions, resulting in the area being policed 'as if it were a dangerous, alien colony in an otherwise wholesome society'.[72]

Manchester Chief Constable James Anderton had already acquired a reputation for his political views and a religious extremism that would intensify in future years. Local Catholic priest Phil Sumner noted how Anderton 'was trying to be the moral person of the area – not just the legal person, but the moral person'.[73] Anderton 'had never been patient with the idea of policing by consent', and undertook tactics and expressed opinions that did nothing to placate local dissatisfaction.[74] While he stated the desire not to 'exacerbate public feeling or create … undue public hostility towards the police', he simultaneously criticised that 'public opinion is often so ill-informed and ambivalent it is necessary occasionally for the police to take initiatives which, to say the least, may not always attract immediate and popular approval'.[75] With Anderton labelled by Defence Committee Chair Gus John as 'a foul human being', and blamed by Sumner for making it 'much harder for the wider community to want to have any sort of relationship with the police', even Whitelaw acknowledged he was 'an individualist … well-known for his outspoken and controversial remarks'.[76] For example, Martin Kettle and Lucy Hodges highlighted a speech Anderton made in September 1980, claiming 'race relations' organisations 'have been infiltrated by anti-establishment factions, one of whose aims is continuously to impede the police'.[77] Moreover, he believed police/community formal liaison committees were worthless, as 'they tend to exist for their own sake'.[78] Tentative attempts in Brixton and Toxteth for such liaison suggested it could be effective, but attitudes like Anderton's undermined such efforts.

Councillor Gabrielle Cox, Police Authority Deputy Chair, recalled a difficult relationship with Anderton: 'just about everything we did, [he] didn't like'. Upon her appointment in May 1981, Cox and others established a number of measures attempting to increase the accountability of the police; noting a close relationship between Anderton and the previous Chair, she characterised prior Police Authority activity as extremely limited, achieving 'no real scrutiny or accountability'.[79] Moreover, as with similar areas, officers in Moss Side were often young and inexperienced, less familiar with the community – being housed outside the area – and one particularly popular officer had been relocated just two weeks before disorders.[80] This lack of foresight, removing a familiar and well-liked community officer, is reminiscent of a drugs raid undertaken without consulting the Police Community Relations Officer in St Pauls, and of the departure on weekend leave of a Community Liaison Officer as the police presence swelled into an already-tense Brixton.[81] This provoked complaints that, 'when trouble brews up, the Community Contact Police isn't there it's the hard-nosed ones that come'.[82] However, community liaison officers did not avoid criticism, accused by black radicals of attempting to win over 'black youths, youth leaders, and the so-called respectable black community', by portraying allegations of police misconduct as 'the work of black extremists who do not represent the majority of law-abiding black citizens'.[83]

Police refusal to address community concerns added to discontent. For example, one police sergeant, questioned during a local school visit about police brutality towards black youth, dismissively responded: 'I'm an honest man, and I can tell you these things don't happen.' As Cox recalled, the inquiring youths thus concluded that their attempts to address the situation 'got nowhere'.[84] Similarly, reports in March 1981 of a cache of illegal weapons found in lockers at Moss Side Police Station prompted calls for a public inquiry, which did not materialise.[85] Demonstrating escalating discontent, a march had been held on 16 August 1980 protesting police harassment of black residents, and representatives of the community warned of the likelihood of unrest due to allegations against the police and impact of events elsewhere.[86] These warning signs were either ignored or unobserved, and Defence Committee member Eloise Edwards later summarised that the disturbances 'were an attempt from people in the area to put a lot of the wrongs to right'.[87] The police and authorities had done nothing to convince local people that progress would occur within the existing system.

Moss Side Disorders

On 6 July 1981, following a weekend of disturbances in nearby Liverpool, the Town Clerk reviewed Manchester City Council's emergency procedure if similar disorders occurred there.[88] This proved a wise precaution, as growing tension erupted in Manchester the following night. Local community worker Barri Potter received consistent accounts of officers taunting local youth on 6–7 July, likely as a response to Toxteth events.[89] Local community organisation the Moss Side Community Action Committee claimed officers shouted that, unlike 'niggers' in Brixton and Liverpool, black people of Moss Side were 'too soft to riot'. While such taunts are unconfirmed, it suggests a clear dispersal and impact of events elsewhere. The Action Committee also suggested that an older officer had been heard declaring younger officers were 'itching for the opportunity to put their recent riot training into practice'.[90] They did not have long to wait.

Disorder began at roughly 3 a.m. on 7 July, involving around 100 people. In the following half-hour, thirteen shops were damaged – three 'absolutely gutted and destroyed' – police and firefighters were stoned, three police cars and two fire-tenders damaged, and extensive looting occurred.[91] Mirroring other disturbances, witnesses suggested that police activity had increased local anger: in this case, the alleged wrongful arrest of seven youths in connection with a supermarket raid some weeks previously.[92] However, police and official reports record that these seven youths were not actually detained until after outbreaks of disorder – a further example of rumour exacerbating inherent discontent with the police.[93]

A press conference the following day saw Anderton decry the 'near anarchy and lunacy' displayed.[94] The Town Clerk offered a less inflammatory reaction, meeting representatives of the Manchester Council for Community Relations (MCCR) to inquire what assistance the City Council could offer. The MCCR, notably described by the Town Clerk as 'Community Leaders', stressed the need for a low police presence in Moss Side and lack of retaliation.[95] The police were identified as a highly visible target for angry and discontented people, and thus requested to refrain from confrontationally 'swamping' the area with high numbers; although, the idea that 'Community Leaders' could truly represent the entire community is problematic.

Police/community meeting

Despite Anderton's provocative reaction, the police were keen to discuss – or at least appear to – the situation with representatives of the local community. Divisional Commander Chief Superintendent Albert Leach arranged a meeting to consider what could be done to prevent recurrences of disorder; such meetings were usual police procedure, aimed at employing older members of the community to discourage younger people from escalating disorders. However, 1980–81 often provoked contradictory responses from different generations, and the ability of older generations to discourage these actions is questionable. Shortly into the meeting, approximately two-dozen local black youths arrived. Anderton's phrasing, that Leach 'had certainly not invited the youths', belies subsequent claims they were 'made most welcome', and Sumner noted he did not know of any local young people aware of the meeting.[96] If a willingness to discuss policing existed, it seemingly did not extend to black youths most likely to be affected.

The first concern of those present was the welfare of arrested youths, again demonstrating distrust of the police. Leach maintained that, as he did not have all requested information, he left to make inquiries believing no progress could be made until such details were presented, and tasked the head of the Police Community Contact Department and a Community Contact Inspector with beginning discussions. Cox remembers it differently:

So we all assembled ... Unfortunately, the Chief Superintendent didn't bother to come to the meeting for ages, so everybody was sitting there getting more and more angry ... After about forty-five minutes, quite a lot of people stormed out – which was unfortunate because all the media was outside, and they were saying 'this is hopeless!'[97]

Leach claimed he returned to the meeting, which had begun to disintegrate, after twenty minutes and faced accusations he had refused to meet representatives of the community – the youths were making the same complaints to assembled journalists outside.[98] The Hytner Inquiry, later established by the Greater Manchester County Council, concluded it was unlikely that Leach would have arranged the meeting just to alienate those present deliberately. If it had been an attempted police 'power play' to establish their authority, it was vastly misjudged. The Hytner Panel refused to make a judgement upon Leach's absence, simply stating there were disagreements as to whether those at the meeting had been provided with adequate explanations, but that, 'rightly or wrongly', they were offended by his absence.[99]

Despite Anderton believing those present 'must have been aware of the reasons' for Leach's absence, Cox and Linbert Spencer suggested that Anderton's personal appearance was necessary to appease them, and he duly arrived at the meeting. Cox informed Anderton that Leach had lost the confidence of the community, offering the opinion that his temporary replacement 'would be helpful to the situation'.[100] Anderton later recorded being 'absolutely dismayed by this appalling proposition', deeming it 'brutal and irregular treatment' to remove a Chief Superintendent in this way. He told Cox and Spencer that he 'would not crucify any of [his] officers in public to please or placate any disgruntled people', concluding in a later report that, if this was an example of 'democratic community policy, God help us!'[101]

Anderton and Leach both offered personal apologies at the meeting, but some present demanded a public apology be made through the press; believing they were seeking 'a sacrificial lamb', Anderton recorded 'they did not get one from me'.[102] Such response is consistent from a Chief Constable known for personally supporting his officers – this support occasionally suggested to extend beyond available levels of evidence. Hytner's Inquiry concluded that, despite Anderton believing complaints about Leach were made 'with malicious intent', they were genuine concerns in a time of emergency.[103] Anderton, however, did not hesitate in believing this to be a sign of broader subversion – indicative of his general reaction to accusations of police misconduct.

Nonetheless, Anderton appeared open to suggestions of a low police profile, reportedly agreeing it was the correct course of action – Hytner even suggested this tactic was Anderton's own suggestion.[104] Journalist Michael Nally instead indicated

Anderton agreed to avoid 'excessive' policing as long as 'hotheads' were restrained, but firm tactics would be employed if necessary to deal with emergencies – to which representatives of the community all reportedly agreed.[105] The general perception of this arrangement was summed up by a local schoolteacher, believing that 'community workers persuaded [Anderton] to assume a low profile' but, once disorders reappeared, Anderton had 'no choice but to initiate firm Police action'.[106]

Anderton received praise for his handling of this meeting. Hytner went so far as to claim he should be 'warmly and unequivocally congratulated' as, thanks to him, 'the day was saved'.[107] Remaining anti-police discontent and simple fact of violent disorder continuing after this meeting might suggest otherwise. Linbert Spencer, later Community Liaison Officer for Greater Manchester Council, sought to minimise the portrayal of this meeting as a great success. He claimed that the police and governmental bodies overestimated the influence of community groups and 'leaders': 'if there is going to be a riot you call the six leaders in and say "let's sort this out" and they go away and they stop the riot. Well the world isn't like that ... [Police are] conferring on ... "community leaders" in quotes, this amazing amount of control'.[108] As noted, assuming any group is truly representative of the wider community is problematic. Nevertheless, a Hytner Panel member later commented the mere fact that the police were willing to discuss the situation 'can only be good news'.[109] However, Anderton's future actions and comments would lead some to question his intentions.

Anderton's own description of the meeting depended upon whom he was addressing. His submission to Hytner's inquiry labelled the meeting 'interesting and informative', stating representatives of the community had declared their ability to 'control their own young people'. Once disorder escalated into confrontation at Moss Side Police Station, Anderton deemed it clear that a stronger police response was required.[110]

Alternatively, in a paper presented to the Police Committee, also released to the press and notably titled 'The Truth about the Moss Side Meeting', Anderton labelled it 'a saga'.[111] Undoubtedly responding to criticism that police tactics had resulted in their absence during disorders, this account was described by Hytner as characterised by 'unrestrained vigour'.[112] For example, Anderton outright dismissed complaints that numerous visible officers within the police station yard were tantamount to provocation. Simply put, he did not appreciate the fundamental local distrust of the police that gave rise to these accusations, which he deemed 'remarkable'. Anderton summarised that the 'heavy pressure' applied to him and officers during the meeting was 'out of all proportion to the problem' – seemingly missing possible parallels with complaints regarding heavy-handed policing tactics. In addition, while confirming he had agreed to the low-profile approach, Anderton posited that some locals wished to see the streets completely free of police. Recording that reports appeared of large gatherings of young people less than one hour after black youths left the meeting, he clearly viewed their attendance as some form of reconnaissance: 'I cannot help but feel that a guarantee of virtually unpoliced streets ... suited and served some terribly ulterior purpose'.[113] Hytner expressed disappointment at this suggestion and, while believing Anderton had not meant to imply that representatives of the community were assisting riotous actions, criticised his phrasing that could be interpreted that way.[114] Anderton's revised account of this meeting was not one that appeared particularly amenable to increased participation from local people in policing matters, instead seeming to suggest that the meeting had been a ploy to allow disorders to escalate unimpeded.

Whichever of Anderton's accounts of the meeting is considered, its main subject and outcome were later believed to have been active deceit. While the police contended that low-profile policing had not worked and events necessitated a stronger police response, many locals believed this had been the plan all along. Moss Side residents contested that, rather than low-profile policing, there had actually been 'no policing whatsoever' because the police 'didn't keep the bargain'.[115] Indeed, the Hytner Panel recorded the 'wild allegation, which we wholly discount', that it had been police policy to 'let Moss Side burn' to endorse a more forceful response.[116] Arnold Spencer was one to level such an accusation, claiming the police wanted to 'let Moss Side burn just a bit before they could move in in their full riot strength'; it is significant that such an allegation was made by a city councillor, even a Labour one.[117] Unsurprisingly, it was fiercely denied by Anderton, who pointed to the average 1,600 emergency calls received at the height of each night's disturbances as evidence that any delay in response was due purely to an overstretched police force.[118] The fact that Anderton had to include such a strong denial in his report of events shows how widely this belief permeated. As with other accusations, its accuracy may never be known; however, that such an immoral police tactic was widely deemed possible, even probable, clearly demonstrates the widespread negative view of the authorities.

A more credible belief, expressed by figures such as Labour City Councillor John Nicholson, was that the disorders were exploited to justify a subsequently more robust police response.[119] The Moss Side Community Action Committee accused Anderton, having recently acquired riot equipment, of using apparent failures of low-profile policing to 'embark on a calculated and brutal attack on the whole Moss Side Community'.[120] Barri Potter expressed the feeling of many locals when insisting Anderton 'knew darn well that the kids would riot that night no matter how many police were on the streets'.[121] Thus, by agreeing to a reduced police presence, Anderton could be seen as willing to co-operate but when disorder continued regardless 'hard'-policing tactics could be employed. Anderton later bluntly countered that the police had been forced into stronger actions by local people's failures: 'when police have to resort to tougher tactics, it is generally the fault of the community and not of the struggling police. We should stop making excuses for conduct that is palpably wicked and nothing else'.[122]

The Hytner Inquiry declared that, as panel member Linbert Spencer attended the meeting, it was unable to consider or comment upon these disputes.[123] For many locals who put weight behind claims of police transgressions, this appeared another example of the authorities not adequately investigating their concerns. While the meeting had ostensibly been an attempt to prevent repeats of disorder through improving the police/community relationship, its lasting legacy was instead to further existing mistrust.

Further disorder

As indicated, this meeting and attempted pacification did not prevent further disturbances. Around 10:22 p.m. on 8 July, approximately 300–1,000 youths 'attacked' Moss Side Police Station. Most of the windows were broken, nine police and seven private vehicles were damaged, and an unsuccessful attempt was made to ignite petrol spilled in the yard.[124] Eyewitnesses even claimed to have seen a crowd, including some identified as outsiders to the area, being led towards the police station by a nine-year-old white boy. Despite this prompting accusations that 'outsiders' had come to target the police, the Hytner Panel 'wholly reject[ed] the implication that the attack had in some way been planned in another city'. This was supported by their connected conclusion that, for a group intending to storm the police station, they seemed 'remarkably ill-prepared' and soon retreated once their 'first and pathetically hopeless attack' failed and police reinforcements arrived.[125]

Others suggested that this crowd was attempting to free the seven previously arrested youths, although these were actually being held at nearby Platt Lane Station; somewhat ironically, reinforcements arriving from this station ended the attack on Moss Side Station.[126] Officer Mike Freeman recalled travelling from Platt Lane and that a relaxed police attitude, that 'it was a bit of a giggle, a bit of a joke', was quickly replaced with fear once the van began to be hit by rocks and bottles.[127] One black youth involved in the attack allegedly proclaimed: 'I'm here to see the pigs get theirs. They've done this for years. Now they know what it's like to be hit back.'[128] The crowd's anger was focused on the police, attempting some form of retribution, but also attempting to change their previous treatment of black residents. The high level of discontent and antipathy in Moss Side towards the police was summed up by a sixty-one-year-old white Conservative-leaning man, who dubbed the attack upon the Moss Side Police Station the best thing to have happened in years.[129]

Many observers were surprised that the attack upon the police station did not immediately alter the police's low-profile approach. Six hundred officers were reportedly waiting in reserve in Platt Lane Station, whereas Moss Side Station contained only fourteen.[130] The police had begun to hear rumours of an attack earlier that afternoon and decided to limit the number of police present in Moss Side Station in the face of a likely attack.[131] However, tensions appeared through negative reaction to the police's absence from the area. For example, Robert William Goldsby, husband of the Moss Side constituency Conservative candidate, complained that local business owners had paid the price for Anderton proving he could keep a low profile.[132] Furthermore, an anonymous witness claimed officers had earlier advised locals to take steps to protect their properties, as more disturbances would occur. When asked why police would not provide protection, officers allegedly replied 'We don't want any confrontation direct with them. You have to protect your own property'.[133]

Evidence suggests that the few officers present in Moss Side withdrew soon after crowds initially assembled on 8 July. Hytner refused to criticise this departure as they 'might have been in considerable danger if they had remained'; indeed, one Police Inspector was struck by a crossbow bolt during this time.[134] At around 10:40 p.m., a police officer, described as 'very young and very afraid', was seen running down the street shouting for cafés and shops to close and for people to leave.[135] Some alleged that no protection against vandalism or looting was provided for two-and-a-half hours, although Hytner recorded that, while 'Much bitter comment' was made about it, police absence had actually lasted only one hour.[136] Just as Chief Constable Brian Weigh was roundly criticised for his withdrawal of officers during the St Pauls disturbances in 1980, disapproval of the police's failure to protect local people and property further galvanised the Government's response of strengthening the police to ensure no repeats of similar situations in the future.[137]

'Hard' policing response

'Eventually', in Hytner's words, the police arrived in numbers, both in vehicles and on foot with riot gear. A large crowd gathered to oppose them and, despite no attempt to disperse it, a number of officers charged the crowd, followed by the entire police line. As Hytner concluded, it is almost impossible to believe this action focused its forcefulness solely against anyone that had warranted it.[138] Furthermore, police vehicles drove at high speed into crowds of people to disperse them: a tactic copied from Northern Irish examples. A number of witnesses were asked by the Hytner Panel whether this was a clever manoeuvre or reckless approach, and in response, stories were recounted of people desperately avoiding oncoming police vans. When questioned what would have happened had they been unable to get out of the way, Arnold Spencer replied 'Well, I think, tough; they would have been dead, I guess'.[139]

If any local people believed such seemingly uncontrolled tactics would be investigated by Hytner's inquiry, they were disappointed. In fact, Hytner determined that it was foolish for residents to be confronting assembled police in the first place, as they had increased the mood of confrontation – although it was nevertheless conceded that, had the police initially made appropriate attempts to disperse the crowd, some might have vacated the streets.[140] Many would likely have remained regardless and faced officers but, without attempting to disperse crowds before employing aggressive tactics, the police prompted further discontentment towards their actions, attitudes and apparent ability to escape unscrutinised.

Merseyside Chief Constable Kenneth Oxford described that traditional police tactics to dissolve large crowds had proven 'completely and utterly ineffective in the face of the tactics adopted by the protagonists in 1981'.[141] Therefore, as opposed to lines of static officers with plastic riot shields providing a police target, Anderton instead employed officers in vans to increase mobility and target influential participants. He later stated that his tactics were influenced by previous large numbers of police injuries, particularly personal experience of his officers deployed in Toxteth, and that similarly high casualty levels 'simply could not be tolerated' in Manchester.[142] It was not only the disturbances themselves spreading in 1981: police tactics evolved following experiences of disorder.

Whitelaw publicly proclaimed his 'fullest support' for Anderton's tactics, which he deemed to have been a 'conspicuous success'.[143] The authorities' opinion can clearly be seen through a Home Office note recording that damage had been less extensive after the 'more positive approach of the police following the disappointing result of their "softly softly" approach'.[144] While the Home Office documented reduced damage when the police employed stronger tactics, it did not reference the negative impact this had upon police/community relations. The collective violence was locally deemed a political protest against a hostile police force and complaints system that had failed black Britons, which in turn was greeted by 'snatch squads' and increasingly aggressive tactics. County Councillor Andrew Fender criticised the move towards 'very heavy-handed' police tactics, flooding the area with officers 'swooping onto people indiscriminately … whatever a situation is, that can't possibly contribute to policing in a civilised society'.[145]

Mike and Trevor Phillips deemed Moss Side 'a watershed in police violence', detailing how fifty-four vans of 'snatch squads', influenced by Northern Irish approaches, went 'speeding through the area … to crack heads and drag their targets away'.[146] The impact of Northern Ireland – of street violence flooding the public consciousness – was considerable, influencing police responses to public disorder. As crowds on English streets were equated with the conflicts of the prolonged 'Troubles', similar methods were utilised to combat them. Indeed, six senior English police officers visited Northern Ireland on 14 July to discuss riot control strategies and, in Robert Reiner's description, learn lessons from the 'success' of Royal Ulster Constabulary tactics.[147]

Conclusion

Mirroring Brixton and Toxteth before it, Moss Side was soon visited by Home Secretary William Whitelaw, who told reporters the disturbances had resulted from local youths' feelings of 'hopelessness' and 'social alienation', in addition to the favoured Conservative explanation of 'criminal hooliganism'.[148] Despite Whitelaw holding a meeting at County Hall, where Police Authority Deputy Chair Gabrielle Cox informed him of the difficult relationship between the police and local youth, community groups criticised his appearance as a 'flying visit' that had not allowed adequate time for them to arrange discussions.[149]

Whitelaw telephoned Thatcher after visiting Manchester and, seemingly disregarding the targeting of the police station and copious evidence of anti-police feeling, informed her that the disorders had been characterised by 'looting and hooliganism, rather than confrontation with the police'. He deemed low-profile policing tactics 'a complete failure', claiming representatives of the community had since admitted as much, and believed the 'relatively little trouble' that greeted the subsequent saturated police presence 'showed the need for decisiveness'. Unsurprisingly from this reading of events, and fitting with the establishment's general response to disturbances, Whitelaw believed the top priority was to ensure the police were suitably equipped to deal with such disorder. This included the threat of water cannons, 'even if it was unlikely to be used in practice', and the possibility of arming the police.[150] This is one of the most obvious examples of how the response at the very highest levels of government focused on criminality and largely unrelated looting that followed initial outbreaks of anti-police disorder. To prevent attention falling upon their policies, the issue was portrayed as one of maintaining law and order – and the answer was ensuring the police were better equipped.[151]

During five days in Moss Side, 135 people were arrested for criminal offences and 106 for public order offences, eighteen officers were injured – of which nine required hospital treatment and 130 days of sick leave were taken – and damage to police vehicles, station, uniforms and equipment totalled over £10,000. Echoing other disturbances, the vast majority of those arrested were aged between seventeen and twenty-four and, despite media reports suggesting otherwise, the majority were white – demonstrating the prevalent involvement of white looters.[152] Despite Whitelaw's omission of this fact, observers noted that violence was directed against specific targets and firefighters recorded that the majority of hostilities were focused towards the police.[153] Some participants had even attempted to prevent looting, reasoning that it shifted focus away from the anti-police sentiment that began the disorders and was turning neutral locals and media against them.[154] As this outcome had been demonstrated in previous disturbances, it can also be viewed as an attempt by participants in collective violence to adapt their tactics and ensure their voices of protest were not drowned out by subsequent looting. Nevertheless, despite such efforts, the general response was once again focused upon criminality.

Attempting to combat this emphasis on criminality, many local people highlighted the extremes that people had to go to make their voices heard. A local social worker concluded that more disturbances might be needed as they were seemingly the only things producing results, and an anonymous witness told the Hytner Panel: 'Look what it's taken to get people like you here to make any inquiry and perhaps listen.'[155] With echoes of previous disorders, it was also noted that local youth felt they had made something happen and, possibly for the first time, forced their issues to be addressed: 'Their actions had been seen to be significant.'[156] H. Warm, District Inspector for Manchester Education Committee, later summarised that the disturbances reflected local people's newfound ability to tell authority that it did not know what was best for them, and that they were going to do things themselves.[157] Thus, this collective violence can be viewed within broader movements towards militancy, Black Power-inspired self-reliance, and range of political responses to achieve an increased level of attention and participation in the political arena for this previously marginalised group.[158]

Disorder returned to Toxteth on 26 July, when twenty-one people were arrested, twenty-six officers were injured, and a disabled man, David Moore, was killed when hit by a police Land Rover.[159] Moore's death was attributed to the Merseyside Police's adoption of the same Northern Irish-inspired crowd dispersal techniques employed in Moss Side.[160] Transferring practices established during the 'Troubles', which seemingly placed more emphasis on maintaining authority, law and order than protecting the public, displayed a hard-line policing approach. Oxford defended his adoption of stronger tactics: 'To put it crudely the people have spat in my face. It is the only way that I can protect them from themselves.'[161] Moore's death would seem to question such protection, tragically answering Hytner's question of what would happen if someone were unable to evade oncoming police vehicles. Michael Smith, then a thirteen-year-old local, witnessed Moore's death:

> The police were getting a lot more violent, a lot more equipped. They were calling it dispersal at the time; it was basically ramming people ... We were running to the fence ... and this guy just went that way and, well, the [police vehicle] just flattened him, and went right over him. I think he died there and then.[162]

Two more men narrowly avoided the same fate, sustaining serious injuries. In response, Oxford bluntly stated: 'They can see the vehicles coming and they know what will happen if they get in the way.'[163] Officers involved in Moore's death were charged with manslaughter, but found not guilty in April 1981; the *Morning Star* alleged that, days after Moore's death, the police van had apparently disappeared from police custody.[164] As disorders spread across the country, coupled with a more aggressive and well-equipped police response, a fatality appeared increasingly likely. The fact that officers involved in Moore's death were not punished proliferated beliefs that the police were not held to sufficient standards of accountability.

While Lord Scarman conducted his investigations into Brixton, several hundred incidents of disorder throughout England had been recorded by the end of August 1981. Three months had passed, but increased tensions undoubtedly played a role in July disturbances – as did the knowledge that Brixton's collective violence had prompted a judicial inquiry, encouraging others to employ such methods to attract similar attention and resources. Because of spreading disorder, Scarman's ongoing Brixton inquiry was widened, purportedly to include examination of these further disturbances, but in reality not including much more than cursory visits and basic discussion of some events. In Manchester, a local inquiry was established by the County Council, but was met with a mixed response, partly due to previous experiences – such as local people angrily storming out of a problematic meeting with the police – having left some local people with the impression such measures were a waste of time. This is discussed in the subsequent chapter.

Despite some private misgivings about the Manchester and Liverpool Chief Constables – blamed by locals for preventing police/community relations improving and allegedly referred to as 'the mad and the bad' by one Home Office official – their forceful responses were publicly backed by the Government as their response remained focused upon law, order and criminality, and the police were essential in enforcing such a focus.[165] Consequently, new methods of police tactics and equipment were utilised to deal with public disorder. English forces had switched their tactics to be more consistent with those seen on the streets of Northern Ireland, such as 'snatch squads', vehicles to disperse crowds and use of CS gas. As Linbert Spencer concluded: 'What happened in Bristol, Manchester, and Liverpool changed the nature of policing forever.'[166]

Notes

1 The National Archives (TNA): PREM 19/484, 'Review of Potential for Civil Disturbance in 1981', 27 April 1981.

2 Black Cultural Archives (BCA): Gutzmore/1/6/1, Brixton Defence Campaign Bulletin No. 2. The Brixton Defence Campaign was established to provide legal aid and support for those arrested in relation to the disturbances.

3 TNA: HO 266/136, James Anderton to P.J.C. Mawer, 16 July 1981.

4 Brain, *History of Policing*, p. 68; Ball, 'The "Bristol Riot"', 33. See: Koopmans, 'Protest in Time and Space'.

5 The author is indebted to John Stevenson, who provided access to a number of sources collected at the time unavailable elsewhere, on which discussions of the following two chapters are largely based.

6 Brixton Defence Campaign Bulletin No. 2.

7 See: Ramamurthy, *Black Star*, pp. 26–7; Scraton and McCulloch, *Deaths in Custody*, pp. 75–8.

8 Ramdin, *Black Working Class*, p. 501; Ramamurthy, *Black Star*, pp. 30–53.

9 Huq, 'Youth Culture and Antiracism', 45. See: Kettle and Hodges, *Uprising!*, pp. 154–7.

10 See: Ramamurthy, *Black Star*, pp. 120–45. Noted human rights lawyer Gareth Peirce also represented defendants in the 1980 St Pauls 'riot' trials, and the men charged with the murder of PC Keith Blakelock during the 1985 Broadwater Farm disturbances.

11 Scarman, *Report*, p. 31.

12 Bowling, 'Emergence of Violent Racism', p. 208. See: Ramamurthy, *Black Star*, pp. 65–96; Shukra, *Black Politics*; Ramdin, *Black Working Class*.

13 TNA: PREM 19/484, C.J. Walters, 'Note of a visit: Liverpool: 7 July 1981', 9 July 1981. See: Belchem, *Before the Windrush*, pp. 251–78; Cooper, 'Merseyside Riots'; Marren, *We Shall not be Moved*, pp. 110–43.

14 Nelson, Jr, *Black Atlantic Politics*, p. 48.

15 *BBC News*, 4 July 2001; Scraton, *Power, Conflict and Criminalisation*, p. 29.

16 Margaret Simey, cited in Kettle and Hodges, *Uprising!*, pp. 55–6; Humphry, *Police Power and Black People*, pp. 13, 17; Fryer, *Staying Power*, pp. 391–2.

17 Nelson, *Black Atlantic Politics*, pp. 203, 237, 263.

18 Cited in *ibid.*, pp. 204–5.

19 'Note of a visit: Liverpool'.

20 Ramdin, *Black Working Class*, p. 455.

21 TNA: PREM 19/484, 'Meeting with Liverpool Community Leaders', 14 July 1981; Oxford, 'Policing by Consent', pp. 114–17.

22 Scraton, *Power, Conflict and Criminalisation*, pp. 26–7.

23 Nelson, *Black Atlantic Politics*, p. 203.

24 'Note of a visit: Liverpool'.

25 Simey, 'Partnership Policing', pp. 135–6; Simey, *Police Accountability*, p. 43.

26 Whitelaw, *Memoirs*, pp. 246–8. See: Dawson *et al.* (eds), *Northern Ireland Troubles*.

27 'Meeting with Liverpool Community Leaders'; TNA: PREM 19/484; 'Meeting with the Church Leaders', 14 July 1981; Thatcher, *Downing Street Years*, p. 145.

28 Thatcher, *Downing Street Years*, p. 146.

29 TNA: PREM 19/484, 'Meeting with local authority representatives', 14 July 1981. Thatcherite 'New Right' ideology redefined national identity around respect for authority, and law and order. See: Mitchell and Russell, 'Race, the New Right and State Policy'.

30 TNA: PREM 19/484, 'Meeting with the Chief Constable of Merseyside', 14 July 1981.

31 Thatcher, *Downing Street Years*, p. 146.

32 'Meeting with the Church Leaders'.

33 *New York Times*, 11 July 1981.

34 Brain, *History of Policing*, p. 73.

35 TNA: PREM 19/484, Michael Heseltine to Margaret Thatcher, 10 July 1981.

36 TNA: PREM 19/578, Heseltine to Thatcher, 13 August 1981. See: Belchem, *Before the Windrush*, pp. 256–66; Marren, *We Shall not be Moved*, pp. 120–1.

37 *BBC News*, 4 July 2001, 3 July 2011.

38 Loveday, 'Government and Accountability of the Police', p. 135; Reiner, *Politics of the Police*, p. 230.

39 TNA: PREM 19/484, 'Notes for supplementaries'.

40 'Note of a visit: Liverpool'; *New Statesman*, 17 July 1981.

41 BCA: Gutzmore/1/6/1, Brixton Defence Campaign Bulletin No. 4; Wegg-Prosser, *Police and the Law*, p. 231; 'Note of a visit: Liverpool'; *New Statesman*, 17 July 1981; *Police Record*, 10 July 1981.

42 Nally, 'Eyewitness in Moss Side', p. 61.

43 Oxford, 'Policing by Consent', p. 118.

44 Whitelaw, *Memoirs*, pp. 246–7.

45 See: Jefferson, *Paramilitary Policing*.

46 *The Times*, 7 July 1981.

47 TNA: PREM 19/484, Anthony Steen to William Whitelaw, 6 July 1981.

48 *New York Times*, 11 July 1981; Benyon, 'Civil Disorder', p. 24.

49 *Time Out*, 17 April 1981; HL Deb 24 March 1982, vol. 428, cc. 1005–6.

50 Benyon, 'Going through the Motions', 410.

51 *New York Times*, 11 July 1981.

52 Murdock, 'Reporting the Riots', pp. 76–8.

53 TNA: PREM 19/484, Willie Rickett to Colin Walters, 13 July 1981.

54 TNA: PREM 19/484, Whitelaw to John Nott, 13 July 1981; Nott to Whitelaw, 30 July 1981.

55 TNA: PREM 19/484, Home Affairs Select Committee, 'Brief for a Debate on Recent Outbreaks of Civil Disorder'.

56 London Broadcasting Company/Independent Radio News Digitisation Archive: Interview with James Anderton, 'Latest Riot Outbreak in Moss Side', 9 July 1981; Home Affairs Select Committee, 'Recent Outbreaks of Civil Disorder'. For policing Northern Ireland, see: Ellison and Smyth, *Policing Northern Ireland*; Sanders and Wood, *Times of Troubles*.

57 Nott to Whitelaw, 16 July 1981.

58 Brain, *History of Policing*, pp. 69–70; *Daily Express*, 1 February 1983.

59 'Notes for supplementaries'.

60 'Meeting with the Chief Constable of Merseyside'.

61 Griffiths, 'One-Tier Policing', p. 130.

62 Waddington, *Public Disorder*, p. 185.

63 Brain, *History of Policing*, pp. 68–9.

64 HC Deb 16 July 1981, vol. 8, cc. 1406–7.

65 *Sunday Telegraph*, 12 July 1981.

66 Thatcher MSS (digital collection), Central Office of Information transcript, 'Press Conference visiting Liverpool', 13 July 1981.

67 John Stevenson's collection (JS): Moss Side Enquiry Minutes of Evidence (MOE), 18 August 1981.

68 JS: MSI, Anonymous resident.

69 JS: MSI, Edwards.

70 Brooke, 'Affective Ecology', 112.

71 Interview with Linbert Spencer, 20 March 2017.

72 Moss Side Defence Committee, *Hytner Myths*, p. 5.

73 Interview with Phil Sumner, 20 April 2017.

74 Phillips and Phillips, *Windrush*, p. 363. See: Prince, *God's Cop*.

75 TNA: HO 266/136, James Anderton, Address to Manchester Luncheon Club, 'Police to Some Purpose', 14 June 1979.

76 Interview with Gus John, 19 May 2017; Interview with Sumner; Whitelaw, *Memoirs*, p. 248.

77 Kettle and Hodges, *Uprising!*, pp. 95–6.

78 Draft of a speech that James Anderton was going to deliver in 1982, but never made as the event was cancelled, in Prince, *God's Cop*, p. 117.

79 Interview with Gabrielle Cox, 19 April 2017.

80 JS: MSI, Edwards.

81 See: chapters 2 and 4.

82 JS: MOE, 21 August 1981; 28 August 1981.

83 George Padmore Institute (GPI): The Black Parents Movement collection (BPM), GB/2904/BPM/3/2/4/2, Manchester Black Parents Organisation, Press Release, 'Cache of Weapons at Moss Side Police Station – What Will Anderton Do Now?'

84 Interview with Cox.

85 'Cache of Weapons at Moss Side Police Station'.

86 Hytner, *Report*, p. 28; *Manchester Evening News*, 8 July 2011.

87 JS: MSI, Edwards.

88 TNA: HO 266/136, Town Clerk, 'Civil Disturbances in Manchester', 20 July 1981.

89 JS: MSI, Barri Potter.

90 TNA: HO 266/136, Moss Side Community Action Committee, Press Statement, 14 July 1981.

91 'Latest Riot Outbreak in Moss Side'; 'Civil Disturbances in Manchester'.

92 JS: MOE, 18 August 1981.

93 James Anderton, 'Serious Incidents of Public Disorder in Greater Manchester 8th to 12th July 1981', 4 September 1981, Appendix 4B, Hytner, *Report*.

94 *Manchester Evening News*, 8 July 2011.

95 'Civil Disturbances in Manchester'.

96 TNA: HO 266/136, James Anderton, 'The Truth about the Moss Side Meeting', 4 September 1981; JS: MOE, 20 August 1981.

97 Interview with Cox.

98 'The Truth about the Moss Side Meeting'.

99 Hytner, *Report*, p. 41.

100 Interview with Cox.

101 'The Truth about the Moss Side Meeting'.

102 *Ibid.*

103 Hytner, *Report*, p. 42.

104 *Ibid.*, p. 41; JS: MOE, 21 August 1981.

105 Nally, 'Eyewitness in Moss Side', pp. 55–6; JS: MOE, 21 August 1981.

106 JS: MOE, 19 August 1981.

107 Hytner, *Report*, p. 41.

108 JS: MSI, Linbert Spencer, 23 August 1983.

109 JS: MOE, 17 August 1981.

110 'Serious Incidents of Public Disorder'.

111 'The Truth about the Moss Side Meeting'.

112 Hytner, *Report*, p. 41.

113 'The Truth about the Moss Side Meeting'.

114 Hytner, *Report*, p. 42.

115 JS: MOE, 17 August 1981; JS: MSI, Mrs L.S.

116 Hytner, *Report*, p. 45.

117 JS: MOE, 17 August 1981.

118 'Serious Incidents of Public Disorder'.

119 JS: MOE, 26 August 1981.

120 Moss Side Community Action Committee, Press Statement.

121 JS: MSI, Potter.

122 Draft of speech, in Prince, *God's Cop*, p. 117.

123 Hytner, *Report*, p. 41.

124 'Civil Disturbances in Manchester'; 'Serious Incidents of Public Disorder'.

125 JS: MOE, 18 August 1981; Hytner, *Report*, p. 45. For 'outsiders' in disorders, see: Murdock, 'Reporting the Riots', pp. 83–5.

126 JS: MOE, 18 August 1981; *Manchester Evening News*, 8 July 2011.

127 *Manchester Evening News*, 4 July 2011.

128 Nally, 'Eyewitness in Moss Side', p. 57.

129 JS: MOE, 17 August 1981.

130 JS: MOE, 20 August 1981.

131 *Manchester Evening News*, 8 July 2011.

132 JS: MOE, 20 August 1981.

133 JS: MOE, 18 August 1981.

134 'Serious Incidents of Public Disorder'; Hytner, *Report*, p. 45.

135 JS: MOE, 27 August 1981.

136 TNA: HO 266/136, Note of a City Council meeting, 16 July 1981; Hytner, *Report*, p. 45.

137 See: chapter 2.

138 Hytner, *Report*, p. 48.

139 JS: MOE, 17 August 1981.

140 Hytner, *Report*, p. 48.

141 Oxford, 'Policing by Consent', p. 123.

142 'Serious Incidents of Public Disorder'.

143 *New York Times*, 11 July 1981.

144 TNA: PREM 19/484, P.J. Honour to Halliday, 10 July 1981.

145 JS: MOE, 17 August 1981.

146 Phillips and Phillips, *Windrush*, pp. 363–4.

147 'The July Riots', 165; Reiner, *Politics of the Police*, p. 86.

148 *New York Times*, 11 July 1981.

149 Interview with Cox; JS: MSI, Martin Bobker.

150 Rickett to Walters, 13 July 1981.

151 See: Rowe, *Racialisation of Disorder*, pp. 156–7; Mitchell and Russell, 'Race, the New Right and State Policy'.

152 'Serious Incidents of Public Disorder'. See: Cooper, 'Merseyside Riots'; Kettle and Hodges, *Uprising!*, pp. 28–9; Keith, *Race, Riots and Policing*, pp. 103–4.

153 JS: MOE, 17 August 1981.

154 Nally, 'Eyewitness in Moss Side', p. 57.

155 JS: MSI, Charlie Harries; JS: MOE, 17 August 1981.

156 JS: MSI, Anonymous Moss Side teacher.

157 JS: MSI, H. Warm.

158 See: Sivanandan, *Different Hunger*, pp. 3–54; chapter 1.
159 *Daily Telegraph*, 28 July 1981.
160 Phillips and Phillips, *Windrush*, p. 365.
161 Kettle and Hodges, *Uprising!*, p. 173.
162 *Observer*, 3 July 2011.
163 Kettle and Hodges, *Uprising!*, p. 173.
164 *Ibid.*, pp. 172–3; *Morning Star*, 1 August 1981.
165 Interview with Cox.
166 Interview with Spencer.

7

'Who the hell's defending if they're going to walk out of here?' The Moss Side Defence Committee

Can't go on no more,
The people getting angry.

The Specials – Ghost Town

REACTION TO the 1981 Moss Side disturbances, as with other locations where anti-police racial disorders appeared in 1980–81, provoked a dichotomous local response concerning the worth of governmental inquiries. Thus, when the Greater Manchester County Council (GMC) established a local inquiry, it was greeted with a far from unanimous response. Some local black community workers, such as Linbert Spencer, Greater Manchester Youth Association Director of Operations, and Louise Da'Cocodia, West Indian Organisation Co-ordinating Committee Manchester Chair, accepted invitations to serve on the inquiry panel, believing they could positively influence its focus and recommendations. Conversely, the Moss Side Defence Committee, formed to aid those arrested in relation to the disturbances, vehemently opposed the inquiry and organised a boycott; Spencer was deemed a 'police spy' and Da'Cocodia was forced to resign from the Defence Committee due to her inquiry involvement.

This chapter provides detailed discussion of the Moss Side Defence Committee, through local and understudied national records and original interviews, which is often overlooked in discussions of 1980–81.[1] Interestingly, it was later suggested that dichotomous local responses allowed progress: that radical groups, such as the Defence Committee, 'being noisy', allowed moderates previously unattainable access to the authorities – but the extent to which this was a conscious tactic is debatable.[2] Tensions raised by disagreements concerning the worth and intention of governmental inquiries were mirrored by conflicting views regarding the very nature of the disorder itself. While the GMC inquiry concluded disorder was the inevitable result of an accumulation of discontent and spreading belief that disturbances were 'bound to happen' in Moss Side, the Defence Committee portrayed them as 'a rational alternative to the more articulate and constitutional, but unsuccessful, protests [from] desperately oppressed and powerless people'.[3] The chapter ends, similarly to chapter 5's examination of Brixton records, by exploring unstudied interviews with residents and inquiry proceedings demonstrating the high level of accusations of police misconduct not appearing in the inquiry report, and the continued discontent created by such exclusions.

The Hytner Inquiry

Soon after disorder subsided in Moss Side, the Manchester City Council resolved to request that the Home Secretary extend Lord Scarman's Brixton disturbances public inquiry to consider events in Manchester; or, if that was not possible, to establish another similar independent inquiry. Town Clerk James Hetherington emphasised the importance of investigations into complaints against the police, needing, most importantly, to be seen to be independent and impartial.[4] The GMC believed a local independent inquiry would better examine the specific case of Moss Side and, as such, declined to submit any observations to Scarman.[5] Following discussions with the Greater Manchester Police Authority, they subsequently established a local inquiry chaired by Benet Hytner QC, a local and distinguished crown court recorder with a reputation for having a social conscience.[6] However, Manchester City Council resented not having been consulted or involved in establishing this inquiry, believing it fell within its jurisdiction. This led City Council leader Norman Morris to claim the inquiry 'started nowhere and it's going nowhere'.[7] Police Authority Deputy Chair Gabrielle Cox later recalled that the lack of overt support from the City Council was 'not helpful'.[8] Certainly, for an investigation desired to be full and independent, things did not start on the best footing.

Hytner's terms of reference were to examine circumstances leading to disorder and the manner they were dealt with, to deliver recommendations that would avoid reoccurrences. Upon opening inquiry proceedings, however, Hytner stressed that it was an investigation into the immediate causes rather than a fuller examination of the underlying conditions. As with similar governmental inquiries, such as Scarman's, this immediately threatened to overlook the accumulation of tensions and discontent at the heart of the disturbances. He also dispelled any hope of this inquiry addressing specific allegations of police misconduct, by declaring it could not provide the strict safeguards that 'basic fairness and justice' required to investigate such public accusations.[9] In fact, Hytner noted the police had accepted the panel's request not to attend public hearings unless invited – a somewhat unsuccessful attempt to encourage residents to provide evidence without fear of legal or police repercussions. Nevertheless, the police subsequently rejected the inquiry's later invitation to appear for questioning, and this local inquiry was incapable of enforcing their attendance. Manchester Chief Constable James Anderton did not believe it was right, 'in view of the statutory relationship between himself and the Police Committee that he should be expected in any way to answer criticisms made to or by' Hytner's inquiry. In a blunter statement to the press, Anderton deemed it 'plainly ridiculous' and 'too intolerable' to address the inquiry's 'petty comments'.[10] It is not difficult to imagine how locals, angered at a lack of police accountability and effective means to voice their concerns, might have viewed this response – although, as previously noted, Anderton had never been fond of the concept of 'policing by consent'.[11]

Jeffrey Wilner, Moss Side Ward City Councillor, accused Anderton of complacency, and the Hytner Report admitted being 'disappointed' by Anderton's response, despite stressing that they understood and in no way resented his refusal to attend. Relatedly, Hytner also noted being 'dismayed' to discover the level of hostility displayed by local youth towards the police.[12] If the inquiry panel was so downhearted by the state of relations between the police and local youth, it is difficult to see why it would not begrudge the police's refusal to attend and discuss this. During the inquiry, Hytner recited a report from Anderton and, wishing to 'avoid disappointment to avoid provoking another riot', assured the assembled public that the police's version of events would not go unchallenged.[13] However, this apparent appreciation of local discontent towards the police did not result in a comparable level of police criticism in the final Report. Hytner later conceded that it would have clearly been helpful if Anderton had co-operated, but he did not believe this absence prevented the inquiry from uncovering the facts.[14] This view was not shared by everyone; indeed, many observers questioned how the truth could be reached or any level of accountability obtained when the police had not even faced the accusations against them.

Hytner often appeared sympathetic to local issues and difficulties, exemplified in requests, while hearing evidence, that locally born people no longer be reductively referred to as 'West Indians'. Furthermore, when the panel received multiple examples of testimony blaming disorder on 'black immigrants who don't know how to behave', Hytner dismissed such accusations by declaring that authors of 'that sort of rubbish' were 'talking through their hat'. The Report similarly noted evidence submitted by 'pathetic, old or sick people who saw themselves threatened by blacks', blaming immigration and demanding deportations, but the panel rejected these 'scurrilous allegations' and was heartened that those espousing such prejudices usually did so anonymously.[15]

Despite this, black Britons still faced having their futures decided by those not living through their circumstances. Local Catholic priest Phil Sumner, who was heavily involved in Moss Side racial issues during the 1980s and 1990s, concluded, 'If somebody comes in from outside ... the question is do they understand the issues in the first place when they actually begin to engage with them?'[16] Going further, Defence Committee Chair Gus John condemned

> the assumption that when these things happen, you get some bloody grandee, who has no understanding whatsoever and has no reason to have an understanding. Why should it be assumed that Ben Hytner was qualified to understand the dynamics of life in Moss Side, or how policing takes place on a routine basis day-by-day in a community like that? The fact that he's a QC and a supposedly intelligent person is not enough qualification for that kind of thing.[17]

Acknowledging the need for such inquiries to be conducted by someone of sufficient eminence without biased links to the area, Cox nonetheless had to remind Hytner, following his declaration he was the only person to have spent his summer in Moss Side, that the local population had also done so.[18]

A picket line, organised by the Defence Committee, protested the inquiry during its open hearing sessions and an angry member of the public threw a jug of water over Hytner.[19] While this was actually regarding an unrelated high court case, the press used it as a metaphor for the local reaction to the inquiry. After the media highlighted the inquiry's generally low attendance, Hytner attempted to portray this rather as evidence that locals did not believe further disturbances would materialise, so did not consider their presence necessary.[20] This, however, did not appear to be the main reason for a low turnout.

Moss Side Defence Committee

During a public meeting of over 300 people on 5 August 1981, it was decided that a legal defence committee would be formed 'around defendants, relatives of defendants, and defendants under curfew to review and prepare legal defence'.

Thus, the Moss Side Defence Committee was established to aid those arrested during and after the disturbances, giving lectures and talks to various unions and organisations to raise money for fines and legal fees, with Gus John concluding 'there were lots of acquittals, because of the quality of the preparation that we did'.[21] Due to his profile and anti-racist campaigns in the area, John was elected Chair. Having worked with other prominent *Race Today* collective figures such as Darcus Howe and John La Rose, John noted that they had 'developed and honed this practice of defence committees ... So I brought of all that'.[22] The Committee's formation followed previous examples in St Pauls and Brixton; it was not named, as a local youth worker seemingly believed, because the Moss Side community needed defending from the police.[23] Whether this was genuine confusion or a pointed comment is unknown, but suggestions that local youth needed an organisation to defend them from police action are extremely illustrative.

Despite their later Hytner boycott, the Defence Committee also initially called for a public inquiry, but committee member Eloise Edwards lamented 'Where we fell down again was that we should have stated the way how we wanted that enquiry to go'. Despite the GMC discussing potential inquiry members with it, the Defence Committee was not granted any further involvement, consequently informing the GMC it disagreed with the inquiry's format and would boycott it.[24] Objecting to a lack of immunity from prosecution for witnesses, and recording 'the way its terms of reference was framed, didn't give us the confidence that they would be objective and open to understanding the entire background', it warned local people against providing evidence in a similar way to the earlier Brixton Defence Campaign.[25] The strength of feeling against the inquiry was clearly demonstrated during the Defence Committee's public meeting on 12 August. After establishing its intention to boycott, it was pointed out that Defence Committee Treasurer Louise Da'Cocodia had agreed to sit on the inquiry panel. When challenged by the committee, Da'Cocodia replied that it was her intention to 'try to influence decisions' through inquiry involvement, as she 'did not think staying away will help anything ... I may be too old to throw stones but I want to show that I can understand the frustration of the youth'. Nevertheless, as Da'Cocodia's 'political position was diametrically opposite to that of the defence committee', her offer to stand down from the Defence Committee was accepted.[26] John later asserted that Da'Cocodia herself was considered part of the establishment, questioning the extent to which she would have been able to 'counteract the sort of unhelpful conclusions or whatever it is that Hytner and that lot would have come to'.[27]

Hytner expressed disappointment at the boycott and, alongside GMC's Labour leader Bernard Clarke, offered to meet the Defence Committee and hear evidence in private to avoid apprehension regarding witnesses being targeted by the police. Hytner further appealed for locals to provide valuable evidence despite their negative opinion of his inquiry: 'if there is evidence that the Chief Constable has not pursued honestly, in the past, complaints of Police conduct, then all I can say is that those who suppress that evidence must be his very best friends'.[28] While to Hytner this may have been a logical and persuasive argument, its failure to convince the boycotters demonstrates the high levels of distrust towards authorities.

Indeed, Hytner recognised the boycott as clear evidence of lack of trust of authorities, and the panel questioned whether this was an indication that no useful dialogue could occur between the police and local community.[29] Panel member Linbert Spencer claimed the danger of boycotting was that the police could later claim local people had sufficient opportunities to voice discontent, and their silence could be used by the police to justify 'cart blanche to do what [they] want'.[30] In a stronger rebuke of the Defence Committee's boycott, Frederick Garside, Lloyd Street Ward Labour Party Chair, called them 'blind', arguing their refusal to provide evidence to the inquiry was a sure way for it to achieve nothing.[31] An anonymous witness further criticised the Defence Committee's boycott, asking during a public hearing: 'Who the hell's defending if they're going to walk out of here and not say anything?'[32]

Hytner believed the most damaging aspect of the boycott was lack of constructive recommendations for the future, and Linbert Spencer later considered it 'sad and counter-productive', concluding: 'Thinking that, when you have no power ... boycotting those with the power is going to change something, I think is just naïve.'[33] Similarly, Cox bemoaned the reluctance to use this 'platform for people to say things' when having 'nowhere else to do it'.[34] This inquiry, however, was not deemed impartial or effective by the boycotters to present such evidence to it.

Alternatively, other witnesses claimed the Defence Committee was not actually representative of the community and that initial exuberance towards it had quickly faded.[35] This highlights problematic characterisations of 'community leaders' and questions how representative such organisations actually were of local people's views. Hytner's Report claimed that the Defence Committee's boycott actually aided the inquiry, as it prevented claims that allegations of police misconduct were coming solely from those branded 'enemies' of the police.[36] While this may have been true to a degree, a lack of detailed information and allegations could only have limited the conclusions the Report could reach.

Hytner's Report

Despite the boycott, after three weeks the Hytner Inquiry had received oral evidence from seventy witnesses in public and over fifty more in private, received almost 100 letters, and visited seven institutions. The Report boasted how they 'were rewarded at the end with a rousing cheer' when visiting local youth, revealingly giving the panel 'the impression [they] were not often asked for their views on anything'.[37]

The Report began by describing itself as an 'unsuitable body to answer a number of the questions implicit in our terms of reference', pointedly highlighting that this had been expressed repeatedly to the GMC. It was suggested that some perceived deficiencies of the Report were due to its being addressed to the Policy Committee of the GMC, rather than the Police Authority or the police themselves.[38] Similar to accusations that Scarman's inquiry was incorrectly established narrowly under the Police Act 1964 rather than examining broader social and political aspects, this appeared to validate the Defence Committee's suggestions that Hytner's inquiry had been unsuitable; undoubtedly fostering anger as it openly admitted it had been an inappropriate response.[39]

The inquiry concluded that, as it believed Scarman would make recommendations regarding policing and political changes, the worth of its Report lay in refuting some myths and misunderstandings that had arisen about the disturbances.[40] The spread of information was indeed characterised by a high degree of rumour. Numerous examples existed, such as that the bus depot was on fire, the police station had been taken over by local youths or went up in flames, and multiple accounts of police activity and alleged impropriety – examined later. These are worthy of comment because, as Anderton summarised, 'The rapid spread of rumour and lies presents as many dangers as any realisation of the truth'.[41] They suggest the general feelings of the local community by highlighting what people were willing to believe and share.

Anderton's response to Hytner

The inquiry was careful 'not to cause the Chief Constable to feel that he is being treated unconstitutionally', so made a point of not drawing judgements on allegations against him.[42] While further aggravating those accusing the inquiry of a pro-police bias, this did not prevent Anderton from disliking his depiction and refusing to make further submissions to Scarman's inquiry. Anderton contended that opinions previously submitted to Scarman had been turned against him in Hytner's Report, and that a number of personal references had been 'unfair and very unkind, to say the least'. He complained of 'damaging conclusions' based on 'the flimsiest and most tentative material', as well as 'personal attitudes and postures [which] have been attributed to me without any justification whatsoever'.[43] This may not have been the case if Anderton had not deemed it 'too intolerable' to attend the inquiry himself, but it is likely he would have criticised the Report regardless and, consistent with his previous attitudes, used its conclusions to allege an anti-police campaign.

The Report did record criticisms, 'amidst a chorus of praise', that Anderton refused to accept complaints against the police. Noting his complete rejection that any complaints could have been stifled at police stations, the Report suggested that such blunt denials 'may be regarded by the public as about on a par with finding, which we do not make, that the allegations were true on the say so of the complainants alone'.[44] This astute observation is supported by available evidence suggesting mounting feelings that the police were covering up their transgressions. A later interview with Anderton further illustrated this point when, addressing Labour Councillor Wilner's suggestion that to improve police/community relations the police must accept their failings, Anderton refused to admit any such problems.[45] Likewise, when Scarman published his Report at the end of 1981, which contained a number of police criticisms, Anderton sent plaques to police stations in Manchester to commend his forces on their handling of disorders.[46] Whether or not this was a direct reaction to Scarman's Report – which would not have been out of character – it certainly reaffirmed that Anderton would seemingly support his officers over any criticism levelled.

Defence Committee's response to Hytner

Initial reaction to Hytner's Report was positive from many areas, with the Police Committee, GMC and media giving a generally favourable response. However, the Defence Committee was predictably less complimentary. Deeming the positive response of others understandable, due to the Report's 'thin veneer of liberalism, humanity and scholarship [and] superficial appearance of a balanced and objective analysis', it instead considered the Report inconsistent, condescending, biased, avoiding the central issues, and attempting to influence Moss Side residents into tolerating largely unchanged policing methods. The Moss Side People's Centre agreed the inquiry had 'evaded the main issues', and the Defence Committee concluded this justified its decision to boycott.[47] In some ways similar to Anderton's criticisms of his portrayal, the Defence Committee boycotted the inquiry but criticised it for not focusing on the aspects it deemed most important. Yet, in the words of Phil Scraton, 'Theirs was a conscious refusal to be incorporated into a politically driven process intended to reinforce and legitimate institutionalised discriminatory policy and practice'.[48] Moreover, Chair Gus John subsequently rejected a proposed meeting with the police, underlining their belief that such action was a pointless endeavour until real change had been demonstrated.[49] As the Brixton Defence Campaign had previously, the Defence Committee launched its own 'People's Inquiry' to examine the situation, which began to collect evidence from local people, but was abandoned due to being 'a mammoth task and we just didn't have the capacity to do it'.[50]

Consistent with broader responses to 1980–81, the Report's focus on the criminality of the disorder was criticised, particularly when no police faced any form of retribution for alleged misconduct. The Defence Committee condemned Hytner's failure to address the 'sausage machine' of court trials that sentenced black youth 'for all kinds of petty stuff'.[51] Its most stringent criticism was directed against the Report's refusal to examine assertions of police harassment fully, instead simply focusing upon the hostility fostered towards the police. Similarly, it attacked labelling Anderton's limited inquiry involvement as simply 'disappointing', querying how the Report could possibly form accurate conclusions without investigating Moss Side policing. Moreover, the Defence Committee argued that if Hytner wished to refrain from passing judgement on Anderton's efficiency, Hytner's Report should not have included references to praise received for his handling of the disturbances. This was seen, in contrast to the simplistic view of 'rioters', as supporting the establishment; by not interrogating officers or examining alleged police racism and misconduct, the focus of the Report was intrinsically upon Moss Side itself, suggesting that this was where the problems lay.[52]

Where the Report made recommendations, such as a proposed community representative to mediate complaints against the police, the Defence Committee dismissed these as superficial changes intended to 'placate' the community and restore confidence in the complaints procedure, rather than actually improve anything. The explanation for disorders forwarded by the Report, that local black youth felt alienated from society and had no stake in their surroundings, was deemed 'deeply insulting'. The Defence Committee believed that unemployment, declining discipline, and divisions between young and old black people were also not the cause; rather, their continuing experience of a discriminatory society and police abuse led to a violent declaration that such a situation was unacceptable. Preceding by some eighteen years the inquiry into the police investigation of Stephen Lawrence's murder, which branded the police 'institutionally racist', the Defence Committee viewed police harassment as simply one of a number of acts 'designed to define black people as a sub-class in white society'. It consequently concluded that local residents could not rely upon the system, 'which has so badly let them down in the past', and, as the disturbances were 'a symptom of collective sanity which finally, and in desperation, [sought] to promote social justice', Hytner's focus threatened to undermine that meaning.[53] This depiction characterises the disturbances firmly within the 'bargaining by riot' framework advanced by this book, as attempts to forward issues previously ignored or overlooked through alternative forms of protest.

The Defence Committee's unfavourable response had already been predicted by the Hytner Panel, who noted difficulties convincing the public that the inquiry was not simply a means of covering-up faults of the police and GMC.[54] As seen by the inquiry's low attendance and critical response from the Defence Committee, it did not appear that the Hytner Panel overcame this. During evidence hearings, the panel had agreed that an inquiry that achieved nothing was worse than no inquiry at all; it is debatable to what extent the Hytner Inquiry did, or could, achieve its goals.[55]

Nature of disorder

Varying responses to the Moss Side disturbances demonstrated a differing view of the nature of disorder itself. While previous uncertainty over whether St Pauls constituted a 'race riot' had disappeared by the July disorders, issues of racism itself were rarely discussed.[56] Home Secretary William Whitelaw labelled many of the 1981 disturbances 'copy-cat', which indicated that youth nationwide followed examples elsewhere to get a 'piece of the action' themselves.[57] Similarly, Richard Clutterbuck firmly maintained that disturbances following the news coverage of Liverpool and Southall disorders on 3 July 'can have no possible explanation other than the copycat phenomenon'.[58] The media was also accused of intensifying beliefs that disorder would erupt specifically within Moss Side, and that the disturbances were thus simply the realisation of that expectation. This view was later espoused by Anderton:

[We] knew as long ago as May and June 1981 that there would be rioting in Moss Side ... not for any sane or defensible reason, but to fulfil a much publicised prophesy ... There were frequent and – in my opinion – thoroughly irresponsible references in the national press and in television programmes to the likelihood of clashes between police and young blacks in Moss Side, although there was no compelling evidence to support it.[59]

Such arguments characterise collective violence as merely irrational and imitative. As Michael Keith summarised, 'There is something slightly insidious in depriving a group of people of historical agency, reducing the considered to the instinctive or automatic and the human to the bestial'.[60]

It would be wrong, however, to claim that events elsewhere had not markedly increased tensions in Moss Side. An anonymous witness argued that such disorder had provided an example of a new way of making the point that local people had been attempting to make for years.[61] Linbert Spencer even concluded 'if Bristol hadn't happened, I think there's a really strong argument that says that Manchester wouldn't have happened'.[62] For many Moss Side residents, St Pauls, Brixton and Toxteth suggested that collective violence towards a common goal had allowed their voices to be heard. Positive outcomes of previous examples of 'bargaining by riot', such as attracting attention or resources, indicated that this could be a successful strategy. In the same way, local priest Phil Sumner noted how, in the years following 1981, residents from other parts of Manchester would proclaim: 'you've got to riot to get attention to get money put in to your area'.[63]

It had become commonplace for residents to discuss the possibility of 'another Bristol'. For example, a Moss Side schoolteacher confirmed that children were talking about events in Toxteth prior to disorder spreading, with reactions ranging from fearing it happening in Manchester to excitement at the possibility.[64] A news report after the first disturbances in Moss Side suggested that, during previous Liverpool disorders, it was assumed Manchester would be next: 'this morning they were proved right'.[65] In fact, in May 1981, a newspaper article had cited youths 'ominously predicting "it is going to blow very soon"', and posters appeared suggesting that, after Brixton, Moss Side would be next.[66] While some argued this demonstrated riots were being planned, Hytner instead characterised it as consistent with the 'mood of inevitability'.[67] David Waddington et al. demonstrated how such expectations could escalate routine interactions between police and locals into 'flashpoints', and consequently outbreaks of disorder.[68]

The Defence Committee rejected the simplification that black residents took to the streets merely because it was expected of them; rather, they did so because they were suffering under the same circumstances as other locations. Committee member Eloise Edwards voiced her rejection of 'copycat' theories, arguing disorder began when it did because people had simply had enough, and an anonymous witness during the Hytner Inquiry furthered this point: 'Why does war happen one year and not the year before? It's just a certain point you reach and then it goes.'[69] Arguing against 'copycat' models, the Defence Committee drew comparisons with early-nineteenth-century Chartist protest erupting in sequence around England and Wales. They reasoned that, in both instances, there was not a 'chain of expectation based on myth', but rather the 'chain reaction … was one which inspired courage: people who might not otherwise have openly protested were inspired to do so by the example of others'. They differentiated this from the sequence of disorder they believed suggested by Hytner, as 'there were real causes of grievance in each of the areas in which it was expressed'.[70] This interpretation is consistent with widespread belief that tensions had been growing for years, and triggers for disorder were seemingly minor clashes with police that sparked a response. Such as Brixton, where Scarman concluded that the plainclothed police saturation action, 'Swamp 81', built upon previous discontent, creating a situation where any relatively minor event would have led to the disturbances.[71]

At least one witness blamed a perceived leniency for the spreading disturbances; claiming the police had been 'absolutely hammered', he concluded that, by not making a sterner example of Brixton, 'you might just as well have issued tickets – "Come to the riots on Wednesday"'.[72] This was something the highest levels of government also felt had been a factor in proliferating disorders. Prime Minister Margaret Thatcher telephoned Whitelaw in July, after visiting Liverpool and Brixton, to stress 'the need to bring some of the rioters before the Crown Courts without delay'. Whitelaw agreed, although he highlighted the 'possible danger' they may be acquitted, as had happened following St Pauls.[73] It is clear that, fitting with their general focus on law and order, authorities believed that an immediate response would simultaneously calm those questioning the police's ability to keep the peace, and act as a deterrent for others. That disorder spread across the country suggests it did neither.

Disturbances also spread throughout the Manchester area, as with Bristol.[74] Moss Side Ward Councillor Patrick Paget recorded a wall-chalked message that read 'Wilmslow Road tonight', and the police observed a small car driving six black men to Wythenshawe, a district some five miles south of Moss Side, where disturbances subsequently occurred.[75] The MCCR had previously asked local newspaper the *Manchester Evening News* not to over-report the incidents, as it was feared this would escalate disorder; however, radio reports after the first night of disturbances in Moss Side ended by questioning: 'will the problems start once more and, if so, where will it happen next?'[76] Foreshadowing recent 'Twitter Revolutions' and 2011 England disorders which utilised social media to spread information, it was also claimed that Moss Side saw the use of CB short-distance radio messages communicating information regarding police locations and tactics.[77] As police were utilising new riot equipment to respond to spreading disturbances, so too were those participating in them.

The role of the media

It was suggested that the media 'glamourised' the disorders, and television and newspaper images were blamed for inspiring locals to copy previous examples, even showing them exactly how to do so.[78] An opinion poll in the *Sun* in July 1981 claimed that 90 per cent of all British city centre residents believed disorders would spread to their areas; as Keith suggested, whether these kinds of stories 'created or reflected such expectation is in some ways not as important as the behaviour that may have resulted from it'.[79] Moreover, Hytner recorded 'almost weekly' television reports of street violence in previous years, invoking comparisons with the Northern Ireland 'Troubles' and a wider context of disorder. Thus, they argued that Moss Side youth had 'become conditioned to those of their own age banding together to smash windows and throw petrol bombs'.[80] One inquiry witness even suggested that the 1977 television miniseries *Roots*, centred upon an African family line's journey from enslavement to emancipation, had 'set a lot of black people against whites'.[81] Similarly, a trend in popular culture over previous years had seen growing attention awarded to apocalyptic themes, no doubt influenced by the nuclear threat during the ongoing Cold War. Television dramas such as *Survivors* (1975), *The Changes* (1975), and most famously *Threads* (1984), as well as films *Dawn of the Dead* (1978), *Mad Max* (1979) and *Planet of the Apes* series (1968–73), all contained depictions of the apocalypse and visions of life after society had crumbled. Peter Hutchings underlined that the growth of apocalyptic themes within British popular culture 'might in some instances be articulating in a covert or unconscious manner a socially and historically specific sense of despair and negativity'.[82]

Perceptions that the media played a significant role in the spread of disorder led the British Broadcasting Corporation and Independent Broadcasting Authority to commission a report from Howard Tumber of the British Film Institute. After conducting interviews with young people, police, and broadcasters themselves, Tumber concluded that television played a minor role, with less than 10 per cent of the 12–19 age group watching television news and seeing reports of the disturbances. He instead argued that youths learnt about disorder through information 'gathered in the classrooms, the streets and the pubs'.[83] However, Graham Murdock contended the media did play a role in spreading disturbances, just a slightly different one than was often claimed:

> Some observers have argued that this kind of coverage raised the consciousness of inner city youth and increased their readiness to take on the police. This is a possibility, but the coverage also had lessons for the police. It primed them to expect major trouble in the cities and strengthened the resolve to crack down on it early by stepping up their activities in inner city areas. This in turn cemented youth resentment at police behaviour and fed local rumours that a riot was imminent. As a result, both sides 'tooled up' for trouble, so that eventually it only took a minor incident on the streets to trigger a confrontation.[84]

Additionally, the media was accused of inherently supporting the authorities, a charge levelled by local community worker Barri Potter: 'In the struggle between oppressed and oppressors the decision to stay neutral is to side with the oppressor.' Citing the brief attack upon the well-protected police station, which caused only minor damage but was used by the media to depict the police as innocent victims of a violent mob, Potter claimed many local community workers and residents purposefully avoided speaking to the media, as they 'knew they would mis-represent us any way'.[85] This was certainly true of the Moss Side Community Action Group, which criticised the media's 'sensationalizing of events', claiming a 'long history of definite mistrust of the media by the Black Community' existed due to its 'totally blind co-operation with Police views and "official Political rhetoric"'.[86]

At the same time, the media's focus upon violence and criminality was criticised, with one resident suggesting a better headline for the disturbances might have been: 'Congratulations to the folk of Moss Side for saying things aren't going right, let's do something about it.'[87] While such a headline appearing in mainstream press was extremely unlikely, their focus upon criminality was in-keeping with the authorities' and media's broader responses. Murdock demonstrated such by abridging the vast majority of newspaper reports into three main points: first, 'rioters' were portrayed as an 'alien black presence threatening the property and safety of established residents'; second, the police were attempting to protect those residents and thus were mutual victims of the 'mob'; third, this exceptional threat necessitated an exceptional response: i.e. heightened police equipment and weaponry. He also cited both Tumber's study of television news and Anders Hansen's analysis of newspaper reports, which established that senior police officers received significantly more post-disorder media attention than representatives of the community, participants or even government ministers.[88]

Conversely, Anderton blamed the media for spreading anti-police hostility, accusing them of often displaying a 'most noticeable bias against the police'. Again, from a Chief Constable famed for his revulsion towards anything approaching police criticism, this is a predictable stance. Using the infamous 'sus' law as an example, he suggested this small issue in a single community in South London had been 'fanned and fanned again with considerable help and attention from the media', spreading to the extent that 'young blacks and Asians everywhere challenged the authority of the police often without really understanding why'. Citing Manchester arrest statistics, that just 0.13 per cent of all recorded crimes in 1980 had fallen under 'sus', he concluded that discontent at its supposed overuse within Manchester was 'therefore, patently absurd'.[89] The characterisation that many participants in disorders did not understand their own motives, and blunt use of numerical statistics – only recording arrests and not the continuous harassment of stops and searches – attempted to relegate the level of dissatisfaction towards the police.

Movement of people

In another parallel to other disorders, locals alleged that 'outsiders' had come into the area to create trouble.[90] It was reported that groups from other cities had travelled to Moss Side, and stories emerged of individuals with Liverpudlian accents attempting to convince local youths to riot. In addition, political extremists, particularly those with left-wing leanings, were observed in the area, accused of manipulating the situation for their own political ends.[91] The Workers' Revolutionary Party and the Socialist Workers' Party were alleged to have played a role in organising the disturbances, although Hytner concluded any influence was marginal.[92] A London black revolutionary had purportedly told a public meeting in Manchester some months previously that 'guns would soon be available' – although Hytner argued that not many local people would consider this an appealing prospect.[93] While some viewed accusations of outsiders to be an attempt to shift blame from local people, others perceived them as another example of Moss Side residents being deemed unable to think or act for themselves. Removing the agency for the Moss Side disturbances away from local people was considered another example of British paternalism and colonial legacy.[94]

One-hundred-and-three Greater Manchester Police officers had previously been drafted into Toxteth during disorders to provide support, returning with personal stories of the ferocity that had greeted them.[95] It was suggested that some Moss Side disorder participants had travelled to 'settle a score' with the police after Toxteth – and, similarly, that Moss Side was a means of police obtaining 'payback', either from officers involved in Toxteth or their colleagues.[96] Officers were affected by previous disturbances through personal experience, media, or word-of-mouth. As addressed by the previous chapter, Anderton utilised tactics designed to minimise police casualties, due to witnessing high levels of injuries in Toxteth. It is likely that officers were also angered, excited or concerned by events elsewhere, leading some to overact in their handling of Moss Side disorders. This generated numerous accusations of police misconduct, which, similar to Scarman's inquiry into Brixton, went unaddressed by Hytner's investigations.

Police misconduct

As with other similar inquiries, one of the main criticisms of the Hytner Inquiry was that it did not examine allegations of police misconduct. Such accusations were instead directed through the normal police complaints procedure: a method that had lost the faith of the community, being deemed at best a waste of time and at worst identification for further police prejudice. There were certainly many claims of police misconduct during the disturbances, which, within broader accusations of police brutality, corruption and a general lack of accountability throughout the period, warrant examination.[97]

If information regarding disorders spread across the country by word-of-mouth, as evidence suggests it did to some extent, the dissemination and credibility of allegations against the police was assisted by pre-existing views. For instance, Sumner argued there was no smoke without fire, and actual examples of police misconduct and brutality gave rise to further stories that were more readily believed.[98] As Hytner summarised: 'You only need 10% [of police] who harass, and the population would get the impression that everybody harasses.'[99] This, coupled with police officials such as Anderton displaying apparently blind support for officers, generated sentiments that the police were not reprimanded for widespread impropriety. Addressing arguments that complaints against the police were manufactured by those with political or ideological axes to grind, Hytner argued that, even if this were the case, the situation could not improve whilst Anderton continued to staunchly dismiss widely believed accusations of police wrongdoing merely as 'fabrications'.[100]

Allegations emerged after the disturbances that police vans drove up and down streets, with officers threatening people with batons and riot gear, shouting 'Nigger, nigger, oi! oi!', calling people 'black bastards', and threatening one man that they would 'kick his fucking black face in'.[101] Police taunts, such as 'you blacks are soft' and 'you've not got the guts of them in Liverpool', were documented, further highlighting how previous disorder influenced subsequent situations.[102] Graphic accounts emerged during Hytner's inquiry, such as police kicking and beating a young boy causing his grandmother to fall over, another of a five-year-old boy being punched by an officer, and a priest even pulling an officer off a civilian.[103] Local GP Donald Bodey treated a number of injured youths following the disturbances, recording cuts and bruises, suspected broken ribs, and an instance of a man's dreadlocks being ripped from his head.[104] He believed many residents were simply too frightened of repercussions to discuss the abuses they had suffered, further suggesting why collective violence was felt to be the last recourse against police misconduct. Local musician DJ Wizzy Dan recalled returning to Moss Side in a car of four young black men, which was surrounded by three vans full of officers. They were beaten both in the police van and at the station, with Dan being hit with a police helmet puncturing his ear-drum, being held under a sink tap, and having his dreadlocks forcibly detached. After a four-year campaign, these four men were awarded damages totalling £9,000, which Dan labelled 'peanuts' compared to the treatment they received.[105]

Officers were accused of attacking assembled crowds without warning them to disperse, and it was widely alleged that there was often no attempt to arrest those caught by the police – they were simply beaten. Another account saw a mother and teenage children chased into their home by three officers emerging from a van, waving their batons and yelling 'You black bastards'. The officers kicked at the locked door and, in the mother's words, 'it looked as if they were just trying to terrorise us'.[106] To local people, already believing the police discriminatorily targeted black Britons, this appeared an escalation of that approach.

Stories spreading of incidents involving those deemed more 'respectable' than black youths gave further credence to claims the police acted improperly. An Irish baker was reportedly badly beaten by four officers, surprising eyewitnesses with their blatancy.[107] Meanwhile, well-known local youth leader Hartley Hanley was arrested outside his own club after attempting conciliation between officers and youths, beaten by officers to the extent of almost losing eyesight in one eye. Councillor Paget believed such actions signalled the abandonment of standard policing methods: 'The Police ... must be in a mood of arresting everything that moves on the street.' Indeed, it appeared that police tactics had been succinctly summarised when a father was informed his son was arrested because 'The good have to suffer for the bad'.[108] Police indiscriminately targeting people, combined with high levels of blatant misconduct, led to an increased willingness of residents to believe accusations of previous police brutality. Such accounts would likely not have been so readily believed or spread had there not already existed common accusations against the police.

This was allegedly merely a continuation of the treatment residents received at the hands of the police. Accusations of previous police brutality were linked with unpopular tactics, such as stops and searches and use of dogs, and black youths had even begun wearing badges declaring: 'Help the police, beat yourself up.'[109] An anonymous local teacher later recounted the ease with which they began to share animosity towards the police after moving to Moss Side, but also how difficult it was for others to believe their stories:

> I know family and friends who don't live in the inner-city, who just disbelieve me. They think I've exaggerated it. You see they take the line, well there's no smoke without fire. They must cause trouble and therefore the police are only doing their job ... The resistance, by people who know me really well, to believe me has really shocked me.[110]

Cox later reinforced this view, stressing it took a long time for public perception to change in order to recognise police misconduct, recalling death threats she'd received that opposed the Police Authority's attempts to introduce greater levels of police accountability.[111]

Even after the disturbances died down, officers allegedly drove around shouting at black youths, drinking alcohol and indiscriminately attacking innocent people.[112] A Moss Side Community Action Committee press statement accused the police of transforming Moss Side into a 'no-go' area by harassing and arresting innocent local inhabitants: '*WE ARE IN EFFECT A COMMUNITY UNDER SIEGE, LIVING THROUGH WHAT AMOUNTS TO MARTIAL LAW!*'[113] The term 'no-go', previously used by a startled public to describe areas where police feared to tread but here used to accuse police of preventing local people from living freely, demonstrates the conflicting perspectives.[114]

As previously noted, Anderton had historically dismissed accusations that complaints against police were stifled or ignored, despite Hytner concluding such was likely. Likewise, Superintendent Robin Oake also refuted suggestions of police racism or brutality, claiming that, if he had been aware of such an incident, the officer would have been disciplined.[115] However, this does not address the possibility of such behaviour occurring either unseen, or that senior officers had turned a blind eye. For local people, ample evidence existed that officers had acted improperly, and they were resolute that something needed to be done.

Ineffective complaints against the police

Discontent towards the police complaints system was cited by Hytner as a 'major source of friction' and, although not deemed a direct contribution to disorders, the panel acknowledged that a lack of a functioning method of addressing police misconduct had added to anger.[116] Indeed, the Moss Side Community Action Group dubbed complaints against the police 'a futile exercise, since they are usually met with a biased and unsympathetic response'.[117]

However, Hytner repeatedly maintained his inquiry was not the place for individual complaints against specific officers and a Court of Law or disciplinary tribunal, where appropriate statutory safeguards could be provided, should be utilised for those accusations. As George Green, who attended Hytner's inquiry in an attempt to make such a complaint, summarised, for the people of Moss Side, the complaints system was so ineffective that it might as well not exist.[118] Other witnesses claimed that those who attempted to make complaints soon found themselves victims of police targeting, and one individual claimed having made over 500 personal complaints without a single positive outcome, suggested to be clear evidence that 'the law supports its own'.[119]

Youth worker Dorothy Lewis claimed community workers 'feel a bit like the coloured youths' when attempting to make complaints, as they were not listened to and never saw complaints have any positive outcome.[120] Comparison with black youths being utilised as a shorthand for complaints going unacknowledged speaks volumes for how black youths themselves must have regarded the complaints system. City Councillor Jeffrey Wilner's experiences had even led him to advise individuals not to waste their time pursuing complaints. Similarly, Councillor Paget and local Labour MP George Morton complained that the complaints system was ineffective, noting if even elected officials could not achieve anything, what hope did local residents have?[121]

Police Authority Chair Councillor Peter Kelly confirmed that the majority of people appeared unaware of a higher authority to complain to, describing the number of civilians who had approached the police authority as 'a little below nil'.[122] When asked why he had not discussed the high level of discontent towards the police complaints system with the Chief Constable, City Councillor Arnold Spencer suggested that Anderton would represent such action as politicians interfering with police operations; thus, 'it was just not worth the bother'. He continued that politicians of 'a certain hue ... not particularly liked by Mr Anderton' would do more damage than good through attempting such campaigns.[123] This is both a sign of a Chief Constable portraying any questioning of the police as an attack upon their independence and undermining of their authority, and that local government and political oversight of the police had failed those needing it the most.

Hytner's Report documented the 'great deal' of evidence alleging police misconduct during the disturbances, noting some was being investigated by the police complaints system. It summarised that evidence suggested officers had used excessive force and indiscriminately arrested people whether they were involved in the disturbances or not, citing repeated charges that officers were 'actively spoiling for trouble with young blacks' and people 'got arrested for not running fast enough'. Evidence directly relating to 9 July, when the police initiated invasive 'hard'-policing tactics, made for 'unhappy listening' for the panel. Hytner also stated that the inquiry was 'satisfied' it was true that, prior to the disturbances, a number of officers had misused stop and search powers and had racially abused black youths.[124] Despite this, Hytner refrained from passing judgement on the police's actions; believing there was sufficient evidence to warrant an 'effective and searching police enquiry', either to prevent recurrences or to redeem the negative police reputation, they left it to the Police Committee. Hytner concluded that, as they had not allowed identification of police, there was no chance to initiate disciplinary proceedings against specific officers, but they hoped the police would not simply discount the amount of evidence presented.[125] To those who had hoped Hytner's inquiry might itself be an 'effective and searching' inquiry into police action, it was another disappointment.

Anderton detailed that twenty-four complaints against the police relating to the disturbances were actually received, alleging assault, criminal damage and abuse of authority. Three complaints were withdrawn, but the remaining twenty-one were investigated and submitted to the DPP and Police Complaints Board.[126] Additionally, an internal police inquiry was launched largely on the strength of evidence provided to Hytner, conducted by Manchester's Assistant Chief Constable John Stalker – later vocal in his denunciations of the 'Scarman agenda' for policing.[127] After a ten-month investigation, all officers were cleared when the DPP deemed the evidence submitted worthy of no further action.[128] Considering the 'great deal' of existing evidence describing police misconduct, this decision demonstrated the defective complaints system.

Conclusion

Following the disturbances, the Moss Side Community Action Group attempted to 'present a clear, unequivocal and incorruptible statement', which incorporated the views of both the youth and 'community workers and concerned adults in the area'. Blaming governmental 'harsh and insensitive policies', which 'have left these young people no alternative but violence and destruction as an expression of their plight', it also accused the police of furthering discontent.[129] However, as with other locations examined throughout this book, there was no unified local black response. While some worked with authorities and participated in the Hytner Inquiry, radical groups 'mercilessly opposed' the police-defined 'respected leaders of the black community'.[130] Interestingly, self-described 'moderate radical' Linbert Spencer portrayed contradictory responses as part of a broader method:

> I only have space ... whilst the Moss Side Defence Committee is kicking off and being noisy. Because if they're not doing that, then the institution isn't bothering about talking to anybody ... if you don't make the noise, we don't get to bring about the change ... But make no mistake, the demands around the table are no less than the demands being made outside the door.[131]

The extent to which such unified tactics consciously existed during these disturbances is debatable – Spencer himself noted becoming more aware of this relationship during the 1990s – but it does demonstrate how disorder was incorporated into broader struggles for progress.

Despite such interpretations, the Defence Committee's boycott of Hytner's inquiry demonstrated prevalent views that such actions were nothing more than diversions, 'means to legitimate state interests', or even methods of obtaining evidence for the police to convict local people.[132] The inquiry was accused of not addressing the main issues and implicitly defending the authorities. A lack of response to seemingly abundant evidence of police misconduct further weakened confidence in the machinery for making complaints against the police or holding them accountable. It still appeared that the constraints and inequalities of the system would not help black Britons: elements of the local black population had demonstrated that they were no longer prepared to suffer unfair and discriminatory circumstances, but authorities remained slow to listen. Following the disorders, central government and the local City Council announced that the entire community should give the police their full support after such 'difficult circumstances'; local youth worker Dorothy Lewis aptly questioned, following the seemingly high-levels of police brutality and discrimination that went unpunished, how anybody could seriously tell black youths to respect the police.[133]

Notes

1 For a notable exception, see: John, *Moss Side 1981*.
2 Interview with Linbert Spencer, 20 March 2017.
3 Moss Side Defence Committee, *Hytner Myths*, p. 2.
4 The National Archives (TNA): HO 266/136, J. Hetherington to P.J.C. Mawer, 4 August 1981; Hetherington to Home Office.
5 TNA: HO 266/136, G.A. Harrison to Mawer, 30 July 1981.
6 John Stevenson's collection (JS): Moss Side Enquiry Minutes of Evidence (MOE), 19 August 1981.
7 *Manchester Evening News*, 6 July 2011.
8 Interview with Gabrielle Cox, 19 April 2017.
9 Hytner, *Report*, p. 1; JS: MOE, 17 August 1981.
10 JS: MOE, 19 August 1981; Hytner, *Report*, p. 4; *Manchester Evening News*, 6 July 2011.
11 See: Phillips and Phillips, *Windrush*, p. 363; Prince, *God's Cop*.
12 JS: MOE, 21 August 1981; JS: Hytner, *Report*, p. 24.
13 JS: MOE, 18 August 1981.
14 *Manchester Evening News*, 6 July 2011.
15 JS: MOE, 20 August 1981; JS: Hytner, *Report*, p. 15.
16 Interview with Phil Sumner, 20 April 2017.
17 Interview with Gus John, 19 May 2017.
18 Interview with Cox.
19 *Manchester Evening News*, 6 July 2011.
20 London Broadcasting Company/Independent Radio News Digitisation Archive (LBC/IRN): 'Hytner Tribunal Investigates Riots on Moss Side', 1981; JS: MOE, 19 August 1981.
21 Interview with John.
22 *Ibid*. See: Bunce and Field, *Darcus Howe*; Smith, 'Conflicting Narratives'.
23 JS: MOE, 20 August 1981.
24 JS: Interviews about Moss Side Riots (MSI), Eloise Edwards.
25 George Padmore Institute (GPI): The Black Parents Movement collection (BPM), GB/2904/BPM/3/2/4/2, Moss Side Defence Committee, Press Release; Interview with John. See: chapter 5.

26 GPI: BPM, GB/2904/BPM/3/2/2/1, Moss Side Defence Committee, Minutes of Public meeting on 12 August.
27 Interview with John.
28 LBC/IRN: 'Benet Hytner and Bernard Clarke to Meet Moss Side Defence Committee', 20 August 1981; JS: MOE, 20 August 1981; 17 August 1981.
29 JS: MOE, 20 August 1981; 17 August 1981.
30 JS: MSI, Linbert Spencer, 23 August 1983.
31 JS: MOE, 20 August 1981.
32 JS: MOE, 17 August 1981.
33 JS: MOE, 20 August 1981; 21 August 1981; JS: MSI, Linbert Spencer; Interview with Spencer.
34 Interview with Cox.
35 JS: MOE, 20 August 1981; JS: MSI, Barri Potter.
36 Hytner, *Report*, p. 6.
37 *Ibid.*, p. 7.
38 *Ibid.*, p. 2; JS: MSI, Linbert Spencer.
39 See: Brain, *History of Policing*, p. 68; chapter 5.
40 Hytner, *Report*, p. 58.
41 TNA: HO 266/136, James Anderton, 'Police/Community Relations in a Multi-Racial Society', 31 July 1981.
42 Hytner, *Report*, p. 26.
43 TNA: HO 266/136, James Anderton to Mawer, 14 October 1981.
44 Hytner, *Report*, p. 30.
45 JS: Written account of 'Arena – Moss Side 5 Months On', *Piccadilly Radio*, Manchester, 1 December 1981.
46 JS: MSI, Potter.
47 Moss Side Defence Committee, *Hytner Myths*, p. 1; *Manchester Evening News*, 6 July 2011.
48 Scraton, 'Official Inquiries', p. 50.
49 'Arena – Moss Side 5 Months On'.
50 Interview with John.
51 *Ibid.*
52 Moss Side Defence Committee, *Hytner Myths*, p. 7.
53 *Ibid.*, p. 1. For Stephen Lawrence, see: Hall, 'From Scarman to Stephen Lawrence'.
54 JS: MOE, 21 August 1981.
55 JS: MOE, 27 August 1981.
56 Solomos, *Race and Racism*, p. 152; Gilroy and Lawrence, 'Two-Tone Britain', pp. 123–6.
57 Brain, *History of Policing*, pp. 68–9.
58 Clutterbuck, 'Terrorism and Urban Violence', 170.
59 Draft of a speech that James Anderton was going to deliver in 1982, but never made as the event was cancelled, in Prince, *God's Cop*, p. 116.
60 Keith, *Race, Riots and Policing*, p. 104.
61 JS: MOE, 17 August 1981.
62 Interview with Spencer.
63 Interview with Sumner.

64 JS: MOE, 19 August 1981.

65 LBC/IRN, 'Latest Riot Outbreak in Moss Side', 9 July 1981.

66 *Mancunion*, 13–19 May 1981.

67 Hytner, *Report*, p. 38.

68 Waddington *et al.*, *Flashpoints*.

69 JS: MSI, Edwards; JS: MOE, 17 August 1981. For 'copycat', see: Keith, *Race, Riots and Policing*, pp. 68–9.

70 Moss Side Defence Committee, *Hytner Myths*, p. 4. See: Thompson, *English Working Class*.

71 Scarman, *Report*, pp. 110–12.

72 JS: MOE, 17 August 1981.

73 TNA: PREM 19/484, Willie Rickett to Colin Walters, 13 July 1981.

74 See: Ball, 'The "Bristol Riot"'.

75 JS: MOE, 19 August 1981; 17 August 1981.

76 TNA: HO 266/136, Town Clerk, 'Civil Disturbances in Manchester', 20 July 1981; 'Latest Riot Outbreak in Moss Side'.

77 Prince, *God's Cop*, p. 111. See, for example: Christensen, 'Twitter Revolutions?'.

78 JS: MOE, 27 August 1981; 24 August 1981.

79 Keith, *Race, Riots and Policing*, p. 69.

80 Hytner, *Report*, p. 37. See: Dawson *et al.* (eds), *Northern Ireland Troubles*.

81 JS: MSI, Ann, Moss Side resident.

82 Hutchings, 'The Idea of Apocalypse', p. 112. See: Newland, 'Babylon'; Friedman (ed.), *British Cinema and Thatcherism*.

83 Tumber, *Television and the Riots*.

84 Murdock, 'Reporting the Riots', p. 87.

85 JS: MSI, Potter.

86 TNA: HO 266/136, Moss Side Community Action Committee, Press Statement, 14 July 1981.

87 JS: MSI, Anonymous resident; H. Warm.

88 Tumber, *Television and the Riots*, p. 38 and Anders Hansen, 'Press coverage of the summer 1981 riots', unpublished M.A. dissertation, University of Leicester (1982), cited in Murdock, 'Reporting the Riots', pp. 73–8.

89 Anderton, 'Police/Community Relations in a Multi-Racial Society'. See: Lawrence, 'The Vagrancy Act'.

90 Murdock, 'Reporting the Riots', pp. 83–5; Solomos, *Race and Racism*, p. 167.

91 JS: MOE, 19 August 1981; 20 August 1981; JS: MSI, Anonymous community worker.

92 Hytner, *Report*, p. 35.

93 *Ibid.*, p. 34.

94 See: Schwarz, *White Man's World*.

95 James Anderton, 'Serious Incidents of Public Disorder in Greater Manchester', 4 September 1981, Appendix 4B, Hytner, *Report*.

96 JS: MOE, 19 August 1981.

97 See, for example: Harvey *et al.*, *The Miners' Strike*; Scraton, *Hillsborough*.

98 JS: MOE, 20 August 1981.

99 JS: MOE, 17 August 1981.

100 Hytner, *Report*, p. 57.

101 JS: MSI, Edwards; JS: MOE, 17 August 1981; 19 August 1981; Kettle and Hodges, *Uprising!*, p. 164; Nally, 'Eyewitness in Moss Side', p. 60.

102 JS: MOE, 26 August 1981; 27 August 1981.

103 JS: MOE, 17 August 1981; 20 August 1981.

104 *Manchester Evening News*, 6 July 2011.

105 *Manchester Evening News*, 5 July 2011.

106 JS: MOE, 19 August 1981; 17 August 1981.

107 JS: MSI, Edwards; Potter.

108 JS: MSI, Anonymous resident; JS: MOE, 20 August 1981; 19 August 1981; 'Arena – Moss Side 5 Months On'.

109 JS: MOE, 18 August 1981; JS: MSI, Mrs L.S., resident of Moss Side; Warm.

110 JS: MSI, Anonymous Moss Side teacher.

111 Interview with Cox. See: Reiner, *Politics of the Police*, pp. 78–96.

112 JS: MOE, 20 August 1981.

113 Moss Side Community Action Committee, Press Statement, emphasis in original.

114 See: Keith, 'No-Go Areas'.

115 Hytner, *Report*, p. 30; *Manchester Evening News*, 8 July 2011.

116 Hytner, *Report*, p. 33. See, for example: Stevens and Willis, 'Ethnic Minorities and Complaints'; Maguire and Corbett, *Police Complaints System*.

117 Moss Side Community Action Committee, Press Statement.

118 JS: MOE, 17 August 1981.

119 *Ibid.*; JS: MOE, 19 August 1981; 18 August 1981.

120 JS: MOE, 20 August 1981.

121 JS: MOE, 21 August 1981; 19 August 1981.

122 JS: MOE, 19 August 1981.

123 JS: MOE, 17 August 1981.

124 *Manchester Evening News*, 8 January 1982.

125 Hytner, *Report*, pp. 49, 54.

126 Anderton, 'Serious Incidents of Public Disorder'. For the Police Complaints Board, see: Reiner, *Politics of the Police*, pp. 223–4.

127 Keith, *Race, Riots and Policing*, p. 13.

128 *Manchester Evening News*, 6 July 2011.

129 Moss Side Community Action Committee, Press Statement.

130 GPI: BPM, GB/2904/BPM/3/2/4/2, Manchester Black Parents Organisation, Press Release, 'Compulsory Police Classes for Black Youths in Moss Side'.

131 Interview with Spencer.

132 Scraton, 'Official Inquiries', p. 50.

133 TNA: HO 266/136, All Party Statement by Councillor Norman Morris on behalf of Manchester City Council, 10 July 1981; JS: MOE, 20 August 1981.

Epilogue: 'Turning point' or 'opportunity lost'? The legacy of 1980–81

What needs fixing is the system,
Not shop windows down in Brixton.
Riots on the television,
You can't put us all in prison.

Plan B – Ill Manors

URING JULY 1981, disturbances reached Birmingham, Blackburn, Derby, Halifax, Leeds, Nottingham, Portsmouth, Reading, Sheffield, Southampton and Wolverhampton – to name but a few locations. As Timothy Brain concluded, 'It was, to say the least, a very tense time for police officers across the country'.[1] The IRR's prominent journal *Race & Class* declared in October 1981 that the summer disorders 'marked a turning point in British politics, [as] black youth on the streets destroyed at a stroke the myth of police invincibility'.[2] Furthermore, black Britons nationwide organised and observed their common struggle through defence committees and appeals for government inquiries, even if their responses were far from uniform.[3] Peter Fryer contended that the 'size and scope of ferocity of the rebellion astonished everyone'. Criticising the resultant turn towards 'hard' policing of public disorder, he concluded that authorities should not underestimate the 'intelligence, determination, and proud traditions of those they desire to control'.[4]

Fryer's conclusions demonstrate how reaction to the disturbances varied drastically between societal groups; while the events empowered black Britons, the authorities attempted to frame reactions around issues of law and order. Accordingly, the first section of this concluding chapter summarises the responses to 1980–81, broadly categorised into conservative and liberal/radical reactions. The second part of this chapter addresses that, as these disturbances occurred almost forty years ago, there have been significant developments since. While examining these to the same level would merit another book in itself, key aspects of direct relevance to the focuses of this study are outlined.

If it is agreed that the 1980–81 collective anti-police violence undertaken predominantly by black Britons discussed here – distinct from looting and arson – was a conscious response to widespread racial discrimination and police harassment in an attempt to improve their situation, it was not particularly successful.[5] These 'collective bargaining by riot' actions, as it has been argued they were, did produce some improvements, such as increased governmental attention and resources – most notably through Environment Secretary Michael Heseltine's attempts at regeneration programmes – and apparent increases in black political participation.[6] Nevertheless, the issues highlighted by the disturbances were marginalised, promised reforms never materialised, and police discrimination that had characterised life for black youth continued largely unabated. Despite widespread collective action and black Britons mobilising to support and defend those arrested following the disorders, Moss Side Defence Committee Chair Gus John lamented the 'opportunity lost [not to] have built a mass movement around all of that', which:

> would have continued to ask further questions about how those same processes and apparatuses that showed their hand so mercilessly in relation to those events, actually operate in normal times … What is that saying about the condition of being young and black in this society? … And, more to the point, how can we take collective action, with a view to bringing about the kind of changes that we think are necessary?[7]

Disturbances had not appeared everywhere in 1981 and notably stayed within England's borders. Why did disorder not follow suit in every inner-city location – for example, Glasgow – where similar conditions were present? Could it be, as Manchester County Council's Hytner Inquiry proffered, just that conditions there were not quite right?[8] David Waddington et al. detailed confrontations between black youth and police in Haymarket, Sheffield, in August 1981, which avoided disorder. They noted the altercation contained many conditions present in other disturbances, such as the use of police dogs, visible arrest of a local youth worker, allegations of police brutality, and officers taunting youths by evoking disorder from other areas. Nevertheless, they reasoned that less clearly segregated black districts prevented the sense of their whole community being under siege, which avoided the situation escalating: 'The flashpoint sparked but it did not ignite. The environment was not conducive to a fire.'[9]

Similarly, disorder did not reoccur in Bristol in 1981. In fact, at the same time as disturbances in Liverpool, more than 15,000 people attended the climax of the annual St Pauls festival in Bristol and witnessed local police joining in with festivities.[10] Likewise, Lewisham in South London, despite minor clashes between small groups of black residents and the police, experienced no serious disorder. The Lewisham Council for Community Relations congratulated the local police's successful employment of 'community policing' by home beat officers, which seemingly prevented disorder.[11]

It appears that more integrationist and restrained police policies, opposed to combative 'hard'-policing reactions demonstrated elsewhere, might have helped avoid further disturbances. Certainly, the areas examined in this study saw specific incidents of police action or misconduct, which built upon pre-existing tensions and 'lit the fuse' leading to disorders – whereas, in other locations, similar conditions did not force escalation in the same manner. Michael Keith argued that many London areas, locally deemed potential 'trouble spots', did not experience disorder, presenting 'ironically, one of the most powerful arguments against the classification of collective violence as irrational'.[12] Assertions regarding why some areas experienced disorders and others did not can tend towards being overly deterministic, and phenomena such as straightforward chance cannot be overlooked.

Nature of disorder

Discussion of why some areas did not experience disorder raises larger questions about the nature of the disturbances themselves. Explanations for disorder spreading across the country were almost as numerous as the locations they reached:

> To some they were the revolt of the underclass and a precursor of the revolution. To some they were race riots, to others they were youth riots or anti-police affrays. To some they were universal events, to others they were highly differentiated outbursts. To some they were a continuation of the American Black ghetto revolts of the 1960s, to others they were a response to a uniquely British situation. To some they were the mindless hooliganism of the unemployables, to others they were a protest against unemployment. Some saw working class insurrection, others criminal vandals enjoying themselves.[13]

John Benyon summarised explanations into two broad groups: liberal/radical or conservative. Characterising liberal and radical perspectives as focusing upon 'basic flaws' in society and politics, he categorised liberal responses as believing improvement could be achieved within current frameworks, whereas radical views advocated a more fundamental restructuring. This grouping reflects divisions suggested by this study: the 'liberal' response of those black organisations and people calling for a public inquiry to advance their position, opposed to the 'radical' actions of 'collective bargaining by riot' participants who believed no advancements would or could be achieved through frameworks deemed inherently discriminatory and racist.

Benyon also abridged interpretations he categorised as conservative, focusing upon law and order rather than social disadvantage or political power, and perceiving 'rioters' to be representing the most disreputable aspects of society, choosing to engage in criminal activity through the desire to loot or for excitement.[14] While certainly apparent, such as largely unconnected looting, initial anti-police disturbances in each case examined can be viewed as a rational response, where conventional alternatives had failed, to protest discrimination and disadvantage.

Unsurprisingly, authorities favoured conservative explanations of the disturbances, characterising them simply as rejections of British law and order. Repeated remarks from Prime Minister Margaret Thatcher contended that any explanation other than 'sheer criminality' were attempts to excuse violence, supported by other government figures such as Home Secretary William Whitelaw: 'No reason, no explanation, for recent troubles justifies what has occurred.'[15] Michael Rowe argued that respect for the law is considered part of the British national character, and arguments regarding broader social, economic or political factors are thus generally not accepted when such public disorder is regarded as 'un-British'.[16] Similarly, Fryer highlighted how prevalent use of terminology such as 'riots' to 'describe what were in fact uprisings … served to obscure the true nature and causes of these events', and Martin Kettle concluded that attempts to depict events as irrational 'denied legitimacy to the rioters, their actions and their views. It made them events without cause, and events that therefore posed no direct threat to any existing assumption'.[17]

Subsequent developments

Almost forty years have passed since the events described, and Winston James correctly summarised that 'Racism persists in various ways, if less crudely than previously'.[18] While impossible in the remaining space to scrutinise subsequent years in similar depth, it is essential to outline relevant developments and consider the lasting legacy of 1980–81. Although what follows is, by necessity, broad discussion, it is nonetheless required to contextualise the events at the heart of this work.

1985 disturbances

John Solomos contended that the most significant message of 1980–81 was that it 'emphasised the role of political protest as a channel for challenging racial injustice after decades of ameliorative reforms'.[19] Accordingly, further disorders and anti-police violence punctuated the following years and widespread disturbances occurred in 1985, the scale of which 'seem to have surprised even some of the most astute commentators'.[20] While important not to aggregate disorders uncritically – Keith highlighted how such action often oversimplifies temporal and spatial racisms – many themes appeared in 1985 similar to those of 1980–81.[21] For example, specific police misconduct or actions that exacerbated existing tensions with black residents, spread of disorder, and subsequent involvement of organisations and defence committees who differed in their opinions of how to respond most effectively. Thus, during an academic conference convened to discuss the 1985 disturbances, the main theme emerged of how little progress had been made.[22] For example, in Liverpool – an area that had received a 'Minister for Merseyside' and some level of governmental expenditure following 1980–81 – William E. Nelson, Jr, argued that disorder returned in 1985 because 'many of the most basic issues remained unresolved'.[23]

Triggers for the 1985 disorders, appearing in Brixton, Toxteth, Handsworth and Tottenham, were police actions aggravating poor relations with the local black population. In Brixton, while searching her home in relation to her son's suspected firearm offence, Metropolitan Police officers shot Dorothy 'Cherry' Groce, which left her paralysed. Rumours spread that Groce had died, and local residents marched on the police station demanding disciplinary action against the officers involved. Anger escalated into two days of disturbances, met with a forceful police response, recording 149 arrests, fifty-five vehicles burnt or damaged, and forty-three civilians and ten officers hurt.[24] Stuart Hall contended that police actions demonstrated the first example of paramilitary policing tactics within mainland Britain, including full riot gear, plastic bullets and CS gas: 'not to contain the violence but to "win" the public-order "war" ' – the roots of which developed throughout 1980–81.[25]

The following week, in Tottenham, Cynthia Jarrett died as officers searched her home in relation to her son's arrest, which likewise sparked protests at the local police station against police actions. The Broadwater Farm Youth Association, an organisation formed in the early 1980s to provide a meeting place for local youth, argued 'the people of Tottenham wanted to exercise their rights to demonstrate peacefully'.[26] Notably, at an ensuing meeting of local councillors and the public, guidance provided by a group Rowe labelled 'established community leaders' – advising that conventional political channels should be utilised to direct complaints through – was rejected in favour of further demonstrations at the police station.[27] Seemingly heightened following experiences following 1980–81, black Britons still deemed traditional political means inadequate for effective protest. Again, tensions grew into disorder, and the subsequent day of disturbances saw the violent death of PC Keith Blakelock at the Broadwater Farm housing estate, the first constable to be killed in public disorder in Britain since 1833.[28]

Despite the long history of disorders throughout British history, including widespread disturbances just four years previously, Metropolitan Police Commissioner Sir Kenneth Newman reportedly labelled the 1985 disorders 'alien to our streets' – as Rowe pointed out, particularly illuminating terminology.[29] In denying British history of public disorder and endorsing 'New Right' redefinitions of national identity around adherence to law and order, it 'reinforced the notion that the blame for the disturbances began and ended with the black community'.[30] Similarly, in his study of the racialisation of disorders throughout the twentieth century, Rowe highlighted how Broadwater Farm had been consistently 'demonised' by media accounts in years preceding the disorder, to the extent that residents even sporadically complained to local press about the negative coverage.[31] In the same way, Broadwater Farm was portrayed as possessing 'something of a proprietorial attachment resenting intrusion, especially by the police to enforce the law'. Demonstrating that the logical outcome of these portrayals leads to what Keith termed 'authoritative policing geographies', Rowe showed how such perceptions of the estate contributed to police action and rumours of disorder apparently spreading prior to the disturbances themselves.[32]

Comparable to 1980–81, commentators reasoned that a breakdown of police/community relations, and the concurrent absence of local 'community leaders' with whom police had regularly liaised, contributed to disorder.[33] An independent inquiry on behalf of Haringey Council chaired by Lord Gifford QC, a Labour peer and barrister who led other similar inquiries and later campaigned for slavery reparations, suggested that senior officers and community organisations enjoyed a generally good relationship. However, high personnel turnover and use of the controversial SPG, prevented positive relations developing between residents and officers policing the estate.[34] Indeed, the Broadwater Farm Youth Association appeared to support community policing ideas, but blamed deployed officers for previous failures: 'Everyone agrees that the police need to be kept in the community as we rely on them for help in many ways. BUT they must be prepared to become a part of the community, not act against it.'[35] It also reasoned that the 'uprising' resulted from increasing police pressure, involving recently intensified drugs raids and tackling of concealed weapons.[36] In remarks often taken out of context that brought widespread condemnation, Bernie Grant, local council leader and Labour MP for Tottenham 1987–2000, similarly stated: 'The youths around here believe the police were to blame for what happened on Sunday and what they got was a bloody good hiding.' Despite criticism for seemingly justifying violence, Grant maintained he was simply summarising the participants' point of view, and spent many subsequent years working to improve police/community relations.[37]

There were certainly attempts at liaison between the police and local people, but these had limited success. Keith described his personal account of a public meeting of the Community Police Consultative Group for Lambeth in Brixton on 1 October 1985, three days after the police shooting of Groce. While characterised by the police, press and the group itself as 'acting as a peaceful outlet for the anger of local people', Keith convincingly contended that this meeting demonstrated the group's inherent failings. Chaired by Astel Parkinson, a respected local youth worker, the meeting was immediately taken over by a militant group who demanded its immediate end, with cries of 'Uncle Tom' directed at Parkinson for co-operating with police 'filth'. Police Commander Marnoch, the senior officer present, was hostilely interrogated by the crowd, eventually breaking down in tears. While Parkinson and Marnoch later portrayed this meeting as successful, Keith viewed it differently:

> both men had been trapped by the contradictions that undermine the whole value of consultation as a mechanism for the resolution of conflict between the police and Black communities ... The roots and nature of this conflict were simply not susceptible to being talked away.[38]

As demonstrated throughout, the response from black residents demonstrated the limitations of liaising with the police or authorities to resolve these tensions. The shooting of Groce and death of Jarrett prompted accusations of police institutional racism and belief they were still not being held accountable. No public apology ever materialised from the police for their role in Jarrett's death, and it was only in 2014, three years after Groce's death and a judicial inquest that found eight separate police failures had contributed to it, that the police accepted liability for their failings in that case.[39]

Despite Labour immediately calling for an independent inquiry into the causes of the 1985 disorders, Thatcher's Government refused to hold another in the mould of Lord Scarman's Brixton public inquiry: demonstrating the difficulty of obtaining such measures, and the disappointment that Scarman had not achieved more. Haringey Council actually invited Scarman to lead their independent inquiry, but, after both he and Mark Bonham Carter – previously chair of both the Race Relations Board and successor the Community Relations Commission – declined, Gifford was approached.[40] The authorities' continued focus on law and order enabled this inquiry refusal as, in Thatcherite Britain, there was no place for questioning the Government's socioeconomic policies. In the context of a strengthened Government, buoyed by recent victory in the prolonged 1984–85 miners' strike, governmental interpretations of disorder portrayed them as purely the indefensible consequence of 'human wickedness' that required a 'hard'-policing response to combat.[41] Indeed, a report by members of Thatcher's policy unit concluded that 'Riots, criminality and social disintegration are caused solely by individual characters and attitudes' – even warning against a proposed £10 million communities programme because '[black] entrepreneurs will set up in the disco and drug trade'.[42]

Their response also confirmed that the Government doubted Scarman's previous conclusions concerning social issues, believing his Report had 'failed to determine the causes of the riots and … contributed towards the eruption of new riots'.[43] Solomos argued that an even-greater focus on criminality was demonstrated than in 1980–81, through a shift in political language that promoted interpretations of disorders as 'criminal enterprise more suited to investigation by the police than by social analysts or judicial experts such as Lord Scarman'.[44] After forging such an environment, the Government's refusal to hold a 'second Scarman' appeared straightforward; but, in doing so, many inherent issues were not addressed. For example, a 1989 Report initiated by Liverpool City Council, also headed by Gifford, found that racism and racial discrimination remained 'uniquely horrific' in the city.[45]

In comparison with refusals to address social issues, six people were immediately charged with PC Blakelock's murder. This included three juveniles, whose cases were all dismissed after their confessions were deemed inadmissible due to the inappropriate conditions they were subjected to during interrogations, and three adults, subsequently sentenced to life imprisonment – despite a lack of eyewitnesses or forensic evidence. The ensuing Broadwater Farm Defence Campaign to exonerate the 'Tottenham Three' bore many similarities to defence organisations established during 1980–81, as black Britons mobilised nationwide and further participated in forms of politics from which they had often previously been excluded. This campaign – which included renowned solicitor Gareth Peirce, support of Brixton inquiry head Lord Scarman, and even an application to the European Court of Human Rights – eventually led to exonerations by the Court of Appeal.[46] In the years since, two more investigations led to multiple arrests and further trials, but Blakelock's death remains hitherto unresolved.

2001 and 2011 disturbances

In 2001, disorder broke out in Oldham, Harehills and Bradford. While Harehills saw anti-police disturbances reminiscent of 1980–81 after the alleged heavy-handed wrongful arrest of a local British Asian man, Oldham and Bradford also demonstrated conflicts between white and British Asian communities. Growing concern regarding 'Asian-on-White' violence had escalated tensions prior to disorders, attracting far-right groups such as the NF who then clashed with the ANL. Deep fracturing and segregation of communities along racial and religious lines increased conflict, as locals 'vented their frustrations on each other as well as the police', reigniting debates regarding the respective merits of assimilation versus integration policies.[47]

In 2011, a protest march in Tottenham against the contentious police killing of Mark Duggan, a local black man, was met with a questionable police response, increasing local tensions and later escalating into disorders. The press immediately reported false information, apparently originating from the Independent Police Complaints Commission (IPCC), that Duggan had died during a 'shootout' with the police, with subsequent media accounts portraying Duggan as a well-known gangster. Duggan's family described such accusations as unsubstantiated, with local residents accusing the police of executing Duggan and deeming the IPCC not an effective or impartial investigatory body.[48] Gus John argued this presentation affected popular memory of the subsequent disorders, increasing sympathy for the police by framing responses around the question: 'if Duggan had not been stopped, would they have been reporting a [civilian] shooting at the end of that day?'[49]

Some commentators made direct comparisons between the 2011 England disturbances and 1980–81, and there are indeed similarities.[50] Both national waves of disorder began the year after a Conservative return to government – albeit, in coalition with Liberal Democrats in 2010 – combined with a background of economic crisis that saw intensifying economic neoliberalism and public spending cuts, through either 'monetarism' or 'austerity', both of which most affected those at the margins of society.[51] During a sensational exchange with a BBC reporter – which generated outrage and forced the BBC to officially apologise – activist Darcus Howe invoked memories of the 1981 Brixton disturbances, drawing parallels with police targeting black youth and a resultant outburst of frustrations.[52] As Kennetta Hammond Perry concluded, Howe argued that the 2011 disturbances were 'intimately connected to a history marked by the state's inability to safeguard the rights of its Black citizens'.[53]

Once disorder began, the police, similarly to Moss Side in 1981, attempted low-profile policing tactics to avoid escalating confrontation, but, like Moss Side, these were deemed a failure as disorder continued unabated.[54] Equally, many accusations emerged of police misconduct and racism. For example, a black youth recorded audio of officers informing him that they had strangled him during his arrest 'because you're a cunt', before proclaiming: 'The problem with you is you will always be a nigger.' The officer in question was later sacked for gross misconduct, but twice avoided sentences for racially aggravated public disorder as both juries were unable to reach a verdict.[55]

The response and media coverage again focused on criminal acts of looting, largely from unrelated persons not involved in anti-police protests, rather than underlying social issues. On 8 August 2011, Home Secretary Theresa May, when asked whether criminals had hijacked a 'genuine cause [to] steal trainers and steal TV's', utilised the exact language of thirty years previously in a blanket condemnation of the 'sheer criminality'.[56] Moreover, similar responses regarding enhanced police equipment and use of water cannon, baton rounds and possibility for police curfews suggested little had changed in the intervening thirty years. Indeed, in the words of Anandi Ramamurthy, 'widespread condemnation of the riots [with] limited discussion on the social justifications for them, is testament to the resilience of Thatcherism as a doctrine that was intent on breaking resistance from communities'.[57]

Although 1980–81 has acquired an air of legitimacy as a rational response to racial discrimination and disadvantage, 2011 seems to have been popularly dismissed purely as, in the recurrent words of Conservative politicians, 'sheer criminality'.[58] For example, Tottenham Labour MP David Lammy, a New Labour minister who replaced Bernie Grant following Grant's death in 2000, labelled the 2011 disorders 'an explosion of hedonism and nihilism'.[59] A far cry from Grant's apparent sympathy with actions in 1985, Lammy's comments and general ability to represent his constituents have been questioned; he certainly appears less popular with black residents than Grant was. One community activist concluded Lammy 'seriously missed the mark and didn't address the wider issue of a failing, racist establishment that had generated such a degree of apathy and distraction. There seems to be a disconnect where there used to be dialogue'.[60]

A lack of legitimacy for 2011 could also be partly due to historical proximity, suggesting that time and distance is needed before such a perspective can be reached: 1980–81 has been framed as successful uprisings against oppression within a broader movement towards political participation and liberation for black Britons, thus far broadly not the case for 2011. Other than Howe, attempts to depict these disorders as rebellions have largely revolved around economic inequalities, with commentators such as Ambalavaner Sivanandan concluding that disconnected youth – 'through unemployment, cuts in education, youth facilities and mentoring schemes' – produced 'neither community-based nor politically-orientated' disorders. However, he did argue they symbolised that 'multiculturalism has succeeded at the point of riot: the rioters came from all communities'.[61]

Black political representation

One discernible result of 1980–81 was the opportunity for some local government authorities to 'place black representation on the mainstream political agenda'.[62] The main avenue for such, the jewel-in-the-crown of the derogatorily termed 'Loony Left', was the Greater London Council (GLC) under Ken Livingstone.[63] Less than a month after the Brixton disturbances, county council elections returned a Labour-controlled GLC, with lawyer Paul Boateng becoming only the second black person to be elected to a county council. Mike and Trevor Phillips asserted that this, alongside other minority ethnic councillors being elected in the West Midlands, showed the electorate had not been wholly alienated by the disorders and even 'hinted at greater possibilities for black politicians'.[64] Programmes of municipal anti-racism that followed provided some advancements, particularly through GLC support for black self-organisation by, in Livingstone's words, providing a political space for oppressed groups to, 'free of the influence of white people, discuss the discrimination they feel, decide how to articulate their demands and then come forward to the movement with proposals for change'. London's County Hall, previously viewed as a symbol of the oppressive and ineffective British state, became depicted in some quarters as the 'People's Palace'.[65]

However, some commentators, such as Sivanandan, criticised these programmes as ineffective at combatting 'monumental and endemic racism', and ethnic politics as weakening the fight against racism by splitting political blackness along class divides, as the black petit-bourgeoisie attempted to further their own specific class interests.[66] The Conservative Government attempted the 'creation of a Black middle class', after Scarman's inquiry recommended creating 'moderate leaders' to aid social stability and for black Britons to gain a stake in the community through business. They arguably also attempted to foster black class division, denying legitimacy to those attempting to develop black consciousness; as Sir George Young, 'minister for race relations', stated in 1982: 'We've got to back the good "guys", the sensible moderate, responsible leaders of the ethnic groups ... If they don't deliver people will turn to the militants.'[67] Similarly, by municipal anti-racism amalgamating diverse communities under the singular heading of 'ethnic minorities', critics decried the alteration of black identity from distinct histories to simply that of their collective relationship with racism.[68] Satnam Virdee agreed with Sivanandan's analysis of the creation of a section of black professionals who occupied a contradictory class position, but noted the lack of detailed assessment of how effective local councils' attempts to tackle racial discrimination and inequality had been. Citing figures showing numbers of black staff in the GLC more than trebled between 1981 and 1986, Virdee concluded that such advancements were somewhat due to black self-organisation and actions, rather than simply concessions from radical Labour-led local authorities.[69]

Paul Gilroy argued that the GLC appeared at a prominent time for the politics of race and movement of such issues towards the centre of political institutions, which altered previous community-level approaches.[70] Anti-racist activists decried the GLC's activities as 'a perfect trap' for defusing street-level militancy, pushing activists into 'filling out applications for grants'.[71] While many anti-racist policies were attacked in the media as 'benefiting blacks "unfairly"', the GLC lacked the resources and authority to effectively promote racial equality and implement real change.[72] Indeed, Shamit Saggar noted the mainstream Labour Party's 'worries over close association with the racial equality lobby (race as a partial metaphor for so-called "loony left" smear politics)'.[73] Perhaps it is fair to describe the fortunes of municipal anti-racism, as Gilroy has, as 'a very, very mixed bag'.[74]

Whereas Labour had previously made little movement towards incorporating black and minority ethnic groups into its organisational structures, towards the end of the 1970s this began to be contested. For example, the Labour Party

Race Action Group was established as an inner-party pressure group in 1975 to spread awareness of the politics of racism, and racial inequality was brought to both local and national party agendas from the late 1970s.[75] 1980–81 helped increase black representation within institutions such as the Labour Party, including calls beginning at the 1983 annual party conference for the recognition of Black Sections to increase black members' influence upon policymaking; although Howe contended this movement was more about the aspirations of black middle-class professionals than 'issues facing the Black working classes'.[76] The significance of the 1980–81 disorders can clearly be viewed when Marc Wordsworth, a prominent Black Sections campaigner, warned of the possible 'tendency, particularly amongst black youth, to redress their grievances through extra-parliamentary action' if not effectively represented within Labour.[77] Party leaders opposed Black Sections, believing they would be seen as divisive – but fears of radical left-wing black groups becoming political liabilities were also apparent.[78]

It has been argued that, during Labour's 'Wilderness Years' when Thatcher battled deeply imbedded working-class cultures such as the miners and trade unions, she destroyed some of the bases of white nationalism within the Labour movement: 'we immigrants had never known those roots, and that left us free to join in the re-building'.[79] While the Black Sections movement failed to achieve the formal recognition it desired, the election of three black British and one British Asian Labour MP in 1987 suggested minority ethnic political participation and inclusion was advancing, and, by 1992, all political parties even 'claimed that race was no longer an issue in British political life'.[80]

Alternatively, Kalbir Shukra criticised developments with her blunt statement in 1998 that 'Radical black politics in Britain is dead'. Asserting that black political activists drew closer to the state from the 1980s, she argued that black professionals and politicians had given the impression that the state could be effective in anti-racism: 'In looking to the state to oppose racism, today's black organisers seem to have forgotten that it was the British state which framed racism in the first place.'[81] This is supported by Bristol activist Simbarashe Tongogara's recollections of being 'dragged' to a government meeting of 'young, intellectual, prominent' black people in 1981 – 'all these people now, all except this one person, are all some establishment figures' – and Gus John's characterisation of New Labour's Cabinet Minister Paul Boateng as having 'lost his way'.[82] While there has arguably been a revival in radical black politics in recent years, discussed later, questions of black political participation and representation remain disputed.

In general, since the 1980s, Britain's public discussions and governmental stances on race and immigration have continued to prove challenging. From Conservative MP Norman Tebbit's 'Cricket Test' demanding people from former colonies support England over 'their home side', New Labour's attempted rebranding of the country in 1997 as chicken tikka masala-loving 'Cool Britannia', to issues associated with post-9/11 and 7/7 terrorism questioning if the concept of multiculturalism is outdated, issues of assimilation and integration have remained controversial.[83] Moreover, Britain's membership of the European Union (EU) incorporated many accompanying changes in immigration controls. Ian Spencer commented that

> changes in immigration law and practice since 1945 have perfectly mirrored the change in Britain's international position ... [from] head of a vast Empire [to] becoming integrated into a European Community heading fitfully and uncertainly towards closer political unity.[84]

Free movement of people within the EU has been restricted to EU citizens and often accompanied by increased efforts to limit immigration from outside of the EU, termed by some observers 'a multi-lateral movement towards the creation of a Fortress Europe'.[85] Evidence suggests that British and EU immigration policy thus disproportionately disadvantages black and ethnic minority populations, both in potential migration and living conditions once in residence.[86] However, due to the 2016 'Brexit' vote to leave the EU, in which the issue of immigration played a significant role, the future of British immigration is currently the most unsure is has been for some time.[87]

In 1998, the Runnymede Trust, an independent organisation established in the 1960s to promote racial equality and generate information on race and ethnicity, established a Commission on the Future of Multi-Ethnic Britain. In 2000, its Report argued in favour of seeing Britain as 'a community of communities and a community of citizens'.[88] It reasoned that, for all its citizens to feel a sense of belonging to the nation, sustained public discussion of what it meant to be British in the twenty-first century was required 'to reflect the current and future, and not just the past, ethnic composition of the country'.[89] However, popular response to this Report, particularly within the media, decried perceived attempts to 'rewrite our history', and numerous newspapers selectively quoted the Report out of context to claim it was suggesting that ' "British" is a racist word'.[90] In a similar way, the rose-tinted nostalgia and imagined past characterising Brexit arguments, as well as a 2014 YouGov poll finding that 59 per cent of respondents believed the British Empire was something to be 'proud' of rather than regretted, demonstrates that discussions of national identity remain well overdue.[91]

Stephen Lawrence and 'institutional racism'

A public inquiry in 1999 similarly suggested that fundamental issues within Britain needed addressing: Sir William Macpherson's inquiry into the death of Stephen Lawrence and the ineffectual police investigation. While waiting for a bus in South East London on 22 April 1993, Lawrence and friend Duwayne Brooks were attacked by white youths who shouted 'What, what nigger?' before Lawrence was stabbed twice and died from his injuries.[92] The police investigation initially disregarded the clear racial aspects of the attack, instead profiling these two young black men as likely involved with gangs and even treating Brooks himself as a suspect. Although five main suspects were soon identified, no arrests took place for two weeks; long enough for suspects to be twice observed by police – but not stopped – removing black plastic rubbish sacks from their homes, potentially destroying evidence. When the five white youths were eventually arrested, charges against them were subsequently dropped due to the Crown Prosecution Service citing insufficient evidence.[93] A private prosecution launched by Lawrence's family resulted in acquittals due to the same conclusions, and it was only in 2012, following a cold case review and new examination of forensic evidence, that Gary Dobson and David Norris were both found guilty of Lawrence's murder. Stephen's mother, Doreen Lawrence, clearly expressed her opinion of the original investigation – characterised by repeated incompetence and discrimination, having squandered time investigating racially stereotyped assumptions and subsequently failing to prosecute suspects. She described it as 'the judicial system making a clear statement saying to the black community that their lives are worth nothing and the justice system will support … any white person who wishes to commit any crime or even murder against a black person'.[94]

Macpherson's public inquiry was only established following a persistent campaign by Lawrence's family and supporters; initially rejected by Conservative Home Office Minister Peter Lloyd, it was later granted by Home Secretary Jack Straw following Labour's landslide return to government in 1997.[95] Many commentators highlighted how this case became a *cause célèbre* due to the impeccable character of Lawrence and his family, which countered the 'unquestioning faith in the police and … that all the talk about "police racism" was really just "a black thing"':

Despite the fact that they were of African/Caribbean origin, the plight of the Lawrences resonated with the sentiments of middle England. The message was clear: anyone could have lost a son in this way, anyone could be confronted by denial, ineptitude by the police and have no means of holding them to account for what had gone wrong.[96]

This was somewhat demonstrated when, in February 1997, notoriously right-wing tabloid the *Daily Mail* identified the five suspects initially prosecuted in 1994 under the headline 'Murderers: The Mail accuses these men of killing. If we are wrong, let them sue us'.[97] None subsequently did.

Macpherson's inquiry report concluded there had been a failure of leadership by senior Metropolitan Police officials, numerous examples of professional incompetence, and that many recommendations from the 1981 Scarman Report had been ignored. The conclusion attracting most attention was its deeming the police 'institutionally racist', almost twenty years after Scarman rejected such accusations; partly due to Macpherson's description of 'institutional racism' being far broader, incorporating 'unwitting prejudice'.[98] Scarman had defended his narrower definition of institutional racism in 1982, which addressed only conscious, 'knowing' discrimination, by deeming the debate 'a matter of semantics'.[99] However, as Ben Bowling pointed out in his discussion of racism, 'naming the problem is not simply a matter of semantics but reflects the intensely political process of conceptualization'.[100] Keith argued that changes in police training proposed by Scarman and later, such as Human Awareness and Race Awareness training, were doomed to fail as they existed upon flawed myths of 'racism as a disease or infection … [that] can be purged by the treatment of individual souls'.[101] Endemic institutional racism, demonstrated by Macpherson to permeate the police force, could not be addressed with responses based on simple assumptions that 'bad apples' needed extracting.

Chris Gifford *et al.* described Macpherson's conclusions as a 'major breakthrough in UK race and ethnic relations', forcing a fundamental rethinking of institutional practices.[102] Public acknowledgement of institutional racism was a result many campaigners had been waiting decades to hear; but, for countless black Britons such as Lawrence and his family, it had come too late – and was by no means an immediate solution. Barry Loveday noted that there has been little evidence of changes in police organisational culture, and Hall summarised popular criticism of the Report, which alleged that such a general definition of institutional racism actually prevented progress: 'if every institution is racist, then there is nothing to do but destroy them and start again – a recipe for inaction'.[103]

Sarah Neal concluded that 'Thatcher paid little heed to Scarman after 1981, and Macpherson, while bringing about legislative reforms, has been subject to police and media challenges since its publication'.[104] Whether these public inquiries actually stimulated the political and social changes being called for is questionable. Popular symbolic measures but with limited successes, they were significant in providing an opportunity for public discourse and allowing those directly affected to contribute to discussions – but failures to implement recommendations and disappointment at lack of progress demonstrates there is much work left to be done.

Policing since 1980–81

There have been many developments in the history of British policing since the events discussed. As a brief illustrative example, Moss Side in Manchester has witnessed a long struggle regarding crime, policing and community relations since 1980–81, obtaining the moniker 'Gunchester' during the 1990s due to high levels of drugs, gang violence and gun crimes. Following the 1981 disturbances, the Police Authority established a complaints committee, encouraging locals to pursue complaints against police misconduct, and sub-divisional community panels for consultation between the police and residents.[105] Linbert Spencer, Community Liaison Officer for Greater Manchester Council, sought to improve police/community relations; however, levels of anti-authority opinion ran deep. While noting advancements, particularly in police addressing complaints, he noted the difficulty of change: 'almost all of the things that people would be voicing at these kinds of meetings would be pretty deeply engrained ... not fixable by one-off or even a series of meetings'.[106] Similarly, deep-seated police racism was slow to diminish. Examples existed of NF stickers on police lockers, a Community Relations Officer for Moss Side warning that black locals will 'take your [car's] wheels', and a Chief Superintendent refuting accusations of police racism because 'I've just been served my dinner by a black woman!'[107] While progress has been slow, the retirement in 1991 of Manchester Chief Constable James Anderton seemed to have a discernible impact. His replacement, David Wilmot, 'gave the impression of being more amenable, more wanting to understand', and acknowledged publicly that the police were part of the problem, enabling the beginnings of a police/community relationship to develop that previously could not: 'The Anderton generation's gradually died out, we've had other people coming in – we're talking 35 years ago.'[108]

Harry Goulbourne argued that 1980–81 led to an increased public interest in the police and desire for them to be more accountable to the communities they served.[109] Indeed, Scarman's public inquiry, although criticised for not having gone far enough, made a number of recommendations to make the police more accountable. The Police and Criminal Evidence Act 1984 was one result: ostensibly attempting to balance police powers with the rights and freedoms of the public, in reality it extended police powers and its complaints system lacked the confidence of both complainants and police.[110]

In the aftermath of 1980–81, however, little actually changed in terms of policing black communities and a number of Scarman's recommendations were either ignored or not effectively implemented. While Hall concluded that, although Scarman's Report 'was no panacea [it] broke the prevailing law-and-order consensus', Scarman himself criticised the lack of implementation of his social and economic recommendations, concluding there had been 'a misdirection of effort [and] a lack of effort'.[111] Considering governmental actions demonstrated throughout this study, this is unsurprising: further to fitting with a government prone to unhesitatingly supporting the police and rejecting conciliation, it has been argued that 'state racism was a crucial ingredient in the toxic cocktail that Thatcherism was constructing around its authoritarian populist agenda'.[112] When Conservative Home Secretary Douglas Hurd claimed, after the 1985 disturbances, that Scarman's recommendations had been largely implemented, John Clare correctly deemed this 'such patent breath-taking nonsense'.[113]

The authorities focused attention upon calls for better equipment and powers to combat social unrest, including strengthening the Public Order Act in 1986, and were averse to attempts at increasing police accountability.[114] Senior police officers further attempted to assert their independence from partly democratically elected police authorities, with Anderton even calling for their eradication.[115] Similarly, there appeared no desire to change previous approaches. At a Conservative Party Monday Club meeting in October 1982, Police Federation Vice-Chair Basil Griffiths proclaimed: 'There is in our inner cities a very large minority of people who are not fit for salvage ... the only way in which the police can protect society is quite simply by harassing these people and frightening them so they are afraid to commit crimes.'[116] The Monday Club was known for long-held controversial beliefs such as voluntary repatriation, leading to its links with the Conservative Party being severed in 2001, and this pronouncement did little to suggest a radical change in police policy. A Police Federation representative would further clarify their position the following month: 'There are two conflicting demands. One is to stop harassing young blacks in inner cities. The other is to stop young blacks harassing other people in the inner cities. Which demand do you respond to? It has to be the second.'[117]

Shukra framed these attitudes as actually an advancement in police tactics, 'targeting of specific black individuals rather than blanket repression'.[118] In years since, police use of stop and search tactics has constantly remained controversial. Despite evidence of limited success and negative impact upon police/community relations, they remain touted as a necessity for combatting crime and terrorism in a post-9/11 world.[119] Equally, minority ethnic groups remain disproportionately overrepresented in the statistics: in 1997–98, rates of stop and search were seven times higher for black Britons and two times higher for British Asians than the white population, a ratio remaining consistent in 2005–6 and returning in 2015–16.[120] Coretta Phillips noted that there was a drop in stops and searches around the time of Macpherson's public inquiry, as police confidence about their legitimate use declined amidst fears of accusations of racism – but similar levels returned within a few years.[121] Racially stereotyped perceptions of black people being more criminally disposed have persisted, with accounts emerging of minority ethnic officers being advised to focus their attention on 'black kids with baseball caps, wearing all the jewellery' because 'if you see four black youths in a car … at least one of them is going to be guilty of something'.[122] Explanations forwarded for ethnic disproportionality in stop and search rates – discussed in chapter 1 – remain inadequate, and it is unsurprising that, until recently, minority ethnic groups retained a lower level of confidence in the criminal justice system than white counterparts.[123]

Recent confidence in the police and criminal justice system appeared to be strengthened somewhat following the Macpherson Report due to governmental attempts under New Labour to be seen tackling racist 'hate crimes'.[124] In February 1981, the cross-party Joint Committee Against Racialism informed Whitelaw of the growing number of racial attacks. Whitelaw agreed to establish a Home Office inquiry, subsequently declaring that 'Racially motivated attacks, particularly on Asians, are more common than we supposed'.[125] Despite previous levels of concern, self-defence and organisation, it had taken until 1981 for racial attacks to be placed on the political agenda and their frequency to be recognised by the British state. While self-organisation and high numbers of racist attacks certainly prompted this inquiry, it was made a 'political necessity' by the 1980–81 disorders.[126] Despite this, there has been mixed success in combatting racial violence. Legislation, such as recognition by the 1998 Crime and Disorder Act of 'racially aggravated' offences, publicly asserted that 'racial harmony and equality are ... among the highest values in our society' and 'such victimisation is considered by the government as abhorrent'.[127] Yet, the number of, and response to, deaths in racist attacks or related to interactions with the police remain a source of great concern and stimulus for black and minority ethnic community activism.

Moreover, the true state of the police in the 1980s is only recently becoming known. Revelations regarding police misconduct and attempts to pervert the course of justice demonstrate their role in forcefully implementing Thatcherite ideology, and a seeming continuation of the sense amongst many officers of having free rein to act without personal negative consequences. Police tactics employed during the particularly bitter dispute between trade unions and the Government during the 1984–85 miners' strike have been widely condemned, with accusations of officers striking protestors and later fabricating or tampering with evidence prompting calls for a public inquiry. Despite the South Yorkshire police in 2012 referring themselves to the IPCC, to investigate accusations of assault, perjury, perverting the course of justice, and misconduct in a public office, the Commission rejected calls for a formal investigation as it was deemed too long ago. Conservative Home Secretary Amber Rudd claimed 'very few lessons [could] be learned from any review of the events and practices of three decades ago'.[128] Similarly, recent revelations about the 1989 Hillsborough disaster, where ninety-six people were crushed to death due to police errors, has revealed that substantial effort was undertaken by the police to conceal the truth, including the alteration of some 116 officer statements to 'remove or alter comments unfavourable' to the police.[129] It is thus hard to argue that 1980–81 positively altered the accountability or attitudes of the police regarding public disorder, and perceived challenges to their authority.

Furthermore, the public's relationship with systems of police accountability have remained complicated. Police authorities in England in Wales were abolished by the coalition Government in November 2012 and replaced with directly elected Police and Crime Commissioners (PCCs), a role ostensibly containing 'phenomenal potential' for greater levels of local accountability.[130] Nonetheless, public reaction was far from enthusiastic and prompted criticism regarding the politicisation of the police. Jenny Watson, United Kingdom Electoral Commission Chair, expressed enormous disappointment at voter numbers, concluding that 'the extremely low turnout – at just 15.1% – must be a concern for anyone who cares about democracy'.[131] While the 2016 PCCs elections saw slightly healthier numbers, the generally low turnout and relatively high numbers of spoiled ballots, as well as conflict between PCCs and chief constables, reprises important questions regarding systems of police administration, accountability, and relationship between the police and politics.

Public inquiries and deaths in police custody

Throughout, this book has considered the perception and role of public inquiries, which are established to examine issues of serious public concern.[132] Deaths related to police action or within custody is one such controversial issue, as questions remain regarding the level of scrutiny focused upon those tasked with physically enforcing the will of the state. When people, such as minority ethnic groups, feel they are not awarded the same treatment as others in society, concern surrounding deaths is unsurprisingly heightened. A number of inquests returning verdicts of unlawful killings in the 1990s led to a United Nations Committee Against Torture report criticising 'the number of deaths in police custody and the apparent failure by [Britain] to provide an effective investigative mechanism to deal with allegations of police and prison authorities' abuse'.[133] At time of writing, figures compiled by Inquest, a charity founded in 1981 concerned with deaths in custody or detention in England and Wales, record that 1,651 persons have died since 1990 in police custody or otherwise following contact with the police. Of these, 176 were classified as being from black or minority ethnic communities.[134] With roughly 14 per cent of the UK population identifying with a black or minority ethnic category in the 2011 Census, a figure just below 11 per cent seems to demonstrate this group is actually slightly underrepresented in deaths related to contact with the police, despite being represented more highly in police shootings – at around 25 per cent. However, distinct research by the IRR suggested that, between 1991 and 2015, at least 509 people from black or minority ethnic, refugee, and migrant communities died 'in suspicious circumstances in which the police, prison authorities or immigration detention officers have been implicated'.[135] A number of controversial cases have compounded existing discontentment regarding deaths of black and minority ethnic people related to police action, demonstrating continued negative perceptions of police attitudes and actions towards these communities.

One such example was that of Joy Gardner in July 1993 who, during attempted deportation by the Metropolitan Police, died after having 'thirteen feet of sticky tape [wrapped] around her mouth'.[136] At the time of her death, Jamaican-born Gardner was appealing a deportation order following the expiration of a six-month visitor's visa. Demonstrators and black residents in Tottenham protested her death and, according to the *Sunday Times*, it was only recently appointed

Metropolitan Commissioner Paul Condon's 'characteristic speed and decisiveness' that prevented rioting by recruiting popular local MP Bernie Grant to call for calm – an approach, of course, unavailable in 1980–81 and 1985.[137] Three of the officers involved in Gardner's death were charged with manslaughter – a decision the Police Federation deemed a 'sad day for British justice' – but were subsequently cleared. Ryan Erfani-Ghettani detailed the UK press's racialised reaction to Gardner's death, with right-wing publications portraying this 'violent uncompromising woman' as a criminal, illegal immigrant: 'Why the hell was she here anyway?'[138] Such portrayals are consistent with attempts to criminalise minority ethnic people, removing the blame away from the police.[139]

Another death in the criminal justice system causing great discontent was nineteen-year-old Zahid Mubarek, attacked and fatally injured at Feltham Young Offenders Institution on 21 March 2000. Serving a three-month sentence for stealing razor blades, just hours before his release he was beaten to death by cellmate Robert Stewart, 'a deeply disturbed skinhead with expressed racist views', who himself later lamented to the CRE: 'Somebody should have thought I was a time bomb waiting to explode.'[140] Stewart had apparently been housed with Mubarek due to it being the last remaining space available, but many observers believed institutional racism and complacency led to this ill-fated decision. Earlier Prison Inspectorate reports on Feltham suggested a history of deep-rooted racism, although no subsequent action had been taken, and evidence surfaced of prison staff instigating racial violence between inmates dubbed 'Gladiator Games'.[141] A prolonged legal campaign by Mubarek's family eventually led the House of Lords to order Labour Home Secretary David Blunkett to hold a public inquiry, which he had previously denied as unnecessary. When its report was published in 2006, it was welcomed as a condemnation of institutionalised racism within the Prison Service, much as Macpherson's Report in 1999 had been for the police. However, Nick Moss observed that the inquiry's conclusions were actually moderate and the issue of racism was sidelined as the inquiry progressed, instead focusing upon procedural failings leading to Mubarek's death. As Moss concluded, 'It remains a remarkable oversight that a skinhead with "RIP" tattooed on his forehead, and who proclaimed association with the KKK, could be considered a safe choice of cellmate for a young, mild, and vulnerable Asian boy'.[142]

In 2014, following the contentious police shooting of Mark Duggan that sparked the 2011 disorders across England, the inquest into his death concluded by a jury majority of eight-to-two that he was lawfully killed. Campaigners again protested outside Tottenham Police Station, opposing this 'perverse' ruling. Stafford Scott, co-founder of the Broadwater Farm Defence Campaign, recounted a previous protest there against police misconduct; in 1999, following his arrest and detainment by the police, Roger Sylvester died following injuries sustained while being restrained by officers during a medical assessment. Though the inquest jury returned a verdict of unlawful killing in 2003, the police appealed to the High Court against what they deemed an 'irrational' ruling, which was subsequently overturned in 2004. As Scott detailed in 2014:

> Fifteen years ago today we came to burn this station down. And the family of Roger Sylvester said don't do it ... we want to go down the justice route ... And they went to a court, they went to an inquest, where the inquest jury said unlawful killing. And the police appealed, and the judge in a high court said 'I believe the jury was confused' ... Well we want a judge to tell us that the jury in the Mark Duggan inquest was confused.[143]

Recent collective action related to deaths of black people either at the hands of US police or going unpunished, most notably Trayvon Martin, Michael Brown and Eric Garner, led to the transnational Black Lives Matter (BLM) activist movement. Following the death of Martin, shot dead in Florida after local resident George Zimmerman seemingly deemed wearing a hoodie whilst being black suspicious behaviour, anger at Zimmerman's acquittal of all charges related to Martin's death – and the state's controversial 'Stand-your-ground' self-defence statute – prompted #BlackLivesMatter to spread on social media. The BLM movement has since seen the mobilisation of black people, provoking similar tensions and disagreement between attempts to work within established political frameworks and militant approaches. Some prominent US civil rights activists, such as Barbara Ann Reynolds and Najee Ali, have expressed reservations about BLM's tactics and actions, exhibiting the same dichotomy that appeared in responses to 1980–81.[144] However, criticism that the movement is simply divisive and racist, by those who immediately retorted with the 'All Lives Matter' slogan, reflects, in the words of David Theo Goldberg, the politics of 'racial dismissal, ignoring, and denial'.[145] In societies where black and minority ethnic lives are continually demonstrated to apparently matter less than white counterparts – through overrepresentation in the criminal justice system, racial discrimination in education and employment, and racial profiling – such response seem to confirm the points.

The recent deaths of Edson Da Costa, Darren Cumberbatch and Rashan Charles have continued a history of contentious deaths of black Britons in relation to police activity. Figures released on 1 August 2017 suggested a disproportionate use of police force against minority ethnic groups, and Da Costa's cousin demonstrated the poor relationship between black residents and the authorities: 'we feel ignored, we feel outraged, we feel hurt'.[146] Similarly, continuing media defamation of victims in deaths related to police action, accusations soon appeared that Da Costa and Charles had swallowed packages of drugs upon detainment, causing severe overdoses when the bags split. While Da Costa's post-mortem did suggest evidence of this, police claims that Charles had similarly swallowed an object upon apprehension have thus far been refuted by the IPCC. The families of these men promised to 'continue to fight for justice' for all who have died in police custody, through political campaigns and 'peace on the streets'. Following the deaths, both peaceful protests and separate violent clashes with police occurred, with a number of arrests and officers injured. Pressure group Stand Up To Racism organised a vigil outside the local police station, describing protestors as 'angry and confused' because they were 'not being represented'.[147] Labour Shadow Home Secretary Diane Abbott believed 'urgent work must be done to rebuild trust and links between the police and the community … but there is absolutely no cause for any more violence'. Similarly, Stafford Scott, coordinator of the Tottenham Rights group, which has campaigned against police oppression since the 1985 Broadwater Farm disturbances, understood the frustrations, but also discouraged rioting: 'Taking to the streets does not give you justice … burning down your neighbourhood is not going to give you justice.'[148] Only time will tell what form future protests will take, but similar contrasts between attempts to work within conventional channels and militant responses demonstrates that the dichotomous response of 1980–81 remains apparent.

A long-awaited official report into deaths in police custody, ordered in 2015, remains unpublished, but is expected to conclude that families of the deceased have been 'failed by the system'.[149] After the death of Kingsley Burrell in Birmingham in March 2011, following a heart attack while forcibly restrained by police and ambulance staff, an inquest found that he had died due to neglect. This led to calls for a public inquiry as the family had 'no faith, no trust' in the police and authorities, arguing: 'Until people are accountable for their actions then there will be no closure.'[150]

However, following the Grenfell Tower fire in North Kensington, West London on 14 June 2017, which caused seventy-one deaths, the ability of public inquiries to hold authorities to account has been widely questioned. When Prime Minister Theresa May ordered a public inquiry, chaired by retired judge Sir Martin Moore-Bick, his first involvement was publicly declaring being 'doubtful' it would be as wide-ranging as residents hoped.[151] Lawyers acting on behalf of the families questioned Moore-Bick's appointment, due to a contentious history regarding housing policies and his unfamiliarity with the lives of poorer, mainly minority ethnic residents. Kensington MP Emma Dent Coad stated Moore-Bick lacked 'credibility' with victims, who required 'somebody we can trust'. Moreover, the public inquiry itself was criticised for seemingly ignoring residents' requests to be involved in setting its terms of reference and choice of lead. Many residents instead demanded an inquest, hoping to avoid a 'whitewash' by establishing an investigation 'truly independent from government, not set up and controlled by government' – in the words of one online petition signed by almost 50,000 people.[152] Phil Scraton, comparing the situation to the chequered history of inquiries into the Hillsborough disaster, demonstrated it was believed that inquest juries could reach 'a verdict independent of government influence'.[153] This demonstrates a shifting perception of public inquiries, which had previously been deemed an independent investigatory mechanism 'symbolic of … an open, transparent society in which, when something goes badly wrong, the powerful are held to account and the powerless cannot simply be ignored'.[154]

Indeed, repeated calls for public inquiries into issues affecting black and minority ethnic people demonstrate that, although not universally accepted, they have retained an enduring place as a key component of the British constitutional system, appearing to provide a level of attention and accountability that other measures simply cannot. As Adam Burgess noted in 2011, in an age of public mistrust of politicians and governments, the credibility and relative authority retained by public inquiries is remarkable.[155] However, current debates suggest this may be changing. Examples outlined throughout demonstrate that public inquiries – when actually forthcoming – have largely failed to live up to expectations or fully address concerns: therefore, their future reputation and effectiveness remains to be seen.

Notes

1 Brain, *History of Policing*, pp. 68–9.
2 'The "Riots"', 225. For *Race & Class*, see: Smith, 'Conflicting Narratives'.
3 Ramdin, *Black Working Class*, pp. 455–6.
4 Fryer, *Staying Power*, p. 399.
5 See: Keith, *Race, Riots and Policing*, pp. 101–4; Kettle and Hodges, *Uprising!*, pp. 28–9.
6 See: Marren, *We Shall not be Moved*, pp. 120–1.
7 Interview with Gus John, 19 May 2017; John, *Moss Side 1981*, pp. 59–60.
8 John Stevenson's collection: Moss Side Enquiry Minutes of Evidence, 21 August 1981.
9 Waddington *et al.*, *Flashpoints*, pp. 115–23.
10 See: chapter 2.
11 Keith, *Race, Riots and Policing*, p. 60.
12 *Ibid.*, pp. 71, 90–5.

13 *Ibid.*, p. 52. See: Smith, 'Conflicting Narratives'.

14 Benyon, 'Civil Disorder', pp. 28–32.

15 HC Deb 16 July 1981, vol. 8, c. 1399.

16 Rowe, *Racialisation of Disorder*, pp. 3–4; Gilroy, *Ain't No Black*, p. 74.

17 Fryer, *Staying Power*, p. 395; Kettle, 'Will 1982 See More Riots', 404.

18 James, 'Black Experience', p. 385; Modood and Berthoud (eds), *Ethnic Minorities*.

19 Solomos, *Race and Racism*, p. 160.

20 *Ibid.*, p. 148.

21 Keith, *Race, Riots and Policing*, p. 188.

22 Benyon and Solomos (eds), *Urban Unrest*.

23 Nelson, Jr, *Black Atlantic Politics*, p. 207. See: Belchem, *Before the Windrush*, pp. 256–66.

24 *Guardian*, 30 September 1985.

25 Hall, 'From Scarman to Stephen Lawrence', 190.

26 Cited in Rowe, *Racialisation of Disorder*, p. 138.

27 Rowe, *Racialisation of Disorder*, p. 138.

28 See: Rose, *Climate of Fear*.

29 Rowe, *Racialisation of Disorder*, pp. 1, 158. See: Stevenson, *Popular Disturbances*; Hampton, *A Radical Reader*.

30 Benyon and Solomos (eds), 'British Urban Unrest', p. 8; Mitchell and Russell, 'Race, the New Right and State Policy'.

31 Rowe, *Racialisation of Disorder*, p. 147.

32 *Ibid.*, pp. 145–6; Keith, *Race, Riots and Policing*, p. 20.

33 Davis, 'Race, Poverty and Policing', 77.

34 Gifford, *Broadwater Farm Inquiry*, pp. 35–64. For the Special Patrol Group, see: chapter 1.

35 *Broadwater Review*, December 1985, cited in Green and Ward, 'Civil Society, Resistance and State Crime', p. 31. For community policing, see: Alderson, *Principled Policing*, pp. 122–33.

36 Rowe, *Racialisation of Disorder*, p. 136; Hall, 'From Scarman to Stephen Lawrence', 190.

37 See: Grant, *Dawn to Dusk*.

38 Keith, *Race, Riots and Policing*, pp. 173–6.

39 *Guardian*, 10 July 2014.

40 Moore, *The Broadwater Farm Riot*, p. 257.

41 Conservative Party Chair Norman Tebbit, cited in Rowe, *Racialisation of Disorder*, pp. 142–3, 158. See, for example: Jackson and Saunders (eds), *Making Thatcher's Britain*; Vinen, *Thatcher's Britain*.

42 *Guardian*, 30 December 2015.

43 Castro, 'Pandemonium Britain', 614.

44 Solomos, *Race and Racism*, p. 175.

45 Gifford *et al.*, *Loosen the Shackles*, p. 23.

46 Rose, *Climate of Fear*, pp. 206–17.

47 Pilkington, *Racial Disadvantage*, p. 258; Ray and Smith, 'Community Conflict', 682. See: Bagguley and Hussain, *Riotous Citizens*; Back *et al.*, 'The Return of Assimiliation'.

48 Erfani-Ghettani, 'Black Deaths in Custody', 110; *Guardian*, 14 August 2011; *New Statesman*, 28 April 2012.

49 Interview with John.

50 For example, for a comparison of Manchester in 1981 and 2011, see: Wain and Joyce, 'Disaffected Communities, Riots and Policing'.

51 See: Jackson and Saunders (eds), *Making Thatcher's Britain*; Cooper and Whyte (eds), *Violence of Austerity*.

52 *BBC News*, 9 August 2011, BBC Television.

53 Perry, *London is the Place for Me*, p. 246.

54 *Guardian*, 8 August 2011.

55 *Guardian*, 30 March 2012; 3 July 2013.

56 *BBC News*, 8 August 2011.

57 Ramamurthy, *Black Star*, p. 123

58 See: Smith, 'Summer of '81'; Frost and Phillips, '2011 Summer Riots'.

59 Lammy, *Out of the Ashes*, p. 17.

60 *Red Pepper*, 10 June 2017.

61 Sivanandan, 'Violence of the Violated'.

62 Shukra, 'New Labour Debates and Dilemmas', pp. 117–18.

63 See: Sofer, *London Left*.

64 Phillips and Phillips, *Windrush*, p. 371.

65 Livingstone, 'Renaissance Labour Style', 22, and Ouseley, 'Resisting Institutional Change', p. 148, cited in Virdee, *Racialized Outsider*, p. 152.

66 Sivanandan, *Communities of Resistance*, p. 148, cited in Virdee, *Racialized Outsider*, pp. 153–4. See: Daye, *Middle-Class Blacks*; Centre for Contemporary Cultural Studies, *The Empire Strikes Back*.

67 *Sunday Times*, 10 October 1982; Daye, *Middle-Class Blacks*, p. 6.

68 Phillips and Phillips, *Windrush*, p. 374.

69 Virdee, *Racialized Outsider*, pp. 153–5.

70 Paul Gilroy in Phillips and Phillips, *Windrush*, pp. 375–6.

71 Tompson, *Under Siege*, pp. 100, 104, cited in Brooke, 'Affective Ecology', 134–5.

72 Phillips and Phillips, *Windrush*, p. 374.

73 Saggar, *Race and British Electoral Politics*, p. 4.

74 Gilroy in Phillips and Phillips, *Windrush*, p. 376.

75 Solomos, *Race and Racism*, p. 207; Phillips and Phillips, *Windrush*, p. 365.

76 Howe, *Black Sections*, pp. 15–16.

77 *The Times*, 16 April 1984, cited in Solomos, *Race and Racism*, p. 208. See: Shukra, *Black Politics*, pp. 70–99.

78 Solomos, *Race and Racism*, p. 208; Mason, *Race and Ethnicity*, p. 127.

79 Phillips and Phillips, *Windrush*, p. 379. See: Virdee, *Racialized Outsider*.

80 Solomos, *Race and Racism*, p. 209.

81 Shukra, *Black Politics*, pp. 110–11.

82 Interview with Simbarasha Tongogara, 4 April 2017; Interview with John. See: Rex and Tomlinson, *Colonial Immigrants*; Sivanandan, *Different Hunger*.

83 See, for example: Pitcher, *Politics of Multiculturalism*.

84 Spencer, *British Immigration Policy*, p. 150.

85 Mitchell and Russell, 'Race, Citizenship and "Fortress Europe"', p. 145.

86 Pilkington, *Racial Disadvantage*, p. 226.

87 See: Ford and Goodwin, 'Britain after Brexit'; Goodwin and Milazzo 'Taking Back Control?'.

88 Parekh, *Multi-Ethnic Britain*, p. 56.

89 Modood, *Multiculturalism*, p. 18.

90 Pilkington, *Racial Disadvantage*, pp. 264–74.

91 'The British Empire is "Something to be Proud of"', YouGov, 26 July 2014.

92 Bowling and Phillips, *Racism, Crime and Justice*, pp. 14–15; Stone, *Stephen Lawrence*.

93 Macpherson, *Stephen Lawrence Inquiry*, 18.1–19.

94 *Ibid.*, 42.23.

95 Hall, 'From Scarman to Stephen Lawrence', 193.

96 *Ibid.*, 196–7; Bowling and Phillips, *Racism, Crime and Justice*, p. 15.

97 *Daily Mail*, 14 February 1997. Brian Cathcart has questioned the newspaper's claim of helping bring about significant social/policy changes and achieve justice: Cathcart, 'Daily Mail'.

98 Macpherson, *Stephen Lawrence Inquiry*, 6.34.

99 Cited in Greaves, 'Brixton Disorders', p. 69.

100 Bowling, *Violent Racism*, p. 2.

101 Keith, *Race, Riots and Policing*, p. 15. See: Bowling and Phillips, *Racism, Crime and Justice*, pp. 115–62; Hall, 'From Scarman to Stephen Lawrence'.

102 Gifford *et al.*, 'Multiculturalism', p. 65.

103 Loveday, 'Police Race Relations', p. 26; Hall, 'From Scarman to Stephen Lawrence', 194. See: Souhami, 'Institutional Racism'; Bridges, 'The Lawrence Inquiry'; Mayberry, *The Failure of the Stephen Lawrence Inquiry*.

104 Neal, 'Scarman Report', 57; Jasper, 'Macpherson', 30–2.

105 Interview with Gabrielle Cox, 19 April 2017.

106 Interview with Linbert Spencer, 20 March 2017.

107 Interview with Cox; Interview with Phil Sumner, 20 April 2017.

108 Interview with Sumner; Interview with Cox. See: Prince, *God's Cop*.

109 Goulbourne, *Race Relations*, p. 69.

110 Burja and Pearce, 'Police on the Line', p. 58; Reiner, *Politics of the Police*, pp. 205–19; Cape and Young (eds), *Regulating Policing*.

111 Hall, 'From Scarman to Stephen Lawrence', 189; Scarman, 'The Quest for Social Justice', pp. 127–8.

112 Virdee, *Racialized Outsider*, pp. 148–9; Gilroy, *Ain't No Black*; Cohen, 'Perversions of Inheritance'.

113 Clare, 'The Ratchet Advances Another Turn', p. 63.

114 Layton-Henry, *Politics of Race*, p. 164; Burja and Pearce, 'Police on the Line', p. 58.

115 McLaughlin, 'Police Accountability and Black People', p. 117.

116 *The Times*, 7 October 1982.

117 *Guardian*, 20 November 1982.

118 Shukra, *Black Politics*, p. 116.

119 See, for example: Miller *et al.*, *Stops and Searches*.

120 Phillips, 'Ethnic Inequalities', pp. 193, 195; Home Office, *Police Powers and Procedures*.

121 Phillips, 'Ethnic Inequalities', p. 195.

122 Cashmore, 'Ethnic Minority Police Officers', 652, cited in Phillips, 'Ethnic Inequalities', p. 194.

123 Criminal Justice System Race Unit, *Race and the Criminal Justice System*.

124 Brain, *History of Policing*, pp. 261–302.

125 Home Office, *Racial Attacks*, p. iii, cited in Bowling, *Violent Racism*, pp. 151–3.

126 Bowling, 'Emergence of Violent Racism', pp. 210–11.

127 Lawrence, *Punishing Hate*, p. 169; Phillips, 'Ethnic Inequalities', p. 192; Ray and Smith, 'Racist Offending, Policing and Community Conflict', 684.

128 *Observer*, 15 June 2014; *Guardian*, 12 June 2015; HC Deb 31 October 2016 vol 616 c 625WS. See: Harvey *et al.*, *The Miners' Strike*.

129 Hillsborough Independent Panel, *Report*, p. 339. See: Scraton, *Hillsborough*.

130 Interview with Spencer. See: Caless and Owens, *Police and Crime Commissioners*.

131 The Electoral Commission, *Police and Crime Commissioner Elections*, p. 3.

132 See: Sedley, 'Public Inquiries'; Elliot and McGuiness, 'Public Inquiry'.

133 Cited in Scraton and McCulloch, 'Deaths in Custody and Detention', 7.

134 INQUEST casework and monitoring, http://inquest.org.uk/statistics (last accessed: 15 March 2018).

135 Athwal and Bourne, *Dying for Justice*, p. 2.

136 Scraton and McCulloch, 'Deaths in Custody and Detention', 6–7; Erfani-Ghettani, 'Black Deaths in Custody', 105.

137 *Sunday Times*, 8 August 1993, cited in Erfani-Ghettani, 'Black Deaths in Custody', 106–7.

138 *Daily Star*, 5 August 1993, cited in Erfani-Ghettani, 'Black Deaths in Custody', 106.

139 See, for example: Scraton and Chadwick, 'Speaking Ill of the Dead'; Rowe, *Racialisation of Disorder*.

140 Moss, 'Racism and Custody Deaths', 142; Gupta, *Gladiator Games*, p. 4.

141 Moss, 'Racism and Custody Deaths', 142, 148.

142 *Ibid.*, 146–7.

143 Erfani-Ghettani, 'Black Deaths in Custody', 102–3; Inquest and Unison, *Roger Sylvester*.

144 See: Lebron, *Black Lives Matter*; Taylor, *#BlackLivesMatter*; Carney, 'Black Lives Matter'.

145 *Huffington Post*, 25 September 2015.

146 *Independent*, 27 June 2017; 1 August 2017.

147 *BBC News*, 29 July 2017.

148 *Guardian*, 29 July 2017.

149 *Guardian*, 4 September 2017.

150 *Guardian*, 15 May 2015.

151 *BBC News*, 29 June 2017.

152 'An Inquest NOT a Public Inquiry', https://you.38degrees.org.uk/petitions/an-inquest-not-a-public-inquiry-for-the-grenfell-tower-fires (last accessed: 6 September 2017).

153 Scraton, 'Learning from Hillsborough'.

154 Burgess, 'Public Inquiries', 7–8.

155 *Ibid.*

Bibliography

Addison, Paul, *The Road to 1945: British Politics and the Second World War* (London, 1977).

Alderson, John, *Principled Policing: Protecting the Public with Integrity* (Hampshire, 1998).

Alibhai-Brown, Yasmin, *Who Do We Think We Are? Imagining the New Britain* (London, 2001).

Alleyne, Brian W., *Radicals Against Race: Black Activism and Cultural Politics* (Oxford, 2002).

Allport, Floyd, *Social Psychology* (Boston, 1924).

Andresen, Knud and Bart van der Steen (eds), *A European Youth Revolt* (Basingstoke, 2016).

Anwar, Muhammad, 'Public Reaction to the Scarman Report', *New Community*, 9 (1981), 371–3.

Aouragh, Miryam and Anne Alexander, 'The Egyptian Experience: Sense and Nonsense of the Internet Revolution', *International Journal of Communication*, 5 (2011), 1344–58.

Ashford, Douglas E., *Policy and Politics in Britain: The Limits of Consensus* (Oxford, 1981).

Athwal, Harmit and Jenny Bourne, *Dying for Justice* (London, 2015).

Avon and Somerset Constabulary, *Annual Report 1980* (Bristol, 1981).

Back, Les, Michael Keith, Azra Khan, Kalbir Shukra and John Solomos, 'The Return of Assimilation: Race, Multiculturalism and New Labour', *Sociological Research Online*, 7:2 (2002), 1–10.

Bagguley, Paul and Yasmin Hussain, *Riotous Citizens: Ethnic Conflict in Multicultural Britain* (Aldershot, 2008).

Ball, Roger, 'The "Bristol Riot" and Its "Other": St Paul's and Southmead in April 1980', *The Regional Historian: Journal of the Regional History Centre*, 22 (2010), 32–41.

Ball, Roger, 'Violent Urban Disturbances in England 1980–81', unpublished PhD thesis, University of the West of England (2012).

Banton, Michael, *Promoting Racial Harmony* (Cambridge, 1985).

Baston, Lewis, 'Roy Hattersley', in Kevin Jefferys (ed.), *Labour Forces* (London, 2002).

Beer, Jason, *Public Inquiries* (Oxford, 2009).

Belchem, John, *Before the Windrush: Race Relations in 20th-Century Liverpool* (Liverpool, 2014).

Benyon, John, 'Going through the Motions, the Political Agenda, the 1981 Riots and the Scarman Report', *Parliamentary Affairs*, 38 (1985), 409–22.

Benyon, John, 'Interpretations of Civil Disorder', in John Benyon and John Solomos (eds), *The Roots of Urban Unrest* (Oxford, 1987).

Benyon, John, 'The Policing Issues', in John Benyon (ed.), *Scarman and After: Essays Reflecting on Lord Scarman's Report, the Riots and Their Aftermath* (Oxford, 1984).

Benyon, John, 'The Riots, Lord Scarman and the Political Agenda', in John Benyon (ed.), *Scarman and After: Essays Reflecting on Lord Scarman's Report, the Riots and Their Aftermath* (Oxford, 1984).

Benyon, John, 'The Riots: Perceptions and Distortions', in John Benyon (ed.), *Scarman and After: Essays Reflecting on Lord Scarman's Report, the Riots and Their Aftermath* (Oxford, 1984).

Benyon, John, 'Scarman and After', in John Benyon (ed.), *Scarman and After: Essays Reflecting on Lord Scarman's Report, the Riots and Their Aftermath* (Oxford, 1984).

Benyon, John (ed.), *Scarman and After: Essays Reflecting on Lord Scarman's Report, the Riots and Their Aftermath* (Oxford, 1984).

Benyon, John and John Solomos, 'British Urban Unrest in the 1980s', in John Benyon and John Solomos (eds), *The Roots of Urban Unrest* (Oxford, 1987).

Benyon, John and John Solomos (eds), *The Roots of Urban Unrest* (Oxford, 1987).

Blake, Charles, 'Citizenship, Law and the State: The British Nationality Act 1981', *The Modern Law Review*, 45:2 (1982), 179–97.

Bland, Lucy, 'White Women and Men of Colour: Miscegenation Fears in Britain after the Great War', *Gender & History*, 17:1 (2005), 29–61.

Bleich, Erik, *Race Politics in Britain and France* (Cambridge, 2003).

Bloch, Alice and John Solomos (eds), *Race and Ethnicity in the 21st Century* (Basingstoke, 2009).

Bloom, Clive, *Violent London: 2000 Years of Riots, Rebels and Revolts* (Basingstoke, 2010).

Boateng, Paul, 'The Police, the Community and Accountability', in John Benyon (ed.), *Scarman and After: Essays Reflecting on Lord Scarman's Report, the Riots and Their Aftermath* (Oxford, 1984).

Bohstedt, John, 'The Dynamics of Riots: Escalation and Diffusion/Contagion', in Michael Potegal and John Knutson (eds), *The Dynamics of Aggression* (New Jersey, 1994).

Bon, Gustave Le, *The Crowd* (London, 1896).

Bowling, Ben, 'The Emergence of Violent Racism as a Public Issue in Britain, 1945–81', in Panikos Panayi (ed.), *Racial Violence in Britain in the Nineteenth and Twentieth Centuries*, third edition (Leicester, 1996).

Bowling, Ben, *Violent Racism: Victimization, Policing and Social Context* (Oxford, 1998).

Bowling, Ben and Coretta Phillips, *Racism, Crime and Justice* (Harlow, 2002).

Brah, Avtar, 'The "Asian" in Britain', in Nasreen Ali, Virinder S. Kalra and Salman Sayyid (eds), *A Postcolonial People: South Asians in Britain* (London, 2006).

Brain, Timothy, *A History of Policing in England and Wales from 1974: A Turbulent Journey* (Oxford, 2010).

Bridges, Lee, 'The Lawrence Inquiry: Incompetence, Corruption and Institutional Racism', *Journal of Law and Society*, 26:3 (1999), 298–322.

Bristol Council for Racial Equality, *Annual Report* (Bristol, 1980).

Bristol Trades Union Congress (TUC), *Slumbering Volcano? Report of an Enquiry into the Origins of the Eruption in St Paul's Bristol on 2nd April 1980* (Bristol, 1981).

Brooke, Peter, 'India, Post-Imperialism and the Origins of Enoch Powell's "Rivers of Blood" Speech', *The Historical Journal*, 50:3 (2007), 669–87.

Brooke, Stephen, 'Living in "New Times": Historicizing 1980s Britain', *History Compass*, 12:1 (2014), 20–32.

Brooke, Stephen, 'Space, Emotions and the Everyday: The Affective Ecology of 1980s London', *Twentieth Century British History*, 28:1 (2017), 110–42.

Brown, Andy R., ' "The Other Day I Met a Constituent of Mine": A Theory of Anecdotal Racism', *Ethnic and Racial Studies*, 22:1 (1999), 23–55.

Buettner, Elizabeth, ' "Would you Let your Daughter Marry a Negro?" Race and Sex in 1950s Britain', in Philippa Levine and Susan R. Grayzel (eds), *Gender, Labour, War and Empire: Essays on Modern Britain* (Basingstoke, 2008).

Bunce, Robin and Paul Field, *Darcus Howe: A Political Biography* (London, 2014).

Bundred, Steve, 'Accountability and the Metropolitan Police', in David Cowell, Trevor Jones and Jock Young (eds), *Policing the Riots* (London, 1982).

Burgess, Adam, 'The Changing Character of Public Inquiries in the (Risk) Regulatory State', *British Politics*, 6:1 (2011), 3–29.

Burja, Janet and Jenny Pearce, 'Police on the Line: Between Control and Correctness in Multi-ethnic Contexts of Urban Unrest', in David Waddington, Fabien Jobard and Mike King (eds), *Rioting in the UK and France: A Comparative Analysis* (Devon, 2009).

Burkett, Jodi, *Constructing Post-Imperial Britain: Britishness, 'Race' and the Radical Left in the 1960s* (Basingstoke, 2013).

Cain, Maureen, *Society and the Policeman's Role* (London, 1973).

Caless, Jane and Jane Owens, *Police and Crime Commissioners: The Transformation of Police Accountability* (Bristol, 2016).

Campbell, James S., 'The Usefulness of Commission Studies of Collective Violence', *The Annals of the American Academy of Political and Social Science*, 391 (1970), 168–76.

Cannadine, David, *Margaret Thatcher: A Life and Legacy* (Oxford, 2016).

Cape, Ed and Richard Young (eds), *Regulating Policing: The Police and Criminal Evidence Act 1984* (Oxford, 2008).

Carney, Nikita, 'All Lives Matter, but so Does Race: Black Lives Matter and the Evolving Role of Social Media', *Humanity & Society*, 40:2 (2016), 180–99.

Carter, Bob and Shirley Joshi, 'The Role of Labour in the Creation of a Racist Britain', *Race & Class*, 25 (1984), 53–70.

Carter, Bob, Marci Green and Rick Halpern, 'Immigration Policy and the Racialisation of Migrant Labour', *Ethnic and Racial Studies*, 19:1 (1996), 135–57.

Carter, Bob, Clive Harris and Shirley Joshi, 'The 1951–1955 Conservative Government and the Racialisation of Black Immigration', *Immigrants and Minorities*, 6 (1987), 335–47.

Carter, Trevor, *Shattering Illusions: West Indians in British Politics* (London, 1986).

Cashmore, Ellis, 'The Experiences of Ethnic Minority Police Officers in Britain: Under-Recruitment and Racial Profiling in a Performance Culture', *Ethnic and Racial Studies*, 24:4 (2001), 642–59.

Cashmore, Ellis, *United Kingdom? Class, Race and Gender since the War* (London, 1989).

Cashmore, Ellis and Eugene McLaughlin (eds), *Out of Order? Policing Black People* (London, 1991).

Castro, Monia O'Brien, 'Pandemonium Britain: Interactions between Formal and Informal Places of Governance in the 1980s', *Journal of Urban History*, 41:4 (2015), 607–24.

Cathcart, Brian, 'The Daily Mail and the Stephen Lawrence Murder', *The Political Quarterly*, 88:4 (2017), 640–51.

Centre for Contemporary Cultural Studies, *The Empire Strikes Back: Race and Racism in 70s Britain* (London, 1982).

Christensen, Christian, 'Twitter Revolutions? Addressing Social Media and Dissent', *The Communication Review*, 14 (2011), 155–7.

Clare, John, 'Eyewitness in Brixton', in John Benyon (ed.), *Scarman and After: Essays Reflecting on Lord Scarman's Report, the Riots and Their Aftermath* (Oxford, 1984).

Clare, John, 'The Ratchet Advances Another Turn', in John Benyon and John Solomos (eds), *The Roots of Urban Unrest* (Oxford, 1987).

Clutterbuck, Richard, 'Terrorism and Urban Violence', *Proceedings of the Academy of Political Science*, 34 (1982), 165–75.

Cohen, Philip, 'The Perversions of Inheritance: Studies in the Making of Multi-Racist Britain', in Philip Cohen and Harwant S. Bains (eds), *Multi-Racist Britain* (Basingstoke, 1988).

Collier-Thomas, Bettye and V.P. Franklin (eds), *Sisters in the Struggle: African American Women in the Civil Rights-Black Power Movement* (New York, 2001).

Commonwealth Immigrants Advisory Council, *Second Report by the Commonwealth Immigrants Advisory Council* (London, 1964).

Comninos, Alex, 'Twitter Revolutions and Cyber Crackdowns: User-Generated Content and Social Networking in the Arab Spring and Beyond', *Association for Progressive Communications* (2011), 1–18.

Cooper, Paul, 'Competing Explanations of the Merseyside Riots of 1981', *The British Journal of Criminology*, 25:1 (1985), 60–9.

Cooper, Vickie and David Whyte (eds), *The Violence of Austerity* (London, 2017).

Copsey, Nigel, *Anti-Fascism in Britain* (Basingstoke, 2000).

Corbally, John, 'The Othered Irish: Shades of Difference in Post-War Britain, 1948–71', *Contemporary European History*, 21:4 (2015), 105–25.

Crick, Michael, *The March of Militant* (London, 1986).

Criminal Justice System Race Unit, *Race and the Criminal Justice System: An Overview to the Complete Statistics 2004–5* (London, 2006).

Critchley, Thomas Alan, *A History of Police in England and Wales* (London, 1978).

Crossman, Richard, *The Diaries of a Cabinet Minister: Volume One: Minister of Housing 1964–66* (London, 1975).

Davies, Carol Boyce, *Left of Karl Marx: The Political Life of Black Communist Claudia Jones* (Durham, 2007).

Davis, Jennifer, 'From "Rookeries" to "Communities": Race, Poverty and Policing in London 1850–1985', *History Workshop Journal*, 27 (1989), 66–85.

Davis, John, 'Rents and Race in 1960s London: New Light on Rachmanism', *Twentieth Century British History*, 12:1 (2001), 69–92.

Dawson, Graham, Jo Dover and Stephen Hopkins (eds), *The Northern Ireland Troubles in Britain: Impacts, Engagements, Legacies and Memories* (Manchester, 2017).

Daye, Sharon J., *Middle-Class Blacks in Britain: A Racial Fraction of a Class Group or a Class Fraction of a Racial Group?* (Basingstoke, 1994).

Deakin, Nicholas, 'The British Nationality Act of 1948: A Brief Study in the Political Mythology of Race Relations', *Race & Class*, 11:1 (1969), 77–83.

Deakin, Nicholas, *Colour, Citizenship and British Society* (London, 1970).

Deakin, Nicholas, 'The Politics of the Commonwealth Immigrants Bill', *Political Quarterly*, 39:1 (1968), 25–45.

Dean, Dennis, 'The Race Relations Policy of the First Wilson Government', *Twentieth Century British History*, 11:3 (2000), 259–83.

Deedes, William, *Race without Rancour* (London, 1968).

Delaney, Enda, *The Irish in Post-War Britain* (Oxford, 2007).

Dierenfield, Bruce J., *The Civil Rights Movement* (Harlow, 2008).

Dresser, Madge, *Black and White on the Buses: The 1963 Colour Bar Dispute in Bristol* (Bristol, 1986).

Dresser, Madge and Peter Fleming, *Bristol: Ethnic Minorities and the City 1000–2001* (Chichester, 2007).

Dyer, Richard, 'The Matter of Whiteness', in *White: Essays on Race and Culture* (London, 1997).

Edelman, Murray, *Politics as Symbolic Action* (Chicago, 1971).

Edmonds, Ennis Barrington, *Rastafari: From Outcasts to Culture Bearers* (Oxford, 2002).

The Electoral Commission, *Police and Crime Commissioner Elections in England and Wales: Report on the Administration of the Elections Held on 15 November 2012* (London, 2013).

Elliot, Dominic and Martina McGuiness, 'Public Inquiry: Panacea or Placebo?', *Journal of Contingencies and Crisis Management*, 10:1 (2002), 14–25.

Ellison, Graham and Jim Smyth, *The Crowned Harp: Policing Northern Ireland* (London, 2000).

Emsley, Clive, *The English Police: A Political and Social History* (London, 1991).

Erfani-Ghettani, Ryan, 'The Defamation of Joy Gardner: Press, Police and Black Deaths in Custody', *Race & Class*, 56:3 (2014), 102–12.

Eskew, Glenn T., *But for Birmingham: Local and National Movements in the Civil Rights Struggle* (London, 1997).

Evans, Neil, 'The South Wales Race Riots of 1919', *Llafur*, 3 (1980), 5–29.

Feagin, Joe R. and Harlan Hahn (eds), *Ghetto Revolts: The Politics of Violence in American Cities* (London, 1973).

Fielding, Nigel, *The National Front* (London, 1980).

Fielding, Steven, *The Labour Governments, 1964–70: Volume 1: Labour and Cultural Change* (Manchester, 2003).

Fogelson, Robert M., *Mass Violence in America: The Los Angeles Riots* (New York, 1969).

Foot, Paul, 'Immigration and the British Labour Movement', *International Socialism*, 22 (1965), 8–13.

Foot, Paul, *Immigration and Race in British Politics* (California, 1960).

Ford, Robert and Matthew Goodwin, 'Britain after Brexit: A Nation Divided', *Journal of Democracy*, 28:1 (2017), 17–30.

Freeman, M.D.A. and Sarah Spencer, 'Immigration Control, Black Workers and the Economy', *British Journal of Law and Society*, 6 (1979), 53–81.

Friedman, Lester (ed.), *Fires Were Started: British Cinema and Thatcherism* (London, 1993).

Frost, Diane and Richard Phillips, 'The 2011 Summer Riots: Learning from History – Remembering '81', *Sociological Research Online*, 17 (2012), www.socresonline.org.uk/17/3/19.html.

Fryer, Peter, *Staying Power: The History of Black People in Britain* (London, 1984).

Gabriel, John, *Whitewash: Racialised Politics and the Media* (London, 1998).

Garnett, Mark and Ian Aitken, *Splendid! Splendid! The Authorized Biography of Willie Whitelaw* (London, 2003).

Geary, Roger, 'Deaths in Custody: Rhetoric and Actuality', *Poly Law Review*, 6 (1981), 36–40.

Geddes, Andrew, *The Politics of Immigration and Race* (Manchester, 1996).

Gifford, Anthony, *The Broadwater Farm Inquiry: Report of the Independent Inquiry into Disturbances of October 1985 at the Broadwater Farm Estate, Tottenham* (London, 1986).

Gifford, Anthony, Wally Brown and Ruth Bundley, *Loosen the Shackles: First Report of the Liverpool 8 Inquiry into Race Relations in Liverpool* (London, 1989).

Gifford, Chris, Jamie Halsall and Santokh Singh Gill, 'The UK's Ad Hoc Multiculturalism and the Rise of Britishness', in Susana Gonçalves and Markus A. Carpenter (eds), *Diversity, Intercultural Encounters, and Education* (New York, 2013).

Gilbert, Tony, *Only One Died* (London, 1975).

Gilroy, Paul, *The Black Atlantic: Modernity and Double Consciousness* (London, 1993).

Gilroy, Paul, 'The Myth of Black Criminality', in Phil Scraton (ed.), *Law, Order and the Authoritarian State* (Milton Keynes, 1987).

Gilroy, Paul, *There Ain't No Black in the Union Jack: The Cultural Politics of Race and Nation* (London, 1987).

Gilroy, Paul, 'You Can't Fool the Youths: Race and Class Formation in the 1980s', *Race & Class*, 23:2–3 (1981), 207–22.

Gilroy, Paul and Errol Lawrence, 'Two-Tone Britain: White and Black Youth and the Politics of Anti-Racism', in Philip Cohen and Harwant S. Bains (eds), *Multi-Racist Britain* (Basingstoke, 1988).

Glass, Ruth, *Newcomers: The West Indians in London* (Michigan, 1960).

Goodhart, David, *The British Dream: Successes and Failures of Post-War Immigration* (London, 2013).

Goodson, Alan, 'Police and the Public', in John Benyon (ed.), *Scarman and After: Essays Reflecting on Lord Scarman's Report, the Riots and Their Aftermath* (Oxford, 1984).

Goodwin, Matthew and Caitlin Milazzo, 'Taking Back Control? Investigating the Role of Immigration in the 2016 Vote for Brexit', *The British Journal of Politics and International Relations*, 19:3 (2017), 450–64.

Goodyer, Ian, *Crisis Music: The Cultural Politics of Rock Against Racism* (Manchester, 2009).

Goulbourne, Harry, *Race Relations in Britain since 1945* (Basingstoke, 1998).

Grant, Eric A., *Dawn to Dusk: A Biography of Bernie Grant MP* (London, 2006).

Greaves, George, 'The Brixton Disorders', in John Benyon (ed.), *Scarman and After: Essays Reflecting on Lord Scarman's Report, the Riots and Their Aftermath* (Oxford, 1984).

Green, Penny and Tony Ward, 'Civil Society, Resistance and State Crime', in Elizabeth Stanley and Jude McCulloch (eds), *State Crime and Resistance* (London, 2013).

Griffiths, Basil, 'One-Tier Policing', in John Benyon (ed.), *Scarman and After: Essays Reflecting on Lord Scarman's Report, the Riots and Their Aftermath* (Oxford, 1984).

Grube, Dennis, 'Administrative Learning or Political Blaming? Public Servants, Parliamentary Committees and the Drama of Public Accountability', *Australian Journal of Political Science*, 49:2 (2014), 221–36.

Gupta, Tanika, *Gladiator Games* (London, 2005).

Gutzmore, Cecil 'Carnival, the State and the Black Masses in the United Kingdom', in Winston James and Clive Harris (eds), *Inside Babylon: The Caribbean Diaspora in Britain* (London, 1993).

Hajer, Maarten, 'Setting the State: A Dramaturgy of Policy Deliberation', *Administration & Society*, 36:6 (2005), 624–47.

Hall, Stuart, *The Hard Road to Renewal: Thatcherism and the Crisis of the Left* (London, 1988).

Hall, Stuart, 'From Scarman to Stephen Lawrence', *History Workshop Journal*, 48 (1999), 187–97.

Hall, Stuart, Chas Critcher, Tony Jefferson, John Clarke and Brian Roberts, *Policing the Crisis: Mugging, the State, and Law and Order* (London, 1978).

Hampshire, James, *The Politics of Immigration: Contradictions of the Liberal State* (Cambridge, 2013).

Hampton, Christopher (ed.), *A Radical Reader: The Struggle for Change in England 1381–1914* (Harmondsworth, 1984).

Hansen, Randall, *Citizenship and Immigration in Post-War Britain* (Oxford, 2000).

Hansen, Randall, 'The Politics of Citizenship in 1940s Britain: The British Nationality Act', *Twentieth Century British History*, 10:1 (1999), 67–95.

Harvey, Mark, Martin Jenkinson and Mark Metcalf, *The Miners' Strike* (Barnsley, 2014).

Hegarty, Angela, 'The Government of Memory: Public Inquiries and the Limits of Justice in Northern Ireland', *Fordham International Law Journal*, 26:4 (2002), 1148–92.

Heineman, Benjamin Walter, *The Politics of the Powerless: A Study of the Campaign against Racial Discrimination* (London, 1972).

Henry, Alistair, 'Looking Back on Police and People in London', in Alistair Henry and David J. Smith (eds), *Transformations of Policing* (Aldershot, 2007).

Hesse, Barnor, 'Diasporicity: Black Britain's Post-Colonial Formations', in Barnor Hesse (ed.), *Un/Settled Multiculturalisms* (London, 2000).

Higgs, Michael, 'From the Street to the State: Making Anti-Fascism Anti-Racist in 1970s Britain', *Race & Class*, 58:1 (2016), 66–84.

Hills, Alice, 'Militant Tendencies: "Paramilitarism" in the British Police', *The British Journal of Criminology*, 35:3 (1995), 450–8.

Hillsborough Independent Panel, *The Report of the Hillsborough Independent Panel* (London, 2012).

Hillyard, Paddy, 'The Normalisation of Special Powers', in Phil Scraton (ed.), *Law, Order and the Authoritarian State: Readings in Critical Criminology* (Milton Keynes, 1987).

Hindell, Keith, 'The Genesis of the Race Relations Bill', *The Political Quarterly*, 36 (1965), 390–405.

Hiro, Dilip, *Black British, White British*, second edition (London, 1992).

Hobsbawm, Eric, 'The Machine Breakers', *Past & Present*, 1 (1952), 57–70.

Hobsbawm, Eric and George Rudé, *Captain Swing* (New York, 1968).

Holdaway, Simon, *Inside the British Police: A Force at Work* (Oxford, 1983).

Holdaway, Simon, 'Police Accountability: A Current Issue', *Public Administration*, 60 (1982), 84–91.

Holdaway, Simon and Megan O'Neill, 'Institutional Racism after Macpherson: An Analysis of Police Views', *Policing and Society*, 16 (2006), 349–69.

Holmes, Colin, *John Bull's Island: Immigration and British Society, 1871–1971* (Basingstoke, 1988).

Home Office, *Police Powers and Procedures, England and Wales, Year Ending 31 March 2016* (London, 2016).

Home Office, *Racial Attacks: Report of a Home Office Study* (London, 1981).

Horne, Gerald, *Fire This Time: The Watts Uprising and the 1960s* (Charlottesville, 1995).

Howe, Darcus, *Black Sections in the Labour Party* (London, 1985).

Hrach, Thomas J., *The Riot Report and the News: How the Kerner Commission Changed Media Coverage of Black America* (Amherst, 2016).

Humphry, Derek, *Police Power and Black People* (London, 1972).

Hunte, Joseph A., *Nigger-Hunting in England?* (London, 1966).

Huq, Rupa, 'Youth Culture and Antiracism in New Britain: From the Margins to the Mainstream?', *International Journal of Sociology*, 38:2 (2008), 43–53.

Hutchings, Peter, 'The Power to Create Catastrophe: The Idea of Apocalypse in 1970s British Cinema', in Paul Newland (ed.), *Don't Look Now: British Cinema in the 1970s* (Bristol, 2010).

Hytner, Benet, *Report of the Moss Side Enquiry Panel to the Leader of the Greater Manchester Council* (Manchester, 1981).

Inquest and Unison, *Black Deaths in Police Custody: The Story of Roger Sylvester 1968–1999* (London, undated).

Institute of Race Relations, *Police against Black People: Evidence Submitted to the Royal Commission on Criminal Procedure* (London, 1979).

Institute of Race Relations, *Policing against Black People* (London, 1987).

Jackson, Ben and Robert Saunders (eds), *Making Thatcher's Britain* (Cambridge, 2012).

Jackson, Louise A., *Policing Youth: Britain, 1945–79* (Manchester, 2014).

Jacobs, Brian David, *Black Politics and Urban Crisis in Britain* (Cambridge, 1986).

James, C.L.R., *A History of Pan-African Revolt* (California, 2012).

James, Leslie, *George Padmore and Decolonization from Below: Pan-Africanism, the Cold War, and the End of Empire* (Basingstoke, 2014).

James, Winston, 'The Black Experience in Twentieth-Century Britain', in Philip D. Morgan and Sean Hawkins (eds), *Black Experience and the Empire* (Oxford, 2004).

Jasanoff, Sheila, 'Restoring Reason: Causal Narratives and Political Culture', in B. Hutter and M. Power (eds), *Organizational Encounters with Risk* (Cambridge, 2006).

Jasper, Lee, 'Macpherson: Was it all a Waste of Time?', *RSA Journal*, 149:5501 (2002), 30–2.

Jefferson, Tony, *The Case Against Paramilitary Policing* (Milton Keynes, 1990).

Jenkinson, Jacqueline, *Black 1919: Riots, Racism and Resistance in Imperial Britain* (Liverpool, 2009).

John, Gus, *Moss Side 1981: More than Just a Riot* (Surrey, 2011).

Jones, Sandra and Michael Levi, 'The Police and the Majority: The Neglect of the Obvious', *The Police Journal*, 41 (1983), 351–64.

Joseph, Peniel E. (ed.), *Black Power Movement: Rethinking the Civil Rights-Black Power Era* (London, 2006).

Joshua, Harris, Tina Wallace and Heather Booth, *To Ride the Storm: The 1980 Bristol 'Riot' and the State* (London, 1983).

'The July Riots', *State Research Bulletin*, 25 (1981), 161–6.

Katznelson, Ira, *Black Men, White Cities: Race, Politics and Migration in the United States, 1900–30, and Britain, 1948–68* (Oxford, 1973).

Katznelson, Ira, 'The Politics of Racial Buffering in Nottingham, 1954–68', *Race*, 11:4 (1970), 431–46.

Kavanagh, Dennis, *Thatcherism and British Politics: The End of Consensus?* (Oxford, 1987).

Kay, Diana and Robert Miles, 'Refugees or Migrant Workers? The Case of the European Volunteer Workers in Britain (1946–1951)', *Journal of Refugee Studies*, 1:3–4 (1988), 214–36.

Keith, Michael, '"Policing a Perplexed Society? No-Go Areas and the Mystification of Police-Black Conflict', in Ellis Cashmore and Eugene McLaughlin (eds), *Out of Order? Policing Black People* (London, 1991).

Keith, Michael, *Race, Riots and Policing: Lore and Disorder in a Multi-Racist Society* (London, 1993).

Kelley, Robin D.G. and Stephen Tuck (eds), *The Other Special Relationship* (New York, 2015).

Kettle, Martin, 'Deaths in Custody', *New Society*, 10 January 1980.

Kettle, Martin, 'The Drift to Law and Order', in Stuart Hall and Martin Jacques (eds), *The Politics of Thatcherism* (London, 1983).

Kettle, Martin, 'Will 1982 See More Riots', *New Society*, 18 February 1982.

Kettle, Martin and Lucy Hodges, *Uprising! The Police, the People and the Riots in Britain's Cities* (London, 1982).

Koopmans, Ruud, 'The Dynamics of Protest Waves: West Germany, 1965 to 1989', *American Sociological Review*, 58:5 (1993) 637–58.

Koopmans, Ruud, 'Protest in Time and Space: The Evolution of Waves of Contention', in David A. Snow, Sarah A. Soule and Hanspeter Kriesi (eds), *The Blackwell Companion to Social Movements* (Oxford, 2004).

Kushner, Tony, *The Battle of Britishness: Migrant Journeys, 1685 to the Present* (Manchester, 2012).

Lambert, John R., *Crime, Police and Race Relations: A Study in Birmingham* (London, 1970).

Lammy, David, *Out of the Ashes: Britain after the Riots* (London, 2011).

Lanning, Greg, 'Television History Workshop Project No 1: The Brixton Tapes', *History Workshop Journal*, 12:1 (1981), 183–8.

Lawrence, Frederick M., *Punishing Hate: Bias Crimes under American Law* (Cambridge, MA, 2002).

Lawrence, Paul, 'The Vagrancy Act (1824) and the Persistence of Pre-emptive Policing in England since 1750', *British Journal of Criminology*, 57:3 (2017), 513–31.

Layton-Henry, Zig, *The Politics of Immigration: Immigration, 'Race' and 'Race' Relations in Post-War Britain* (Oxford, 1992).

Layton-Henry, Zig, *The Politics of Race in Britain* (London, 1984).

Lea, John, 'From Brixton to Bradford: Official Discourse on Race and Urban Violence in the United Kingdom', in George Gilligan and John Pratt (eds), *Crime, Truth and Justice* (Cullompton, 2004).

Lea, John and Jock Young, 'The Riots in Britain 1981: Urban Violence and Political Marginalisation', in David Cowell, Trevor Jones and Jock Young (eds), *Policing the Riots* (London, 1982).

Lea, John and Jock Young, *What Is to Be Done About Law and Order?* (London, 1984).

Lebron, Christopher J., *The Making of Black Lives Matter: A Brief History of an Idea* (New York, 2017).

Leishman, Frank and Paul Mason, *Policing and the Media: Facts, Fictions and Factions* (Devon, 2003).

Lindop, Fred, 'Racism and the Working Class: Strikes in Support of Enoch Powell in 1968', *Labour History Review*, 66:1 (2001), 79–100.

Lipsky, Michael, 'Social Scientists and the Riot Commission', *The Annals of the American Academy of Political and Social Science*, 394 (1971), 72–83.

Lipsky, Michael and David J. Olson, *Commission Politics: The Processing of Racial Crisis in America* (New Brunswick, 1977).

Litton, Ian and Jonathan Potter, 'Social Representations in the Ordinary Explanation of a "Riot"', *European Journal of Social Psychology*, 15 (1985), 371–88.

Livingstone, Ken, 'Renaissance Labour Style', *Marxism Today* (December 1984), 19–22.

Loveday, Barry, 'Government and Accountability of the Police', in R.I. Mawby (ed.), *Policing across the World: Issues for the Twenty-First Century* (London, 1999).

Loveday, Barry, 'Must Do Better: The State of Police Race Relations', in Alan Marlow and Barry Loveday (eds), *After Macpherson: Policing after the Stephen Lawrence Inquiry* (Lyme Regis, 2000).

Lunn, Kenneth, 'The British State and Immigration, 1945–51: New Light on the Empire Windrush', in Tony Kushner and Kenneth Lunn (eds), *The Politics of Marginality: Race, the Radical Right and Minorities in Twentieth Century Britain* (London, 1990).

Macilwee, Michael, *The Teddy Boy Wars: The Youth Cult that Shocked Britain* (Preston, 2015).

Macmillan, Harold, *The Macmillan Diaries: The Cabinet Years, 1950–1957* (London, 2003).

Macpherson, William, *The Stephen Lawrence Inquiry* (London, 1999).

Maguire, M. and C. Corbett, *A Study of the Police Complaints System* (London, 1991).

Malik, Kenan, *The Meaning of Race: Race, History and Culture in Western Society* (Basingstoke, 1996).

Malik, Michael Abdul, *From Michael de Freitas to Michael X.* (London, 1968).

Marable, Manning, *Malcolm X: A Life of Reinvention* (London, 2010).

Marren, Brian, *We Shall not be Moved: How Liverpool's Working Class Fought Redundancies, Closures and Cuts in the Age of Thatcher* (Manchester, 2016).

Mason, David, *Race and Ethnicity in Modern Britain* (Oxford, 1995).

Mayberry, David, *Black Deaths in Police Custody and Human Rights: The Failure of the Stephen Lawrence Inquiry* (Hertford, 2008).

Maylor, Uvanney, 'What Is the Meaning of "Black"? Researching "Black" Respondents', *Ethnic and Racial Studies*, 32 (2009), 369–87.

McAdam, Doug, '"Initiator" and "Spin-Off" Movements: Diffusion Processes in Protest Cycles', in Mark Traugott (ed.), *Repertoires and Cycles of Collective Action* (Durham, 1995).

McCabe, Sarah and Peter Wallington, *The Police, Public Order and Civil Liberties: Legacies of the Miners' Strike* (London, 1988).

McGowan, Jack, '"Dispute", "Battle", "Siege", "Farce"? Grunwick 30 Years On', *Contemporary British History*, 22 (2008), 383–406.

McLaughlin, Eugene, 'Police Accountability and Black People: Into the 1990s', in Ellis Cashmore and Eugene McLaughlin (eds), *Out of Order? Policing Black People* (London, 1991).

McNee, David, *McNee's Law* (London, 1983).

McPhail, Clark and Ronald T. Wohlstein, 'Individual and Collective Behavior within Gatherings, Demonstrations and Riots', *Annual Review of Sociology*, 9 (1983), 579–600.

McWhorter, Diane, *Carry Me Home: Birmingham, Alabama, the Climactic Battle of the Civil Rights Revolution* (New York, 2001).

Mead, Matthew, '*Empire Windrush*: The Cultural Memory of an Imaginary Arrival', *Journal of Postcolonial Writing*, 45:2 (2009), 137–49.

Mikardo, Ian, *Back-Bencher* (London, 1988).

Miles, Robert, 'Nationality, Citizenship, and Migration to Britain, 1945–1951', *Journal of Law and Society*, 16:4 (1989), 426–42.

Miles, Robert, 'The Riots of 1958: Notes on the Ideological Construction of "Race Relations" as a Political Issue in Britain', *Immigrants and Minorities*, 3:3 (1984), 252–75.

Miles, Robert and Annie Phizacklea (eds), *Racism and Political Action in Britain* (London, 1979).

Miles, Robert and Annie Phizacklea, *White Man's Country: Racism in British Politics* (London, 1984).

Miller, Joel, Nick Bland and Paul Quinton, *The Impact of Stops and Searches on Crime and the Community* (London, 2000).

Mitchell, Mark and Dave Russell, 'Race, the New Right and State Policy in Britain', in Tony Kushner and Kenneth Lunn (eds), *The Politics of Marginality: Race, the Radical Right and Minorities in Twentieth Century Britain* (London, 1990).

Mitchell, Mark and Dave Russell, 'Race, Citizenship and "Fortress Europe"', in Phillip Brown and Rosemary Crompton (eds) *Economic Restructuring and Social Exclusion* (London, 1994).

Modood, Tariq, *Multiculturalism: A Civic Idea* (Cambridge, 2007).

Modood, Tariq and Richard Berthoud (eds), *Ethnic Minorities in Britain: Diversity and Disadvantage* (London, 1997).

Moore, Tony, *The Killing of Constable Keith Blakelock: The Broadwater Farm Riot* (Hampshire, 2015).

Moss, Nick, 'Comment: Racism and Custody Deaths in the U.K.: The Zahid Mubarek Inquiry', *Social Justice*, 33:4 (2006), 142–50.

Moss Side Defence Committee, *The Hytner Myths: A Preliminary Critique of the Hytner Report* (Manchester, 1981).

Mullard, Chris, *Black Britain* (London, 1973).

Murdock, Graham, 'Reporting the Riots: Images and Impact', in John Benyon (ed.), *Scarman and After: Essays Reflecting on Lord Scarman's Report, the Riots and Their Aftermath* (Oxford, 1984).

241

Murphy, Andrea, *From the Empire to the Rialto: Racism and Reaction in Liverpool, 1918–1948* (Birkenhead, 1995).

Myers, Daniel J., 'The Diffusion of Collective Violence: Infectiousness, Susceptibility, and Mass Media Networks', *American Journal of Sociology*, 106 (2000), 173–208.

Myrdal, Gunnar, *An American Dilemma: The Negro Problem and Modern Democracy* (New York, 1944).

Nally, Michael, 'Eyewitness in Moss Side', in John Benyon (ed.), *Scarman and After: Essays Reflecting on Lord Scarman's Report, the Riots and Their Aftermath* (Oxford, 1984).

National Advisory Commission on Civil Disorders, *Report* (Washington, 1968).

National Council for Civil Liberties, *Southall 23 April 1979: The Report of the Unofficial Committee of Inquiry* (London, 1980).

Neal, Sarah, 'The Scarman Report, the Macpherson Report and the Media', *Journal of Social Policy*, 32 (2003), 55–74.

Nelson, William E., Jr, *Black Atlantic Politics: Dilemmas of Political Empowerment in Boston and Liverpool* (Albany, 2000).

Newburn, Tim and Stephanie Hayman, *Policing, Surveillance and Social Control* (Devon, 2002).

Newland, Paul, 'We Know Where We're Going, We Know Where We're From: Babylon', in Paul Newland (ed.), *Don't Look Now: British Cinema in the 1970s* (Bristol, 2010).

Newman, Mark, *The Civil Rights Movement* (Edinburgh, 2004).

Nocon, Andrew, 'A Reluctant Welcome? Poles in Britain in the 1940s', *Oral History*, 24:1 (1996), 79–87.

Northam, Gerry, *Shooting in the Dark: Riot Police in Britain* (London, 1988).

Oberschall, Anthony, 'The 1960 Sit-Ins: Protest Diffusion and Movement Take-Off', *Research in Social Movements, Conflict and Change*, 11 (1989), 31–53.

Offe, Claus, *Contradictions of the Welfare State* (London, 1984).

Oliver, Pamela E., 'Bringing the Crowd Back In: The Nonorganizational Elements of Social Movements', *Research in Social Movements, Conflict and Change*, 11 (1989), 1–30.

Olusoga, David, *Black and British* (London, 2016).

Olzak, Susan and Suzanne Shanahan, 'Deprivation Race Riots: An Extension of Spilerman's Analysis', *Social Forces*, 74 (1996), 931–61.

Ouseley, Herman, 'Resisting Institutional Change', in Wendy Ball and John Solomos (eds), *Race and Local Politics* (Basingstoke, 1990).

Oxford, Kenneth, 'Policing by Consent', in John Benyon (ed.), *Scarman and After: Essays Reflecting on Lord Scarman's Report, the Riots and Their Aftermath* (Oxford, 1984).

Panayi, Panikos (ed.), *Racial Violence in Britain in the Nineteenth and Twentieth Centuries*, third edition (Leicester, 1996).

Parekh, Bhikhu, *The Future of Multi-Ethnic Britain: Report of the Commission on the Future of Multi-Ethnic Britain* (London, 2000).

Patterson, Sheila, *Dark Strangers: A Sociological Study of the Absorption of a Recent West Indian Migrant Group in Brixton, South London* (London, 1963).

Patterson, Sheila, *Immigration and Race Relations in Britain, 1960–1967* (London, 1969).

Paul, Kathleen, 'From Subjects to Immigrants: Black Britons and National Identity, 1948–62', in Richard Weight and Abigail Beach (eds), *The Right to Belong: Citizenship and National Identity in Britain, 1930–1960* (New York, 1998).

Paul, Kathleen, *Whitewashing Britain: Race and Citizenship in the Postwar Era* (London, 1997).

Pearson, Geoffrey, *Hooligan: A History of Respectable Fears* (London, 1983).

Peplow, Simon, 'The "Linchpin for Success"? The Problematic Establishment of the 1965 Race Relations Act and its Conciliation Board', *Contemporary British History*, 31:3 (2017), 430–51.

Perry, Kennetta Hammond, *London is the Place for Me: Black Britons, Citizenship and the Politics of Race* (New York, 2015).

Perry, Kennetta Hammond, '"U.S. Negroes, Your Fight is Our Fight": Black Britons and the 1963 March on Washington', in Robin D.G. Kelley and Stephen Tuck (eds), *The Other Special Relationship* (New York, 2015).

Phibbs, Cheryl, *The Montgomery Bus Boycott* (Oxford, 2009).

Phillips, Coretta, 'Ethnic Inequalities: Another 10 Years of the Same?', in John Hills, Tom Sefton and Kitty Steward (eds), *Towards a More Equal Society? Poverty, Inequality and Policy since 1997* (Bristol, 2009).

Phillips, Mike and Trevor Phillips, *Windrush: The Irresistible Rise of Multi-Racial Britain* (London, 1998).

Phizacklea, Annie and Robert Miles, 'The British Trade Union Movement and Racism', in Peter Braham, Ali Rattansi and Richard Skellington (eds), *Racism and Antiracism: Inequalities, Opportunities and Policies* (London, 1992).

Pilkington, Edward, *Beyond the Mother Country: West Indians and the Notting Hill White Riots* (London, 1988).

Pilkington, Edward, *Racial Disadvantage and Ethnic Diversity in Britain* (Basingstoke, 2003).

Pitcher, Ben, *The Politics of Multiculturalism: Race and Racism in Contemporary Britain* (Basingstoke, 2009).

Prince, Michael, *God's Cop: The Biography of James Anderton* (London, 1988).

Profitt, Russell, 'Equal Respect, Equal Treatment and Equal Opportunity', in John Benyon (ed.), *Scarman and After: Essays Reflecting on Lord Scarman's Report, the Riots and Their Aftermath* (Oxford, 1984).

Pryce, Ken, *Endless Pressure: A Study of West Indian Life-Styles in Bristol* (Harmondsworth, 1979).

Race Relations Board, *Report for 1966–67* (London, 1967).

Rachel, Daniel, *Walls Come Tumbling Down* (London, 2016)

Ramamurthy, Anandi, *Black Star: Britain's Asian Youth Movements* (London, 2013).

Ramdin, Ron, *The Making of the Black Working Class in Britain* (Aldershot, 1987).

Ramdin, Ron, *Reimaging Britain: Five Hundred Years of Black and Asian History* (London, 1999).

Ray, Larry and David Smith, 'Racist Offending, Policing and Community Conflict', *Sociology*, 38:4 (2004), 681–99.

Rees, Tom, 'Immigration Policies in the United Kingdom', in Charles Husband (ed.), *Race in Britain* (London, 1982).

Reicher, S.D., 'The St. Pauls Riot: An Explanation of the Limits of Crowd Action in Terms of a Social Identity Model', *European Journal of Social Psychology*, 14 (1984), 1–21.

Reiner, Robert, 'Black and Blue: Race and the Police', *New Society*, 57 (1981), 466–9.

Reiner, Robert, *The Politics of the Police*, fourth edition (Oxford, 2010).

Renton, Dave, *When We Touched the Sky: The Anti-Nazi League, 1977–81* (Cheltenham, 2006).

Rex, John, 'Black Militancy and Class Conflict', in Robert Miles and Annie Phizacklea (eds), *Racism and Political Action in Britain* (London, 1979).

Rex, John, 'Disadvantage and Discrimination in Cities', in John Benyon (ed.), *Scarman and After: Essays Reflecting on Lord Scarman's Report, the Riots and Their Aftermath* (Oxford, 1984).

Rex, John, 'Life in the Ghetto', in John Benyon and John Solomos (eds), *The Roots of Urban Unrest* (Oxford, 1987).

Rex, John and Sally Tomlinson, *Colonial Immigrants in a British City: A Class Analysis* (London, 1979).

Rhodes, Jane, *Framing the Black Panthers: The Spectacular Rise of a Black Power Icon* (Illinois, 2017).

Rich, Paul B., *Race and Empire in British Politics* (Cambridge, 1989).

'The "Riots"', *Race & Class*, 23 (1981), 223–9.

Roberts, Pat and Christina Drury, *Police out of Brixton!*, Revolutionary Communist Pamphlets, 10 (London, 1981).

Rodrigues, Jeff, 'The Riots of '81', *Marxism Today* (October 1981), 18–22.

Rogers, Everett M., *Diffusion of Innovations*, fourth edition (New York, 1995).

Rollo, Joanna, 'The Special Patrol Group', in Peter Hain (ed.), *Policing the Police* (London, 1980).

Rose, David, *A Climate of Fear: The Murder of PC Blakelock and the Case of the Tottenham Three* (London, 1992).

Rose, E.J.B., *Colour and Citizenship: A Report on British Race Relations* (London, 1969).

Rose, Paul, *Backbencher's Dilemma* (London, 1981).

Rough, Elizabeth, 'Policy Learning through Public Inquiries? The Case of UK Nuclear Energy Policy 1955–61', *Environment and Planning C: Politics and Space*, 29:1 (2011), 24–45.

Rowe, Michael, *Policing, Race and Racism* (Devon, 2004).

Rowe, Michael, *The Racialisation of Disorder in Twentieth Century Britain* (Aldershot, 1998).

Rowe, Michael, 'Sex, "Race" and Riot in Liverpool, 1919', *Immigrants and Minorities*, 19:2 (2000), 53–70.

Royal Commission on Tribunals of Inquiry, *Report of the Royal Commission on Tribunals of Inquiry* (London, 1966).

Rudé, George, *The Crowd in History 1730–1848: A Study of Popular Disturbances in France and England* (New York, 1964).

Russel, Trevor, *The Tory Party: Its Policies, Division and Future* (Harmondsworth, 1978).

Rutherford, Jonathan, *Forever England: Reflections on Race, Masculinity and Empire* (London, 1997).

Saggar, Shamit, *Race and Politics in Britain* (London, 1992).

Saggar, Shamit, *Race and British Electoral Politics* (London, 1998).

Said, Edward W., *Orientalism* (London, 1978).

Sanders, Andrew and Ian S. Wood, *Times of Troubles: Britain's War in Northern Ireland* (Edinburgh, 2012).

Scarman, Lord Leslie, 'An Epilogue', in John Benyon (ed.), *Scarman and After: Essays Reflecting on Lord Scarman's Report, the Riots and Their Aftermath* (Oxford, 1984).

Scarman, Lord Leslie, 'The Quest for Social Justice', in John Benyon and John Solomos (eds), *The Roots of Urban Unrest* (Oxford, 1987).

Scarman, Lord Leslie, *The Red Lion Square Disorders of 15 June 1974: Report of Inquiry* (London, 1975).

Scarman, Lord Leslie, *The Scarman Report: The Brixton Disorders, 10–12 April 1981* (Harmondsworth, 1981).

Schaffer, Gavin, 'Legislating against Hatred: Meaning and Motive in Section Six of the Race Relations Act of 1965', *Twentieth Century British History*, 25 (2014), 251–75.

Schofield, Camilla, *Enoch Powell and the Making of Postcolonial Britain* (Cambridge, 2013).

Schwarz, Bill, ' "Claudia Jones and the West Indian Gazette": Reflections on the Emergence of Post-Colonial Britain', *Twentieth Century British History*, 14:3 (2003), 264–85.

Schwarz, Bill, *Memories of Empire: The White Man's World* (Oxford, 2011).

Scraton, Phil, 'From Deceit to Disclosure: The Politics of Official Inquiries', in George Gilligan and John Pratt (eds), *Crime, Truth and Justice* (Cullompton, 2004).

Scraton, Phil, 'The Grenfell Tower Inquiry: Learning from Hillsborough', *The Conversation*, 22 June 2017, https://theconversation.com/the-grenfell-tower-inquiry-learning-from-hillsborough-79505.

Scraton, Phil, *Hillsborough: The Truth*, third edition (Edinburgh, 2016).

Scraton, Phil, *Power, Conflict and Criminalisation* (London, 2007).

Scraton, Phil and Kathryn Chadwick, 'Speaking Ill of the Dead: Institutionalised Responses to Deaths in Custody', *Journal of Law and Society*, 13:1 (1986), 93–115.

Scraton, Phil and Jude McCulloch, 'Deaths in Custody and Detention', *Social Justice*, 33:4 (2006), 1–14.

Scraton, Phil and Jude McCulloch, *In the Arms of the Law: Coroner's Courts Deaths in Custody* (London, 1987).

Sedley, Stephen, 'Public Inquiries: A Cure or a Disease?', *The Modern Law Review*, 52 (1989), 469–79.

Sewell, Terri, *Black Tribunes: Black Political Participation in Britain* (London, 1993).

Seyd, Patrick, *The Rise and Fall of the Labour Left* (New York, 1987).

Shepherd, Robert, *Enoch Powell* (London, 1997).

Sherwood, Marika, *Claudia Jones: A Life in Exile* (London, 1999).

Shukra, Kalbir, *The Changing Pattern of Black Politics in Britain* (London, 1998).

Shukra, Kalbir, 'The Death of a Black Political Movement', *Community Development Journal*, 32:3 (1997), 233–43.

Shukra, Kalbir, 'New Labour Debates and Dilemmas', in Shamit Saggar (ed.), *Race and British Electoral Politics* (London, 1998).

Simey, Margaret, *Democracy Rediscovered: A Study in Police Accountability* (London, 1988).

Simey, Margaret, 'Partnership Policing', in John Benyon (ed.), *Scarman and After: Essays Reflecting on Lord Scarman's Report, the Riots and Their Aftermath* (Oxford, 1984).

Sivanandan, Ambalavaner, 'Challenging Racism: Strategies for the 80s', *Race & Class*, 25:2 (1983), 1–11.

Sivanandan, Ambalavaner, *Communities of Resistance: Writings on Black Struggles for Socialism* (London, 1990).

Sivanandan, Ambalavaner, *A Different Hunger: Writings on Black Resistance* (London, 1982).

Sivanandan, Ambalavaner, 'Race, Class and the State: The Black Experience in Britain', *Race & Class*, 17 (1976), 347–68.

Sivanandan, Ambalavaner, 'The Violence of the Violated', *IRR News* (16 August 2011).

Smith, David J., 'Policing and Urban Unrest', in John Benyon and John Solomos (eds), *The Roots of Urban Unrest* (Oxford, 1987).

Smith, David J. and Jeremy Gray, *Police and People in London, Vol. iv: The Police in Action* (London, 1983).

Smith, Evan, 'Conflicting Narratives of Black Youth Rebellion in Modern Britain', *Ethnicity and Race in a Changing World: A Review Journal*, 1:3 (2010), 16–31.

Smith, Evan, 'Once as History, Twice as Farce? The Spectre of the Summer of '81 in Discourses on the August 2011 Riots', *Journal for Cultural Research*, 17:2 (2013), 124–43.

Smith, Evan and Marinella Marmo, *Race, Gender and the Body in British Immigration Control: Subject to Examination* (Basingstoke, 2014).

Smith, Martin J., 'From Consensus to Conflict: Thatcher and the Transformation of Politics', *British Politics*, 10 (2015), 64–78.

Sofer, Anne, *The London Left Takeover* (London, 1987).

Solomos, John, *Black Youth, Racism and the State: The Politics of Ideology and Policy* (Cambridge, 1988).

Solomos, John, *Race and Racism in Britain*, second edition (London, 1993).

Souhami, Anna, 'Institutional Racism and Police Reform: An Empirical Critique, *Policing and Society*, 24:1 (2014), 1–21.

Spencer, Ian, *British Immigration Policy since 1939: The Making of Multi-Racial Britain* (London, 1997).

Squires, Peter and Peter Kennison, *Shooting to Kill? Policing, Firearms and Armed Response* (Chichester, 2010).

Strang, David, 'Adding Social Structure to Diffusion Models: An Event History Framework', *Sociological Methods and Research*, 19 (1991), 324–53.

Steel, David, *No Entry: The Background and Implications of the Commonwealth Immigrants Act, 1968* (London, 1969).

Stevens, P. and C.F. Willis, 'Ethnic Minorities and Complaints against the Police', Home Office Research and Planning Unit Paper 5 (London, 1981).

Stevenson, John, *Popular Disturbances in England 1700–1832* (London, 1992).

Stone, Richard, *Hidden Stories of the Stephen Lawrence Inquiry* (Bristol, 2013).

Tabili, Laura, *'We Ask for British Justice': Workers and Racial Difference in Late Imperial Britain* (Ithaca, 1994).

Tarrow, Sidney, *Democracy and Disorder: Protest and Politics in Italy, 1965–1975* (Oxford, 1989).

Tarrow, Sidney, *Power in Movement. Social Movements, Collective Action and Politics* (Cambridge, 1994).

Taylor, David, *The New Police in Nineteenth-Century England: Crime, Conflict and Control* (Manchester, 1997).

Taylor, Keeanga-Yamahtta, *From #BlackLivesMatter to Black Liberation* (Chicago, 2016).

Taylor, Stan, *The National Front in English Politics* (London, 1982).

Taylor, Stan, 'The Scarman Report and Explanations of Riots', in John Benyon (ed.), *Scarman and After: Essays Reflecting on Lord Scarman's Report, the Riots and Their Aftermath* (Oxford, 1984).

Thatcher, Margaret, *The Downing Street Years* (London, 1993).

Thomas, Devon, 'Black Initiatives in Brixton', in John Benyon (ed.), *Scarman and After: Essays Reflecting on Lord Scarman's Report, the Riots and Their Aftermath* (Oxford, 1984).

Thomlinson, Natalie, *Race, Ethnicity and the Women's Movement in England, 1968–1993* (Basingstoke, 2016).

Thompson, E.P., *The Making of the English Working Class* (London, 1963).

Thurlow, Richard, *Fascism in Britain: A History, 1918–1998* (London, 1998).

Tilly, Charles, 'Collective Violence in European Perspective', in Ivo K. Feiarabend, Rosalind L. Feirabend and Ted Robert Gurr (eds), *Anger, Violence and Politics: Theories and Research* (Hemel Hempstead, 1972).

Tilly, Charles, *The Politics of Collective Violence* (Cambridge, 2003).

Tompson, Keith, *Under Siege* (Harmondsworth, 1988).

Toye, Richard, 'From "Consensus" to "Common Ground": The Rhetoric of the Postwar Settlement and its Collapse', *Journal of Contemporary History*, 48:1 (2013), 3–23.

Tuck, Stephen, 'Malcolm X's Visit to Oxford University: U.S. Civil Rights, Black Britain, and the Special Relationship on Race', *The American Historical Review*, 118:1 (2013), 76–103.

Tuck, Stephen, *The Night Malcolm X Spoke at the Oxford Union: A Transatlantic Story of Antiracial Protest* (California, 2014).

Tumber, Howard, *Television and the Riots: A Report for the Broadcasting Research Unit of the British Film Institute* (London, 1982).

Venner, Mary, 'What the Papers Said About Scarman', *New Community*, 9 (1981), 354–63.

Verney, Kevern, *Black Civil Rights in America* (London, 2000).

Vinen, Richard, *Thatcher's Britain: The Politics and Social Upheaval of the Thatcher Era* (London, 2009).

Virdee, Satnam, *Racism, Class and the Racialized Outsider* (Basingstoke, 2014).

Waddington, David, *Contemporary Issues in Public Disorder: A Comparative and Historical Approach* (London, 1992).

Waddington, David, Karen Jones and Chas Critcher, *Flashpoints: Studies in Public Disorder* (London, 1989).

Waddington, P.A.J., 'The Case Against Paramilitary Policing Considered', *The British Journal of Criminology*, 33:3 (1993), 353–73.

Waddington, P.A.J., *Liberty and Order: Public Order Policing in a Capital City* (London, 1994).

Wain, Neil and Peter Joyce, 'Disaffected Communities, Riots and Policing: Manchester 1981 and 2011', *Safer Communities*, 11 (2012), 125–34.

Walvin, James, *Passage to Britain* (Harmondsworth, 1984).

Waters, Chris, ' "Dark Strangers" in our Midst: Discourses of Race and Nation in Britain, 1947–1963', *Journal of British Studies*, 36:2 (1997), 207–38.

Wegg-Prosser, Charles, *The Police and the Law*, third edition (London, 1986).

Whitaker, Ben, *The Police in Society* (London, 1979).

Whitelaw, William, 'Serious disturbances in St. Paul's, Bristol on 2 April, 1980: a memorandum placed in the Library of the House of Commons by the Secretary of State for the Home Department, following the report made to him by the Chief Constable of the Avon and Somerset Constabulary' (London, 1980).

Whitelaw, William, *The Whitelaw Memoirs* (London, 1989).

Wild, Rosalind Eleanor, ' "Black Was the Colour of Our Fight." Black Power in Britain, 1955–1976', unpublished PhD thesis, University of Sheffield (2008).

Wild, Rosalind Eleanor, '"Black Was the Colour of Our Fight": The Transnational Roots of British Black Power', in Robin D.G. Kelley and Stephen Tuck (eds), *The Other Special Relationship* (New York, 2015).

Wilson, Harold, *The Labour Government, 1964–1970: A Personal Record* (London, 1971).

Winder, Robert, *Bloody Foreigners: The Story of Immigration to Britain* (London, 2004).

Woodhouse, Diana, 'Matrix Churchill: A Case Study in Judicial Inquiries', *Parliamentary Affairs*, 48 (1995), 24–39.

Wraith, R.E. and G.B. Lamb, *Public Inquiries as an Instrument of Government* (London, 1971).

Young, Hugo, *One of Us: A Biography of Margaret Thatcher* (London, 1993).

Index

RACE AND RIOTS IN THATCHER'S BRITAIN

Manchester University Press

RACISM, RESISTANCE AND SOCIAL CHANGE

Race and riots in Thatcher's Britain

Simon Peplow

Manchester University Press

Published by Manchester University Press
Altrincham Street, Manchester M1 7JA
www.manchesteruniversitypress.co.uk

British Library Cataloguing- in- Publication Data
A catalogue record for this book is available from the British Library

ISBN 978 1 5261 2528 6 hardback
ISBN 978 1 5261 5168 1 paperback

First published 2019

Typeset by Out of House Publishing

Lightning Source UK Ltd.
Milton Keynes UK
UKHW041517271120
374223UK00009B/68